FoxPro 2.5 for Windows
Inside & Out

Edward Jones

FoxPro 2.5 for
Windows Inside & Out

Osborne **McGraw-Hill**

Berkeley New York St. Louis San Francisco
Auckland Bogotà Hamburg London Madrid
Mexico City Milan Montreal New Delhi Panama City
Paris São Paulo Singapore Sydney
Tokyo Toronto

Osborne **McGraw-Hill**
2600 Tenth Street
Berkeley, California 94710 U.S.A.

For information on translations and book distributors outside of the U.S.A., please write to Osborne **McGraw-Hill** at the above address.

FoxPro 2.5 for Windows Inside & Out

234567890 DOC 99876543

ISBN 0-07-881898-2

Publisher
Kenna S. Wood

Acquisitions Editor
Elizabeth Fisher

Associate Editor
Scott Rogers

Technical Editor
David Nesbitt

Project Editor
Cindy Brown

Copy Editors
Michael Katz
Janna Hecker Clark

Proofreaders
Lindy Clinton
Scott Brown

Indexer
Richard Shrout

Computer Designer
Stefany Otis

Illustrator
Susie Kim

Cover Designer
Mason Fong
Bay Graphics Design

Contents at a Glance

Contents

17 *Programming for Data Retrieval* **433**

18 *Advanced Programming Topics* **447**

Acknowledgments

As with any detailed book, this one exists due to the combined work of many individuals. I would like to offer sincere thanks to the following persons: Liz Fisher and Scott Rogers, who guided the project to completion at a time when the publishing world was being deluged with Windows applications; David Nesbitt of the Nesbitt Group, for his thorough technical review; Cindy Brown, for her skillful management as project editor; Michael Katz, for the job of copy edit; and Brent Serbus at the FoxPro division of Microsoft, for clearing up questions and keeping me supplied with beta software during the writing process.

Introduction

FoxPro is, technically, a "relational database manager." However, that term doesn't tell the full story regarding what FoxPro has to offer. FoxPro provides speed, dBASE compatibility, and an outstanding environment for the development of business applications. Multiple windows, pull-down menus, mouse support, and more are all here within FoxPro.

About This Book

This book is designed to present the features of FoxPro in an easy-to-learn format. At the same time, "easy-to-learn" does not mean that you will be shortchanged in terms of depth; this book delves well into the more advanced uses of FoxPro, detailing programming techniques and concepts you'll need for effective development of your business applications. Most exercises throughout this book are presented in a step-by-step tutorial format, so you can follow along with your copy of FoxPro.

How This Book Is Organized

This book is divided into 19 chapters. The first two-thirds of the book cover the use of FoxPro in building databases, performing queries and generating reports, and working with multiple files. The last third of the book covers programming in FoxPro and provides the necessary skills for building complete applications.

Chapter 1 gets you started with the software. It explains the concepts of relational databases; illustrates how you will use FoxPro; and provides instructions for installing FoxPro, using the keyboard and (optional) mouse, choosing menu selections, and entering FoxPro commands. In Chapter 2, you begin creating databases, entering data, and using various FoxPro options and commands to get information from a database.

Chapter 3 provides details on changing databases. In this chapter, you'll learn how to edit records, how to make effective use of the Browse mode, how to delete unwanted records, and how to change the structure (or overall design) of a database. Chapter 4 provides details on how to sort or index a database to place records in any order you desire.

Chapter 5 covers the important area of performing queries. In a nutshell, you'll learn how to get the precise data you want out of a database. Chapter 6 shows how users of FoxPro 2 can also use the RQBE window to quickly design sophisticated queries. Chapter 7 introduces the topic of reports. You'll learn how to produce customized reports with the Report Generator built into FoxPro. And you will also learn to use various commands for creating quick listings of data with a minimum of hassle.

Chapter 8 covers how you can store and manipulate data in General fields of a FoxPro database. FoxPro lets you store graphics, sound, and any objects that can be pasted from other Windows applications into General fields.

Chapter 9 covers file operations, such as copying, erasing, and renaming files. Here, you'll learn to use the Filer feature of FoxPro to easily perform file operations. In Chapter 10, you'll learn to use the macro features of FoxPro to automate often-used tasks.

Chapter 11 builds on the topics introduced in Chapter 7 by covering advanced reporting needs. In Chapter 11, you'll learn how the Report Generator can be used for more varied reporting tasks, such as form letters and invoices. You will also learn how to create and modify mailing labels and how various parts of commands (called expressions) can enhance the flexibility of the reports that you create. Chapter 12 provides coverage of the relational capabilities of FoxPro. Here, you'll learn to manage multiple files simultaneously and how to produce reports based on more than one database file at a time.

Chapter 13 details the use of FoxPro's ability to create complete applications, using the FoxPro Applications Generator. With the Applications Generator, you can create moderately complex applications to manage a database and produce reports without writing any program code.

Chapter 14 starts off the portion of the book on programming with FoxPro. In Chapter 14, you'll learn to create command files (or programs) to perform tasks in FoxPro. You will also learn how functions, variables, expressions, and operators can be used within a FoxPro program. Chapters 15 through 18 build on this programming knowledge by covering various aspects of programming in detail. In Chapter 15, you will become familiar with various commands that control the flow of execution inside a FoxPro program. Chapter 16 covers how programs can be written specifically for data entry and editing needs. Chapter 17 examines the specifics of programming for data retrieval, or the generation of reports. And Chapter 18 covers an assortment of advanced programming topics you will find useful when designing your own applications.

Chapter 19 provides tips on using FoxPro with other popular software packages, including Excel for Windows, Lotus 1-2-3, and WordPerfect. The appendixes provide a detailed listing of FoxPro commands and functions and a list of dBASE IV commands that are not compatible with FoxPro.

Conventions Used In This Book

Throughout this book, you will be instructed to enter various commands. Each of these entries will either appear in boldface or be visually set apart from the text. Menu selections you should make will be detailed within the text in a step-by-step format.

CHAPTER

Getting Started with FoxPro

Welcome to FoxPro for Windows, a high-powered relational database manager for the IBM PC and compatible computers. You can use FoxPro for Windows to create database files that contain the necessary categories (fields) for your data. And you can display information in a format that best meets your needs with the custom form and report capabilities built into FoxPro for Windows.

FoxPro displays information in a tabular format (known as Browse mode) or in a screen format (known as Edit or Change mode). The commonly used Browse mode is shown in the example in Figure 1-1.

Note   Throughout this book, the term "FoxPro" will be used as a shorthand for "FoxPro for Windows." It does not refer to the program's DOS cousin, which has always been called simply, "FoxPro."

Creating a database to store your data is a straightforward process. After choosing the New option from the File menu and selecting Table/DBF in the dialog box that appears, you define the names and types of fields you will use. Seven different data types can be used in FoxPro: *character* (combinations of alpha and numeric characters), *numeric, floating, date,*

FIGURE
1-1

FoxPro in use (Browse mode)

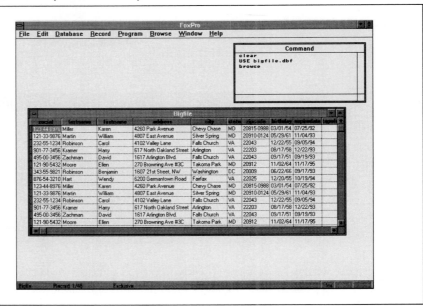

logical (true or false), *memo* (which contain characters in varying lengths), and *general*. (General fields can be used to store graphics, sound, or any other kinds of objects that can be pasted in from other Windows applications.) Figure 1-2 shows the process of creating a database in FoxPro.

Once you have created a database, you can enter data by using on-screen forms that resemble the paper forms used in an office. You can also design custom forms, with fields placed at specific locations you desire, and optional enhancements like borders or descriptive text.

To get more detailed information from your FoxPro databases, you will want to build detailed reports. For maximum flexibility in reporting, you can use the powerful Report Writer, built into FoxPro to design custom reports in either a columnar or a free-form format. The Report Writer has a Quick Report option that lets you quickly design and produce a report.

If you are an advanced user, you will find that FoxPro has the power to match your complex database management needs. Using the relational capabilities of FoxPro, you can draw complex relationships between multiple database files. You can also write programs that perform

FIGURE
1-2

Creating a FoxPro database

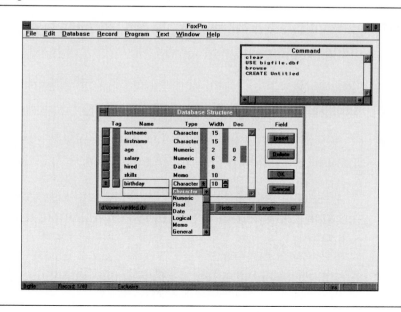

complex tasks using the command language that is an integral part of FoxPro. If you have existing programs written for dBASE III, dBASE III+, or dBASE IV, you can use these programs with FoxPro, since FoxPro understands the dBase command language. In addition to being "command compatible" with dBASE, FoxPro also provides many new commands that take full advantage of the Windows environment.

What Is a Database?

Although database management is a computer term, it can also apply to the ways in which information is catalogued, stored, and used. At the center of any information management system is a database. Any collection of related information grouped together as a single item, as in Figure 1-3, is a database. A metal filing cabinet containing customer records, a card file of names and phone numbers, and a notebook containing a penciled listing of a store inventory are all databases. However, a file cabinet or a notebook does not itself make a database; rather, the way pieces of information are organized makes the difference between random data and a database. Containers, like cabinets, notebooks, or computer programs like FoxPro, are only aids in organizing information.

Information in a database is usually organized and stored in the form of *tables*, with rows and columns in each table. A database, or a FoxPro *database file*, may consist of one such table or several.

FIGURE 1-3

A simple database

Name	Address	City	State	ZIP	Phone No.	Cust. No.
J. Billings	2323 State St.	Bertram	CA	91113	234-8980	0005
R. Foster	Rt. 1 Box 52	Frink	CA	93336	245-4312	0001
L. Miller	P.O. Box 345	Dagget	CA	94567	484-9966	0002
B. O'Neill	21 Way St. #C	Hotlum	CA	92346	555-1032	0004
C. Roberts	1914 19th St.	Bodie	CA	97665	525-4494	0006
A. Wilson	27 Haven Way	Weed	CA	90004	566-7823	0003

For example, in the mailing list shown in Figure 1-3, each row contains a name, an address, a phone number, and a customer number. Each row is related to the others because they all contain the same types of information in the same places. Because the mailing list is a collection of information arranged in a specific order—with a column of names, a column of addresses, and a column of customer numbers—it is a database. Rows in a database table are called *records*, and columns are called *fields*.

Figure 1-4 illustrates this idea by comparing a simple one-table database to an address filing system kept on 3x5 file cards. Each card in the box is a single record, and each category of information on a card is a field. Fields can contain any type of information, as long as each field always contains the same type. In the card box, each record contains six fields: a name, address, city, state, ZIP code, and phone number. Since every card in the box has the same type of information, the card box is a database. Figure 1-5 identifies a record and a field in the mailing list database.

FIGURE 1-4

Each card represents a record; information is separated into fields

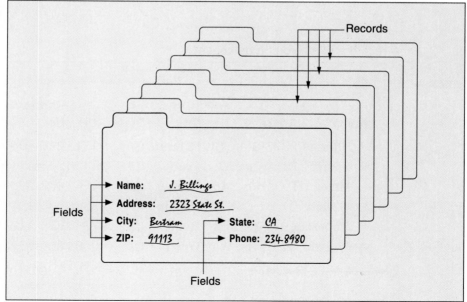

Using a Database

A database, or computerized filing system, can make information storage and retrieval more efficient than a traditional paper filing system. Tasks that would be time-consuming to accomplish manually are more practical with the aid of a computer. In principle, a database in a computer is not different from a database recorded on paper and filed in cabinets. But the computer does the tedious work of maintaining and searching through a database, and it does so quickly. A computerized database that can do all of this is known as a *database management system,* or DBMS for short.

Several shortcomings are associated with manual database systems. A telephone book, for example, is fine for finding telephone numbers, but if all you have is an address and not the name of the person who lives there, the telephone directory becomes useless for finding that person's telephone number. A similar problem plagues conventional office filing systems: if the information is organized by name and you want to find all the clients located in a particular area, you could be in for a tedious search. In addition, storing massive amounts of information into written directories and filing cabinets can consume a great deal of space.

FIGURE 1-5

A record and a field of a database

					Phone	Cust.
Name	**Address**	**City**	**State**	**ZIP**	**No.**	**No.**
J. Billings	2323 State St.	Bertram	CA	91113	234-8980	0005
R. Foster	Rt. 1 Box 52	Frink	CA	93336	245-4312	0001
L. Miller	P.O. Box 345	Dagget	CA	94567	484-9966	0002
B. O'Neill	21 Way St. #C	Hotlum	CA	92346	555-1032	0004
C. Roberts	1914 19th St.	Bodie	CA	97665	525-4494	0006
A. Wilson	27 Haven Way	Weed	CA	90004	566-7823	0003

Field

Record

A manual database can also be tedious to modify. For example, inserting a new phone number into a list may mean rearranging the list. Or, if the phone company were to assign a new area code, someone would have to search for all phone numbers having the old area code, and replace it with the new one. Any volunteers?

When a database is teamed with a computer, many of these problems are eliminated. A computerized database provides speed: finding a phone number from among a thousand entries or putting the file in alphabetical order takes just seconds with FoxPro. A computerized database is compact: a database with thousands of records can be stored on a single floppy disk. A computerized database is flexible: it has the ability to examine information from a number of angles, so you can search for a phone number by name, by address, or by zip code and then name.

Relational Databases

There are a number of ways to store information in a computer, but not all of these are *relational database management systems* like FoxPro. A *relational database manager* is one that can draw information from different tables linked by a common field.

Consider an example of two tables; one contains a record of auto parts, and the other contains purchasers who have ordered certain parts. These tables are typical examples of tables that could benefit from the use of a relational database. The parts table contains part numbers, descriptions, and the cost of each part. The orders table, on the other hand, contains the names of customers who have ordered certain parts, as well as the part numbers and quantities of the parts that have been ordered.

If you used a single table to track all of this information, then each time a customer ordered a part that had been ordered previously, you would have to duplicate the part description and the part cost. To avoid such unnecessary duplication, a relational database manager lets you link the two tables together based on a common field (in this example, the field containing the part number).

A word processing program can be used to organize data in the form of a list; however, it offers only limited flexibility to manipulate that data once you've entered it. A step up from word processors are the simple file managers and spreadsheets with basic database management capabilities. Most such programs can also perform sorting and other data management tasks.

Relational database managers like FoxPro can also store information in database files. But in addition to being more sophisticated than file managers, they can access two or more database files simultaneously. By comparison, simple file managers can access only one database file at a time, which is a severe constraint.

Consider: if a file manager is accessing information from one table but needs three pieces of information from a second table, the file manager can't continue unless the second table is open. But the file manager cannot open the second table until it is finished with the first one! The only way for the file manager to get information from both tables simultaneously is to duplicate the three fields from the second table in the first table. This will probably mean re-entering data, and making the database file needlessly large—which can slow down search times considerably.

Fortunately, this is not a problem with a relational database manager like FoxPro, which can access both tables at once.

How You Will Use FoxPro

Figure 1-6 shows the relationship between the database, the user, and the database software. At the core is the database from which you will retrieve, add, and delete information. The database must somehow be accessible to the user, and that is accomplished by the available menu options and commands provided within FoxPro. FoxPro lets you carry out operations in one of two ways: by choosing the options from a series of menus that appear at the top of the window running FoxPro, or by typing in a series of commands within the Command window. Whatever you want done to the database has to be communicated to the computer by means of the correct command or menu option.

FoxPro's commands and menu options offer you a host of ways to manage information. Among all these commands and menu options, however, you won't find a one-shot, all-purpose command that creates a database, enters information into it, and prints the database on the

Mailing list and customer order databases

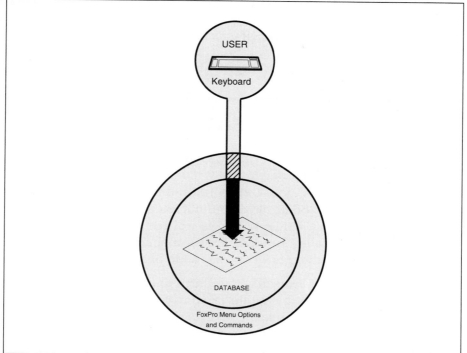

printer. Instead, you have to divide the task into smaller chores that FoxPro will handle—just as you would with any other database manager. For example, to create a mailing list, you need to perform the following steps:

1. Create the database structure.

2. Enter information into the database.

3. Print the contents of the database.

Even after breaking down the problem this far, you need to segment the process further, since, for example, there is no single command that inputs information into the database. How does one know when the task is divided into sufficient steps for FoxPro to cope with it? Experience. You have to know the program, and you have to know what you can and can't get away with. This book is designed to provide that knowledge.

System Requirements

To use FoxPro for Windows, you need an IBM PC or other 100%-IBM compatible computer. Your PC must also have Windows installed, which means your PC must meet the minimum hardware requirements for Windows (80286 or higher-numbered processor, hard disk, and EGA or VGA monitor). While Windows will technically run with one megabyte (Mb) of installed random access memory (RAM), FoxPro for Windows requires that you have at least 4 Mb of RAM installed.

FoxPro can be used with either a monochrome or a color monitor, and with any compatible printer. FoxPro is designed to take advantage of extra memory, and can use the AST RAMPage, Intel Above Board, or any other memory board meeting the LIM (Lotus-Intel-Microsoft) specifications.

Designing a Database

At this point, you may be anxious to load FoxPro into your computer and begin using the program. Resist the temptation to use FoxPro if you are new to the task of database design; there's an excellent reason for approaching the job of designing a database with patience. Planning is vital to effective database management. Many a buyer of database management software has started with the software, created a database, and stored data within that database, only to discover—to their disappointment—that their database does not provide all of the needed information, because they hadn't carefully thought through the database's design.

Although powerful databases like FoxPro let you make up for mistakes you might make during the design process, correcting such errors can be a tedious job. To help you avoid such time-consuming mistakes, much of the remainder of this chapter focuses on database design. If you are experienced at database design but new to FoxPro, you may want to skip ahead to the "Installing FoxPro" section later in this chapter.

Tip   Creating a database without proper planning often results in a database with too few or too many fields.

Just as you would not haphazardly toss a bunch of files into a filing cabinet without designing some type of filing system, you cannot place information into a database file without first designing the database. Database design requires that you think about how the data should be stored, and how you and others will ask for data from the database file. During this process, your solution (which FoxPro was purchased to facilitate) will be outlined on paper. As you do so, you must define the kinds of information that should be stored in the database.

About Data and Fields

Data and fields are two important terms in database design. *Data* is the information that goes into your database. An individual's last name—Smith, for example—is data. *Fields* are the types of data that make up the database. A field is another name for an attribute or category, so an entire category of data, such as a group of names, is considered to be a field. Names, phone numbers, customer numbers, descriptions, locations, and stock numbers are common fields that your database might contain.

Besides determining what kinds of information will go into the database, you must give careful consideration to the ways in which information will come out of the database. Information comes from a database in the form of *reports.* When you ask the computer for a list of all homes in the area priced between $100,000 and $150,000, or for a list of employees earning less than $15.00 per hour, you are asking for a report. When you request John Smith's address, you are also asking for a report. A report is a summary of information. Whether the computer displays a few lines on the screen or hundreds of lines on a stack of paper, it is providing a report based on the data contained within the database file.

To practice the techniques of database design, the example sessions in this text demonstrate how you can design and use a database with various hypothetical examples. Throughout much of this text, the database needs of a video rental store, Generic Videos, are used to illustrate many of the basics behind database management with FoxPro. From time to time, successive chapters of this text will show how the staff at Generic Videos successfully uses FoxPro to manage information. By following along with these examples, you will learn how to put FoxPro to work within your particular application.

Three Phases of Database Design

Designing a database file, whether it is for Generic Videos or for your own purposes, involves three major steps:

1. Data definition (analyzing existing data)
2. Data refinement (refining necessary data)
3. Establishing relationships between the fields

Data Definition

During the first phase, data definition, you should list on a piece of paper all the important fields involved in your application. To do this, you must examine your application in detail, to determine exactly what kinds of fields, or categories of data, will be stored in the database.

In discussing the design for the database, the staff at Generic Videos determined that certain things must be known about each member: the member's name, address, date of birth, and the date their membership expires. The resulting list of fields is as follows:

Member name
Member address

Date of birth
Expiration date

An important point to remember is that during this database design phase, you should list all possible fields of your database. You may list more fields than are actually needed by your particular application, but this isn't a problem, because unnecessary fields will be eliminated during the data refinement stage.

Data Refinement

During this phase, you refine the list of fields on your initial list, so that the fields form an accurate description of the types of data that will be needed in the database. At this stage, it is vital to include suggestions from as many other users of the database as possible.

 Tip   The people who use the database are likely to know what kinds of information they will want to manage with the database.

When the staff of Generic Videos took a close look at their initial list of fields, they realized that most of the refinements were obvious. The address field, for example, should be divided into street address, city, state, and ZIP code. This will make it a simple matter to sort or select records based on a specific category, such as all persons living in a particular ZIP code. In your own case, some refinements may quickly become evident and others may not be as evident, but going over your written list of fields will help make any necessary refinements more obvious.

For example, when the staff of Generic Videos further examined the initial field list, they realized that the index-card system of members contained several cases of members who had the same last name. To avoid confusion, the name field was further divided into last name and first name. Also, the managers wanted a field indicating whether the member rented tapes in the older "Beta" format, and a comments field for member preferences. The following shows the refined list of fields:

Member last name
Member first name

Street address
City
State
ZIP code
Date of birth
Expiration date
Beta?
Preferences

Establishing the Relationships Between Fields

During the third phase, drawing relationships between the fields can help determine which fields are important and which are not so important. One way to determine such relationships is to ask yourself the same questions that you will ask your database. As an example, suppose that a personnel agency develops a database to track its employees and their work assignments. If the personnel manager of the agency wishes to know which employees worked on a particular job for Mammoth Telephone & Telegraph, the database must draw a relationship between a member identifier (such as the social security number) and the types of jobs that the employees worked.

Relationships can be more complex. A company vice president, using the same database, might want to know how many employees who are data entry operators worked for Mammoth Telephone between July and October. The database management system must compare fields for the type of job worked, with fields for the time at which the job was performed. These types of questions can help reveal which fields are unimportant, so that they can be eliminated from the database.

During this phase, it is particularly important that you determine which, if any, relationships between data will call for the use of multiple databases, keeping in mind the fact that FoxPro is a relational database. In a nutshell, relational capability means that the data within one database can be linked, or related, to the data in another. When you are designing a database, it is important not to lose sight of that fact. Too many users take relational database management software and proceed to create bulky, nonrelational databases, an approach that results in unneeded repetitive data entry and drastically increased amounts of work.

As an example, the proposed database for Generic Videos has fields that will be used to describe each video store member. A major goal of computerizing the records at the store is to support automated billing: by creating another database showing which tapes are checked out to a particular member, the store can quickly generate rental receipts, and track needed inventory. If we take the nonrelational approach of adding another field for the name of a tape, we could store all of the information needed in each record. However, we would also have to fill in the name, address, and other information for each tape rental, every time a member rents a tape. The better solution is to create two databases; one containing the fields already described, detailing each member, and the other containing a listing of rented tapes, along with a field that identifies the member who has rented each one.

When establishing the relationships, you may determine that an additional field is necessary as a "match" field. Generic Videos decided to match members with rented tapes by means of members' social security numbers, so a field for this purpose was added to the proposed list of fields, resulting in the finalized list shown here:

Member social security number
Member last name
Member first name
Street address
City
State
ZIP code
Date of birth
Expiration date
Beta?
Preferences

The sample database created in the next chapter is based on this list. A social security number is needed because in a relational database, the field you use to link the files must be unique in at least one of the files. Since under normal circumstances no two social security numbers are the same, the social security number serves as a unique method of identification. Using fields like last name and first name for linking files could present problems later, because the fields' contents might not always be unique. If two people with the same name joined the video club, a relational link based on name only might result in one member getting billed for the other member's rentals.

During the design phases, it is important that potential users be consulted to determine what kinds of information they will expect the database to supply. Just what kinds of reports are wanted from the database? What kinds of queries will members make of the database? By continually asking these types of questions, you'll think in terms of your database, and this should help you determine what is important and what is unimportant. It often helps, while you design the database, to consider examples of the data you will store. For example, if your database contains many names that include salutations like "Dr." or "Honorable," you may need to create a separate title field to allow selections based on such information; you might, for example, want to provide a mailing to all doctors based on the contents of a sales database.

Tip Look at examples of your data before finalizing your list of fields. This should help you track down variations that may not have been allowed for, fields that may have been omitted, and other potential problems.

Keep in mind that even after the database design phases, the design of the database file is not set in stone. Changes to the design of a database file can be made later if necessary. But if you follow the systematic approach to database design for your specific application, you will be less likely to create a database that fails to provide some of the information you need, and that must then be extensively redesigned. Although FoxPro lets you make such design changes at any time, they are often inconvenient to make once the database is in use. Here is an example.

If you were to create a FoxPro database file to handle a customer mailing list, you might include fields for names, addresses, cities, states, and ZIP codes. At first glance this might seem sufficient. You could then begin entering customer information into the database and gradually build a sizable mailing list. However, if your company later decides to begin telemarketing with the same mailing list, you may suddenly realize that you have not included a field for telephone numbers. Using FoxPro, you could easily change the design to include such a field, but you would still face the mammoth task of going back and adding a telephone number for every name currently in the mailing list. If this information had instead been added as you developed the mailing list, you would not face the inconvenience of having to enter the phone numbers as a separate operation. Careful planning, and time spent, during the database design process can help avoid such pitfalls.

Installing FoxPro

FoxPro comes in the form of assorted manuals and quick reference guides, and a set of either 5 1/4-inch or 3 1/2-inch disks, depending on which version you purchased. If you are not sure whether all your disks are present, refer to your FoxPro documentation to be sure that you have the correct number of disks.

If your computer is attached to a local area network, contact your network administrator for help in installing FoxPro on the network. Refer to the FoxPro documentation for step-by-step directions regarding installation on different types of networks.

 Tip   Before installing the software, it is a wise idea to make a complete backup copy of your program disks. If you do not know how to copy disks, refer to your Windows or DOS documentation for directions.

During the installation process, you will need to have the following information available:

☐   The serial number of your copy of FoxPro (it is printed on disk 1)

☐   The drive (or directory) from which you are installing FoxPro. Assuming that you are installing from a floppy disk drive, this will usually be either drive A or drive B.

☐   The directory name where you want the FoxPro system files installed. (By default, the installation program puts these files in C:\FOXPROW.)

To install FoxPro, perform the following steps.

1.   Start Windows in the usual manner.

2. Insert the FoxPro system disk 1 in your floppy disk drive. (If you have more than one drive, you can use any floppy disk drive that matches the size of the disk that you are using.)

3. From the Windows Program Manager menu bar, choose File/Run. This causes the Run dialog box to appear.

In the Command Line text box, type **a:\setup** if the floppy is in drive A, or type **b:\setup** if the floppy is in drive B. Then, click OK. In a moment, the FoxPro for Windows User Information dialog box appears.

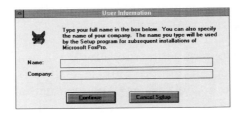

Enter the requested information in the text boxes. You can move from box to box with the TAB key, or by clicking in the desired box with the mouse. The Name, Company Name, and Serial Number boxes must be filled in.

Note   If you do not have sufficient disk space on your drive C, but you have sufficient disk space on other hard disk drives, then you will want to change the default selections for where FoxPro installs the program. For example, instead of installing the program in C:\FOXPROW, you might want to enter D:\FOXPROW or E:\FOXPROW in the Install To text box. If the directory does not yet exist on the hard disk you specify, the installation program will create it automatically.

Tip   If you are short on disk space, you can reduce FoxPro's installed size by turning off the options for installing the sample tables and the sample application. Do this by clicking the corresponding check boxes. The exercises in this book do not make use of any of these options;

however, the exercises provided in the FoxPro documentation do make use of these options.

After filling in all the options, click the Continue button in the dialog box to start the installation process. From time to time, the installation program will display a dialog box requesting another disk. When this occurs, insert the requested disk in the floppy drive you have been using, and click OK.

Starting FoxPro

Once the installation program is complete, a new program group named FoxPro for Windows will be added to your Windows desktop. You can start FoxPro by opening that program group, then double-clicking on the FoxPro for Windows icon contained within.

When the program starts, you briefly see an introductory screen and a copyright message. Within a moment, the FoxPro menus and Command window appear, as shown in Figure 1-7. The application window containing FoxPro contains a menu bar with menu options, a Command window, and a "desktop" working surface (the remainder of the window). You can enter FoxPro commands in the Command window, or you can select menu options that have the same results as entering FoxPro commands. Both methods for using FoxPro—the menus and the Command window—are covered in detail throughout this text.

If you have worked with other applications running under Microsoft Windows, you may be familiar with the concept of parent windows and child windows. As with other Windows applications, FoxPro's desktop is a 'parent' window. You can create files and other objects (such as tables, forms, or reports) in various child windows. The child windows are dependent on the parent window; you could not close the parent window and still have child windows open on the screen.

The top line of the screen shows the menu bar, which contains eight choices. You can open any of the menus by clicking the desired menu heading with the mouse, or by pressing ALT and the first letter of the menu name; for example, pressing ALT+F opens the File menu. Such ALT+*key* combinations are known as *shortcut keys*. An alternative method

FIGURE
1-7

FoxPro menu options and Command window

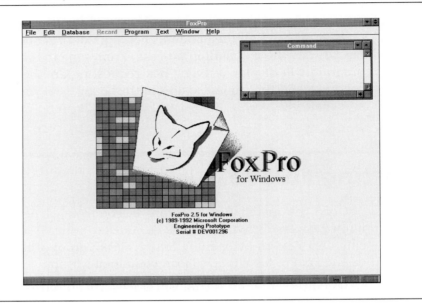

of opening a menu is to press F10, use the LEFT ARROW and RIGHT ARROW keys to highlight the desired menu, and then press ENTER to open the menu. When a menu is open, the appropriate menu options appear in a rectangular box called a pull-down menu.

Selecting Menu Options

Once a menu has been opened, you can choose any option on that menu by clicking it with the mouse. (You can also open menus and simultaneously choose a menu option, by clicking and dragging to highlight the desired menu option; if clicking and dragging is an unfamiliar term, see "About the Mouse" later in this chapter.) From the keyboard, you can choose menu options from an open menu by pressing the UP ARROW or DOWN ARROW key to highlight the option and then pressing ENTER. (An alternative is to press the highlighted letter in the desired menu option; this is usually, but not always, the first letter of the option.)

As an example, if you open the File menu with ALT+F, you see the letter P highlighted within the Print option. Pressing P will choose the Print command from that menu. Note that not all of the menu options are available at all times. For example, you cannot access the Record menu until you open a database file.

Canceling a Menu

You can click anywhere outside of the menu, or press the ESC key to close a menu without selecting any option. In a similar fashion, you can use the ESC key to exit from many options within FoxPro without performing the operation you've started. However, you should be aware that some operations (like copying files) cannot be canceled once the process has actually begun.

 Tip   ESC is your most useful key whenever you are somewhere you don't want to be. In most cases, repeatedly pressing ESC gets you out of an operation.

The Keyboard

If you're already familiar with the PC keyboard, skip this section and begin reading at the next section.

FoxPro uses a number of special-purpose keys for various functions. In addition to the ordinary letter and number keys, you may often use the function keys. On most older IBM PCs and compatible computers, the function keys are the double row of gray keys at the left side of the PC keyboard, as shown in Figure 1-8. On newer IBM PCs and most newer compatibles, the function keys are placed in a horizontal row at the top of the keyboard, as shown in Figure 1-9. The function keys on the older PCs are labeled F1 through F10, for Function 1 through Function 10. The newer machines have 12 function keys. Usually grouped on the left side of the keyboard are four commonly used keys: the ESC (Escape) key, the TAB key (it may have double arrows on it), the SHIFT key (it may have a hollow upwards-pointing arrow), and the ALT (Alternate) key. Some keyboards

FIGURE
1-8
The IBM PC keyboard

have the ESC key in a different location. Find these keys before going further; they will prove helpful for various operations.

You should locate the function key template supplied with your FoxPro package, and place it where you can easily refer to it when using the function keys. The uses of the various function keys are detailed in later chapters, as pertinent operations are discussed.

Towards the right side of the keyboard is another SHIFT key. Located below it on some keyboards is a key labeled CAPS LOCK; it is used to change all typed letters to uppercase. Newer IBM PCs and many compatible keyboards have the CAPS LOCK key above the left SHIFT key. (The CAPS LOCK

FIGURE
1-9
The enhanced IBM PC keyboard

key does not change the format of the numbers in the top row of the keyboard.) Just above the right SHIFT key is the ENTER, or RETURN key; it performs a function that is similar to the Return key of a typewriter. Above the ENTER key is the BACKSPACE key.

On the right side of the keyboard, in the numeric keypad area, is a key labeled DEL. The DEL (Delete) key can be used to delete characters. Finally, the far right side of the keyboard has two gray keys with plus (+) and minus (-) labels. These keys produce the plus and minus symbols when pressed.

The far right side of the keyboard contains a numeric keypad. On some computers, this area serves a dual purpose. The keys in this area containing the up, down, left, and right arrows can be used to move the cursor in these directions. By pressing the NUM LOCK key, you can then use the same keys to enter numbers. Some keyboards have one area with separate arrow keys, and a separate area with a numeric keypad.

When NUM LOCK is pressed, the arrow keys on many keyboards create numbers instead of moving the cursor. If you press an arrow key and get an unwanted number, check the status of the NUM LOCK key.

The Mouse

Like other Windows packages, FoxPro makes excellent use of a mouse in performing many tasks. There are three basic operations you perform with the mouse: pointing, clicking, and selecting (also called dragging). The mouse controls the location of a special cursor called the mouse pointer. In FoxPro, the mouse pointer usually takes on the shape of a small, upwards-pointing arrow.

To point at an object with the mouse, simply roll the mouse in the direction of the object. As you do so, the mouse pointer moves in the same direction on the screen. The term *clicking* refers to pressing the left mouse button. By pointing to different objects and clicking on them, you can select many of the objects while in FoxPro. The term *dragging* refers to pressing and holding down the left mouse button while moving the mouse. This is commonly done to choose menu options within FoxPro.

If you have just purchased your mouse for use with Windows and with FoxPro, a few hints are in order. Most mice require software drivers to be installed before they will work properly; the Windows installation automatically installs software for most mice. If your mouse works with Windows, it will work with FoxPro; if your mouse is not working with Windows, it will not work with FoxPro either. (If your mouse is not functioning, refer to your Windows documentation for suggestions.)

Obviously, you'll need a clear area on your desk on which to manipulate the mouse. What is not so obvious is that some desk surfaces work better than others. A surface with a small amount of friction seems to work better than a very smooth desk. Mouse pads are available if your desktop is too smooth to obtain good results. Also, the mouse will probably require cleaning from time to time. (Some mice do not require regular cleaning, so check your manual to be sure.) If you turn the mouse upside down, you will probably see instructions that indicate how the ball can be removed for cleaning. A cotton swab dipped in alcohol works well for cleaning the ball. If your mouse uses an optical sensor design instead of a large ball underneath, you should refer to the manual that accompanied the mouse for any cleaning instructions.

Using FoxPro Commands

The menus provide one way in which you can use FoxPro, but another method is to enter commands directly in the Command window. Most menu options have equivalent commands that can be entered in this window. You get acceptable results from FoxPro regardless of which method you choose, but it does help to know a little about both methods.

If you do not use the mouse, an ALT key combination, or F10 to open a menu, FoxPro assumes that any entry you type is a command, and it will appear within the Command window. FoxPro's basic command structure becomes obvious after you try a few commands. To print information on the screen, you use the question mark. As an example, type

? "FoxPro Inside and Out"

Once you press ENTER, the response

FoxPro Inside and Out

appears in the lower left portion of the desktop, outside of the Command window. The ? command prints everything between the quotation marks. To clear the entire screen of information, enter

CLEAR

Note that you can go from Command mode back to the menus at any time simply by clicking a desired menu option, or by pressing the ALT key combination for the desired menu.

FoxPro also accepts commands in abbreviated form. Only the first four letters of any command are necessary, so you could use CLEA instead of CLEAR to clear the screen. However, all commands in this book will be used in their complete form.

Conventions

Before you start working with FoxPro, you need to know some conventions that are used throughout the book.

All commands are printed in UPPERCASE, but you can type them in either uppercase or lowercase. Any part of a command surrounded by left ([) and right (]) brackets is optional, and any command followed by ellipses (...) can be repeated. Parameters in the command are in italics. Every command that you enter is terminated by pressing ENTER (or RETURN). Pressing ENTER indicates to FoxPro that you have finished typing the command and that you want it to execute. So whenever you are asked to enter a command, finish it by pressing ENTER, unless you are instructed otherwise.

Getting Help

Should you need help, FoxPro provides information on subjects ranging from basic database concepts to the use of programming commands and functions. This information is stored in a file that is always accessible to FoxPro, so you can get help at any time by pressing F1.

The help system in FoxPro is context-sensitive, meaning that if you are in a particular area (such as in the process of creating a database file) and you ask for help, you are provided with help regarding that particular topic. If you are not in any particular area when you ask for help, FoxPro displays the contents page of the help system, as shown in Figure 1-10. From anywhere in the help system, you can click on the Contents button to display the contents page. Once the contents page is visible, you can click on any of the headings in that page, to move to the named topic. You can also click on the Search button and then enter a search term, or scroll through the list box of topics that appears.

The help file is quite extensive, so by all means take some time to rummage through it, view the different options, and understand how it is set up. Knowing where to locate information about a particular operation or command can be a great aid when you work with some of the more difficult operations in this book.

Contents page of Help window

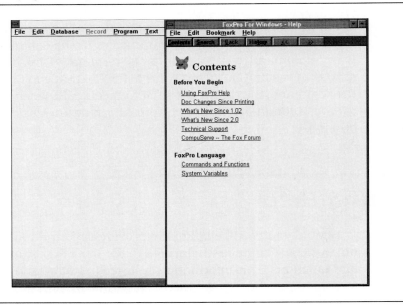

Windows

FoxPro makes extensive use of windows. In FoxPro, you can manipulate windows with either the keyboard or the mouse. Open the Help menu now and choose Filer. In a moment, the FoxPro Filer appears within its own window, as shown in Figure 1-11. The operation of the Filer is covered in detail in Chapter 12; for now, you may want to take a few moments to try various window operations using the Filer and Command windows.

With the Filer window open, there are currently two windows on your screen: the Filer window and the Command window. Although FoxPro can display as many windows as you can comfortably work with at the same time, only one window can be active. Whichever window contains the highlighted title bar is the active window; since the last window you opened was the Filer window, it is currently active.

FIGURE 1-11

Command Window and Filer Window

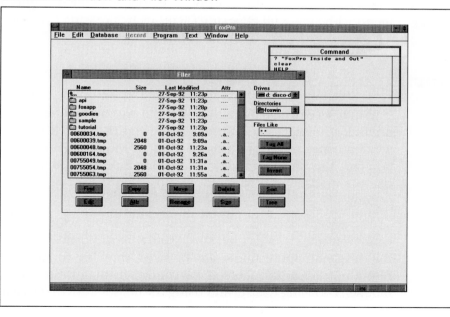

If you open the Window menu now, you see the options shown here.

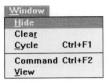

This menu contains various commands that let you manipulate windows. The first option, Hide, hides the active window. The window remains open, but it is not visible. Once hidden, a window appears by name in the Window menu; you can open the Window menu and choose the window by name to unhide or redisplay it. If you choose Hide from the Window menu now, the Filer window vanishes; open the Window menu again and notice that the window name, Filer, is shown at the bottom of the Window menu. Choose Filer from the menu now, to redisplay the Filer window.

Note that hiding a window and closing a window are two different things. If you hide a window, it is still open in memory. If you close a window, it is no longer active, and you have to reopen the window (by choosing Filer from the Help menu, in the case of the Filer window) to redisplay it. Windows can be closed by double-clicking the Control menu icon at the upper-left corner of the window, or by opening the Control menu with ALT+- and choosing Close, or by pressing CTRL+F4.

Moving and Sizing Windows

Windows can be moved around the screen and resized at will. To move a window, simply click anywhere on the title bar (the top bar of the window containing its name) and drag the window to the desired location. You can also move a window by opening its control menu (press ALT+- or use the mouse), choosing Move, and using the arrow keys to move the window.

To resize a window, click at any edge of the window, and drag the window frame to its desired size. (Note that while most windows, including the Command window, can be sized, the Filer cannot.) You can also resize a window by opening its control menu (press ALT+- or use the mouse), choosing Resize, and using the cursor keys to resize the window.

The Maximize and Minimize icons can be used to maximize a window (increase it to its fullest possible size), and to minimize a window (reduce it to the size of an icon on the screen). Click the Maximize icon to bring the window currently in use, or *active window,* to full size. You can also maximize a window by opening its Control menu and selecting the Maximize command, or by pressing ALT+F10. Click the Minimize icon to reduce the active window to a small icon that appears at the bottom of the screen. You can also minimize a window by opening the Control menu and selecting the Minimize command, or by pressing ALT+F9.

Changing Windows

When more than one window is displayed, you can switch between windows by clicking on the desired window to make it active, or by using the Cycle option on the Window menu. (The CTRL+ key equivalent for this menu option is CTRL+F1.) If you open the Window menu now and choose Cycle, you see that the Command window becomes the active window. The Cycle option moves through all windows currently displayed on the screen; if you have more than two windows displayed, using Cycle causes each window to be activated in the sequence in which the windows were opened.

The View option on the Window menu can be used to create a view that lets you establish relationships between database files. The use of this option, as well as the dialog box that appears when you select it, is covered in detail in Chapter 12.

Before proceeding, close the Filer (if it is still open in a window), by double-clicking the Control menu icon in the upper-left corner of the Filer window.

The Command Window

As mentioned earlier, the Command window is where FoxPro commands normally appear when you enter them. If you click anywhere in the Command window (or open the Window menu and choose the Command option), the Command window is made the active window. (CTRL+F2 is the shortcut key for this menu option.) The Command option and its CTRL+F2 equivalent can also be used to display the Command window if it has been hidden.

By means of the Command window, you can control FoxPro operations in the interactive, or Command, mode. All commands that you type appear in the Command window. Try entering the following commands now:

? 2 * 4

DIR *.*

HELP

When the Help window appears, press ALT+F4 to close it, and again make the Command window the active window. In response to each of your commands, FoxPro performed some sort of action: displaying the result of two times four on the screen, showing a directory of files in response to the DIR *.* command, or bringing forward the Help window. With the Command window now active, you can see that the commands you just entered are still displayed within the window.

You can scroll through the Command window by clicking the up or down arrows in the scroll bar at the right edge of the window, or by using the UP ARROW and DOWN ARROW keys. All the commands you see in the Command window are remembered by FoxPro, so you can repeat a command by moving the cursor up to that command and pressing ENTER. For example, if you now move the cursor back up to the command ? 2 * 4 and press ENTER, the calculation is again performed and the result displayed at the left edge of the screen.

This capability of remembering commands can be quite useful for correcting mistakes. If you make an error when entering a command, simply move the cursor back up to that line; then use BACKSPACE, DEL, and the cursor keys to correct the error. When done with the correction, press ENTER to repeat the command.

You can resize the Command window, like other windows. You may find this helpful, as many of the more complex commands that you enter will extend beyond the visible width of the default Command window size. Note that the length of the command you can type is not restricted by the size of the Command window; when you enter a long command, it simply scrolls to the left when you reach the right side of the window. If you make a mistake in entering a long command, you can go back to the incorrect line and use the left or right arrow in the scroll bar at the bottom edge of the window to scroll horizontally in the window. Keyboard users have to settle for using the cursor keys; however, you can use CTRL+LEFT ARROW and CTRL+RIGHT ARROW to move left or right a word at a time.

You can also cut and paste information within the Command window, using the same techniques that are used universally in Windows applications for cutting and pasting information. (Refer to your Windows documentation if you are unfamiliar with such techniques.)

If you hide the Command window (or close it by clicking on the Control menu icon or by choosing Close from the File menu), you can still enter commands. However, you will in a sense be "flying blind," because you will not be able to see the commands you enter. The CTRL+F2 key combination can be used to quickly restore the Command window to view (remember that you can also open the Window menu and choose Command from that menu).

The Scroll Bars

You can use the scroll bars at the bottom and right edges of a window to move to other areas of the window. If the window contains a table, clicking the arrows located within the scroll bar will move you by one row or column at a time. Clicking the up or down arrow in the right (or vertical) scroll bar moves you up or down a row at a time. Clicking the left or right arrow in the scroll bar at the bottom of the window (the horizontal scroll bar) moves you left or right by a column at a time. You can also drag the boxes located in the scroll bars to move by a relative amount; for example, if you drag the box in the vertical scroll bar halfway down the bar, you will move halfway down the window's contents.

Open dialog box

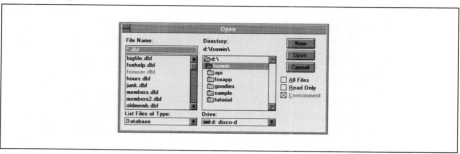

Dialog Boxes

In FoxPro, choosing certain menu options will open a dialog box asking for additional information. Figure 1-12 shows an example of a dialog box that appears when File/Open is chosen from the menu bar.

Other dialog boxes may contain some or all of the options shown in this example. A dialog box may contain a number of different options, such as check boxes, list boxes, command buttons, and text boxes. Here is a description of these items, which are illustrated in the figure:

A check box is a small square box that you use to turn an option on or off. To select a check box, just click it.

A list box is a rectangular area used to display a list of available names, such as file names. List boxes may have scroll bars to aid you in viewing the box's contents.

A drop-down list box shows the currently selected option only. To display more options, click the down arrow and drag down the list until you have highlighted the option you want.

A command button is a rectangular button (with rounded edges) that lets you implement a command or other action. Many dialog boxes contain at least three command buttons: an OK or Save button, a Cancel button, and a Help button. The OK button, when present, is used to accept the options chosen within the dialog box, and the Save button, when present, is used to save a file. The Cancel button is used to cancel the current operation and remove the dialog box from the screen. Some dialog boxes may contain other buttons (such as New or Save As) for performing various operations. Select the desired command button by clicking it.

A text box is a rectangular area in which text that is needed for a command can be entered. (As an example, when saving files, you enter desired filenames into text boxes.) Within the text box, you can type text, and you can edit or delete text with the BACKSPACE and/or DEL keys.

Desktop Accessories

FoxPro offers some desktop accessories, which are available from the Help menu. Since most of these accessories don't deal specifically with database management, they aren't covered in detail in this book. However, you should be aware of their existence. The following paragraphs provide a brief description; you can learn more details on the accessories from the FoxPro documentation.

If you open the Help menu with the mouse or with ALT+H, you see options for a calculator, a calendar/diary, a filer, and a puzzle. The filer can be used for DOS file management, such as erasing and renaming files. Its operation is discussed further in Chapter 9.

The Calculator option, when selected, provides a desktop calculator. Modeled after a pocket calculator, its operation is fairly obvious. To enter numbers, you can use your keyboard's numeric keypad (after pressing NUM LOCK), or you can use the numbers on the top row of the keyboard.

The Calendar/Diary option, when chosen, displays the current month (based on the computer's clock) along with a Diary area in which you can type notes of your choosing. To enter a note, click anywhere in the right side of the Calendar/Diary and begin typing. When you close the calendar (by double-clicking on the Control menu icon at the upper-right corner or by pressing CTRL+F4), the note is automatically saved. You can click the Month buttons or the Year buttons to move between months or between years, and you can click the Today button to return from anywhere to the current date.

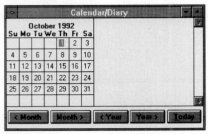

The Puzzle option displays an entertaining puzzle, resembling a child's number puzzle. You can click any number adjacent to the empty square to move the number around. Clicking the Shuffle button causes the numbers to be remixed in a random order. The object of the game is to align the numbers in order from 1 through 15. Good luck.

CHAPTER

Creating and Displaying Databases

*T*his chapter assumes that you have installed FoxPro and know how to start the program. It also assumes that you know how to make selections within dialog boxes, move and resize windows, and use the keyboard and the mouse. If you are unfamiliar with any of these areas, you should review the latter half of Chapter 1 before proceeding.

Creating a Database

FoxPro gives you two ways to create a database. In the Command window, you can enter **CREATE** *filename*, where *filename* is the name for the new database you wish to create. Or you can open the File menu, choose New, and then select Table/DBF from the dialog box that appears. Either method has the same result: the appearance of the Table Structure dialog box in which you define the database or table by entering the field names, types, and widths. As an example, you can now create the sample database used throughout this chapter by opening the File menu and selecting the New option. When you do this, the New dialog box, shown in Figure 2-1, appears.

The various options in the dialog box allow for the creation of new databases (or tables), programs, text files, index files, reports, labels, or screen forms. (Unless an existing database has already been opened for use, the Index option is unavailable; hence, it is dimmed.) Of interest to programmers are additional options for creating menus, queries, or projects; these are discussed in the programming portion of this text.

Once you select the Table/DBF option and click New (or simply press ENTER while the Database option is chosen), FoxPro displays a screen with highlighted blocks for the entry of each field's name, field type, field width, and number of decimal places. This box, known as the Table Structure dialog box, is shown in Figure 2-2.

When naming a field, use a name that best describes the contents of the field. Field names can be made up of letters, numbers, and under-score characters, but they must start with a letter, and may not contain spaces. Field names can contain up to 10 characters. FoxPro does not allow the entry of field names that are too long or that contain illegal characters.

FIGURE 2-1   Dialog box for a new file

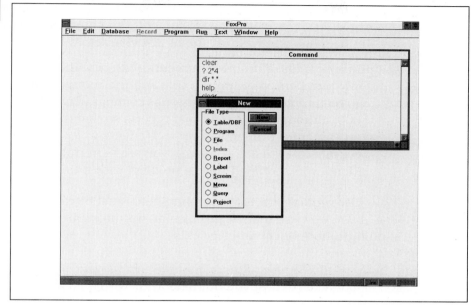

The first field on the list for the example database is the member's social security number. If you are following the example, enter **Social** for the field name, then press TAB. Once you press the TAB key, the cursor automatically moves to the Type column. FoxPro allows for the entry of seven types of fields:

FIGURE 2-2   Table Structure dialog box

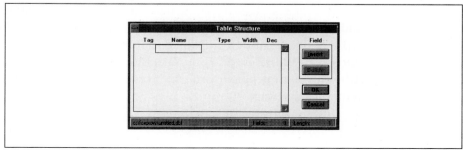

☐ *Character fields* These can be used to store any characters, including letters, numbers, special symbols, and blank spaces. A character field has a maximum size of 254 characters.

☐ *Numeric fields* These use numbers, with or without decimal places. Only numbers, a decimal point, and the minus sign (the hyphen) can be entered; FoxPro does *not* use commas in numbers larger than 1000, although you can format reports so that the commas appear. You can enter numbers of up to 20 digits in length, and FoxPro is accurate to 15 digits, so unless you are performing scientific calculations, you shouldn't have a problem with numeric accuracy.

Tip Use numeric fields for numbers that must be calculated. Numbers that you never need to perform calculations on (such as phone numbers) should be stored in character fields.

☐ *Float fields* These are numeric fields with a floating decimal point. As with numeric fields, you can enter numbers and an optional minus sign, and accuracy extends to 15 digits.

☐ *Date fields* You use date fields to store dates. FoxPro automatically inserts the slashes if you enter all six digits of a date into a date field. You must include any leading zeros for the day and month; if you do not, you must type in the slashes.

☐ *Logical fields* These consist of a single letter representing a true or false value. T or Y represents true, and F or N represents false.

☐ *Memo fields* FoxPro can store large blocks of text for each record in the form of memo fields. An unlimited amount of text can be stored in a memo field (you are limited only by available hard disk space).

☐ *General fields* This type of field can be used to store pictures, sound, word processing documents, spreadsheets, or any other types of data that can be pasted in from other Windows applications (including Windows OLE, or object linking and embedding, objects). (Chapter 8 shows how you can use General fields along with other Windows software.)

Most fields in a database are of the character or numeric type, although there may be times when you need the other different field types that FoxPro offers.

When the cursor is in the Type column of the Database Structure dialog box, you can either enter the first letter of the desired field type, or you can click the arrow in the drop-down list box to display a drop-down menu showing the available field types. When this menu is visible, you can press the first letter of the desired field type, followed by ENTER, or you can simply click the desired field type. Note that you can also use the left and right arrow keys to cycle through the various field types within the menu.

The social security numbers in our example database consist of numbers, so at first thought it might seem sensible to use a numeric field. However, this is not practical. If you include the hyphens that normally appear as part of a social security number, FoxPro ignores everything typed after the first hyphen, and the result is an incorrect entry. You will never use a social security number in a numerical calculation, so it makes sense to store such entries, like phone numbers, as character fields rather than numeric fields. A number stored in a character field cannot be used directly in a numerical calculation, although you could later use a FoxPro function to convert the value to a number.

The next step in the example is to choose Character. Since Character is the default type, you can press TAB to move to the Width box, or click in the Width box. Remember, character fields can be up to 254 characters in length, while numeric and float fields are limited to 20 digits. Logical fields are fixed at 1 character, and date fields are fixed at 8 characters. In Chapter 1, the example structure for the video store database indicated that the social security field would require 11 characters, so enter **11** as the field width. (You can type **11** in the width box, or you can click on the up and down arrows to the right of the width box to change the value inside to 11.) Finally, press TAB to move the cursor to the Name column for the next field.

For this example, enter **Lastname** for the second field name, and press TAB. In the Type area, leave Character as the default setting for the field type. Press TAB again, and enter **15** for the field width. Press TAB again, and the cursor moves to the beginning of the third field definition. For the third field, enter **Firstname** as the field name and press TAB. Again, leave Character as the default setting for the field type, press TAB, and enter **15** for the field width. Press TAB to begin defining the fourth field.

To follow the example, enter **Address** for the fourth field name, Character for the field type, and **25** for the field width. For the fifth field, enter **City**, choose Character for the field type, and enter **15** for the width. For the next field, enter **State**, choose Character for the field type, and enter **2** for the field width.

The next field will be ZIP code. ZIP codes contain numbers, but ten-digit ZIP codes also contain hyphens. So, like social security numbers, they should be treated as character data. Enter **Zipcode** as the field name, Character as the field type, and **10** as the width.

You may recall from Chapter 1 that two of the fields in the example database will take the form of dates: the date of birth and the date the membership expires. FoxPro lets you use date fields to enter dates. By doing so, you can perform date arithmetic (as in subtracting one date from another to come up with the difference in days between the two). You can also arrange records chronologically based on date fields.

Enter **Birthday** for the name of the next field, press TAB, and type **D** in the Type column to select the Date field type. Note that FoxPro automatically supplies a width of 8 for this type of field. Press TAB again to get to the next field name.

Enter **Expiredate** for the name of the next field, press TAB, and type **D** in the field type column to indicate a date field. Press TAB again, and for the next field name, enter **Tapelimit**. Press TAB to move to the field type box, and type the letter **N** (for numeric), then press TAB again. For the field width, enter **2**. This creates a numeric field with a maximum width of two digits. You will be able to store numbers from 0 to 99 in this field. (Generic Videos assumes it will never need to simultaneously rent more than 99 tapes to one member.)

Note that when you next press TAB, the cursor moves next to the decimal column. You could, if desired, specify a number of decimal places for the numeric field. In this example, whole numbers are used to describe the number of tapes, so you can press TAB to bypass the decimal entry, and move to the next field.

Whenever you are using numeric fields to track dollar or other currency amounts (such as salaries or costs), you should include one digit in the width to contain the decimal point. For example, to track salaries of up to $999.99, you would need a numeric field with a width of 6; 3 for the dollar amount, 1 for the decimal point, and 2 for the cents values. Whenever you include decimal amounts, allow one digit for the decimal point, and if you are working exclusively with decimal numbers, include one extra digit so the decimal point can be preceded by a zero (for example, 0.1). Thus, the minimum field width for a decimal number is 3. Note that if you plan to enter negative numbers in a numeric field, an additional space is needed for the minus symbol.

If you are following the example, enter **Beta** as the next field name and choose Logical as the field type. Note that after you choose a logical field, FoxPro automatically assigns a width of 1.

Depending on the member's tastes, the next field (Preference) may need to store a lengthy series of comments. The most economical way to store any large group of information is to use a memo field. Use the TAB key to get to the next field name, enter **Preference**, and then type **M** (for memo) as the field type. FoxPro automatically supplies 10 as the field width.

While you are creating a database, you may notice the statistics listed at the bottom of the dialog box, as shown in Figure 2-3. In the lower-right corner of the dialog box is the length of each record, in bytes. This figure is calculated by adding the widths of all fields in the database structure. (Memo fields, of course, can store unlimited amounts of data, but only ten characters are stored in the actual database for each memo field; the text of the memo is stored elsewhere by FoxPro.)

The number shown near the bottom middle of the dialog box indicates the number of fields created so far. Both figures, the length and the number of fields, change as you add fields to the database.

FIGURE
2-3

Dialog box with Statistics

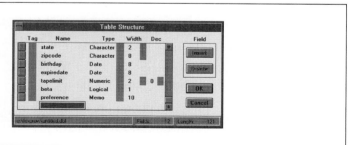

Correcting Mistakes

If you make any mistakes while defining the structure of the database, you can correct them before completing the database definition process. To correct mistakes, click in the column, or use TAB or SHIFT+TAB to move to the desired column, and use the BACKSPACE key, along with the character keys, to make any desired corrections. To insert new characters between existing characters, place the cursor at the desired location and then type the correction. Pressing the INS key takes you out of insert mode. When you are not in insert mode, any characters that you type will write over existing characters.

Saving the Database

To tell FoxPro that you have finished defining the database structure, click the OK button in the dialog box. (As an alternative, you can also just leave the final field name blank and press ENTER, in which case the cursor automatically moves to the OK button and you can press ENTER. Or, you can press CTRL+W.) The screen displays the Save As dialog box shown in Figure 2-4. In this box, you are prompted for a name for the file. Each database file must have a name, and the name must not contain more than eight characters. FoxPro automatically assigns an extension of .DBF to the name. For database files that include memo fields, FoxPro also automatically creates a corresponding file with an .FPT extension.

FIGURE
2-4

Save As dialog box

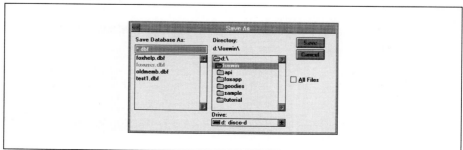

Tip In many operations (including saving a database), CTRL+W is an alternate key combination that tells FoxPro you are ready to save.

If you have been following the example, enter **MEMBERS** as the name of the file. To save the new file structure, you must next click the Save button (or TAB over to the Save button in the dialog box and press ENTER). Once you have done this, you will see a message asking if you want to add new records now, as shown here:

Choosing either Yes or No completes the database definition process, but choosing Yes leaves the file open for adding new records. You can click the Yes button (or just press ENTER) to begin adding records. If you are following the example, choose Yes, and FoxPro enters Append mode.

Note Databases with memo fields are stored in two files, with .DBF and .FPT extensions. Keep this in mind if you use DOS commands to copy or erase files.

Adding Information to a File

As with nearly all operations in FoxPro, you can add data by using a menu choice or by typing a command. From the Command window, the command you use is APPEND. (Note that a database file must first be opened with the USE command before you can type APPEND to add data.) From the menus, you can open the File menu, select the Open option, and then choose the file by name from the dialog box that appears. Once the file has been opened, you open the Record menu and choose the Append option to begin adding data.

Whether you enter **APPEND** in the Command window or choose Append from the Record menu, the result is the same: a window opens containing a simple on-screen form (Figure 2-5), with blank spaces beside each field name. In FoxPro, this is the default screen used for adding and

On-screen data entry form

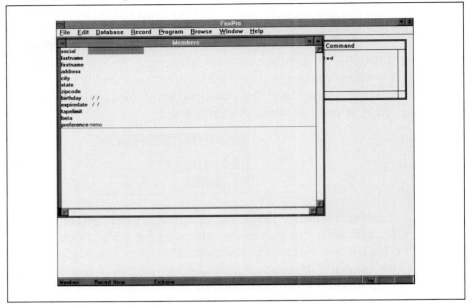

editing records. Its layout matches the structure of the database currently in use.

If you are following the example, enter the following information, pressing TAB after each entry is completed.

Social:	123-44-8976
Lastname:	Miller
Firstname:	Karen
Address:	4260 Park Avenue
City:	Chevy Chase
State:	MD
Zipcode:	20815-0988
Birthday:	03/01/54
Expiredate:	07/25/93
Tapelimit:	6
Beta:	F

If you make a mistake during the data entry process, you can click in the offending field to place the insertion pointer there, and use the BACKSPACE key to correct and retype the entry. When you have entered all of the information, the cursor should be at the start of the memo field.

Entering Data in a Memo Field

Entering data in a memo field is different from entering data in other fields. Whenever the cursor is in a memo field (as it is now), you are at the entry point for a Memo window that can hold a theoretically unlimited amount of text. (In practice, you are limited only by the available hard disk space.) You can enter the Memo window by double-clicking in a memo field, or by pressing CTRL+PGDN whenever the cursor is in a memo field. Once you use either method the entry form is partially covered by a Memo window, as shown in Figure 2-6, and you will be editing the memo field.

FIGURE
2-6

Editing within a memo field

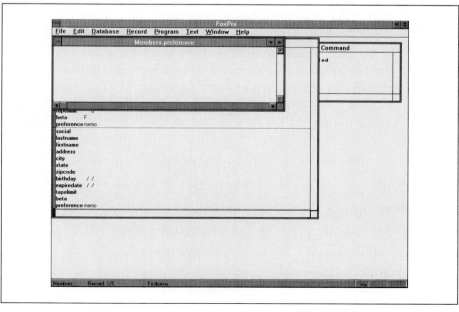

When in a Memo window, FoxPro lets you type text as you would with any word processing software. It isn't necessary to press the ENTER key at the end of every line; as you reach the end of a line, FoxPro automatically moves the cursor to the next line. The BACKSPACE key erases any mistakes, and you can use the mouse or the arrow keys to move the cursor around the screen for editing.

The various ways to edit text while in a window receive more detailed treatment in Chapter 14. For now, you'll use just the text entry capabilities and the simple editing possible with the BACKSPACE and DEL keys to add a few comments in the memo fields. As an example, type the following:

```
Prefers science fiction, horror movies. Fan of Star Trek films.
```

When you have finished typing the text, you need to get back to the data entry screen. You can do so either by choosing Close from the File menu or by double-clicking the Control menu icon at the upper-left corner of the window. Another method is to use the CTRL+F4 key combination. Use any of these methods to get back to the data entry window.

Tip   CTRL+PGDN gets you into a memo window, as does double-clicking the memo field with the mouse. Double-clicking on the Memo window's Control menu icon or using CTRL+F4 saves the changes, and gets you back out of the Memo window.

You can continue adding records by using the TAB key to move to the next (blank) record. To follow the example, fill in the following additional records for the video members' database. Double-click the Control menu icon or use CTRL+F4 to complete each memo field entry, and use the TAB key to move to each new record as the prior one is completed.

Social:	121-33-9876
Lastname:	Martin
Firstname:	William
Address:	4807 East Avenue
City:	Silver Spring
State:	MD
Zipcode:	20910-0124

Birthday:	05/29/61
Expiredate:	07/04/93
Tapelimit:	4
Beta:	F
Preference:	Enjoys Clint Eastwood, John Wayne films.
Social:	232-55-1234
Lastname:	Robinson
Firstname:	Carol
Address:	4102 Valley Lane
City:	Falls Church
State:	VA
Zipcode:	22043
Birthday:	12/22/55
Expiredate:	09/05/94
Tapelimit:	6
Beta:	F
Preference:	Likes comedy, drama films.
Social:	901-77-3456
Lastname:	Kramer
Firstname:	Harry
Address:	617 North Oakland Street
City:	Arlington
State:	VA
Zipcode:	22203
Birthday:	08/17/58
Expiredate:	12/22/93
Tapelimit:	4
Beta:	T
Preference:	Big fan of Eddie Murphy. Also enjoys westerns.

When you finish the last record, double-click the Control menu icon in the upper-left corner of the Memo window (or press CTRL+F4) to close the window. Then double-click the Control menu icon of the form's window (or press CTRL+F4 again) to leave Append mode.

An Introduction to Browse

Viewing and entering records in this manner gets the job done, but as you can see, it is often difficult to view a number of records on the screen at one time. FoxPro can also display information in table form, an important advantage because most users find it easier to grasp the concept of a database when it is shown in a tabular manner. It is easy to see a number of records at once, and the records and fields are clearly distinguished. There will be times when you prefer to see the information in the form of a table, and there will be times when you prefer a form view like the one you have been using until now.

If you are following the example, open the Database menu and choose Browse. (You can also choose Browse from the Browse menu; however, unless you are already appending to or editing a file, the Browse menu would not yet appear as a menu option.) When you select the Browse option from either the Database or the Browse menu, the database currently in use appears in table form, as shown in Figure 2-7. (If the data does not appear as a table, open the Browse menu and choose Browse. Also, note that you may need to scroll upwards using the vertical scroll bar, or press the PGUP key, to see all of the records.) This style of display is known as Browse mode. Another way to display data in this format is to enter the BROWSE command in the Command window.

Moving around in the database is different when you are in Browse mode than when you are in Append or Edit mode and using a data entry form. Try PGUP and PGDN, and then try using the UP ARROW and DOWN ARROW keys. Where previously (in Edit mode) PGUP and PGDN would move you up and down by a record at a time, they now move you up and down by a screenful of records. (Actually, since you now have less than a screenful of entries, the PGUP and PGDN keys have no effect yet.) Also, the UP ARROW and DOWN ARROW keys now move the cursor between records instead of between fields. You can use the TAB and SHIFT+TAB keys to move the cursor between fields. Using the mouse, you can also click any desired field or record to place the cursor at that location. And, you can use the scroll bars to navigate within the window; by clicking the left, right, up,

FIGURE
2-7

Tabular view of record (Browse mode)

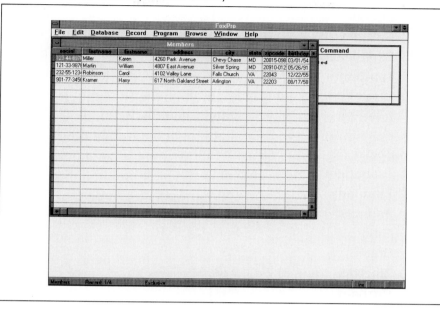

or down arrow in the window's scroll bars, you can move in the respective directions. You can also add new records to a database while in Browse mode, by choosing the Append Record option from the Browse menu, or by pressing its CTRL+N shortcut key combination.

There are a number of other options for using Browse mode, and these are covered in detail in the next chapter. If you are following along with the example, use the Append Record option on the Browse menu to add the remaining records to the table now.

Tip When working in Browse mode, use the CTRL+N key combination to add records; it is faster than using the menus.

Social:	121-90-5432
Lastname:	Moore
Firstname:	Ellen
Address:	270 Browning Ave #3C
City:	Takoma Park

State:	MD
Zipcode:	20912
Birthday:	11/02/64
Expiredate:	11/17/95
Tapelimit:	6
Beta:	F
Preference:	Drama, comedy.

Social:	495-00-3456
Lastname:	Zachman
Firstname:	David
Address:	1617 Arlington Blvd
City:	Falls Church
State:	VA
Zipcode:	22043
Birthday:	09/17/51
Expiredate:	09/19/93
Tapelimit:	4
Beta:	T
Preference:	Science fiction, drama.

Social:	343-55-9821
Lastname:	Robinson
Firstname:	Benjamin
Address:	1607 21st Street, NW
City:	Washington
State:	DC
Zipcode:	20009
Birthday:	06/22/66
Expiredate:	09/17/94
Tapelimit:	2
Beta:	T
Preference:	Westerns, comedy. Clint Eastwood fan.

Social:	876-54-3210
Lastname:	Hart
Firstname:	Wendy
Address:	6200 Germantown Road
City:	Fairfax
State:	VA
Zipcode:	22025
Birthday:	12/20/55
Expiredate:	10/19/94
Tapelimit:	2
Beta:	T
Preference:	Drama, adventure. Likes spy movies, including all James Bond series.

After the last memo field entry has been made, you can double-click the Control menu icon or use CTRL+F4 or to close the window.

Getting a Quick Report

You can create *quick reports* by selecting a few menu options. The options you use are part of the report creation process that is described in detail in Chapter 7. However, the example in the following paragraphs demonstrates how easily this can be done.

To create a quick report, choose New from the File menu. The New dialog box that appears, as shown here, offers a choice of different types of files to create.

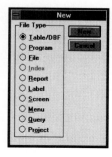

Click Report, then click New in the dialog box. Once you have selected the New button, the report design screen appears. This screen can be used to create custom reports, a process detailed in Chapter 7. For a quick report, you simply choose Quick Report from the Report menu, and the report is designed automatically for you. Open the Report menu now, and choose Quick Report. The Quick Report dialog box appears, as shown in Figure 2-8.

The Column Layout and Form Layout buttons allow you to select either a columnar layout, with data appearing in tabular columns as in Browse view, or a form layout, where each record's fields appear stacked on top of each other. For the purposes of this example, choose Form by clicking the Form button; it's the one on the right side of the dialog box. (The Titles option can be used to control whether or not field names appear as titles beside their contents, and the Fields option is used to select specific fields for inclusion in the report. You can ignore these options if

FIGURE 2-8

Quick Report dialog box

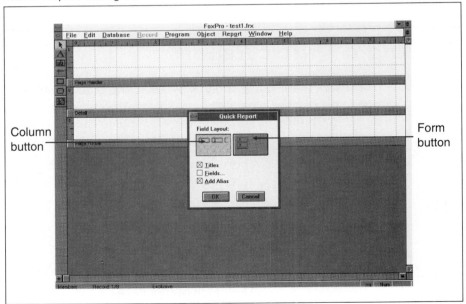

Column button

Form button

you want to include all fields in the report, as is the case here. The Add Alias option is used with reports of a relational nature. Such reports are covered in detail in Chapter 12.)

Click OK in the dialog box. You will see a report design appear, with field names laid out in a form layout, as shown in Figure 2-9. Open the File menu and choose Save. In a moment, the Save As dialog box appears.

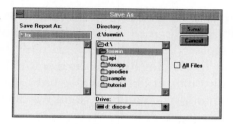

FIGURE
2-9

Report Design with fields included

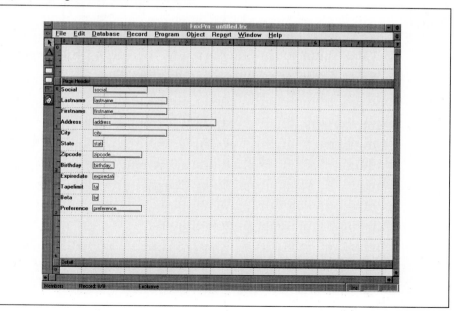

You must now enter a name for the report file. Enter **RSAMPLE** and then click the Save button. In a moment, you will be asked whether you want to save the environment information; answer Yes. (Environment information is discussed in detail in Chapter 7.) Finally, choose Close from the File menu to exit the report design process.

To run the report, you use the Report option of the Database menu. Open the Database menu and choose Report. When the Report dialog box appears, click the Form button, choose RSAMPLE from the list box which appears, then click Open. If you would like the report printed as well as displayed on your screen, turn off the Page Preview option in the dialog box (by clicking it), then turn on the To Printer option in the dialog box. Finally, click OK in the dialog box to print the report. In a moment, the Print dialog box (common to all Windows applications) appears.

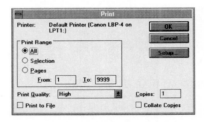

Make sure your printer is ready, then click OK to begin printing. The results should resemble those shown here:

Social:	123-44-8976
Lastname:	Miller
Firstname:	Karen
Address:	4260 Park Avenue
City:	Chevy Chase
State:	MD
Zipcode:	20815-0988
Birthday:	03/01/54
Expiredate:	07/25/92
Tapelimit:	6
Beta:	F
Preference:	Prefers science fiction.

Social:	121-33-9876
Lastname:	Martin
Firstname:	William
Address:	4807 East Avenue
City:	Silver Spring
State:	MD
Zipcode:	20910-0124
Birthday:	05/29/61
Expiredate:	07/04/93
Tapelimit:	4
Beta:	F
Preference:	Enjoys Clint Eastwood, John Wayne films.

You can produce far more detailed reports in FoxPro. Such reports can include customized headers and footers, customized placement of fields, word-wrapping large amounts of text, and numeric results based on calculations of fields. These report features are covered in Chapters 7 and 11.

Before going further, close the window containing the MEMBERS table, by either pressing CTRL+F4 or double-clicking the window's Control menu icon.

Command-Level Options for Displaying a Database

A few shortcuts for displaying your data with commands may prove useful. While using commands in the Command window requires a precise recall of how the commands should be entered, many users find commands to be faster than menu options. If the Command window is not currently the active window, click in the Command window to make it the active window.

When you first start FoxPro, you must choose a database file for use. This action can be performed with the USE command. The syntax for this command is

USE *filename*

If you now enter

```
USE MEMBERS
```

FoxPro opens the MEMBERS database file.

Viewing a Database

You can use the LIST or DISPLAY command to examine the contents of a database. Typing **LIST** by itself shows the entire contents of a database unless you specify otherwise, but you can limit the display to certain fields by including the field name after the word LIST. If you specify more than one field, separate them by commas. For example, if you are using the example database and you enter

```
LIST LASTNAME, EXPIREDATE
```

FoxPro shows only the last names and expiration dates contained in the database, as shown here. If you had entered **LIST** without any field names, you would have seen a list of all the fields.

```
Record#      LASTNAME      EXPIREDATE
1            Miller        07/25/93
2            Martin        07/04/93
3            Robinson      09/05/94
4            Kramer        12/22/93
5            Moore         11/17/95
6            Zachman       09/19/93
7            Robinson      09/17/94
8            Hart          10/19/94
```

The DISPLAY command lets you view selected information. By default, the LIST command shows you all records, while the DISPLAY command shows only the current record. To see more than one record with DISPLAY, you must add an optional "scope" clause, such as ALL or NEXT 5. Enter the following:

```
GO 3
DISPLAY
```

You will see the third record in the database. (The GO command, followed by a record number, tells FoxPro to move to that record.) Note that the record may be partially hidden by the Command window. You can move the Command window; to do so, use the mouse to drag the window in the usual manner, as outlined in Chapter 1. If you try the following commands, you will see three records, beginning with record number 2:

```
GO 2
DISPLAY NEXT 3
```

You can see an entire database by entering

```
DISPLAY ALL
```

There is one significant difference between DISPLAY ALL and LIST. If the database is large, the LIST command causes the contents to scroll up the screen without stopping. If you use the DISPLAY ALL command, the screen pauses after every screenful, and you can press any key to resume the scrolling.

The DISPLAY command can also be used to search for specific information, if it is followed by a specific condition. For example, you could display only the name, city, state, and tape-limit fields for only those members with a tape limit of four or more by entering

```
DISPLAY FIELDS LASTNAME, FIRSTNAME, CITY, STATE,
TAPELIMIT FOR TAPELIMIT > 3
```

(This command appears on two lines here, but you must enter it all on one line in the Command window.)

You can find more detailed coverage on performing selective queries in Chapter 5, "Performing Queries."

Searching Within a Field

There may be occasions when you want to search for information that is contained within a field, but you know only a portion of that information. This can cause problems, because FoxPro does not search "full text," or within a field, unless you give it specific instructions to do so. To demonstrate the problem, if one of the Generic Videos managers calls and asks for the name of "that member who lives on North Oakland Street," how do you find "that" record? The manager can't recall the member's name.

Try searching for a member who lives on North Oakland Street by entering the following:

```
DISPLAY FOR ADDRESS = "North Oakland"
```

Don't feel that you've done something wrong when the record does not appear. FoxPro normally begins a search by attempting to match your characters with the first characters of the chosen field. In our database, there is no record that begins with the characters "North Oakland" in the Address field. As a result, FoxPro failed to find the data.

To get around this problem, you can search within a field. The generic layout, or syntax, for the necessary command is

DISPLAY FOR "*search text*" $ *fieldname*

where *search text* is the actual characters that you want to look for, and *fieldname* is the name of the field that you wish to search. To try an example, enter the following command:

```
DISPLAY FOR "North Oakland" $ ADDRESS
```

This time, FoxPro should find the desired information.

You can use this technique to search for data within the text of a memo field. For example, the command

```
DISPLAY LASTNAME, PREFERENCE FOR "comedy" $
PREFERENCE
```

displays all records containing the word "comedy" anywhere in the Preference field. Figure 2-10 shows the results of such a search.

Results of text search

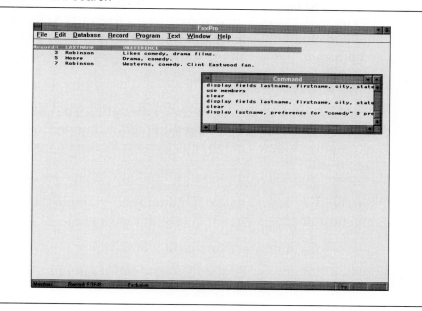

Keeping Track of Records

Whenever FoxPro looks at a database, it examines one record at a time. Even when you list all of the records in the database, FoxPro starts with the first record in the file and then examines each additional record, one by one. The program keeps track of where it is by means of a *pointer*. The FoxPro pointer is always pointing to a particular record whenever you are using a database. You can move the pointer to a specific record with the GO command.

Enter **GO TOP**, and then enter **DISPLAY**. The pointer will be at the first record in the file:

```
1   123-44-8976 Miller     Karen       4260 Park Avenue...
```

To move the pointer to the fourth record, enter **GO 4**. Enter **DISPLAY**, and you will see the fourth record:

```
4  901-77-3456 Kramer     Harry      617 North Oakland Street...
```

You can go to the first record by entering **GO TOP**, or you can go to the end of a database by entering **GO BOTTOM**. If you don't know the record number but need to find a particular record, you can use the LOCATE command to find it. The use of the LOCATE command is detailed in the following chapter.

If this is a good time for a break, enter **QUIT**. The QUIT command saves any work in progress and exits the program. For your reference, the menu alternative to leave FoxPro is to open the File menu and choose Quit from that menu.

Now that you have a file containing some data, you'll want to know how you can manipulate that data to better obtain the results you want. The next chapter covers this area in more detail.

CHAPTER

Changing Your Database

*F*oxPro has a number of menu options and commands that you can use to change records and fields. You can edit information in a record, such as a person's name or phone number on a mailing list, and you can change the structure of a database, adding fields for items that you did not plan for, or deleting fields that you no longer use. You can also shorten or expand the width of a field. Let's begin by editing records in the Generic Videos database.

Editing a Database

From the Record menu, you can use the Change option to make changes to records. (This assumes that you are already at the desired record, but there are many ways to find a record you wish to change; you will learn more about that later.) After opening a database for use, you open the Record menu and select Change. This menu option is equivalent to entering **CHANGE** in the Command window. With either method, a record in the database appears within the default form in a window, as shown in Figure 3-1.

Remember   You can open a database file for use by choosing File/Open from the menu bar, or by entering **USE <filename>** in the Command window.

At this point you are in Change mode, and you can make changes to the data within the chosen record. If you repeatedly press the arrow keys, you will note that each keypress moves the cursor one row at a time. If you keep pressing the DOWN ARROW key, FoxPro takes you to the next record in the file. Pressing the UP ARROW key repeatedly eventually takes you to the prior record in the file, unless you are already at the first record. You can use the arrow keys to move the cursor to any location in the record.

While you are in Change mode, you can also use the PGUP and PGDN keys to move around in the database. The PGDN key takes you one record forward, and the PGUP key takes you one record back. At the first record in the file, PGUP has no effect, and at the last record in the file, PGDN has no effect.

Result of Change option or CHANGE command

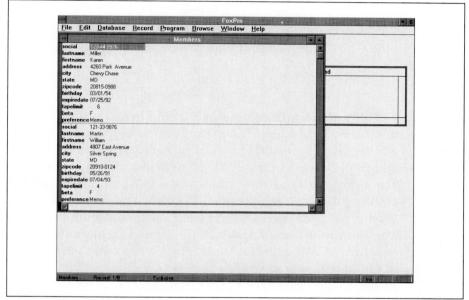

You can make changes to any field by clicking in the desired field, and typing your desired corrections. As an example of changing a file, an address change might be needed for Ms. Ellen Moore, a member of the video club. If you have not already done so, open the MEMBERS file by choosing the Open option from the File menu, or by entering **USE MEMBERS** in the Command window. Then enter **CHANGE** or choose the Change option from the Record menu. Next, use the PGDN key to find the record for Ms. Ellen Moore. The final steps in the correction are to click in the Address field to place the insertion pointer next to the apartment number, use the BACKSPACE key to delete the old apartment number, and enter **#2A** as the new apartment number.

Once you make changes you can make them permanent either by pressing CTRL+F4 or by moving to another record (with the mouse, the arrow keys, or the PGUP and PGDN keys). For now, consider the menu options available for changing records.

If you open the Record menu now, you see the options shown here:

This menu contains options that are useful when you are changing a database. The Append option puts you in the Append mode, allowing the addition of new records as detailed in the previous chapter. The Change option puts you in Change (or Edit) mode, allowing records to be edited. The Goto and Locate options can be used to quickly find a record for editing. Goto can take you to a specific record by record number, and Locate can perform a search based on the contents of a particular field. The Goto and Locate options are covered in more detail in Chapter 5; however, a brief introduction to the Locate option is useful for the task of finding records to edit.

When you select Locate from the Record menu, another dialog box appears:

The dialog box contains three options: Scope, For, and While. For your basic search, all you need is the For option (Scope and While are covered in Chapter 5). When you click For, another dialog box appears, as shown in Figure 3-2. The use of all the options in this dialog box are covered in detail in Chapter 5. For the purposes of a simple search, you should know that you can enter a search expression in the For Clause window and then click the OK button.

A *search expression* is simply a combination of a field name, operator (usually an equal sign), and search term or value you are looking for. For example, say you are seeking the record for Ms. Robinson. Enter the expression

```
LASTNAME = "Robinson"
```

FIGURE 3-2

Expression Builder dialog box

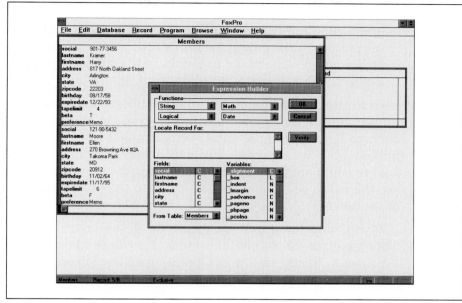

in the Locate Record For portion of the dialog box, and then click the OK button. The For Clause dialog box disappears, and the previous dialog box (with the Scope, For, and While choices) is again visible. You next click the Locate button to begin the Locate operation. Assuming you are still in Change mode, the desired record appears, as shown in Figure 3-3.

Note that the cursor stays in the field it was in when you initiated the search. For example, if the cursor was in the Address field after you edited Ellen Moore's address, it would move to the Address field of Robinson's record. In some cases, you might need to use the vertical scroll bar or the arrow keys to see the name field.

You can use similar search expressions to find any desired record. For example, within the For Clause window you could enter

```
TAPELIMIT = 4
```

to find the first record in the database with a value of 4 in the Tapelimit field. And you could use an expression like

```
LASTNAME = "Smith" .AND. FIRSTNAME = "Susan" .AND. CITY =
"Raleigh"
```

to find a person with that name living in that specific city. (Note the use of the periods surrounding the word "AND"; these are required. Chapter 5 offers more details on the use of the .AND. clause in expressions.)

The Locate option finds the first occurrence of the search term; if you wish to look for additional records meeting your search criteria, choose Continue from the Record menu. For example, after the earlier Locate operation, you could use the Continue option from the Record menu to find each successive record in which the value of Tapelimit was 4. If FoxPro could not find any records meeting the search criteria, you would see the message "End of Locate scope" in the Status Bar at the bottom of the window.

If you know the record number of the desired record, you can use the Goto option of the Record menu to find the desired record. For example, if you want to edit record number 6, open the Record menu, select the

FIGURE 3-3

Results of search

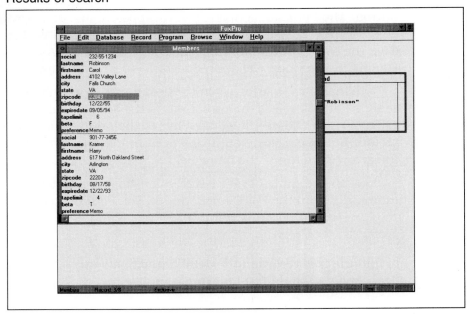

Goto option, and from the dialog box that next appears, choose Record and enter **6** in the text box. Click the Goto button. You will see that FoxPro jumps to record 6, which happens to be the record for Mr. David Zachman.

As with all menu operations, you can also perform these tasks with commands. From the Command window, once you have opened a file for use with the USE command, you can edit a record by using the command CHANGE *n*, where *n* is the record number of the record you want to edit. Users who are familiar with the dBASE language may know that EDIT is an equivalent command. Entering **EDIT 5** accomplishes the same result as entering **CHANGE 5**: record number 5 appears, ready for editing.

You can also use the command GO *n*, where *n* is the record number of the record you wish to edit, and then enter the CHANGE or EDIT command without any record number after the command. For example, in the Command window, you could enter

```
GO 3
CHANGE
```

to edit the contents of record number 3. Once in Change mode, you can save your changes by using CTRL+F4 or by double-clicking the window's close box.

From the Command window, you can also use the LOCATE command to perform a search in a manner similar to the search options of the menus. By default, LOCATE starts its search from the top of the file rather than from the current record. However, you can conduct a forward search by using the CONTINUE command after the LOCATE command. For example, if you use the command

```
LOCATE FOR LASTNAME = "Robinson"
```

and the name you find is not the Robinson you want, you can then enter

```
CONTINUE
```

to find additional occurrences of the same last name.

Editing in Browse Mode

Another useful way of editing data is from Browse mode, which was introduced in the previous chapter. Browse mode displays more than one record at a time on the screen, so you can conveniently access a number of records for editing. To use Browse mode, enter **BROWSE** in the Command window or choose the Browse option on the Database menu. You'll see a screenful of records, as shown in Figure 3-4 (you may need to press PGUP to see all of the records).

Browse mode displays as many fields as will fit on the screen. If there are more fields in a record than will fit on a screen, only the first few fields appear. With most monitors and graphics hardware, this is the case with the Generic Videos database. (Users running very high video resolutions on multi-scan monitors may be able to see the entire table at once.) In cases where you cannot see all of the fields, the other fields are to the right of the display. When in Browse mode, you can scan across the database to bring other fields or additional records into view by using the scroll bars, or the TAB and SHIFT+TAB key combinations. Using the scroll bar at the right edge, you can click the up and down arrows to scroll the database vertically. You can also drag the square box within the scroll bar; this provides a vertical movement relative to the location of the indicator. For example, if you drag the box three-fourths of the way down

FIGURE 3-4   Browse mode

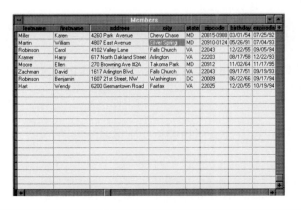

the vertical scroll bar and release it, you will be positioned about three-fourths of the way down the database.

The scroll bar at the bottom edge works in a similar manner for horizontal movement. Clicking on the left and right arrows scrolls the database columns horizontally, and dragging the box provides a horizontal movement relative to the location of the indicator. Other mouse features work the same with Browse as they do with other windows; you can resize the window by dragging any edge or corner of the window, and you can use the Maximize and Minimize buttons (detailed in Chapter 1) to expand the window to full size, or to reduce it to an icon.

Try pressing the TAB key repeatedly. As you continue to press the TAB key, fields on the left side of the window disappear as remaining fields come into view. Tabbing at the end of the table will take you back to the start of the table.

Press SHIFT+TAB repeatedly, and you'll notice the opposite effect. The fields that disappeared at the left of the window reappear, as the fields on the right side disappear. Continue pressing SHIFT+TAB until the Social field returns to view within the window.

Try using the PGUP and PGDN keys. These two keys move the cursor through the database one screenful at a time. Since Generic Videos' list of members is rather short, pressing PGDN moves the cursor to the end of the database. To move the cursor up or down by one record, use the UP ARROW and DOWN ARROW keys.

You can also edit the records while in Browse mode. You can type changes in a field, and they will take effect just as they did when you were using Edit mode. However, it is usually easier to access a particular field when in Change (or Edit) mode.

Memo fields can be edited in Browse mode, in the same manner as in Change mode; double-click the memo field to open a window containing its contents, and edit the contents as desired. (An alternate method is to place the cursor in the memo field, and press CTRL+PGDN.) When done with the memo field, double-click the Control menu icon to close it, or press CTRL+F4, or open the Control menu with ALT+HYPHEN and choose Close.

In Browse mode, records can be added to a database by opening the Browse menu and choosing Append Record. (Note that a shortcut key, CTRL+N, exists for this menu option.) When you choose this option, a new, blank record appears at the end of the file, and the cursor appears in the first field of that record. You can enter the desired information, and then exit Browse mode when you are done by double-clicking the close box, or by choosing Close from the File menu, or by pressing CTRL+F4.

Note You might think that choosing Append from the Record menu would also let you add a record. It will do so, but you will not remain in Browse mode with this option; if you use it to add a record, FoxPro switches to Append mode, with the familiar Edit/Change form displayed in a window.

Browse Menu Options

While in Browse mode, note that a new option, Browse, has been added to the menu bar at the top of the screen. Open the Browse menu now, and you will see the options shown here:

Its options are covered in detail in the following pages, and here is a brief overview of them. Note, too, that many of these operations can be performed quickly with the mouse, so you may find the menu options unnecessary (unless you prefer to use the keyboard).

☐ *Change* This option shows the database in the Browse window but in full-screen (edit) format, similar to the display that appears with the CHANGE or EDIT command.

☐ *Grid* This option hides or displays the vertical and horizontal lines that normally appear between the columns and rows. The option is a toggle, so selecting it will alternately hide and display the vertical lines.

☐ *Link Partitions* When a window is split into two parts or partitions, this option alternately "links" or "unlinks" the two portions of the window. Unlinking allows you to move the cursor independently in the two partitions, whereas linking scrolls both partitions in synchronization. The Link Partitions option is a toggle, so selecting it will alternately link and unlink partitions.

☐ *Change Partition* When a window is split into two partitions, this makes the active partition of the window inactive and the inactive partition active.

☐ *Font* When chosen, this option opens a dialog box from which you can select the desired font, font style, and font size to use in the Browse window.

☐ *Size Field* This resizes the field that contains the cursor. TAB to the desired field, select the option, and use the arrow keys to change the size; then press any key (except the arrow keys) to complete the resizing.

☐ *Move Field* This moves a field to a new location. TAB to the desired field, select the option, and use the LEFT ARROW or RIGHT ARROW key to relocate the field. When done, press any key except the LEFT ARROW or RIGHT ARROW key.

☐ *Resize Partitions* This lets you split a window into two parts, or if it is already split, lets you change the size of the partitions. (It is generally easier to do this with the mouse, by dragging the Split Bar—as is discussed shortly.) You can also use this option to restore a split window back to a single window. Choose the option, and then use the LEFT ARROW and RIGHT ARROW keys to open, close, or change the size of the partitions. When done, press any key except the LEFT ARROW or RIGHT ARROW key.

☐ *Goto* This option is the equivalent of the Goto option of the Change menu; you can use it to go to a specific record.

☐ *Seek* This option is used with indexed files to quickly find a record. The subject of indexed files is covered in the next chapter.

☐ *Toggle Delete* This lets you mark a record for deletion while in Browse mode. Place the cursor at the desired record, and then choose Toggle Delete (or press CTRL+T) to mark the record for deletion.

☐ *Append Record* This adds a blank record to the end of the database.

Before proceeding, you will find it helpful to have a database to work with that contains more records than the sample one you created earlier. There is a simple way to create such a database: you can create a new file based on the existing Videos file, and duplicate records from the existing file into the new file a number of times. Double-click the Control Menu icon to exit the Browse window, and enter the following commands in the Command window now to create a larger database for use with Browse:

```
COPY STRUCTURE TO BIGFILE
USE BIGFILE
APPEND FROM MEMBERS
APPEND FROM MEMBERS
APPEND FROM MEMBERS
APPEND FROM MEMBERS
APPEND FROM MEMBERS
APPEND FROM MEMBERS
```

This creates a file with 48 records, enough to fill a screen while in Browse mode. Enter **BROWSE** to get back into Browse mode now. (You may want to press the PGUP key so you can see a window full of records.)

Changing the Fonts

You may prefer to change the font or font size used by the Browse window, to make the type easier to read. You can quickly do so by choosing the Font option of the Browse menu. When you choose Browse/Font, a Font dialog box appears, as shown here:

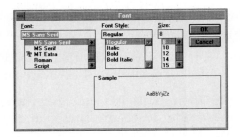

Click the desired font by name in the Font list box to select it, and click the desired point size in the Size list box. In the Font Style box, you can choose from among Regular, Italic, Bold, or Bold Italic. When done choosing your options, click OK. Your choice of fonts, styles, and sizes can make a significant difference in the appearance of data in the Browse window; as an example, Figure 3-5 shows a Browse window using a Sans Serif font and an 8-point size, while Figure 3-6 shows a Browse window using a Times New Roman font and a 12-point size.

Manipulating the Window

FoxPro offers you several options for manipulating the size and contents of the Browse window. Click the window's Maximize button, which allows the display of a maximum number of records at a time, to open the window to full size, as seen in Figure 3-7. You can now try the PGUP and PGDN keys to move throughout the database.

You can split the window into two portions with the mouse, or with the Resize Partitions option. Try splitting the Browse window with the mouse now, by dragging the split bar in the bottom scroll bar. Place the mouse pointer over the split bar; when you do so, the pointer changes shape to resemble an arrow with two heads. Click and drag the split bar to the right until the mouse pointer is just past the Social, Lastname, and Firstname fields. When you do so, your screen will resemble the example shown in Figure 3-8.

Browse window using 8-point Sans Serif font

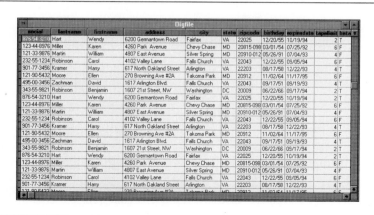

FIGURE
3-6

Browse window using 12-point Times New Roman font

From the keyboard, you can split a window by opening the Browse menu and choosing Resize Partitions. Begin pressing the RIGHT ARROW

FIGURE
3-7

Browse mode after maximizing window

FIGURE
3-8

Browse window after split

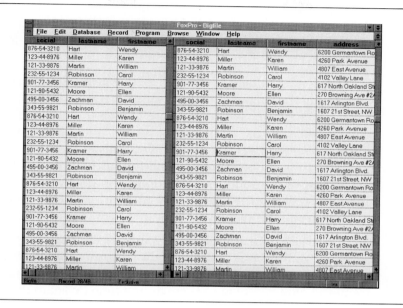

key, and the window splits in two. Continue pressing the RIGHT ARROW key until the desired fields are visible. Then press any key (other than the arrow keys) to complete the operation.

With the split window, the portion of the window containing a high-lighted cursor, or an insertion pointer, is the *active partition*. With the mouse, you can make the inactive partition active simply by clicking anywhere inside it. From the keyboard, you can swap active partitions by choosing Change Partition from the Browse menu. Note that there is a shortcut key combination (CTRL+H) for this menu option. Try repeatedly pressing CTRL+H now to see how you can change partitions.

Using Edit in Browse

The Change option of the Browse menu can be used to display a record in Edit mode, while you are still in a Browse window. This is particularly useful for seeing records in both a tabular view and a full-record view at the same time (which you can do once you split a window). Make the right partition active now by clicking anywhere in the right partition, or by pressing CTRL+H. Next, choose Change from the Browse menu. Note that the screen layout of the right partition changes to Edit mode, as shown in Figure 3-9.

A major advantage of this type of display is that you can easily locate a record in the left partition, and see all of the fields for that corresponding record in the right partition. Press CTRL+H to make the left partition the active one, and try using the UP ARROW and DOWN ARROW keys to view different records. As you do this, you will see the selected record appear in the right partition. Note that once you are using the Edit style of display in the active partition, the first option on the Browse menu changes to Browse. You can then use this menu option to change the display back to a Browse-style display.

The Grid option of the Browse menu can be used to remove the vertical and horizontal lines that normally appear between fields and records when you use the Browse style of display. Once the lines have been removed, you can restore them at any time by again choosing Grid from

FIGURE
3-9

Edit mode in Browse window

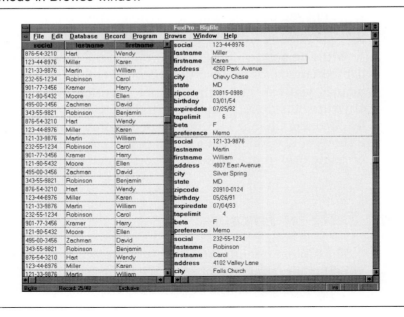

the Browse menu. (A check mark appears in the menu beside the word Grid when the lines are turned on.)

Mouse users should note that when a window is split, two vertical scroll bars appear; the center vertical scroll bar controls movement in the left partition, and the right vertical scroll bar controls movement in the right partition.

Unlinked Partitions

As you move the cursor between records, both partitions move in the same direction. This happens because partitions are normally *linked,* or synchronized to the same record. There may be times when you prefer to maintain independent control over the partitions. You can do so by choosing Link Partitions from the Browse menu. Once you do so, you can switch between partitions with CTRL+H or with the mouse, and move around in each partition independently.

 Tip You can tell whether partitions are linked or not by looking at the Link option in the Browse menu. If a check mark appears beside the option, partitions are linked; if the check mark does not appear, the partitions are unlinked.

Open the Browse menu again, and now choose Link Partitions to restore the link before proceeding. Then click anywhere in the left partition (or use CTRL+H) to make the left partition the active one.

Changing Field Sizes and Positions

You can change field widths and rearrange the position of the fields while you are in Browse mode. (Changing the position of the field does not affect the field's position in the database; only the screen display is affected.) You change field widths by clicking and dragging the border in the field heading area, or by using the Size Field option of the Browse menu. You change field locations by clicking the field heading itself and dragging it to the desired location, or by using the Move Field option.

Try sizing the Firstname field now, by placing the mouse pointer in the field heading area, at the right edge of the field. When you do so, the mouse pointer changes to the shape of a double-headed arrow. Click and drag this edge to the left slightly, release the mouse button, and you will see the field narrow by a corresponding amount.

If you prefer to use the keyboard, you can size a field by placing the cursor in the desired field, and choosing Size Field from the Browse menu. Use the LEFT ARROW key to narrow the field size to the desired amount, and then press ENTER to complete the resizing.

To move a field, simply click on the field's heading, and drag it to the desired location. You can try this now by clicking the Firstname field heading and holding down the mouse button, and then dragging the field over to the Lastname column. When you release the mouse button, the Firstname field will be relocated, and will appear ahead of the Lastname field. If your window is still split between a Browse-style display and an Edit-style display, note that the field position has changed in both, as shown in Figure 3-10.

FIGURE 3-10

Fields after movement

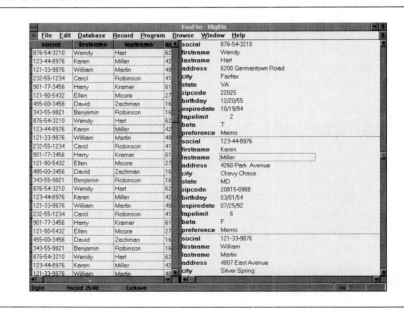

The normal procedure for moving a field using the keyboard is to place the cursor in the desired field, choose Move Field from the Browse menu, and relocate the field with the LEFT ARROW or RIGHT ARROW key. When the field is in the desired position, press ENTER to end the process.

Before proceeding, double-click the Browse window's Control menu icon to exit Browse mode.

Using Browse with Commands

You can enter the BROWSE command in the Command window to get into Browse mode, and then use the same Browse menu options and key combinations described earlier to update records. There are also options that you can specify in the Command window along with the BROWSE command. These options provide ways to lock certain fields in place so that they are not lost from view when you pan with the CTRL and arrow keys. Other command-level options let you show or edit selected fields when using BROWSE.

Tip The BROWSE options available at the command level give you more flexibility than those on the Browse menu.

Using the FIELDS option of the BROWSE command, you can name the specific fields that you want to display with BROWSE. This option is particularly helpful when you want to edit only specific information while using BROWSE. The syntax for this form of the command is

BROWSE FIELDS *field1, field2,...field3*

As an example, you might wish to change the tape-limit amounts to reflect new tape limits for some video club members. You want to see only their names and tape-limit amounts. Click anywhere in the Command window to get to the command level, and then try this command:

```
BROWSE FIELDS LASTNAME, FIRSTNAME, TAPELIMIT
```

The resulting display, shown in Figure 3-11, shows only those fields that you named within the command. Since these are the only fields that are displayed, they are the only fields that can presently be edited.

The FREEZE option of the BROWSE command lets you limit any editing to a specific field. This is a useful command to know, because there is no equivalent from the Browse menu. The FREEZE option comes in particularly handy when you must change one field in a number of records; when you use the option, DOWN ARROW moves you to the next record rather than the next field. When you use FREEZE, other fields are displayed, but only the specified field can be changed. The syntax for the command is

BROWSE FREEZE *fieldname*

To try the effect of this option, press CTRL+F4 to exit the current Browse window, and then enter

```
BROWSE FREEZE EXPIREDATE
```

You will see that only the Expiredate field can be edited. The UP ARROW and DOWN ARROW keys will move you between records, but pressing TAB or SHIFT+TAB does not cause you to leave the field, as it normally does, and the LEFT and RIGHT ARROW keys have no effect.

FIGURE 3-11

Browsed fields

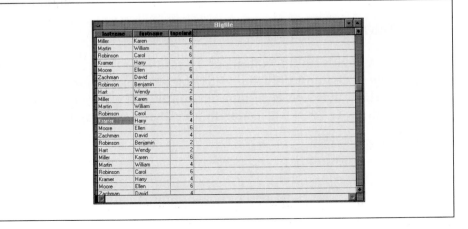

You can use the command-level options of the BROWSE command in combination with each other. For example, the command

```
BROWSE FIELDS LASTNAME, CITY, STATE, EXPIREDATE
FREEZE EXPIREDATE
```

results in a display with the Lastname, City, State, and Expiredate fields visible, and just the Expiredate field available for editing. (The above command is printed on two lines, but you must enter it on one line.)

Before proceeding, press CTRL+F4 to close the Browse window. Then enter the command **USE MEMBERS** to close the larger file you created earlier and get back into the video database.

Deleting Records

FoxPro uses a combination of two menu options, or two commands, to delete records. From the menus, these are the Delete option of the Record menu and the Pack option of the Database menu. From the command level, the two commands are DELETE and PACK.

Remember   Records you mark for deletion are still visible (unless you use SET DELETED ON). You must perform a PACK to permanently remove the records.

The Delete option of the Record menu (or its command-level equivalent, the DELETE command) prepares a record for deletion but does not actually delete the record. This method allows you to mark as many records as you wish at one time for later deletion. By letting you identify records in this manner, FoxPro provides a built-in safeguard: you have the opportunity to change your mind and recall the record.

To mark a single record for deletion, first find the desired record with any of the search techniques discussed previously. Then open the Record menu and choose the Delete option. A dialog box appears, as shown in Figure 3-12. If you just want to mark the current record for deletion, you can ignore all of the options, and click the Delete button to delete the record.

Delete dialog box

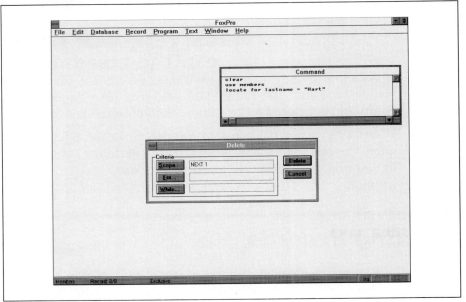

For future reference, the Scope option lets you choose a larger group of records for deletion; you can choose All records, Next n (where *n* is a number, such as the next five records), Record n (where *n* is the record number of the record to be deleted), or Rest (which deletes all records from the current record to the end of the file). The While option in the dialog box is used with indexed files; it is discussed in Chapter 5, but it is not appropriate for use with simple deletions.

You can repeat the technique just described as often as necessary, deleting unwanted records. The records remain in the database until you use the Pack option of the Database menu to make the deletions permanent. (If you are using the example database, do *not* permanently remove any records with Pack—they are used in additional examples later in the text.) Because the Pack option involves copying all records not marked for deletion to a temporary file, it can be quite time-consuming with large databases.

Note that while you are in a Browse window, FoxPro provides another quick way to delete a record. You can click the mouse pointer in the rectangular shaded area to the immediate left of the record's leftmost field. When you click in this area, the shaded area turns from gray to black, indicating that the record has been marked for deletion. You can delete as many records as you want using this method, and then use the Pack command (or the Pack option of the Database menu) to make the deletions permanent.

Command window users can use the LOCATE command to find desired records, followed by the DELETE command to mark the records for deletion. To see how this works, get to the Command window, if you are not already there. You may recall from earlier in the chapter that the format of the LOCATE command, when used with a simple search, is

LOCATE FOR *fieldname* = "*search-term*"

If you are searching a character field, you must surround the search term with quotes. Capitalization inside the quotes must also match the target record; you will not find the desired record if you enter **Jackson** when what's really stored within the field is "jackson". If you are searching a numeric field, enter the number alone without any quotes. (The syntax for searching dates and memo fields is discussed in Chapter 5.) As an example, if you are working with the video database, try the following:

```
LOCATE FOR LASTNAME = "Hart"
```

FoxPro should respond with the message "Record = 8" in the lower-left corner of the Status Bar. If you instead see an error message, or the message "End of Locate scope," recheck your spelling of the command or the last name, and try the command again. Then, since record 8 is the one you want to mark for deletion, enter

```
DELETE
```

and the confirmation "1 record(s) deleted" briefly appears in the Status Bar.

If you know the record number, you can specify the command DELETE RECORD *n*, where *n* is the number of the record to be deleted. Suppose that Mr. Kramer, listed in record 4, also needs to be removed from the list. Enter the command

```
DELETE RECORD 4
```

Again, the "1 record(s) deleted" message briefly appears. Now enter the command

```
LIST LASTNAME, FIRSTNAME
```

and the listing that results should resemble the one shown here:

```
Record#   LASTNAME        FIRSTNAME
      1   Miller          Karen
      2   Martin          William
      3   Robinson        Carol
      4  *Kramer          Harry
      5   Moore           Ellen
      6   Zachman         David
      7   Robinson        Benjamin
      8  *Hart            Wendy
```

You can see from the listing that the marked records have not been removed from the database. When the LIST command is used, an asterisk appears beside the marked records, indicating that the records are marked for deletion.

If you decide that deleting a record is not the thing to do, you can use the RECALL command to undo the damage. For example, enter the following command to recall the fourth record:

```
RECALL RECORD 4
```

The confirmation "1 record recalled" briefly appears in the Status Bar. Now re-enter the LIST LASTNAME, FIRSTNAME command. A shortcut is available here: by pressing the UP ARROW key while the Command window is active, you can move the cursor back up to the commands you entered earlier. When the cursor is beside the desired command (in this case, LIST LASTNAME, FIRSTNAME), just press ENTER to repeat the command. Once you do so, the database shows that only record 8 is still marked for deletion. Note that the RECALL ALL command can be used to recall all records marked for deletion. (For now, leave record 8 marked.)

When a record has been marked for deletion, it remains in the database, and operations like SUM and COUNT (which are covered later) can still use the record in calculations, as if it had never been deleted. Also, the deleted record will still appear in your reports, which may not be what you had in mind. To avoid displaying and using records that have been marked for deletion, you can use the SET DELETED command. Enter

```
SET DELETED ON
```

Now repeat the LIST LASTNAME, FIRSTNAME command by pressing the UP ARROW key until you are at the command, and then pressing ENTER. You will see that record 8, which is still marked for deletion, does not appear. To make the record visible again, enter

```
SET DELETED OFF
```

When you try the LIST command again, the record marked for deletion will be visible in the database.

There is no need to delete records one by one with the DELETE command. You can mark more than one record for deletion by specifying the number of records to be deleted. For example, enter the commands

```
GO 5
DELETE NEXT 2
LIST LASTNAME, FIRSTNAME
```

GO 5 moves the pointer to record 5; then DELETE NEXT 2 marks records 5 and 6 for deletion.

The RECALL command can be used in the same manner. Enter

```
GO 5
RECALL NEXT 2
LIST LASTNAME, FIRSTNAME
```

and records 5 and 6 will be unmarked. Before proceeding, enter the command

```
RECALL ALL
```

to recall any records that are still marked for deletion. Remember that after deleting records in your files, you must enter **PACK** (or choose the Pack option of the Database menu) to make your deletions permanent.

Note A pack operation can be time-consuming with large databases.

Deleting Files

You can also delete whole files from within FoxPro. From the command level, you can use the DELETE FILE command. For example, the command

```
DELETE FILE NAMES2.DBF
```

would erase a file called NAMES2.DBF from the disk. Use care in deleting files, because once a file has been deleted, you cannot recall it without special programs or techniques that are beyond the scope of this book.

Global Replacements with Commands

Suppose that you wanted to replace the five-digit ZIP codes with the new nine-digit ZIP codes for both members named Robinson. You can change the ZIP code for every Washington, D.C., entry by adding options to the CHANGE command. With these options, you need to use CHANGE only once because it becomes a global command. A *global command* performs the command on the entire database, not just on a single record.

When used with the global options, the CHANGE command becomes a two-step process: first, CHANGE finds the proper field, and then it asks you to enter the correction. The generic format of the command is

CHANGE FIELDS *fieldname* FOR *keyfield* = "*keyname*"

where *fieldname* is the field where you want the changes to occur, and *keyfield* is the field where CHANGE searches for the occurrence of *keyname.* You must surround keyname with quotes.

In the following example you use the CHANGE command to change the Zipcode field for each record in the database that has the word "Robinson" in the Lastname field. Enter the following:

```
CHANGE FIELDS LASTNAME, FIRSTNAME, ZIPCODE FOR LASTNAME =
"Robinson"
```

The first record with "Robinson" in the Lastname field appears. Notice that FoxPro displays only the fields that you named as part of the CHANGE command.

The cursor is flashing in the Lastname field, so you can move down to the Zipcode field and enter **22043-1234** as the new ZIP code for this record. After you fill the field, you can move down to the next record with "Robinson" in the Lastname field. Enter **20009-1010**, press CTRL+F4, and the screen form vanishes. To see the results, enter

```
LIST LASTNAME, CITY, ZIPCODE
```

The new ZIP codes you entered are displayed, as shown here:

Record#	LASTNAME	CITY	ZIPCODE
1	Miller	Chevy Chase	20815-0988
2	Martin	Silver Spring	20910-0124
3	Robinson	Falls Church	22043-1234
4	Kramer	Arlington	22203
5	Moore	Takoma Park	20912
6	Zachman	Falls Church	22043
7	Robinson	Washington	20009-1010
8	Hart	Fairfax	22025

REPLACE operates very much like CHANGE, except that REPLACE doesn't ask you to type in the change after it finds the field. Instead, you specify the change within the command, and it is made automatically. The format of the command is

REPLACE [*scope*] *fieldname* WITH *field-replacement* FOR *condition*

The *scope* parameter is optional and is used to determine how many records REPLACE will look at. If ALL is used as the scope, REPLACE looks at all records; but if NEXT 5 is used as the scope, REPLACE looks only at the next five records from the pointer's current position. NEXT is always followed by the number of records REPLACE will look at. The *fieldname* parameter is the field where the change will occur, and *field-replacement* is what will be inserted if *keyfield*, which is the field REPLACE is searching for, matches *keyword*.

There is plenty going on with REPLACE, so it might be best described by an example. Enter the following:

```
REPLACE ALL CITY WITH "Miami" FOR CITY = "Falls Church"
```

This means "Search for all City fields containing the words 'Falls Church' and then replace those fields with the word 'Miami'." Next, enter

```
LIST LASTNAME, CITY
```

You'll see that the Falls Church members have been relocated to Miami. They probably would not enjoy the commute to work, so let's move them back. Enter the command

```
REPLACE ALL CITY WITH "Falls Church" FOR CITY = "Miami"
```

Again, enter

```
LIST LASTNAME, CITY
```

Now the City fields are restored to their original contents. The REPLACE command is very handy for updating salaries or prices on a global basis. If every employee in a personnel file is to receive a 50-cent per hour increase, do you really want to manually update each record? It is much faster to use the REPLACE command to perform the task. Assuming a field named Salary in a personnel file, you could use a command like

```
REPLACE ALL SALARY WITH SALARY + .50
```

to quickly increase all salary amounts by 50 cents.

 Tip The REPLACE command can be used much like a word processor's search-and-replace feature. You can change values in a group of records, or in all records, depending on the structure of the REPLACE command.

As you work with FoxPro, you'll find that REPLACE is a handy command for changing area codes, dollar amounts, and for other similar applications. But you should be careful: REPLACE can wreak havoc on a database if used improperly. If you doubt whether REPLACE will have the desired effect, make a copy of the database file under a different name and experiment on the copy instead of the original. Or you can use the CHANGE command as described earlier. CHANGE is a better command to use when you want to see the data and exercise some discretion regarding the changes.

Modifying the Structure of a Database

You'll often use a database for a while and then decide to enlarge a field, delete a field, or add a field for another category. You can make these changes in the structure of a database. From the command level, this is done with the MODIFY STRUCTURE command. From the menus, you choose the Setup option of the Database menu; when the dialog box appears, you click the Modify button. When you change the structure of a database, FoxPro creates a new, empty database according to your instructions and then copies all the records from the old database into the new database.

If the manager at Generic Videos suddenly decides that the database should include all of the members' phone numbers, you can add a field for them. To make this change, in the Command window enter

```
MODIFY STRUCTURE
```

or open the Database menu and choose the Setup option. When the dialog box appears, click Modify. With either approach, you will see the structure of the Generic Videos database as shown in Figure 3-13.

You will enter the field name, type, and width exactly as you did when you created the database in Chapter 2. But before you do, you need room to add a new field. While it is easiest to add new fields at the end of the existing list of fields, you can add them anywhere you desire by using the Insert and Delete buttons at the right side of the dialog box.

Click anywhere in the Birthday field to select it. Then click Insert, and a new field appears above the Birthday field. Since you want to enter phone numbers, the word "Phone" would be a good title for the field. Enter **Phone**, then press TAB. Once you press TAB, the cursor moves to the field type column. You want to use C for the Character type (since phone numbers are never used in calculations, they need not be numeric), so press TAB again to select this default and move on to the next column.

At the Width category, enter **12**. This leaves room for a ten-digit phone number and two hyphens. You could, if needed, change any of the field widths for the existing fields by moving to the desired field and entering a new value in the Width column.

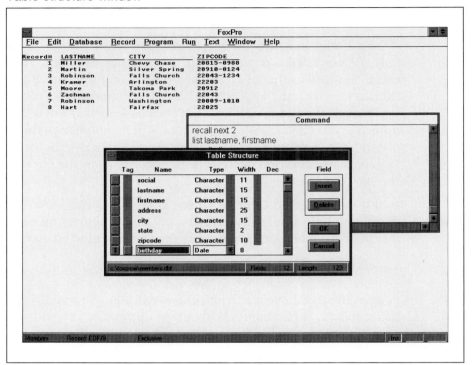

FIGURE
3-13   Table structure window

Moving Fields

While it is not necessary in this example to move a field to a different location in the structure, you can easily do so if you desire. To move an existing field, click and hold the button at the far left side of the window, adjacent to the field's name, and drag the button along with the entire field up or down to the desired new location.

Saving the Changes

When you modify a database, data is automatically returned from the fields of the temporary file to the fields in the modified database, but only if the field names and field types match. If you change the type of a field,

FoxPro may not restore the data in that particular field, since it doesn't always know how to convert the data type. FoxPro makes the conversion when it can. For example, if you change a character field into a numeric field, all valid numeric entries are converted. However, if you were to change a numeric field into a logical field, the data in the numeric field would be lost because the two field types have nothing in common.

Once you have completed your desired changes to the database structure, click the OK button in the dialog box. You will see the dialog box shown here:

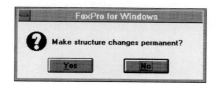

This indicates that FoxPro is ready to copy the data from the old file into the modified database. Click Yes, and after a short delay (during which FoxPro automatically rebuilds the database), you are returned to the Command window. Now enter the command

```
BROWSE FIELDS LASTNAME, FIRSTNAME, PHONE FREEZE PHONE
```

Press PGUP, and you'll see that all of the Phone fields are present but empty. To complete the database, type in the phone numbers for the members as shown here:

Lastname	Firstname	Phone
Miller	Karen	301-555-6678
Martin	William	301-555-2912
Robinson	Carol	703-555-8778
Kramer	Harry	703-555-6874
Moore	Ellen	301-555-0201
Zachman	David	703-555-5432
Robinson	Benjamin	202-555-4545
Hart	Wendy	703-555-1201

Had this field been planned in advance, during the database design stage outlined in Chapter 1, you wouldn't have the inconvenience of returning to each record to type in a phone number.

 Note If you change a field's name and its location in the database structure at the same time, by inserting or deleting fields, FoxPro doesn't restore the data in that particular field because it doesn't know where to find the data. FoxPro uses either the field name or the position of the field in the database structure to transfer existing data. If both are changed, the existing data is discarded. If you need to change both the name and location of a field, perform the task in two steps. Change the field name, and exit the Modify Structure process; then re-enter the MODIFY STRUCTURE command and change the field's location.

Creating the Rentals File

Before proceeding to the next chapter, you should create an additional database. This database, called RENTALS, will contain a listing of videotapes rented by the members of Generic Videos. Later chapters will make use of this file in various examples of working with more than one database file.

To create the file, click in the Command window, and enter the command

```
CREATE RENTALS
```

When the Database Structure window appears, enter the following field information.

Field	Field Name	Type	Width
1	Social	Character	11
2	Title	Character	30
3	Dayrented	Date	8
4	Returned	Date	8

Once the fields have been entered in the structure, save the new database structure by clicking OK. When the "Input Data now?" dialog box appears, click Yes to begin adding new records to the file. Add the following records, and when you are done, press CTRL+F4 to exit Append mode.

Social	Title	Day Rented	Returned
123-44-8976	Star Trek VI	03/05/93	03/06/93
121-33-9876	Lethal Weapon III	03/02/93	03/06/93
232-55-1234	Who Framed Roger Rabbit	03/06/93	03/09/93
901-77-3456	Doc Hollywood	03/04/93	03/05/93
121-90-5432	Fried Green Tomatoes	03/01/93	03/06/93
495-00-3456	Wayne's World	03/04/93	03/09/93
343-55-9821	Prince of Tides	03/06/93	03/12/93
876-54-3210	Lethal Weapon III	03/07/93	03/08/93
123-44-8976	Friday 13th Part XXVII	03/14/93	03/16/93
121-33-9876	Mambo Kings	03/15/93	03/17/93
232-55-1234	Prince of Tides	03/17/93	03/19/93
901-77-3456	Coming to America	03/14/93	03/18/93
121-90-5432	Prince of Tides	03/16/93	03/17/93
495-00-3456	Star Trek VI	03/18/93	03/19/93
343-55-9821	Wayne's World	03/19/93	03/20/93
876-54-3210	Mambo Kings	03/16/93	03/18/93

You'll use this database along with the MEMBERS database you created in Chapter 2 in most of the examples used throughout the rest of this text.

CHAPTER

Sorting and Indexing a Database

When you want to produce reports from your data, you seldom want the data coming out to be in the same order as the data going in. Most databases contain records entered in a random manner; as different customers sign up or as different employees are hired, new records are added to the database. When you want a report, on the other hand, you usually want it in a specific order—perhaps alphabetically by name or by expiration date. With an inventory database, you may want to see the records arranged by part number. For a mailing list, a database might need to generate labels by order of ZIP code.

Databases can be arranged in a number of ways with the SORT and INDEX commands. The first portion of this chapter teaches you how to sort and discusses some disadvantages that accompany the sorting process. The second portion of the chapter covers indexing, which offers some advantages over sorting while accomplishing the same overall result.

Most of the commands in this chapter are executed at the Command level, rather than through the menus. You can perform sorting and indexing tasks with either method, but many of the more complex sorting and indexing operations can be performed more quickly with commands. Once you are familiar with the syntax of the commands, you can use them within your own FoxPro programs. Because it is good to have an idea of both methods, the chapter includes both; use whichever method you are comfortable with for your own use.

Sorting

When FoxPro sorts a database, it creates a new file with a different file name. If you were to sort a database of names in alphabetical order, the new file would contain all the records that were in the old file, but they would be arranged in alphabetical order, as shown in Figure 4-1.

The format for the SORT command is

SORT ON *fieldname* [/A/C/D] TO *new-filename*

From the menus, you open the Database menu, choose the Sort option, and then fill in the desired fields for the sort order. A new file by the name of *new-filename* is created, sorted by the field that you specify. If you specify the /A option, the file will be sorted in *ascending order.* This

Sorting records in a database

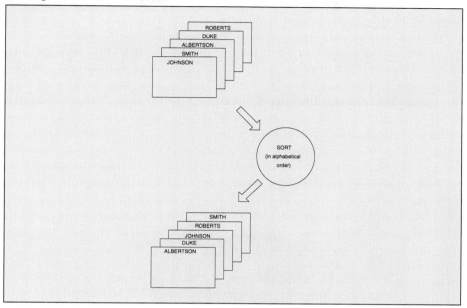

order places character fields in alphabetical order, numeric fields in numerical order, and date fields in chronological order (earliest to latest). If you use the /D option, character fields are sorted in *descending order* (Z to A), numeric fields from highest to lowest, and date fields in reverse chronological order (from latest to earliest). You cannot sort on memo fields. If you do not use either /A or /D, FoxPro assumes that ascending order is your preference. Sorts are also normally in ASCII order, with uppercase letters treated differently from lowercase letters. ASCII order ascending specifies A through Z, then a through z. ASCII order descending specifies Z through A, then z through a. If you want uppercase and lowercase letters to be treated equally in the sorting order, include the /C option for character/dictionary.

Use the SORT command to alphabetize the Generic Videos database by members' last names. Enter the following:

```
USE MEMBERS
SORT ON LASTNAME TO MEMBERS2
```

The file has been sorted, but you are still using the original MEMBERS file at this point. To see the results, you must open the new file. Try the following commands:

```
USE MEMBERS2
LIST LASTNAME
```

The results are shown here:

```
Record#     LASTNAME
      1     Hart
      2     Kramer
      3     Martin
      4     Miller
      5     Moore
      6     Robinson
      7     Robinson
      8     Zachman
```

The old file, MEMBERS, still exists in its unchanged form. The sorting operation has created a new file (called MEMBERS2) that is in alphabetical order. Remember, a file cannot be sorted into itself in FoxPro; each time a sort is performed, a new file must be created. Before proceeding, enter **USE MEMBERS** to switch back to the original file.

Now try a sort option from the menus. Open the Database menu and choose Sort. The Sort dialog box is displayed (Figure 4-2). In the upper-left part of the dialog box is the All Fields list box, which lets you choose desired fields on which the sort will be based. The center portion of the dialog box contains a Field Options box; this lets you select ascending or descending order and whether FoxPro should ignore case (sorting upper- and lowercase letters together) or sort uppercase before lowercase. As you select fields from the All Fields list box, they are added to the Sort Order box on the right side of the dialog box.

The Input box at the bottom center of the dialog box lets you add a Scope, For, or While clause to limit records included in the sorted file. The Output box at the lower-right corner of the dialog box contains a Save As button and text box for the file name to be assigned to the sorted file, along with a Fields option. When chosen, the Fields option brings up another dialog box which lets you specify a list of fields that will be included in the sorted file. When this option is not used, all fields are included in the sorted file (the default).

FIGURE
4-2

Sort dialog box

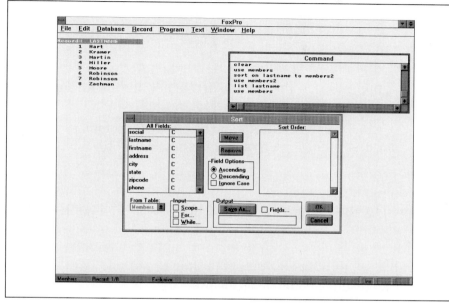

For this example, a sort is needed on the expiration-date field. In the All Fields list box, use the scroll bar to bring the Expiredate field into view, and click it to select the field. Then, click Move. When you do so, the field name, preceded by the database name (MEMBERS), appears in the Sort Order list box. Ascending order, which is the default shown in the Field Options box, is fine for this example. No Scope or For clauses are needed, since all records are desired. Click in the text box underneath the Save As button, and enter **MEMBERS3** as the file name. Then click Save from the Save As dialog box, and click OK in the Sort dialog box.

In a few moments, you'll see a message in the Status Bar indicating the completion of the sorting process. Enter

```
USE MEMBERS3
LIST LASTNAME, EXPIREDATE
```

You will then see the following:

Record#	LASTNAME	EXPIREDATE
1	Martin	07/04/93
2	Miller	07/25/93

```
3       Zachman      09/19/93
4       Kramer       12/22/93
5       Robinson     09/05/94
6       Robinson     09/17/94
7       Hart         10/19/94
8       Moore        11/17/95
```

It shows that the records in this new file are arranged in the order of expiration date, with the earliest dates first.

Enter **USE MEMBERS** and try the SORT command with the /D option (for descending order) on the Lastname field by entering:

```
SORT ON LASTNAME /D TO MEMBERS4
```

To see the results, you need to list the new file you created. Enter this:

```
USE MEMBERS4
LIST LASTNAME
```

The results should be as follows:

```
Record#    LASTNAME
      1    Zachman
      2    Robinson
      3    Robinson
      4    Moore
      5    Miller
      6    Martin
      7    Kramer
      8    Hart
```

Return to MEMBERS by entering **USE MEMBERS**. For an example of numerical sorting, enter

```
SORT ON TAPELIMIT TO MEMBERS5
```

When the sorting process is complete, enter

```
USE MEMBERS5
LIST LASTNAME, TAPELIMIT
```

You should then see the following:

```
Record#    LASTNAME    TAPELIMIT
      1    Robinson    2
      2    Hart        2
      3    Martin      4
      4    Kramer      4
      5    Zachman     4
      6    Miller      6
      7    Robinson    6
      8    Moore       6
```

This shows the records arranged by the contents of the Tapelimit field, in ascending order.

Remember Sorting always creates a duplicate of the original file. You must put the new file in use to view or print the sorted records.

Before going on to consider sorting on multiple fields, you may want to perform some housekeeping by deleting the example files you just created. This can easily be done from the Command level. First, enter

```
USE MEMBERS
```

to close the file you are currently working with and open the original MEMBERS database. (Database files must be closed before you can erase them.) Then enter these commands to erase the database and accompanying memo field files:

```
DELETE FILE MEMBERS2.DBF
DELETE FILE MEMBERS3.DBF
DELETE FILE MEMBERS4.DBF
DELETE FILE MEMBERS5.DBF

DELETE FILE MEMBERS2.FPT
DELETE FILE MEMBERS3.FPT
DELETE FILE MEMBERS4.FPT
DELETE FILE MEMBERS5.FPT
```

Note You can also erase files with the Filer. The use of the Filer is covered in Chapter 9.

Sorting on Multiple Fields

Sometimes you may need to sort on more than one field. For example, if you alphabetize a list of names that is divided into Firstname and Lastname fields, you would not want to sort only on the Lastname field if there were three people with the last name of Williams. You would also have to sort on the Firstname field to find the correct ordering of the three Williamses. Fortunately, FoxPro can sort on more than one field. From the Command level, this can be done by listing the fields as part of the SORT command, separating them with commas. The field that is sorted first would be listed first. From the menus, you can sort on multiple fields by choosing more than one field name from the dialog box for the database fields. You can also sort on a combination of different types of fields, such as a numeric field and a character field, at the same time.

As an example, consider the recent sort shown by tape limit. While the tape limits were in order, there were a large number of members with the same tape limit, and the members within the tape-limit group fall in random order. Sorting the file in order of tape limit, and within equal tape-limit groups by order of their last names, would provide a more logical listing.

First try it from the menus. Open the Database menu and choose Sort. When the dialog box appears, in the All Fields list box, scroll down to the Tapelimit field, click to select it, and then click Move. Then click the Lastname field to select it, and click Move again. The Tapelimit and Lastname fields will appear in the Sort Order list box at the right side of the dialog box.

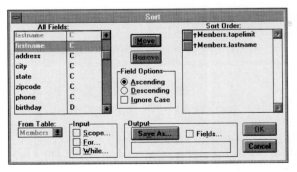

This indicates that the sort will take place by tape limit, and where the tape limits are the same, by last name.

Click in the text box located within the Output portion of the dialog box, and enter **MEMBERS2** as the file name. Then click OK. When the sorting process is complete, choose Open from the File menu, and choose MEMBERS2 as the name of the new file to open. Click Open in the dialog box to open the file. Next, open the Database menu and choose Browse. You will see the data sorted in order of tape limit and last name, as shown in Figure 4-3. (In the figure, the Browse window has been split to allow the Lastname and Tapelimit fields to be viewed at the same time.) When you're done viewing the data, press CTRL+F4 to get out of Browse mode.

To do this type of sort from the Command level, the format for the command is

SORT ON *1st-field* [/A/C/D],*2nd-field* [/A/C/D]...
last-field [/A/C/D] TO *new-filename*

File sorted by Tapelimit and Lastname fields

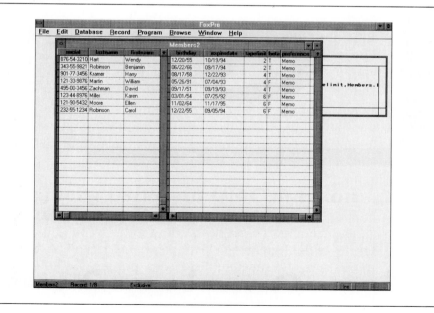

so you could perform the same sort by getting to the Command level and entering commands like this:

```
USE MEMBERS
SORT ON TAPELIMIT, LASTNAME /C TO MEMBERS2
```

The database would be sorted on both fields, in ascending order because the /D option has not been specified. The /C option was included, so the sort would be in character/dictionary rather than ASCII order.

To see the results of a descending-order sort on multiple fields, enter these commands:

```
USE MEMBERS
SORT ON TAPELIMIT /D, LASTNAME /D TO MEMBERS2
```

Because you are now trying to overwrite a file you've already created (MEMBERS2.DBF), you will see a dialog box warning you that the file exists. Click Yes from the dialog box to tell FoxPro that you want to overwrite the previous file, and the sort will occur. To see the results, enter

```
USE MEMBERS2
LIST LASTNAME, TAPELIMIT
```

The results this time resemble the following:

```
Record#     LASTNAME     TAPELIMIT
      1     Robinson     6
      2     Moore        6
      3     Miller       6
      4     Zachman      4
      5     Martin       4
      6     Kramer       4
      7     Robinson     2
      8     Hart         2
```

The file is sorted in descending order by tape limit and, where the entries in the Tapelimit field are equal, in descending order by last names. In this sort, the Tapelimit field is the primary field. A *primary field* is the field that will be sorted first by the SORT command. After the database has been sorted by the primary field, if there is any duplicate information in the first field, SORT will sort the duplicate information by the second field listed in the command, known as the *secondary field.* It is possible to sort further with additional secondary fields; you can, in fact, sort with all fields in the database. For example, the commands

```
USE MEMBERS
SORT ON STATE, CITY, TAPELIMIT, LASTNAME TO MASTER
```

would create a database called MASTER that alphabetizes records by states, sorts each state by city, and sorts each city by tape-limit amounts. If there were any duplicate entries at this point, the last names would be sorted in ascending order. In this example, State is the primary sort field, while City, Tapelimit, and Lastname are secondary sort fields.

Sorting a Subset of a Database

Adding a qualifying FOR statement to a SORT command lets you produce a sorted file that contains only a specific subset of the records in the database. The format for the SORT command when used in this manner is

SORT ON *fieldname* [A/C/D] TO *new-filename* FOR *condition*

For an example, let's produce a new database sorted by last names and containing only those records with Virginia addresses. Enter the following commands:

```
SORT TO VAPERSON ON LASTNAME FOR STATE = "VA"
USE VAPERSON
LIST LASTNAME, STATE
```

The results are shown here:

Record#	LASTNAME	STATE
1	Hart	VA
2	Kramer	VA
3	Robinson	VA
4	Zachman	VA

This display shows the result of the qualifying FOR condition. The new database contains only the records of members located in Virginia.

More examples of conditional use of the SORT command include the following:

```
SORT TO MYDATA ON LASTNAME, TAPELIMIT FOR TAPELIMIT < = 4
SORT TO PACIFIC ON ZIP FOR ZIP >="90000"
```

Once you know the syntax of these commands, using them can be much faster than using the menus. To do this type of selective sort from the menus, you would have to select various field names and For clauses from the pick lists within the dialog box. In the time it takes to get through half the options, you could have entered the entire command from the Command level to do the job.

Sorting Selected Fields to a File

You can create a sorted file that includes selected fields from a database by including a list of fields with the SORT command. This can be quite useful for creating files that will be used by other software, such as a word processor for creating form letters. You might want to create a file in alphabetical order containing only names and addresses and excluding all other fields. The syntax of the SORT command, when used in this manner, is

SORT TO *filename* ON *expression* FIELDS *list-of-fields*

As an example, you could create a file with only the names and addresses from the MEMBERS database with commands like the following:

```
USE MEMBERS

SORT TO MYFILE ON LASTNAME, FIRSTNAME FIELDS LASTNAME,
FIRSTNAME, ADDRESS, CITY, STATE, ZIPCODE
```

The resultant sorted file, called MYFILE, would contain only the Lastname, Firstname, Address, City, State, and Zipcode fields.

Why Sort?

Once you've learned all about sorting with FoxPro, you should know why you should not sort a database—at least not very often. Sorting can be very time-consuming, particularly when you are sorting large files. Sorting also uses a lot of disk space. Each time a sort occurs, FoxPro creates a new file that will be as large as the original unless you limit the fields included or the records processed with a For clause. For this reason, you must limit the database to no more than half the free space on the disk if you are going to sort it.

Adding records to a database merely complicates matters. After you add records, chances are that the database must be sorted to maintain the desired order. If you are sorting multiple fields, the sorting time can become noticeable. However, there is a more efficient way of arranging a database alphabetically, numerically, or chronologically: by using index files.

Indexing

An *index file* consists of at least one field from a database. The field is sorted alphabetically, numerically, or chronologically, and with each entry in the field is the corresponding record number used to reference the record in the *parent database* (Figure 4-4). In effect, an index file is a virtual sort of the parent database, since none of the records in the parent database are sorted.

Just as a book index is a separate section that indicates where information is located, a FoxPro index file is a separate file that contains information regarding the location of individual records in the parent database. When the database file is opened along with the index file, the first record to be retrieved is not the first record in the parent database; instead, it is the first record listed in the index. The next record retrieved is the second record listed in the index, and so on. Remember, indexing does not affect the order of the parent database.

Index file alphabetized by last name and parent database that is organized by ZIP code

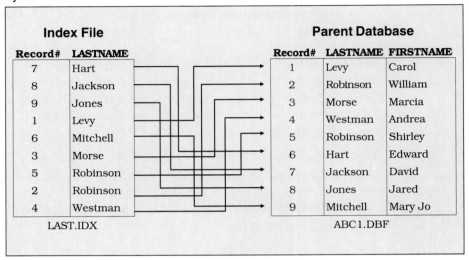

Types of Indexes

FoxPro for Windows, and all versions of FoxPro for DOS from version 2 on, can maintain index information in one of two ways; either method accomplishes the same result of keeping things in order. The first method uses a *compound index file* with an extension of .CDX. This file maintains information on the different indexes that you create within a single file. FoxPro can have more than one compound index file open at a time, and each compound index (.CDX) file can contain data about more than one index. However, only one index file—the active index file—controls the order of the records you see. (You will learn more about this in "Using SET INDEX" later in the chapter.)

By default, the TAG option of the INDEX command (which is discussed shortly) stores the index information in a compound index file that is automatically given the same name as the database. This .CDX file, known as the *structural .CDX file*, is opened and updated automatically whenever the database is opened.

The second method of indexing your files is to create individual .IDX index files for each index desired. With this approach, the information for each index is stored in a separate file. If you wanted to index a file on last names and also on ZIP codes, you would need two separate .IDX files to do this. The individual .IDX files can be one of two types: compact .IDX files and noncompact .IDX files. The compact .IDX files take up less disk space than the noncompact types, but the noncompact .IDX files are compatible with other versions of FoxPro.

The two methods of indexing exist for an important reason: compatibility with earlier versions of FoxPro. The first method of indexing, using the compound index file to hold all the index information, is more efficient. However, FoxPro for DOS versions 1.x cannot use the compound index files. Therefore, all versions of FoxPro for Windows, and FoxPro for DOS from version 2 on, provide menu options and commands that let you work with .IDX index files, which are the style of index files used with all DOS versions of FoxPro below version 2. If you must share data with other users of FoxPro, you may want to create and use the .IDX-style index files to maintain compatibility. Keep in mind that you must use noncompact .IDX index files if you want to use the index files with FoxBase+, FoxBase Mac, or FoxPro for DOS versions 1.*x.*

From the Command level, the general format of the INDEX command is similar to the format of the SORT command:

INDEX ON *expression* TO *index-filename*
[FOR *condition*][UNIQUE][COMPACT]

This variation of the index command produces a single .IDX index file containing the index information. FoxPro appends the extension .IDX to all index files. Note that Ashton-Tate's dBASE III and III PLUS products use an .NDX extension for index files. dBASE IV can use index files with either an .NDX extension or an .MDX extension. If you attempt to open a dBASE database and accompanying .NDX or .MDX index file under FoxPro, FoxPro immediately rebuilds the index, using its own .IDX extension.

A simple use of the syntax

INDEX ON *fieldname* TO *index-filename*

creates an index file based on the named field, with all records included in the index. The UNIQUE clause, if added, causes a *unique index* to be constructed. Such an index will not contain any duplicates of the index expression. You would use this type of index to intentionally hide any accidental duplicate records. For example, if a social security field were used to build the index and two records contained the same social security number, the second occurrence would be omitted from the index. The FOR expression lets you build a selective index, which contains only those records that meet a specified condition. The COMPACT clause, if added, causes the index file to be stored as a compact-type .IDX file. If omitted, a noncompact .IDX file is created. The TAG statement can be used with the INDEX command to add index tags to a compound index file. The general format of the INDEX command then becomes

INDEX ON *expression* TAG *index-tag name* [FOR *condition*]
[UNIQUE] [COMPACT]

This version of the INDEX command adds an index tag to the structural compound (.CDX) index file. If the file does not exist, it will be created; if it exists, the new index tag will be added to the file.

Creating an Index

Suppose you need to arrange the membership list in order by city for Generic Videos. You can create an index file by entering the following commands:

```
USE MEMBERS
INDEX ON CITY TAG TOWNS
```

Enter **LIST LASTNAME, CITY** and you will see the result of the new index file:

```
Record#     LASTNAME     CITY
      4     Kramer       Arlington
      1     Miller       Chevy Chase
      8     Hart         Fairfax
      3     Robinson     Falls Church
      6     Zachman      Falls Church
      2     Martin       Silver Spring
      5     Moore        Takoma Park
      7     Robinson     Washington
```

If you want compatibility with earlier versions of FoxPro, you can accomplish the same results by using the command

```
INDEX ON CITY TO TOWNS
```

The only difference is that the index data is stored in an .IDX-style index file.

Notice that the record numbers that indicate the order of the records in the database itself are not in order. The command you entered creates an index containing the index information. Any index you create is automatically made active immediately after its creation; so the order of the records displayed with the LIST command is now controlled by the new index.

It's good practice to give index files or index tags a name related in some manner to the field that has been indexed. This helps you and others keep track of how the file was indexed and what field was used.

From the menus, you can index a file by choosing the New option of the File menu. When the dialog box appears, click Index, and then click New. This causes the Index dialog box to appear, as shown in Figure 4-5. The dialog box contains a field list from which you can select a field to base the index on. If you need to base the index on an expression (such as a combination of fields), you can manually enter the expression in the text box beside the Index Key button. Or you can click the Index Key button to bring up the Expression Builder that can be used to create the index expression. Expressions can be complex and can include field names, functions, and operators. (Examples of indexing with complex expressions are provided later in this chapter.) After you enter the expression used to build the index, you click OK in the dialog box to exit the Expression Builder and return to the Index dialog box.

The Unique check box lets you select a unique index, in which duplicate entries of the indexed field or expression are ignored. (This is equivalent to the UNIQUE clause used with the INDEX ON command.) The Index Filter button brings up a For clause in an Expression Builder dialog box, which lets you specify an expression to limit records that are stored in the index; this is the equivalent of adding a FOR clause to the

Index dialog box

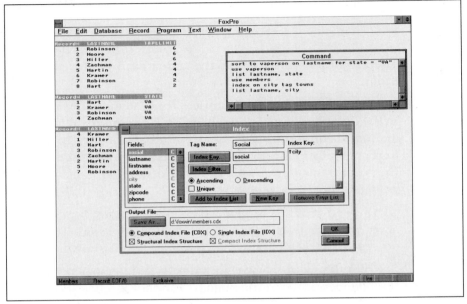

INDEX ON command. For example, clicking the Index Filter button and entering an expression like

```
STATE = "MD"
```

in the For Clause box would limit the resultant index to those records with MD in the State field.

At the lower left corner of the dialog box is an area with Output options; this controls what type of index is created. You can select .CDX (compound) or .IDX (single) index files, and you can choose compact-type index files by checking the Compact check box. (Remember, compact indexes take up less space but are not compatible with earlier versions of FoxPro.) If you choose compound (.CDX) type files, you can also choose whether the tag will be added to the structural compound index (the .CDX file having the same name as the database).

To try indexing from the menus, select New from the File menu. When the dialog box appears, click Index, and then click New. In a moment, the Index dialog box will appear. Click Lastname in the Fields list box at the left side of the dialog box and then click the Add to Index List button. When you do so, you see the field name appear in the list box at the right side of the screen. You may also notice that Lastname appears by default as a tag in the Tagname area of the dialog box. While you can change this to any tag that you desire, for this example you can leave the tag name as is.

In the Options area of the screen, you may notice that a compound (.CDX) index file is chosen as the default. You can leave the options in this area as is for now. Select OK to create the index. When the indexing is completed, choose Browse from the Database menu to view the file. It will appear in order by last name. Before continuing, press CTRL+F4 to leave Browse mode.

Selective Indexing

You can use the FOR clause with the INDEX ON command (or the Index Filter button of the Index dialog box) to add a clause that limits the records stored in the index. When used from the Command level, the syntax for this INDEX command is

INDEX ON *expression* TAG *tagname* FOR *condition*

where the condition used with FOR is any expression that evaluates to a logical "True" or "False." If you desire compatibility with earlier versions of FoxPro, you can also use the FOR clause with .IDX-style index files by using a similar syntax.

INDEX ON *expression* TO *filename* FOR *condition*

This is a powerful FoxPro option that can, in effect, filter unwanted records from the database and place records in order at the same time. The SET FILTER command along with a simple use of the INDEX command would accomplish the same result, but assuming an updated index already exists, using FOR with INDEX ON is faster than using SET FILTER. As an example, if you wanted to produce a report of members in the videos database who lived in Maryland or Virginia, indexed in ZIP code order, you could use a command like the following to accomplish such a task:

```
INDEX ON ZIPCODE TAG ZIPS FOR STATE = "MD" .OR. STATE = "VA"
```

Indexing on Multiple Fields

You can index files based on several fields. The process is similar to sorting on multiple fields. There is a limitation, however; you cannot directly index on multiple fields that are not of the same field type. For example, you could not index by Lastname and Tapelimit because Tapelimit is a numeric field and Lastname is a character field. However, there is a way to do this; you use special operators known as functions. (This technique is discussed shortly.)

To see how indexing on multiple fields works and to be sure the index file or tag that you created earlier is still active, take a look at the Lastname and Firstname fields by entering **LIST LASTNAME, FIRSTNAME**. Now notice that Carol Robinson is listed before Benjamin Robinson, which is not correct. Because you indexed the file on last names only, the order of the first names was ignored. To correct the situation, enter

```
INDEX ON LASTNAME + FIRSTNAME TAG ALLNAMES
```

or (for compatibility with all earlier versions of FoxPro):

```
INDEX ON LASTNAME + FIRSTNAME TO ALLNAMES
```

Records having the same last name are now indexed by last names and then by first names. To see the results, enter

```
LIST LASTNAME, FIRSTNAME
```

 Tip Press the UP ARROW key to repeat the LIST command you used earlier.

The listing should be as follows:

```
Record#    LASTNAME    FIRSTNAME
      8    Hart        Wendy
      4    Kramer      Harry
      2    Martin      William
      1    Miller      Karen
```

```
5     Moore        Ellen
7     Robinson     Benjamin
3     Robinson     Carol
6     Zachman      David
```

You can use this technique to create an index file on any number of fields within a record. The plus symbol (+) is always used with the INDEX command to tie the fields together. For example, the command

```
INDEX ON ZIPCODE + LASTNAME + FIRSTNAME TAG ZIPNAMES
```

would result in a database that is indexed three ways: by ZIP codes, by last names for records having the same ZIP code, and by first names for records having the same last name. As you might expect, multiple indexes are valuable aids when you are dealing with a large database and must organize it into comprehensible subgroups.

As with sorting, when you index on multiple fields, the first field named takes priority.

Indexing on Fields of Different Types

One limitation of the basic use of the INDEX command, as noted earlier, is the inability to directly index on combinations of fields that are of different types. For example, you cannot index on a combination of the Lastname and Tapelimit fields in the Generic Videos database. To see the problem, at the Command level, try either of the following commands:

```
INDEX ON LASTNAME + TAPELIMIT TO TEST
INDEX ON LASTNAME + BIRTHDAY TO TEST
```

The resulting error message, "Operator/operand type mismatch," tells you that FoxPro cannot index on a combination of fields that are of differing data types (such as date and character fields). The secret to indexing on fields that are not of the same type is to use functions to convert fields that are not character fields into character fields. Functions perform special operations that supplement the normal FoxPro commands. They are explained in greater detail in the programming portion of this text. For now, it is sufficient to know about two functions: the DTOS (Date-To-String) function and the STR (String) function.

The DTOS function converts the contents of a date field into a string of characters that follow a year-month-day format. The STR function converts the contents of a numeric field into a string of characters. You can use the DTOS and STR functions in combination with your INDEX commands to accomplish the same results as indexing on combinations of different types of fields.

The normal format for an index command, when combined with these functions, is

INDEX ON *character-field* + STR(*numeric-field*) +
DTOS(*date field*) TO *index-filename*

As with all indexing commands, you can use a combination of additional fields, in whatever order you prefer, to build the index. For an example of using these functions to build an index file that is indexed in alphabetical order by state and in numeric order by tape limit within each group of states, enter this command:

```
INDEX ON STATE + STR(TAPELIMIT) TO TEST
```

Enter **LIST LASTNAME, STATE, TAPELIMIT** to see the results of the index file; they should resemble the following.

Record#	LASTNAME	STATE	TAPELIMIT
7	Robinson	DC	2
2	Martin	MD	4
1	Miller	MD	6
5	Moore	MD	6
8	Hart	VA	2
4	Kramer	VA	4
6	Zachman	VA	4
3	Robinson	VA	6

You can also use these functions within the menus by manually entering the functions along with the field names in the Expression Builder window.

Note For more details on functions, see the programming portion of this text.

Opening Databases and Index Files

When opening databases with the USE command, you can simultaneously open one or more index files by adding the word INDEX and the index file names after the USE *filename* portion of the command. The syntax for the USE command, when used with the INDEX option, becomes

USE *filename* TAG *tagname*

and if you desire compatibility with earlier versions of FoxPro, you can optionally use the command

USE *filename* INDEX *index-name1* [,*index-name2*]

You could simultaneously open the MEMBERS database along with the TOWNS and ALLNAMES index files with a command like

```
USE MEMBERS INDEX TOWNS, ALLNAMES
```

If you are working with a compound index file with the same name as the database (or the structural compound index file), you need not specify the index file name along with the USE command. The structural compound index file, if it exists, is automatically opened by FoxPro whenever you open a database. If you choose to add index tags to compound index files that have other names, you can activate such an index file at the same time that you open the database with this variation of the USE command:

```
USE filename INDEX .cdx filename
```

The compound index file named as part of the command will be opened along with the database.

Note that the first index file you list (when working with separate index files) is the controlling index, so in this example the TOWNS index file would control how the records were displayed or printed in a report.

Using SET INDEX

In many cases you'll create and work with more than one index for a database, but the order in which the records appear or are printed is controlled by only one index. For an index to control the order of the records, it must be active. An index that has just been created is active, and the SET INDEX command makes a dormant index active. The SET INDEX command is the Command-level equivalent of choosing Open from the File menu and then selecting Index from the Type button in the dialog box that appears.

Suppose that you need three lists from the MEMBERS database. The first list must be in order by tape limit, another list by last name, and a third list by ZIP codes. Create the indexes from these three fields now using the .IDX-style index file format with the following commands:

```
INDEX ON LASTNAME TO NAME
INDEX ON TAPELIMIT TO TAPES
INDEX ON ZIPCODE TO ZIP
```

These commands create three .IDX-style indexes on your hard disk: NAME, TAPES, and ZIP. Each index file contains the appropriate field from each record and the corresponding record numbers. NAME, for example, contains last names in alphabetical order and the matching record numbers for each last name.

Since ZIP was the last index created, it is the active index. By using the SET INDEX command, you can activate any index. For example, to activate the TAPES index file and display the database organized by tape limit instead of by ZIP code, enter

```
SET INDEX TO TAPES
LIST LASTNAME, TAPELIMIT
```

The display should appear as follows:

```
Record#     LASTNAME     TAPELIMIT
      7     Robinson     2
      8     Hart         2
      2     Martin       4
      4     Kramer       4
      6     Zachman      4
      1     Miller       6
```

```
     3      Robinson      6
     5      Moore         6
```

Now try the same method to activate and display the ZIP file:

```
SET INDEX TO ZIP
LIST LASTNAME, ZIPCODE
```

The display should appear as follows:

```
Record#      LASTNAME     ZIPCODE
      7      Robinson     20009-1010
      1      Miller       20815-0988
      2      Martin       20910-0124
      5      Moore        20912
      8      Hart         22025
      6      Zachman      22043
      3      Robinson     22043-1234
      4      Kramer       22203
```

Remember, ZIP codes are stored as characters, so they are indexed "alphabetically," which explains why the nine-digit ZIP codes are not at the bottom of the list.

Using SET ORDER

When you are working with multiple tags in a compound index file, you can make any index tag the active index with the SET ORDER command. For an index tag to control the order of the records, it must be active; the SET ORDER command makes a dormant index tag active.

As an example, consider the MEMBERS database. If you have followed the example, there is already an index tag called ALLNAMES in your structural compound index file; it is organized on a combination of last and first names. Suppose that you need another list from the Generic Videos database, and it must be in order of expiration date. Create the needed index now by entering the following command:

```
INDEX ON EXPIREDATE TAG DAYS
```

By using the SET ORDER command, you can activate any tag in the index file. For example, the index tag based on expiration dates is currently active because you created it last. To activate and display the database organized by names instead of by expiration dates, enter

```
SET ORDER TO TAG ALLNAMES
LIST LASTNAME, FIRSTNAME, EXPIREDATE
```

The display should appear as follows:

```
Record#      LASTNAME      FIRSTNAME      EXPIREDATE
      8      Hart          Wendy          10/19/94
      4      Kramer        Harry          12/22/93
      2      Martin        William        07/04/93
      1      Miller        Karen          07/25/93
      5      Moore         Ellen          11/17/95
      7      Robinson      Benjamin       09/17/94
      3      Robinson      Carol          09/05/94
      6      Zachman       David          09/19/93
```

Since the ALLNAMES index tag is active, the members are arranged in order of names. Now try the same method to activate the index tag based on expiration dates, and display the data in that order:

```
SET ORDER TO TAG DAYS
LIST LASTNAME, FIRSTNAME, EXPIREDATE
```

The display should appear as follows:

```
Record#      LASTNAME      FIRSTNAME      EXPIREDATE
      1      Martin        William        07/04/93
      2      Miller        Karen          07/25/93
      6      Zachman       David          09/19/93
      4      Kramer        Harry          12/22/93
      3      Robinson      Carol          09/05/94
      7      Robinson      Benjamin       09/17/94
      8      Hart          Wendy          10/19/94
      5      Moore         Ellen          11/17/95
```

Open Index Files

Although only one index can be active at a time, you can have up to seven open *files.* You can easily tell which indexes are in use at any time by using the LIST STATUS or DISPLAY STATUS command. If an index file is open, any changes you make to the parent database are updated automatically in that index file. For example, adding a record to MEM-BERS places the Lastname field of the new record and the record number in the NAMES index and then realphabetizes the index file, provided that the NAME.IDX index file is open.

You can also open an index file with either the USE *filename* INDEX *index-names* command, or the SET INDEX command. You can open a database and index files at the same time with USE *filename* INDEX *index-names*. For example, the command

```
USE MEMBERS INDEX NAME, ZIP
```

opens the MEMBERS database, along with the NAME.IDX and ZIP.IDX index files. SET INDEX TO NAME, ZIP also opens the NAME.IDX and ZIP.IDX files if they are not already open. (You do not have to supply the .IDX extension to the command.) An active index file is also an open index file, so using SET INDEX opens a file that is closed. If you list more than one file with SET INDEX, all files are opened, but only the first is active.

In general, use the USE *filename* INDEX *index-names* command to open your databases along with as many index files as needed; once they are open, use the SET INDEX command to make different index files active. For example, if you need three lists, one in order of name, one in order of ZIP code, and one in order of tape limit, you could use commands like these:

```
USE MEMBERS INDEX NAME, ZIP, TAPES
SET INDEX TO NAME
LIST LASTNAME, FIRSTNAME, CITY, ZIP, TAPELIMIT
SET INDEX TO ZIP
LIST LASTNAME, FIRSTNAME, CITY, ZIP, TAPELIMIT
SET INDEX TO TAPES
LIST LASTNAME, FIRSTNAME, CITY, ZIP, TAPELIMIT
```

To get an idea of why it is important to keep needed index files open, you can use the index files you created earlier, NAMES and TAPES. Use the SET INDEX command to open these files by entering this command:

```
SET INDEX TO TAPES, NAME
```

The two index files (TAPES.IDX, containing Tapelimit, and NAME.IDX, containing Lastname) are now open. Now enter **LIST LASTNAME,**

TAPELIMIT. The display shows that the index you specified by naming the TAPES file first is the active index, but NAMES.IDX is also open. This is important if you add or edit records in the database because as long as the index files are open, they are updated automatically. See how this works by entering

```
APPEND
```

When the new blank record appears, enter this data:

```
Social:            111-22-3333
Lastname:          Roberts
Firstname:         Charles
Address:           247 Ocean Blvd
City:              Vienna
State:             VA
Zipcode:           22085
Tapelimit:         3
```

The remaining fields in the record may be left blank for now. Press CTRL+F4 to store the new record and get back to the Command level. Now enter this command again:

```
LIST LASTNAME, TAPELIMIT
```

The index file now includes the new entry, in the proper order of tape limits, as shown here:

```
Record#      LASTNAME      TAPELIMIT
      7      Robinson      2
      8      Hart          2
      9      Roberts       3
      2      Martin        4
      4      Kramer        4
      6      Zachman       4
      1      Miller        6
      3      Robinson      6
      5      Moore         6
```

This brings up an important point: speed. Whenever you make changes or add records to a database, FoxPro automatically updates all open index files. This may slow down the entire operation, particularly if more than one index file is open at once. If you wish, you can close all open index files without closing the database with the CLOSE INDEX command.

Using REINDEX

If you changed a database and didn't remember to open an .IDX-style index file, you can update the index with the REINDEX command. You will want to do this with the ZIP index file, for example; because you did not open the ZIP index file, it does not include the newly added record. You can verify this by using the ZIP index and looking at names in the database. Enter the following:

```
SET INDEX TO ZIP, NAME, TAPES
LIST LASTNAME
```

As you can see, the name Roberts does not appear in the database because the ZIP index was not open when you added the record:

```
Record#     LASTNAME
      7     Robinson
      1     Miller
      2     Martin
      5     Moore
      8     Hart
      6     Zachman
      3     Robinson
      4     Kramer
```

Try the REINDEX command now by entering

```
REINDEX
```

To display the updated result, enter **LIST LASTNAME**. The results are shown here:

```
Record#     LASTNAME
      7     Robinson
      1     Miller
      2     Martin
      5     Moore
      8     Hart
      6     Zachman
```

```
    3      Robinson
    9      Roberts
    4      Kramer
```

The Roberts entry is now in the indexed ZIP file. Mr. Roberts is no longer needed in the database. Enter **DELETE RECORD 9** and then enter **PACK** to remove him from the list. Since the ZIP, NAME, and TAPELIMIT index files are open, the entry for Roberts will be removed from each of the index files.

Remember   The PACK command automatically reindexes all open index files.

Caution   A power failure or hardware malfunction can damage an index file. If this happens, REINDEX may not work properly. Use the INDEX command instead to rebuild the index from scratch.

Using CLOSE INDEX

If you decide that you do not want to use any index file (other than the structural compound index), use the CLOSE INDEX command to close the index file and leave the associated database open. To execute the command from the Command level, you enter

```
CLOSE INDEX
```

Note that the REINDEX command is available from the menus, while the CLOSE INDEX command is not. To rebuild an index file while at the menus, open the Database menu and choose the Reindex option. To close an index file through the menus, you could choose the Open option of the File menu and open the same database a second time, without opening the corresponding index file.

Searching for Specifics

You can use two additional FoxPro commands with indexed files: FIND and SEEK. These commands quickly find information in an indexed file.

The commands are discussed briefly here, since they do pertain to indexed files. Chapter 5, which deals with querying your database, covers these commands in additional detail.

Both commands operate only on the active index. The format for the FIND command is FIND *character-string,* where *character-string* is a group of characters that do not have to be surrounded by quotation marks. The format for SEEK is SEEK *expression.* Here, *expression* can be a number, a character string (which must be surrounded by single or double quotes), or a variable (variables are discussed in the programming portion of this text).

FIND and SEEK search the active index file and find the first record that matches your specifications. The record itself is not displayed; the FIND and SEEK commands simply locate the record pointer at the desired record. If no match is found, FoxPro responds with a "Find not successful" error message. To try the FIND command, enter

```
SET INDEX TO NAME
FIND Moore
DISPLAY
```

The result is as follows:

```
Record_#    SOCIAL       LASTNAME  FIRSTNAME  ADDRESS...
      5     121-90-5432  Moore     Ellen      270 Browning Ave...
```

To try the SEEK command, enter

```
SET INDEX TO TAPES
SEEK 4
DISPLAY
```

The result is as follows:

```
Record_#    SOCIAL       LASTNAME  FIRSTNAME  ADDRESS...
      2     121-33-9876  Martin    William    4807 East Avenue...
```

Remember The menu equivalent of the SEEK command is available by choosing SEEK from the RECORD menu.

The FIND and SEEK commands offer the advantage of speed over the LOCATE command (introduced in Chapter 3). LOCATE is simple to use but slow. In a database containing thousands of records, a LOCATE command can take several minutes. A FIND or SEEK command can accomplish the same task in a matter of seconds.

When you are searching for a character string, both FIND and SEEK allow you to search on only the beginning of the string. However, you should keep in mind that both the FIND and SEEK commands search for an exact match in terms of capitalization. For example, if the Generic Videos database index is set to NAME, the two commands

```
FIND Mo
FIND Moore
```

would both find the record for Moore. However, the command

```
FIND mo
```

would not find the record, because FoxPro considers uppercase and lowercase letters to be different characters. As far as FoxPro is concerned, "Moore" and "moore" are different names. One way of preventing problems with the case-significance of FoxPro is to design entry forms that store your character data as all uppercase letters. Another method is to use a FoxPro function called the UPPER function. The use of this function is discussed in "Using Functions to Standardize Case" later in this chapter.

Index Tips and Unusual Cases

With all the different ways to arrange a file, you may occasionally run into some unusual requests relating to indexing. The following sections cover some of the more unusual areas of indexing, along with hints for making your indexing as efficient as possible.

The Multiple Numeric Field Trap

With multiple numeric fields, things may not always turn out as you expect because of the way FoxPro builds an index expression. Consider a database of department store sales, with fields for customer name, high credit amounts, and balance amounts. You are preparing a mailing, and you want to target customers who have high credit lines and low account balances; they are likely prospects for heavy spending. You'd like to get an idea of who these customers are, so you prepare a report showing records sorted by high credit amounts. Where the high credit amounts are the same, you'd like to order the records by outstanding balance. If you use the INDEX command to do something like

```
USE SALES
INDEX ON HIGHCREDIT + BALANCE TO MAILER
LIST STORE, CUSTNAME, CUSTNUMB, HIGHCREDIT, BALANCE
```

the results will look like this:

STORE	CUSTNAME	CUSTNUMB	HIGHCREDIT	BALANCE
Collin Creek	Artis, K.	1008	1200.00	0.00
Oak Lawn	Jones, C.	1003	900.00	350.00
Galleria	Johnson, L.	1002	1200.00	675.00
Six Flags	Keemis, M.	1007	2000.00	0.00
Collin Creek	Williams, E.	1010	2000.00	0.00
Prestonwood	Smith, A.M.	1009	2000.00	220.00
Prestonwood	Allen, L.	1005	2000.00	312.00
Downtown	Walker, B.	1006	1300.00	1167.00
Prestonwood	Smith, A.	1001	2000.00	788.50
Downtown	Jones, J.	1011	2000.00	875.00
Collin Creek	Jones, J.L.	1004	2000.00	1850.00

Rather than concatenating the two numbers, FoxPro has added them and indexed in the order of the sum, which may not be what you had in mind. To FoxPro, the plus symbol means something different for numeric expressions than for string (character-based) expressions. The plus symbol adds numbers, but it combines character expressions. If you instead use the SORT command, with commands like

```
USE SALES
SORT ON HIGHCREDIT,BALANCE TO SALES1
USE SALES1
LIST STORE, CUSTNAME, CUSTNUMB, HIGHCREDIT, BALANCE
```

you will get these results:

STORE	CUSTNAME	CUSTNUMB	HIGHCREDIT	BALANCE
Oak Lawn	Jones, C.	1003	900.00	350.00
Collin Creek	Artis, K.	1008	1200.00	0.00

```
Galleria        Johnson, L.  1002      1200.00        675.00
Downtown        Walker, B.   1006      1300.00       1167.00
Six Flags       Keemis, M.   1007      2000.00          0.00
Collin Creek    Williams, E. 1010      2000.00          0.00
Prestonwood     Smith, A.M.  1009      2000.00        220.00
Prestonwood     Allen, L.    1005      2000.00        312.00
Prestonwood     Smith, A.    1001      2000.00        788.50
Downtown        Jones, J.    1011      2000.00        875.00
Collin Creek    Jones, J.L.  1004      2000.00       1850.00
```

What you get is what was expected: a file in numeric order by high credit, and where high credit is the same, in order of the outstanding balance. The unexpected results when using INDEX occur because the INDEX command, when used with multiple fields, depends on a math expression. In this case, FoxPro is adding the amounts, building the index on a value that is the sum of the amounts. To index on the combined numeric fields and get the desired results, you would have to first convert the numeric expressions into string values and then use the plus symbol to combine the string values. In the previous example, you could issue a command like

```
INDEX ON STR(HIGHCREDIT) + STR(BALANCE) TO CSALES
```

to accomplish the same result as the SORT command.

Using Functions to Standardize Case

The UPPER function and, less commonly, the LOWER function are often used to avoid problems arising from the case-sensitive nature of FoxPro. These functions can also be used as part of an index expression, resulting in an index containing characters that are all uppercase or all lowercase. The potential problem that can arise when the data entry people are not consistent with methods of data entry is shown in the following example. In this database of names, some of the names start with initial capital letters, some are entered as all caps, and some are all lowercase:

```
USE SAMPLE
INDEX ON NAME TAG NAMES
LIST
```

```
Record#      NAME                   AGE
       1     ADDISON, E.            32
       2     Addison, a.            28
       3     Carlson, F.            45
       4     McLean,R.              28
       5     Mcdonald, s.           47
       7     Smith, S.              55
       8     Smith, b.              37
      10     adams, j.q.            76
       6     de laurentis, m.      25
       9     edelstein, m.          22
```

Unless told otherwise, FoxPro puts lowercase letters after uppercase letters in the index, and the results are probably not what you had in mind. If you use the UPPER function to build the index, you get acceptable results, as shown with the following commands:

```
USE SAMPLE
INDEX ON UPPER(NAME) TAG NAMES
LIST
```

```
Record#      NAME                   AGE
      10     adams, j.q.            76
       2     ADDISON, A.            28
       1     Addison, E.            32
       3     Carlson, F.            45
       6     de laurentis, m.      25
       9     edelstein, m.          22
       5     Mcdonald, s.           47
       4     McLean,R.              28
       8     Smith, b.              37
       7     Smith, S.              55
```

To find such records in the index, simply enter all uppercase letters in the expression used along with the FIND or SEEK command. For example, the command

```
SEEK "ADDISON"
```

would find the records in this database, regardless of the case of the letters in each actual record.

Indexing on a Date Field

When you need an index based partially on a date field, FoxPro can present a bit of a challenge. It's no problem when you want to see the database in order by just one date field. Consider the example of a small medical database, containing patient names and a field with the date of admission to a hospital. You can use commands like these, with the results shown:

```
USE PATIENT
INDEX ON ADMITTED TAG DATESIN
LIST PATIENT, ADMITTED

Record#      PATIENT        ADMITTED
      1      Smith, A.      04/05/85
      2      Johnson, L.    04/15/85
      3      Jones, C.      04/15/85
      4      Jones, J.L.    04/15/85
      5      Allen, L.      05/20/86
      6      Walker, B.     05/20/86
      7      Keemis, M.     05/20/86
      8      Artis, K.      05/20/86
      9      Smith, A.M.    05/20/86
     10      Williams, E.   06/14/86
     11      Jones, J.      06/22/86
```

You get a database indexed in the order of the entries in the date field. Things get more complex, however, when you want a database indexed on a combination of fields, and one of the fields is a date field.

Since FoxPro doesn't let you index directly on multiple fields of different types, you must use functions to convert the date into a character string. Assuming the database contains a date field named Diagnosed and a character field named Patient, and you want it indexed by date and then by the name of the patient, you would use the DTOS function. This function is specifically designed to store date values in true chronological order. It converts a date value to a character value of *YYYYMMDD*, where *YYYY* is the year, *MM* the month, and *DD* the day. When an index is built with the DTOS function, the result comes out in true chronological order. Using the sample database just described, the commands

```
USE PATIENT
INDEX ON DTOS(DIAGNOSED) + PATIENT TAG COMBO
LIST PATIENT, DIAGNOSED
```

provide an index based on date and patient name, in the correct chronological order:

Record#	PATIENT	DIAGNOSED
3	Jones, C.	02/08/85
4	Jones, J.L.	03/02/85
2	Johnson, L.	03/06/85
1	Smith, A.	03/17/85
9	Smith, A.M.	02/03/86
7	Keemis, M.	02/23/86
8	Artis, K.	04/19/86
5	Allen, L.	05/12/86
6	Walker, B.	05/16/86
10	Williams, E.	06/01/86
11	Jones, J.	06/13/86

Tips for Indexing

A few tips when you are using index files will help speed things along in FoxPro.

☐ *Use short keys when you don't need long ones* Most indexes are directly based on a series of character fields, and in real life, most character fields get unique around the tenth character, if not sooner. If you can get by with indexing on fewer characters, do so. FoxPro will manage the index in less time. Let's look at a real-world example. You are building a customer file for a store in a medium-sized city of about 100,000 people, so you do not need to deal with the duplication of names that you get in New York or Los Angeles. The customer base is manageable: you might see a maximum of 5000 to 10,000 records in the file over the next ten years. The store manager despises labels with names cut off for lack of field width, so you've specified a width of 30 characters each for the Lastname and Firstname fields. You are going to index on a key field of customer number as the primary index, but you also want an index based on a combination of last and first names so you can quickly find a record when a customer is on the phone and does not have his or her customer number handy.

In this situation, do you really need an index based on the Lastname and Firstname fields? Quite likely not, but this is often done out of force of habit, and FoxPro must work harder for it. If you instead do something like

```
INDEX ON LEFT(LASTNAME,10) + LEFT(FIRSTNAME,10)
```

the use of the LEFT function results in an index that contains 20 characters per entry, as opposed to an index that contains 60 characters per entry. Given the customer base, having the first ten characters of the last and first names should be more than enough to keep the records in order and find a given record. Also, the index file uses considerably less disk space.

☐ *Store numbers in character fields if you are never going to perform calculations on those numbers* If you use numbers as unique identifiers (as in part numbers, employee numbers, invoice numbers, and so on), and you plan to use this data as a part of the index, don't store it in a numeric field. Use a character field instead. It makes a difference to FoxPro, because FoxPro does a better job of indexing on character fields than on numeric fields. When you try indexing with very large files, it becomes apparent that FoxPro takes longer to index a numeric field than a character field of equivalent size. Assuming you are not going to calculate such fields, they don't need to be numeric fields.

☐ *Perform routine maintenance often* When FoxPro must perform sequential operations while your index files are open, it has to work harder. You can cut down processing times by regularly putting your database files back in their natural order. To do this, open the file along with the index you most often use for sequential reporting or processing, and use the COPY TO *filename* command to copy the contents of the file to another file. Then delete the original database, give the new database the same name as the original database, and rebuild the necessary indexes. In applications using large files that are regularly updated, this simple step can make a dramatic difference to users in terms of response time when they are performing any reporting or processing based on sequential operations in FoxPro. Part of the speedup may also be due to the fact that the creation of a new database with the COPY command results in a new file under DOS, which may have its data arranged in sectors located side by side on the hard disk. Often, when a file has been updated over months of time, it is arranged in sectors that are scattered all over the hard disk. You can use the technique just described to reduce such fragmentation of files over a hard disk, or you can use one of the many "disk optimizer" software packages available to clean up your hard disk and make all of your files more accessible to your software.

CHAPTER

Performing Queries

This chapter covers an important subject: getting the desired data out of your database. Performing *queries,* or the fine art of asking questions, is the most common task done with computer databases. With so much time spent in this area, it pays to know the best ways to query a database in FoxPro. There are many ways to get desired data out of a database. Some are faster than others, and different ways are often best suited to different tasks.

As with most activities in FoxPro, data can be retrieved both with the menus and with commands. When it comes to queries, you're likely to see a distinct advantage in the use of commands over menus. The commands, once learned, tend to be faster to carry out; querying a database through the menus often involves making a large number of menu selections. Also, the command structure can be used as an integral part of programs written in FoxPro, and the programming language (which you will begin to learn about in Chapter 14) is a major FoxPro resource. The first portion of this chapter highlights queries performed through menu selections, and the second half covers queries performed with commands.

Performing Queries With the Menus

All of your data retrieval tasks will involve one of two scenarios: either you will need to select a single record, or you will need to isolate a subgroup of records (a process that often precedes the printing of a report). If a single record is all you need, the Goto, Locate, and Seek options, found on the Record menu, are what you are after.

Using Goto

The Goto option lets you move to the top or bottom of a file, move by a set number of records, or move to a specific record (by record number). For example, if you know that record 7 needs to be edited, you can (after opening the database with a USE command or with the Open option of the File menu) open the Record menu and choose Goto. When you do this, the dialog box shown in Figure 5-1 appears. Four options are provided: Top,

FIGURE
5-1

Go to dialog box

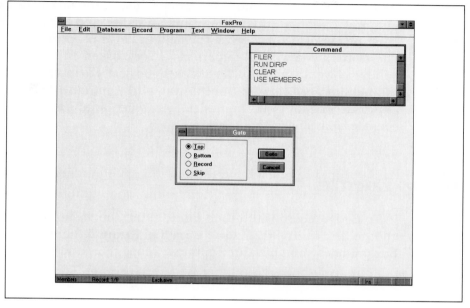

Bottom, Record, and Skip. You must select the desired option, and then select the Goto button in the dialog box to implement your choice.

Choosing Top moves the record pointer to the top of the database, while the Bottom option moves the record pointer to the last record in the database. The Skip option lets you move the record pointer by a certain number of records. If you choose Skip, the number 1 appears in an entry field, because the Skip option assumes you want to skip forward by one record. You can enter any other number you want, including negative numbers; for example, entering **–5** would move you back five records in the database, and entering **42** would move you forward 42 records. If you choose the Record option, the number 1 appears in an entry field, and you can enter the record number of the desired record. Once you make your choice of ways to move the record pointer, you can click the Goto button, and the pointer will move to the desired record.

These methods are fine when you know (by its record number) where a record is located. Unfortunately, this is usually not the case; most users performing queries have no idea where a desired record may be. Thus, you need some sort of search operation. Searches can be performed with the Locate, Continue, and Seek options, also found on the Record menu. The Seek option assumes the use of an index, and the resulting search must be performed based on the field or fields used to build the index. Therefore, if you wanted to perform a Seek based on the last name, the database would need to be indexed on the Lastname field (or on a combination of fields that begins with the Lastname field). Locate and Continue do not need an index, but with large databases, they are considerably slower than Seek.

Using Locate

To find a record without an index in use, open the Record menu and choose Locate. The dialog box shown in Figure 5-2 appears. This dialog box provides you with three options: Scope, For, and While.

FIGURE 5-2   Locate dialog box

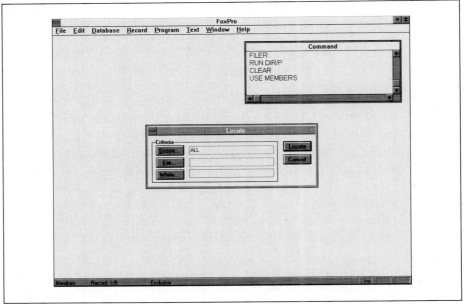

Clicking the Scope option reveals yet another dialog box with four options: All, Next, Record, and Rest.

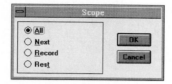

The optional use of a scope lets you impose a further limit on the operation of the Locate option. You can choose All to specify that the Locate operation should span all records; this is the default. You can choose Next, and then enter a number that specifies a span of records starting with wherever the pointer is now located; for example, entering **10** tells FoxPro to look at only the next ten records. You can choose Record and enter a number, which again selects a specific record by its record number. (In the case of Locate, this is a useless option, since if you knew the record number, you wouldn't need a search.) Or you can choose Rest, which applies the Locate to all records located between the pointer and the end of the file. Again, none of these options are much help unless you know something about where the desired record is located.

The For and While options that appear after you choose Locate are the options likely to prove most useful. The While option works best with an index, but the For option can easily be used on any field, whether an index exists or not. Click For in the dialog box, and the Expression Builder containing a Locate Record For text box appears next, as shown in Figure 5-3.

In the Locate Record For text box, you enter the expression that will locate the record you want. An *expression* is a combination of field names, operators, and constants that evaluate to a certain value. The term

```
LASTNAME = "Morris"
```

is an expression, as is

```
TAPELIMIT > 3
```

which evaluates to a tape limit of more than 3. If the parts of the expression do not make sense at this point, don't be too concerned; they are explained in more detail later in this chapter.

FIGURE
5-3

Expression Builder with Locate Record For text box

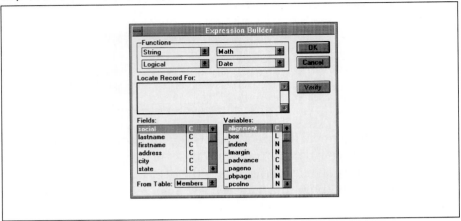

Field names, which are normally used to build search expressions, can be selected by double-clicking the desired field in the Fields box, in the lower-left corner of the dialog box. Once you double-click a field name, it appears in the Locate Records For text box. (As an alternative, you may choose to enter the field name in the Locate Records For text box by typing it.) The next step is usually to enter an operator, such as an equal sign. You can choose from most of the commonly-used operators by clicking on the Logical drop-down list; however, it is usually faster to just type the symbol into the Locate Records For text box. Finally, enter the desired search value. Text expressions are always entered with quotes surrounding them; numbers are entered exactly as they are stored in the numeric field; and dates may be entered with the CTOD (Character To Date) function. For example, CTOD("12/20/90") would be evaluated as a date value of 12/20/90. Memo fields can also be used within your search expression.

You will make use of logical operators (covered in more detail in later chapters) to apply multiple conditions to a search. Two common logical operators are .AND. and .OR., which specify whether all the conditions must be met (.AND.), or whether only one of the conditions must be met (.OR.). For example, the condition

```
LASTNAME = "Robinson" .AND. TAPELIMIT = 2
```

specifies that the last name must be Robinson, and the tape limit must be equal to 2. The condition

```
CITY = "Falls Church" .OR. CITY = "Arlington"
```

specifies that the City field must contain either Arlington or Falls Church. Note that the logical operators are always surrounded by periods.

You can check your expression for correct syntax, if desired, by clicking the Verify button. If the expression is a valid one, FoxPro briefly displays an "Expression is valid" message in the Status Bar. Finally, click the OK button to finish your entry, and the Locate dialog box will reappear. You can now click the Locate button to implement the search. Remember, the process only locates the record—it does not display it, although you can confirm that the record has been located by looking at the Status Bar. You can now choose the Change option of the Record menu to view the record.

Remember   With large databases, LOCATE can be slow. If the field you are searching is indexed, use FIND or SEEK instead.

Consider a simple example, which you can carry out if you've created the MEMBERS database outlined in Chapter 2. Perhaps you need to locate Mr. Kramer, a member of the video club. Assuming the MEMBERS file is open, you can open the Record menu, choose Locate, and click the For button when the Locate dialog box (shown in Figure 5-2) appears. The Expression Builder dialog box next appears (Figure 5-3); your desired expression will be LASTNAME = "Kramer". You can simply type this into the Locate Record For text box, or you can double-click Lastname in the list of fields, type an equal sign or choose one from the Logical drop-down list, and then type **"Kramer"** (you must include the quotation marks). An alternative to typing the quotation marks is to click the String drop-down list, select Text, and then type the name; but again, it is usually faster to just type in the quotation marks.

Once all this is done, the Expression Builder dialog box resembles the example shown in Figure 5-4. If you entered the field name manually, you probably won't have the filename prefix (Members.) in your example; it is added if you select the field name from the list box. Such prefixes are needed for working with multiple files, as covered in Chapter 12; when

FIGURE 5-4

Filled-In Expression Builder dialog box

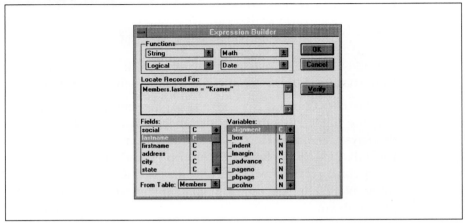

you are working with just one file, it does not matter whether they are included or not.

You next select the OK button, and the Locate dialog box reappears. Finally, click the Locate button in the Locate dialog box to implement the search. If you then choose Change from the Record menu, the desired record appears.

Probably the strongest argument for using commands, rather than the menu options, appears in the Command window after you've completed the operation just described. These two commands appear:

```
LOCATE ALL FOR members.lastname = "Kramer"
CHANGE
```

They could have been entered from Command mode to perform the same task. Even the "members." could have been omitted, as this identifies the file, and such identifiers are optional when you have only one file open. Hence, the command

```
LOCATE ALL FOR LASTNAME = "Kramer"
```

would have worked just as well as the menu options.

When you use Locate, FoxPro searches by examining the characters in your search term from left to right, so you need enter only as much of the term as is necessary to find the record. For example, the command

```
LOCATE FOR LASTNAME = "Jo"
```

would be enough to find a person named Jones if there were no other names with "Jo" as the first two letters of the name.

When selected, the While option in the Locate dialog box (see Figure 5-2) causes the same Expression Builder to appear; the only difference is that the center text box is labeled "Locate Record While." Figure 5-5 shows an example of the Expression Builder containing the Locate Record While text box. Using the While option takes a little more planning than using the For option, because the While clause is effective only "while" a condition exists. For example, if you were to enter **LASTNAME = "Kramer"** as an expression in the Locate Record While text box, FoxPro would locate the record only while the condition was true; in other words,

Expression Builder with Locate Record While text box

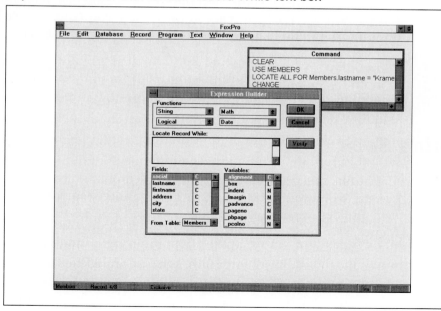

the database pointer would need to already be at a record with Kramer in the Lastname field.

"While" clauses are normally used with indexed files, where records matching a certain condition are likely to be grouped together. For example, with a database indexed by tape limit, you could find the first record with a tape limit of 6 and then perform a Locate operation while the tape limit was 6.

Using Continue

The Locate option finds the first occurrence of what you are looking for. If there is more than one occurrence, you can use the Continue option to find successive records with the same search term. For example, your database might contain two persons with a last name of Robinson, and the use of Locate might turn up the wrong one. You can again open the Record menu and choose Continue. The Continue option is available on the menu only after you have used the Locate option. It continues the search, seeking the next record that meets the condition you specified when using Locate. If no further records meet the specified condition, an "End of Locate scope" message briefly appears in the Status Bar. (You will see the same error message if an initial use of Locate fails to find a record.)

 Remember You can use the CONTINUE command only after using a LOCATE command.

Using Seek

If a file has been indexed, you can search the index with the Seek option. When you open the Record menu and choose Seek, the Expression Builder appears, containing a Value to SEEK text box, as seen in Figure 5-6. Again, the Seek option's Expression Builder works just like those used with the Locate For and Locate While options. Seek simply works much faster with large files, because an indexed file takes less time to search.

You enter the desired expression into the Value to SEEK text box. However, you need enter only the expression itself, since FoxPro knows

FIGURE
5-6

Expression Builder with Value to SEEK text box

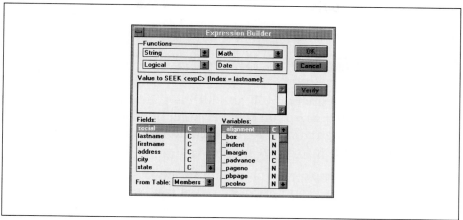

which field (or fields) the index is based on. For example, assume that the active index is based on the Lastname field. Instead of entering LASTNAME = "Kramer" as was done with Locate, you would only enter **"Kramer"** in the Value to SEEK text box. Remember that since Seek is designed to work with an index, you must search for data based on the indexed field or fields. (You could not, for example, use Seek to search for a last name if the database were indexed only by social security number.)

Text expressions are always entered surrounded by quotes; numbers are entered exactly as they are stored in the numeric field; and dates may be entered with the CTOD function. As an example of Seek, if the video database were indexed on the Tapelimit field, you could enter **4** in the Value to SEEK window, and the Seek option would find the first record with a value of 4 in the Tapelimit field. If the database were indexed on the Expiredate field, you could enter **CTOD("12/20/93")** in the Value to SEEK window to find the first record with the expiration date of 12/20/93.

After entering the search value, click the OK button, and the Seek will take place. You can then use the Change option of the Record menu to view the desired record. Keep in mind that the Seek option finds the first occurrence in the index. If there are duplicate occurrences of that index expression (such as more than one last name of Robinson in a file indexed only on Lastname), you may want to use Browse to aid you in finding the desired record.

Selecting Subsets of Data

Often, a query involves selecting a group of records. You should note that such queries can be done either by using the techniques that follow, or by using FoxPro's RQBE (Relational Query By Example) window. The use of RQBE to create queries is covered in the following chapter.)

For example, you may want to see all members who live in Maryland or Virginia. From the menus, this can be done with the Setup option of the Database menu. This option, among other things, lets you set a filter that restricts the available records; in effect, the records shown must meet the conditions of the filter that you specify.

When you open the Database menu and choose Setup, the Setup dialog box shown in Figure 5-7 appears. This dialog box is used for many tasks; the one this chapter will explore is the Filter Data option, shown in the lower-left corner of the dialog box.

If you click the Filter Data button, the Expression Builder appears with a SET FILTER Expression text box, as shown in Figure 5-8. By now, the design of the Expression Builder should be quite familiar; you enter

**FIGURE
5-7**

Setup dialog box

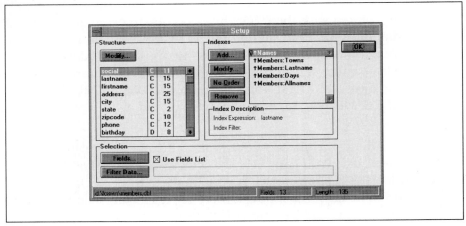

FIGURE 5-8

Expression Builder with SET FILTER Expression text box

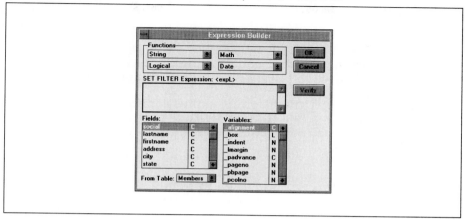

an expression in the same manner as with the For option of the Locate command. Field names can be selected by double-clicking the desired field in the Fields box in the lower-left corner of the dialog box. Once a name is selected, it appears in the SET FILTER Expression text box. (As an alternative, you can type the name into the SET FILTER Expression text box directly.) Next, you enter the desired operator, such as the equal sign. Finally, enter the desired search value. Remember to surround text expressions with quotes, and to enter any dates with the CTOD function. As an example, the expression

```
TAPELIMIT = 6
```

would select a group of records with a value of 6 in the Tapelimit field. The expression

```
STATE = "MD" .OR. STATE = "VA"
```

would select records with either Maryland or Virginia in the State field.

Once you enter the expression and choose the OK button, the Setup dialog box reappears. Click the OK button in this dialog box, and the needed SET FILTER command appears in the Command window, and is executed. You can then perform a Browse to see records meeting your condition, or you can use the LIST command to produce a simple on-screen report.

Again, consider our simple example. Perhaps you need a list of all customers in the video database who live in Maryland or Virginia. Open the Database menu, choose Setup, and click the Filter Data button in the Setup dialog box. The Expression Builder will appear.

Next, enter the following expression in the SET FILTER Expression window:

```
STATE = "MD" .OR. STATE = "VA"
```

Then click the OK button here, and again click the OK button in the next dialog box that appears. The resulting command, which is

```
SET FILTER TO STATE = "MD" .OR. STATE = "VA"
```

now appears in the Command window, and the filter is set. Next, choose Database Browse to see the records meeting your filter condition, as shown in Figure 5-9. If the records don't appear in tabular format, choose Browse/Browse from the menus.

Results of filter condition

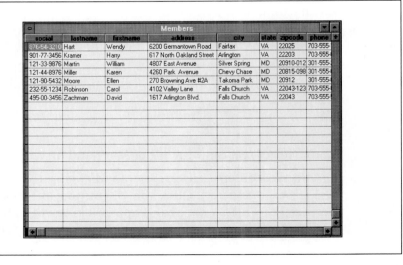

Reporting Needs

If you need to create a report based on a select group of data, one method is to set a filter using the menu options just described, as the middle step in a three-step process. First, design and save a report, as detailed in Chapters 7 and 11 (this needs to be done only once). Then use the menu options just described to set the desired filter conditions. Finally, select the Report option from the Database menu to print the report.

Another method works well if a simple columnar report with no fancy headings will suffice. Set the filter as described earlier, then use the LIST command with the desired fields, and add the TO PRINT option to route the output to the printer. For example, after setting the filter condition described in the prior example, you could enter the command

```
LIST LASTNAME, FIRSTNAME, STATE, EXPIREDATE TO PRINT
```

to produce a columnar listing of the above named fields at the printer. Such a list would resemble the example shown here:

```
Record#   LASTNAME       FIRSTNAME        STATE EXPIREDATE
      8   Hart           Wendy            VA    10/19/94
      4   Kramer         Harry            VA    12/22/93
      2   Martin         William          MD    07/04/93
      1   Miller         Karen            MD    07/25/93
      5   Moore          Ellen            MD    11/17/95
      3   Robinson       Carol            VA    09/05/94
      6   Zachman        David            VA    09/19/93
```

You will find additional details on using the LIST command with the TO PRINT option in Chapter 7. Before proceeding, enter the command

```
SET FILTER TO
```

with no expression following the command, and press ENTER. This clears the effects of the previous filter. (You will learn more about the SET FILTER command later in this chapter.)

Performing Queries with Commands

At FoxPro's Command level, you can use four commands to search for items: LOCATE, CONTINUE, FIND, and SEEK. The LOCATE and CONTINUE commands perform a sequential search (checking one record at a time) and work with any database. The FIND and SEEK commands perform a much faster search than LOCATE, but work with indexed files only.

Using LOCATE

The LOCATE command can be used to find the first occurrence of a record. The syntax for the command is

LOCATE [*scope*] FOR *condition*

where *condition* is a logical expression (such as LASTNAME = "Morris") that defines your search. The scope, which is optional, can be used to limit the number of records searched. If the scope is omitted, FoxPro assumes that you want to search all of the records in the file. You can enter **ALL** to specify that LOCATE should look at all records; this is the default. You can enter **NEXT**, and then enter a number that specifies a span of records starting with wherever the pointer is now located; for example, entering **NEXT 10** as the scope would tell FoxPro to look at only the next ten records, starting with the current record. Or you can enter **REST**, which applies the LOCATE to all records from wherever the pointer is located, to the end of the file.

Note that LOCATE does not find all matches, or even the second match—only the first match. Its companion command, CONTINUE, is used to continue the search as many times as desired, assuming that the first record found was not the one you really wanted. LOCATE and CONTINUE carry on a sequential search until either a record is found or you reach the end of the database. If a LOCATE or CONTINUE command is unsuccessful, you get the message, "End of LOCATE scope."

For an example, a simple search can be entered in the Command window to search the Tapelimit field of the video database:

```
LOCATE FOR TAPELIMIT = 4
DISPLAY
```

The result, shown in part here, demonstrates that the record found does indeed contain a value of 4 in the Tapelimit field:

```
121-33-9876    Martin    William    4807 East Avenue...
```

If this is not the desired record, the search can be continued with the CONTINUE command. As an example, if you enter the commands

```
CONTINUE
DISPLAY
```

the result shows that the CONTINUE command found the next occurrence of the desired record:

```
901-77-3456    Kramer    Harry    617 North Oakland Street...
```

You can add the logical conditions .AND. and .OR. to get closer to the precise data you want. (The periods must be included around the words AND and OR when they are used as part of an expression.) The .AND. condition specifies that both conditions on each side of the word AND must be true, while .OR. specifies that either one or the other condition must be true. As an example, if you needed to find a record where the last name was Miller and the tape limit was 6, you could try the command

```
LOCATE FOR LASTNAME = "Miller" .AND. TAPELIMIT = 6
```

If you were seeking a record with an expiration date of 12/31/93 or 1/1/94, you could try the following command:

```
LOCATE FOR EXPIREDATE = CTOD("12/31/93") .OR.
EXPIREDATE = CTOD("01/01/94")
```

When using LOCATE, keep in mind that FoxPro searches by examining the characters in your search term from left to right. Therefore, you need to enter only as much of the term as necessary to find the proper record. For example, the command

```
LOCATE FOR LASTNAME = "Jon"
```

would be enough to find a person named Jones if there were no other names with "Jon" as the first three letters of the name. Sometimes, this left-to-right tendency of a search may be troublesome; for example, the command

```
LOCATE FOR LASTNAME = "Mills"
```

would locate names like Millson or Millsap, which might not be what you had in mind. If you want FoxPro to look for your precise search term, you can first enter the command

```
SET EXACT ON
```

and then enter the desired LOCATE command. The SET EXACT command tells FoxPro to execute any LOCATE, FIND, or SEEK operation by comparing all characters in the search term with all those in the actual data. You can later enter **SET EXACT OFF** to disable this effect.

Using FIND and SEEK

FIND and SEEK work very differently from LOCATE and CONTINUE. Both FIND and SEEK make use of index files to perform a very fast search. (FoxPro may not find anything, but you will know about it very quickly!) Either a record matching the specified condition is found, or the end of the database is reached. This type of search is common with database management software; it is popular because it is extremely fast. Even with a very large database, FoxPro can usually find a record in this manner in well under two seconds. The time that a LOCATE command takes, by comparison, grows progressively worse as the database grows in size.

The syntax for the two commands is similar:

FIND *character-string*
SEEK *expression*

where *character-string* is a group of characters that do *not* need to be surrounded by quotation marks.

The expression can be a number, a character string (which *must* be surrounded by quotation marks), or a variable. The expression can also be a combination of constants, variables, and operators (including functions).

The FIND and SEEK commands search the active index file and find the first record matching your specifications. The record itself will not be displayed; the FIND and SEEK commands simply move the record pointer to the desired record. Try the commands with the sample video database, entering the following:

```
USE MEMBERS
INDEX ON LASTNAME TO NAMES
FIND Moore
DISPLAY
```

The result is as follows:

```
5    121-90-5432 Moore     Ellen     270 Browning Ave #2A...
```

To try the SEEK command, enter

```
USE MEMBERS
INDEX ON TAPELIMIT TO TAPES
SEEK 4
DISPLAY
```

The result is shown here:

```
2    121-33-9876 Martin    William    4807 East Avenue...
```

Note that the index need not be created anew for every search; if an index already exists, you need only ensure that it is opened before you attempt to use FIND or SEEK.

Comparisons, Comparisons: FIND and SEEK Versus LOCATE and CONTINUE

Since FIND and SEEK are usually so much faster than LOCATE, why not use FIND or SEEK in every case? Simplicity sometimes plays a part. First, remember that none of these commands is guaranteed to find what you really want. In many cases, it is easier for novice users to get close with LOCATE and CONTINUE than with FIND or SEEK, because FIND and SEEK find only the first matching record. If you're searching for Jim Smith in a 12,000-name mailing list with 75 Jim Smiths, a FIND command will find the first one. It's then up to you to figure out how to find the one you want. This can be done by using a WHILE qualifier along with the LOCATE command, which will then tell FoxPro to start its search at the current position in the database. As an example, you could use commands like these, assuming that the database is indexed by last names:

```
FIND "Smith"
LOCATE WHILE LASTNAME = "Smith" FOR FIRSTNAME = "Jim"
.AND. CITY = "New York"
```

This helps you narrow the search down to the desired record without wasting a great deal of time. An inherent advantage to LOCATE and CONTINUE is that these commands find every matching record (and, sooner or later, the desired one).

Another advantage of LOCATE is its ability to search within a field, using the $ operator. For example, the statement

```
LOCATE FOR "East Avenue" $ ADDRESS
```

would search for the words "East Avenue" anywhere inside the Address field. If you are using FIND or SEEK, you must know the starting characters or values in the index field; you cannot search for something in the middle of a field with FIND or SEEK.

Tip You can use LOCATE to search the contents of memo fields.

One more problem with FIND and SEEK is the index file requirement. The problem arises when you need to make a search based on something different from what you've indexed your file on. Suppose you index by social security number as well as by a combination of last and first name, and you pride yourself for being efficient. Then a co-worker comes along and wants to find "this customer I spoke with last week, and I can't remember her name, and I don't know her social security number, but she lives somewhere on Myterra Avenue." Armed with this knowledge, your index files are fairly worthless. And in a database containing tens of thousands of records, FoxPro will spend some time on a command like

```
LOCATE ALL FOR "Myterra Ave" $ ADDRESS
```

while you mutter under your breath, thinking there must be a better way. This is brought out to emphasize one point: the LOCATE and CONTINUE commands are in the language because there may be times you will need them (although with good planning, you can minimize those times). Knowing how to effectively use all of the available commands reduces the amount of time FoxPro must spend searching for your data.

The secret to a quick find, if there is one, is to use an index file and a FIND or SEEK, rather than a LOCATE. This may seem like elementary knowledge to some, but it is surprising how many FoxPro users are still using LOCATE when it isn't necessary. When indexing on one field, using FIND or SEEK is rarely a problem. If, for example, a personnel list is indexed by last names and you are looking for Ms. Samuels, you would simply use

```
FIND Samuels
CHANGE
```

and unless the database is a sizeable one, you're probably at the record or close enough to use PGDN to get to it. The problem arises when you have large databases and you index on multiple fields to get a more precise match.

Let's say you're working with a large mailing list, and you index on a combination of Lastname + Firstname + City. The Lastname and Firstname fields are each 15 characters long. This means that the records in the index get stored like this:

Smith	Art	Raleigh
Smith	Louise	Tampa
Smith	Louise	Washington
Sodelski	Thomas	St. Louis

The contents of the index precisely match the structure of the field, spaces included. To use FIND or SEEK from the Command window with such an index, and be assured of finding the correct record, you would have to enter something like the following:

```
FIND Smith          Louise          Washington
```

including the exact number of spaces to match the index; otherwise, you get a "no find." There are ways to get around this when writing programs that find records. However, if you do much of your work from the Command level, you should be aware of this potential problem. One simple way around it is to search the first field in the index (in this case, Lastname) with a FIND command; when the first matching record is found, use BROWSE to visually scan for the exact record desired.

Using SET FILTER with Commands

The SET FILTER command is a popular one, and it has both advantages and disadvantages. SET FILTER hides records that do not meet the condition specified. The syntax for the command is

SET FILTER TO *condition*

where *condition* is a logical expression (such as LASTNAME = "Morris") that defines your search. Once this command is entered, other commands that would normally use records from the entire database, will instead use only records that meet the condition specified by the filter. In effect, this lets you work with a subset of a database, as though it were the entire database. A command like

```
SET FILTER TO CITY = "Washington" .AND. STATE = "DC"
```

limits a database to those records located in Washington, D.C. In effect, this is the equivalent of the Filter Data button of the Setup dialog box, available through the Database/Setup menu choices. You can isolate a group of records by issuing a SET FILTER command; then you can use the LIST or BROWSE command to view the data, or the REPORT FORM command (covered in the next chapter) to produce a printed report.

As an example, consider the following commands, used with the video database:

```
USE MEMBERS

SET FILTER TO EXPIREDATE >= CTOD("01/01/94") .AND.
```

```
EXPIREDATE <= CTOD("12/31/94")

LIST LASTNAME, FIRSTNAME, SOCIAL, EXPIREDATE
```

(The second command appears on two lines here due to printing limitations, but you should enter the entire command on a single line.) The SET FILTER command in this example restricts the listed records to only those with expiration dates that fall in the year 1994. You can enclose parts of the expression in parentheses to build very complex expressions. For example, the command

```
SET FILTER TO ( EXPIREDATE >= CTOD("01/01/94") .AND.
EXPIREDATE <= CTOD("12/31/94") ) .OR. STATE = "MD"
```

would limit the records available to those with an expiration date sometime in 1994, or those with the letters "MD" in the state field.

You can see whether a filter is in effect at any time by using the LIST STATUS or DISPLAY STATUS command. The listing that results from either of these commands will include the filter condition for any filter that is in effect. And you can cancel the effects of an existing filter by entering

```
SET FILTER TO
```

without including a condition in the command, as shown above.

One point sometimes overlooked, until you get used to this abnormality, is that when you set a filter, the current record is not immediately affected by the filter. The filter does not take effect until you move the record pointer. If the next command causes the record pointer to move before data is displayed or printed, fine. If not, you may wind up with a record you don't really want. This problem can be illustrated by imagining a large personnel database containing a Lastname field. When the following commands are entered, note the result:

```
SET FILTER TO LASTNAME = "Robinson"
LIST LASTNAME NEXT 10

Record#   LASTNAME
      1   Miller
      3   Robinson
      7   Robinson
     11   Robinson
```

```
15   Robinson
19   Robinson
23   Robinson
27   Robinson
31   Robinson
52   Robinson
```

The first name in the display obviously isn't Robinson—it is the name from the record that was current when the LIST command was entered. Once you take any action that causes the record pointer to move, the invalid record disappears.

You'll have to think about whether the commands you use immediately after the SET FILTER command will move the record pointer before displaying any data. The REPORT FORM and LABEL FORM commands automatically move the pointer to the top of the database before printing any reports or labels, so you will get the proper results if no NEXT or WHILE clauses are included in the REPORT FORM or LABEL FORM command. Similarly, a LIST command normally moves the pointer before displaying data, but it won't if you include a NEXT or WHILE scope along with the command. If you try a command like LIST NEXT 20 immediately after a SET FILTER command, you will get 19 records that meet the condition, and one that may not. The solution, simply enough, is to move the record pointer by issuing a GO TOP command immediately after the SET FILTER command. This automatically moves the record pointer to the first record meeting the filter condition, and you can then use the desired commands.

Before you become too fond of the SET FILTER command, you should be aware of its disadvantages. The SET FILTER command appears to perform a rapid sequential qualification of every record in the database, starting from record 1 and moving to the highest record number. Because FoxPro performs a rapid internal search during this process, it is not a problem if the record numbers happen to be in sequential order (which means that no index files are open). However, if an index file is open, and one usually is, FoxPro examines each record in the order of the index, which is usually not the same as sequential order. This means that FoxPro must now check both the index and the database in sequential order for each record, so any operation that uses SET FILTER will be terribly slow for a large, indexed database. Understandably, the larger the database, the more interminable the delays with an indexed file.

You can avoid opening the index files while using SET FILTER, which is fine if you don't mind having to update the indexes after changes have been made. Another problem arises when you want a report with an odd selection of records. You probably want it in some kind of sorted order, and the alternative of sorting the database and then setting a filter is about as appealing as the slow index.

The answer, like so many things in life, is a compromise. When using indexes, stay away from filters wherever possible; when using filters, stay away from indexes wherever possible. If you want to find records for editing and updating, don't use filters. Open indexes and use FIND or SEEK instead. Save the SET FILTER command for showing lists of data, and for serving your reporting needs. It is less annoying to see a delay during reporting; most users turn on the printer, choose the report, and go off to do something else while FoxPro does all the work. Also, in reporting, often a large percentage of your records may meet the filter criteria, and performance improves as more records match the criteria outlined with the SET FILTER command. An alternative to using SET FILTER is to use the FOR clause with the INDEX command to build a selective index file. This topic was covered in detail in Chapter 4.

Using View Files

The conditions placed in effect with a SET FILTER command can be stored in the form of a *view file* for additional use at a later time. A view file will also contain a record of any open database and index files, as well as any screen format file in use at the time the view file was created. You can think of a view file as a "snapshot" of your overall FoxPro environment. Once you have opened your database and index files, loaded any desired format file, and set a filter condition with the SET FILTER command, you can create a view file by entering

CREATE VIEW *filename* FROM ENVIRONMENT

where *filename* is the name for the view file. Once you have done this, you no longer need to repeat the same set of commands for opening these files and setting this filter during later FoxPro sessions. Instead, you can simply issue the SET VIEW command, using the following syntax:

SET VIEW TO *filename*

Here, *filename* is the name of the view file you saved earlier, and FoxPro will open the same database and index files (if any indexes are in use). Any filter condition that was in effect when the view file was created will be placed back into effect.

Not only is this useful for sparing yourself the tedious entry of a number of commands, but it can also be used with reports. As Chapter 7 will show, an ENVIRONMENT option of the REPORT FORM command can automatically open the settings in a view file before a report is produced. And a view file will also contain any relations that have been established between multiple files. (Relations between multiple files are covered in Chapter 12.)

CHAPTER

Creating Queries with RQBE

*A*s mentioned in the last chapter, a significant part of managing your data consists of finding specific groups of information, or *making queries.* The commands and menu options detailed in the last chapter provide one way in which you can find records and to isolate groups of records. However, you can also make use of FoxPro's RQBE feature to quickly isolate groups of records for browsing or reporting.

RQBE has an important advantage over the methods described in the prior chapter: speed. When you use RQBE to implement a query, FoxPro interprets your selections within the RQBE window as SELECT commands. (The SELECT command is a command in a computer language called SQL, originally implemented by IBM on mainframe computers in the 1970s.) FoxPro uses advanced programming logic to optimize the query, creating the most efficient type of SELECT command for your particular query. Hence, queries performed using selections from the RQBE window (or using the equivalent SELECT commands) are likely to execute much faster than any commands you enter by using the LOCATE and SET FILTER commands described in the previous chapter.

 Tip   Queries designed by using the RQBE window operate much faster than retrievals implemented with SET FILTER commands or FOR clauses.

Creating a Query with RQBE

Creating a query is a simple matter with RQBE. The basic steps involved in this process are as follows:

1. Open the RQBE window, either by choosing New from the File menu and choosing Query, or by entering the command CREATE QUERY.

2. Choose the database for use in the query (if you already have a database open, it is chosen by default).

3. Choose the fields that you want to see in the results of the query.

4. If desired, change the order in which the fields will be displayed in the results.

5. Choose the desired destination for the results (by default, the output is to a Browse window).

6. Specify any selection criteria for the records.

7. Perform the query.

8. Save the query (if desired) for re-use later.

As mentioned, queries are designed by using the RQBE window (Figure 6-1). You can get to this window in one of two ways. From the menus, you can choose New from the File menu. When the dialog box appears, you can select Query and then select New. Or from the Command level, you can enter the command CREATE QUERY. Either method opens the RQBE window.

The upper-left portion of the RQBE Window contains a list box for databases (tables) that are to be used by the query. (Chapter 12 shows how you can perform a query using more than one database file; for now, only the MEMBERS database is used.) The upper-middle portion of the

RQBE Window

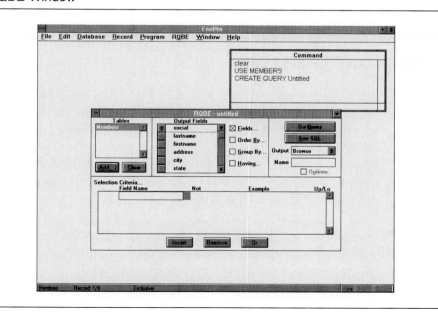

window displays a list box called Output Fields. This list box is used to determine which fields should be included in the results of the query. At the upper-right side of the window, the Output drop-down list is used to control where the results of the query are sent. By default, the results appear in a Browse window; however, you can have them appear in the form of a printed report or as a new database file.

The lower portion of the window is the Selection Criteria area. In this area, you choose the conditions that will limit the records provided by the query, such as "all members living in Maryland" or "all employees earning more than $9.00 per hour."

Note that when the RQBE window is active, FoxPro's menu bar also contains a new menu heading, titled RQBE. This menu contains the same options that appear as selection buttons in the RQBE window; you can either select the desired button, or choose the option from the menu. The various buttons (and their equivalent menu options) are discussed throughout this chapter.

Once you have chosen the desired options in the RQBE window, you click the Do Query button at the right side of the window, and the query is performed. Depending on your selection in the Output menu, your results appear on-screen, are printed, or are stored in a new database file.

Practice Queries

Assuming you are following along with the example of the MEMBERS database, you can perform some queries now to see how the RQBE window is used. As an example, perhaps you need to see all members living in Virginia. Open the File menu and choose New. From the dialog box that appears, select Query, and then click New. If a database is not currently open, you will see another dialog box asking you to select a database; if so, click MEMBERS and then click Open.

In a moment, the RQBE window, as shown in Figure 6-1, appears. The MEMBERS database should appear in the Tables box. Also, notice (at the upper-middle area of the window) that all fields appear by default in the Output Fields box. FoxPro assumes that you want all fields available in the query; you will see how to change this assumption later.

For this simple example, all that's needed is to make the criteria selections at the bottom of the screen. Click anywhere in the Field Name text box, and a drop-down list of fields appears (Figure 6-2).

When specifying fields to control the selection criteria, you can simply pick the desired field from this list. In this case, you want all records from a particular state, so click **state** in the menu. When you do so, notice that the Like clause automatically appears beside the Field Name entry.

Take a close look at the Like entry box. This is also a drop-down list box, and Like is just one of many choices. For this example, this choice is fine, but you should be aware of the possible choices here. Click the arrow to the right of Like, and you will see choices for Like, Exactly Like, More Than, Less Than, Between, and In. You can use this menu to further refine the conditions in your queries.

Since Like is fine for this example, press TAB twice, to move to the Example box. In this box (directly underneath the word "Example") you enter the desired example for your query. Since you want all records where the state is Virginia, enter **VA** in this box. At this point, your query should resemble the example shown in Figure 6-3.

Click the Do Query button at the right side of the window. In a moment, a Browse window will appear, containing the results of the query (Figure 6-4). If you examine the State field within the Browse window, you will

Menu of fields

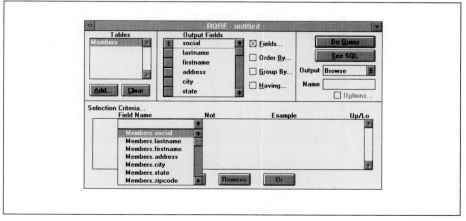

Completed query

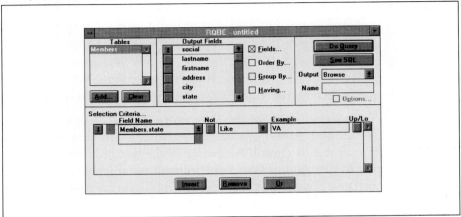

see that only those members residing in Virginia have been included in the query results.

Results of query

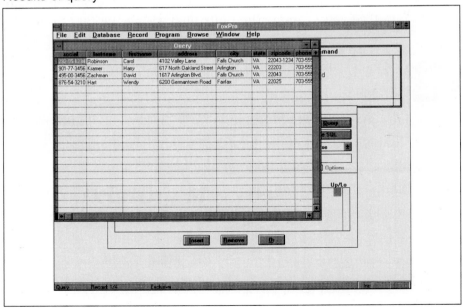

Press CTRL+F4 to close the Browse window. You can remove the existing criteria by selecting the Remove button at the bottom of the window. (Note that an alternate method of clearing the criteria is to open the RQBE menu and choose Remove.)

A Sample Query Using an AND Condition

By default, the RQBE window assumes that any series of conditions should be an AND query; that is, a query where each of the named conditions must prove true for the record to appear in the results. For example, perhaps you need to see all members who live in Maryland and have a value of more than three in the Tapelimit field. This denotes an AND condition; in order for a record to qualify, the member must live in Maryland AND have a tape limit value greater than three.

Click anywhere in the Field Name box to open its drop-down list. From the list, click **state**. TAB over to the Example box and enter **MD**.

You may have noticed that once an entry is made in the Field Name box, a new space appears below that entry in the same column. This space lets you enter additional conditions. Click anywhere in the new space in the Field Name box. From the list of fields, choose Tapelimit.

Click the arrow to the right of the Like entry to display the list of possible choices. Since you want all members with more than three in the Tapelimit field, choose More Than. TAB over to the Example field, and enter **3**. Finally, click Do Query to perform the query. Your results should resemble those shown in Figure 6-5.

A Sample Query Using an OR Condition

The other type of query you'll commonly create is an OR query; that is, a query where if any one of the named conditions proves true, the record appears in the results. For example, perhaps you need to see all members who live in Maryland or in Washington, D.C. This denotes an OR condition; in order for a record to qualify, the member must live in Maryland OR in Washington.

FIGURE 6-5

Results of AND query

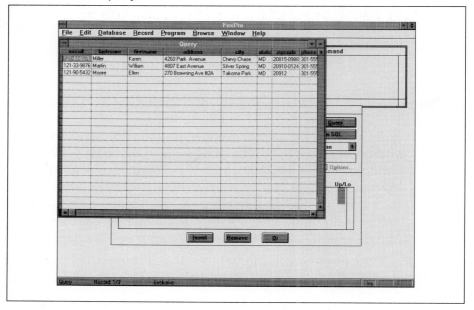

Press CTRL+F4 to clear the Browse window containing the previous results, and click the Remove button twice to clear the existing conditions.

Click anywhere in the Field Name box. From the drop-down list of fields, click **state**. TAB over to the Example box, and enter **MD**.

To specify an OR condition between criteria, you use the Or button at the bottom of the window (or the Or option of the RQBE menu). Click the Or button. You should see the designation "OR" appear under your existing criteria.

Click anywhere in the new Field Name box that has just appeared. From the list of fields, again choose **state**. TAB over to the Example box, and enter **DC**. Finally, choose Do Query to perform the query. Your results should resemble those shown in Figure 6-6.

Results of OR query

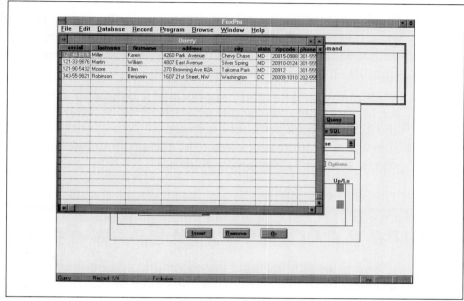

A Sample Query Using a Date Range

You've seen sample queries using both text (the names of states) and numbers (the contents of the Tapelimit field); you should be aware that you can also build queries that use dates as conditions. For example, you might want to see all members whose video memberships expire in 1994; this would help you to prepare a letter encouraging them to renew. Press CTRL+F4 to clear the Browse window of the prior results, and click Remove repeatedly until all conditions have been cleared from the criteria area. Click the Field Name area, and click Expiredate in the fields list. Click the arrow to the right of the Like entry, and choose More Than from the list. In the Example column, enter **12/31/93**.

Click in the second Field Name area, and again click Expiredate in the fields list. Click the arrow to the right of the Like entry, and choose Less Than from the menu. In the Example column, enter **1/1/95**. Finally, click Do Query. The results should resemble those shown in Figure 6-7; note that the contents of the Expiredate fields for these records are all from 1994. Before continuing, press CTRL+F4 to clear the Browse window.

One advantage of queries performed with FoxPro's Query-By-Example facility is evident when working with dates; you can enter the dates in the RQBE Window without needing the CTOD() function. Recall that with the types of queries described in the previous chapter, functions are required when working with dates.

Adding a Sort Order to Query Results

You can easily specify that the results of a particular query appear in a certain order. To do this, use the Order By check box. When you turn on the check box, a dialog box appears, and you can select the field or

FIGURE
6-7

Results of date-based query

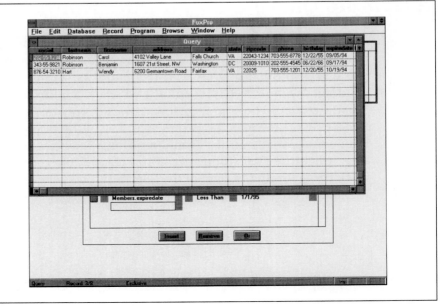

fields that will control the order of the results. For example, if you wanted the records in a query to appear in order of last name, you could choose the Lastname field from the dialog box.

To see how this works, you can reuse the example that was last entered. Close the Browse window by pressing CTRL+F4. With the criteria still entered in the lower half of the dialog box, click the Order By check box. You will see the RQBE Order By dialog box, shown in Figure 6-8.

To define the order in which the records should appear, you simply select the desired field or fields, and use the Move button to move the field name(s) into the Ordering Criteria list box at the right side of the screen. (You can also select the field name and press ENTER.) In this example, click **lastname** and then click the Move button. The field (Members.Lastname) will appear in the Ordering Criteria list box on the right side of the screen.

For this example, ordering simply on the basis of last names suffices. However, note that you could add additional field names if desired; for example, choosing Lastname followed by Firstname would result in an order based on last names, and where last names were the same, on first

FIGURE
6-8

Order By dialog box

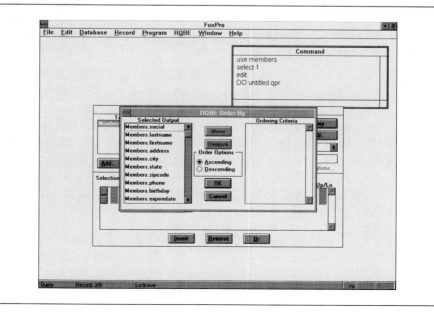

names. Also, note the Order Options of Ascending and Descending. You can choose the desired option to determine whether the order is ascending (letters A-Z, numbers 0-9, and dates earliest to latest), or descending (letters Z-A, numbers 9-0, and dates latest to earliest). For this example, the default choice of ascending is fine.

Click the OK button. When the Order By dialog box disappears, click the Do Query button in the RQBE window. The same records (with an expiration date of 1994) will appear. But this time, they will appear in alphabetical order, by last names. Before continuing, press CTRL+F4 to clear the Browse window.

Selecting Fields for Query Results

You can choose to display only certain fields for the results of a query, omitting all fields that you did not select. To do this, click the Fields check box. When you do this, a dialog box appears, and you can add or remove fields that will then appear in the results.

As an example, perhaps you are only interested in the member's name, city, and membership expiration date. Again use the search criteria that were previously entered. Click the Fields check box now. In a moment, the RQBE Select Fields dialog box that appears shows that all fields have been selected for output; they all appear in the Selected Output portion of the dialog box (Figure 6-9).

Now, click the Remove All button in the dialog box to remove the fields from the Selected Output list box. With no fields selected, you can now proceed to select only the desired fields at the left side of the dialog box, and use the Move button (or just double-click the desired field) to move the field to the right side of the dialog box. Select the Lastname, Firstname, City, and Expiredate fields by double-clicking each, in succession. When you are done, the four named fields should be the only fields visible in the Selected Output box at the right side of the screen.

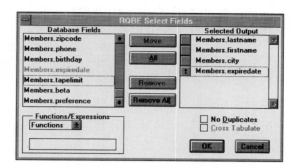

Click OK, and then click Do Query. The results, shown in Figure 6-10, contain only those fields you selected. Before continuing, press CTRL+F4 to clear the Browse window of the results.

RQBE Select Fields dialog box

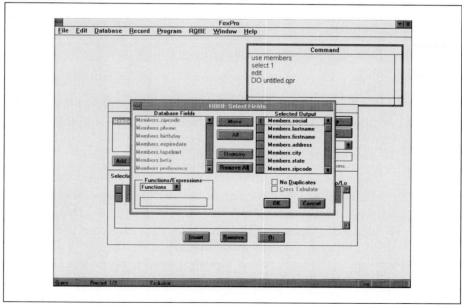

Query with selected fields

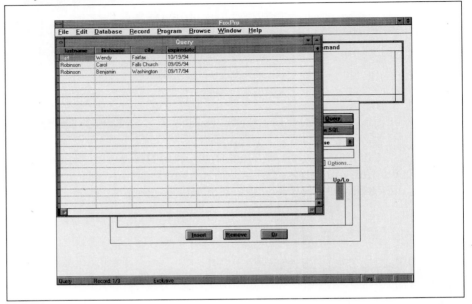

Changing the Output of a Query

Until now, all of your queries have appeared in the form of a Browse display. But you are likely to need the results of many queries in printed form. To accomplish this, you can use the available options in the Output To area of the RQBE window.

As an example, with the criteria for the last sample query still present in the window, click the arrow at the right edge of the Output drop-down list box, and a menu appears with five choices: Browse, Report/Label, Table/DBF, Cursor and Graph. The first choice is the one that you have been using; this causes the output of the query to appear in a Browse window. The last choice, Graph, requires the use of a utility known as Graph Wizard; see your FoxPro documentation for details. The cursor choice is for advanced programming use and is not discussed here. The second choice, Report/Label, can be used to direct the output to your printer in the form of a report, or as mailing labels. The third choice, Table/DBF, is used if you want the results of the query to be stored as a new database file.

You'll learn more about designing reports and labels in later chapters. For now, note that you can generate a printed copy of the results of a query by using the Reports/Labels option of this menu and then choosing Options from the dialog box. To see how this works, click the Report/Label choice in the menu now, and then click the Options check box just below the Output area. In a moment, the RQBE Display Options dialog box appears, as shown in Figure 6-11.

Most of the options in this dialog box will make more sense after you have seen the material in Chapters 7 and 11. For now, all you need to keep in mind is that the Output Destinations area at the bottom of the dialog box can be used to get a printed copy of the results of your query.

Click the To Printer option under Output Destinations, and then click OK. Make sure your printer is ready, and choose Do Query. This time, the results are printed instead of appearing in a Browse Window. (Note that if you are using a laser printer, you may have to press your printer's On Line button, followed by the Form Feed button, to get the page to eject from the printer.)

FIGURE 6-11   RQBE Display Options dialog box

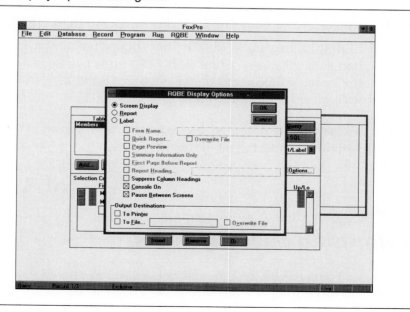

Saving Queries for Reuse

FoxPro lets you save queries for repeated use. This feature proves useful if you perform the same queries often, such as when printing the same type of report on a daily or weekly basis. Whenever a query is open in the active window, you can choose Save or Save As from the File menu, and if the query has not been saved previously, FoxPro will prompt you for a name for the query. Another way to save queries is to simply press CTRL+F4 or double-click the Query window's Control menu icon; before exiting, FoxPro always asks if you want to save a query that has not been saved. As an example, with the RQBE window still visible, press CTRL+F4. FoxPro will ask you if you want to save the changes.

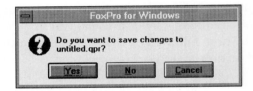

Choosing Yes causes another dialog box to appear, prompting you for a name for the query. Choosing No discards the current query without saving it. And choosing Cancel returns you to the RQBE window.

In this case, click Yes. The next dialog box that appears will ask for a name for the query. Enter **SAMPLE1** and click Save from the dialog box; the query will be saved under the name SAMPLE1. (All queries are saved with an extension of .QPR.)

Remember You must save your queries if you want to reuse them later without re-entering all of the information.

Performing Saved Queries

To repeat the results of a query you have saved, use the command

DO *query-name*.QPR

where *query-name* is the name of the stored query. Hence, if you wanted to repeat the results of the stored query SAMPLE1, you could enter the command

```
DO SAMPLE1.QPR
```

in the Command window.

From the menus, you can run a query by choosing File/Open, and in the Open dialog box which appears, clicking the List Files of Type list box, and choosing Query. Then, click the desired query by name in the File Name list box, and click Open. Finally, when the RQBE Window appears, click Do Query.

Modifying Existing Queries

If you want to modify an existing query, use the MODIFY QUERY command. In the Command window, enter the command

MODIFY QUERY *query-name*

where *query-name* is the name of the stored query. The RQBE window appears, and you can make whatever changes are desired to the query. Remember that you must save the query again if you want to keep a permanent copy of the modifications.

To modify a query from the menus, choose File/Open, and in the Open dialog box which appears, click the List Files of Type list box, and choose Query. Then, click the desired query by name in the File Name list box, and click Open. The RQBE Window appears, and you can make the desired changes to the existing query.

A Note About RQBE and the SELECT Command

As noted earlier, the RQBE feature of FoxPro translates your selections into equivalent SELECT commands. If you are familiar with the use of the SELECT command, and with the SQL language that the command is derived from, you may prefer to enter your own SELECT commands at the Command level. You can enter a SELECT command by typing it directly into the Command window, just as you enter any other command in FoxPro.

If you are not familiar with the SQL language, you can still get an idea of what FoxPro is doing behind the scenes by choosing the See SQL option of the RQBE menu, after you have designed a query. When you design a query and then choose See SQL from the RQBE menu, a window containing the equivalent SQL command appears. If you want to see how this works, bring the query you just saved back into the RQBE window now by entering the command

```
MODIFY QUERY SAMPLE1
```

When the RQBE window appears, click the See SQL button. The window that appears contains the SELECT command that is equivalent to the stored query. If you followed the example, it should read something like this:

```
SELECT MEMBERS.LASTNAME, MEMBERS.FIRSTNAME, MEMBERS.CITY,;
MEMBERS.EXPIREDATE;
FROM MEMBERS;
WHERE MEMBERS.EXPIREDATE > CTOD("12/31/93");
AND MEMBERS.EXPIREDATE < CTOD("01/01/95");
ORDER BY MEMBERS.LASTNAME;
TO PRINTER NOCONSOLE
```

If you were to type this SELECT command into the Command window, the query would be performed. And as you will learn in later chapters, the contents of one FoxPro window can be copied into another; hence, the command that you see in the window could now be copied into another window where a program was being designed. (You can get rid of the window and the query now by pressing CTRL+F4 twice.)

Most users of FoxPro will probably find it easier to compose queries using the RQBE window. But keep in mind that FoxPro offers you the option of direct entry of SELECT commands. If you are not familiar with the SQL language, you can learn much about how SELECT commands should be structured by designing queries in the RQBE window and using the See SQL option of the RQBE menu to view the equivalent SELECT commands.

CHAPTER

Introducing Reports

Creating reports is, for many users, what database management is all about. You can readily perform queries to gain immediate answers to specific questions, but much of your work with FoxPro will probably involve generating reports. Detailed reports are easy to produce with FoxPro, thanks in part to the program's Quick Report option, which can be combined with queries, or with selective commands such as SET FILTER and SET FIELDS, to fine-tune your reports.

FoxPro also provides several ways to print reports. You can design and print quick reports in just a few steps. From the Command window, you can also use a combination of the LIST and DISPLAY commands to print information. You can use FoxPro's sophisticated Report Writer to create custom reports. And you can print form letters or mailing labels.

This chapter provides an introduction to the many ways you can produce reports. More advanced reporting topics, including mailing labels and form letters, are covered in Chapter 11. Before going any further, be sure that your printer is turned on and ready; otherwise, you may lock up your system when you try to print.

Reports available through FoxPro's Report Writer can be divided into two overall groups: quick reports and custom reports. FoxPro creates *quick reports* immediately, when you start the Report Writer and choose the Quick Report option from the Report menu. Quick reports normally include all of the fields in the database. (You can limit the fields included by clicking the Fields check box in the Quick Report dialog box; this technique is covered later in this chapter.) By default, the field names that were chosen during the database design phase are used as headings for the fields.

Custom reports, by comparison, are reports that you create or modify to better fit your specific needs. A significant plus of the Report Writer is that it doesn't force you to design custom reports from scratch, starting from a blank screen. You can use the Quick Report option to create a report layout containing all fields, and then proceed to modify that layout as you wish, deleting fields, moving the location of fields, changing headings, or adding other text.

Custom reports that you design with the Report Writer can contain any data you desire from the fields of the database. They can include numeric information, such as totals or other calculations based on numeric fields. Reports can also include headings that print the report's assigned title, the date on which it is printed (as determined by the PC's clock), and the page number for each page. Such headings are commonly used with *columnar reports*. The following shows an example of such a report, in which the data is arranged in columns.

```
SOCIAL          TITLE                     DAYRENTED   RETURNED
123-44-8976     Star Trek VI              03/05/93    03/06/93
121-33-9876     Lethal Weapon III         03/02/93    03/06/93
232-55-1234     Who Framed Roger Rabbit   03/06/93    03/09/93
901-77-3456     Doc Hollywood             03/04/93    03/05/93
121-90-5432     Fried Green Tomatoes      03/01/93    03/06/93
495-00-3456     Wayne's World             03/04/93    03/09/93
343-55-9821     Prince of Tides           03/06/93    03/12/93
876-54-3210     Lethal Weapon III         03/07/93    03/08/93
123-44-8976     Friday 13th Part XXVII    03/14/93    03/16/93
121-33-9876     Mambo Kings               03/15/93    03/17/93
232-55-1234     Prince of Tides           03/17/93    03/19/93
901-77-3456     Coming to America         03/14/93    03/18/93
121-90-5432     Prince of Tides           03/16/93    03/17/93
495-00-3456     Star Trek VI              03/18/93    03/19/93
343-55-9821     Wayne's World             03/19/93    03/20/93
876-54-3210     Mambo Kings               03/16/93    03/18/93
```

By contrast, here is an example of a report in a *form layout. Form layouts* often resemble paper-based forms.

```
SOCIAL          123-44-8976
TITLE           Star Trek VI
DAYRENTED       03/05/93
RETURNED        03/06/93

SOCIAL          121-33-9876
TITLE           Lethal Weapon III
DAYRENTED       03/02/93
RETURNED        03/06/93

SOCIAL          232-55-1234
TITLE           Who Framed Roger Rabbit?
DAYRENTED       03/06/93
RETURNED        03/09/93

SOCIAL          901-77-3456
TITLE           Doc Hollywood
DAYRENTED       03/04/93
RETURNED        03/05/93

SOCIAL          121-90-5432
```

```
TITLE          Fried Green Tomatoes
DAYRENTED      03/01/93
RETURNED       03/06/93
```

One of the fastest ways to produce printed reports in FoxPro is to enter the Report Writer and use the Quick Report option, since this report needs no designing in advance. To produce a quick report, simply open the desired database and, in the Command window, enter **CREATE REPORT** *filename*. (Or, from the menus, you can choose New from the File menu and then select Report.) When the Report Writer appears in a window, open the Report menu and choose Quick Report. This causes the Quick Report dialog box to appear.

Click the column-oriented Field Layout button on the left (if a columnar-style report is desired) or click the form-oriented Field Layout button on the right (if a form-style report is desired). Click the OK button, and then choose Save from the File menu (or press CTRL+S). Exit the Report Writer by choosing Close from the File menu, or by double-clicking the window's Control menu icon, and the report will be stored on disk and ready for use.

You can display the report on the screen, or print it, at any time with the REPORT FORM command. Entering REPORT FORM *filename* as a command displays the report on the screen, while entering REPORT FORM *filename* TO PRINT sends the report to the screen and printer at the same time. The menu equivalent for generating the report is to open the Database menu and choose Report; then click the Form button, and choose the name of the stored report in the dialog box. Check any desired options in the next dialog box that appears (see the following section), and click the OK button to produce the report.

The first report shown was produced from the RENTALS database (which was created in Chapter 2) by means of the Quick Report option. It illustrates the design of a columnar-style quick report. Field names appear as column headings, and the data appears in single-spaced rows beneath the headings.

If you generate your own quick report by opening the MEMBERS file (not the RENTALS file) and following the procedure described in the preceding paragraphs, you may notice one trait of a quick report that may not be very appealing to you. Depending on the number of fields in the file, one or more columns of data may be cut off at the right margin. You could solve this problem in a custom report by changing column widths, or by changing column locations.

If you don't want all the fields included in the report, you have two ways of obtaining a quick report containing only selected fields. One way is to click the Fields check box in the Quick Report dialog box, which was shown earlier. When you click this check box, a Field Picker dialog appears.

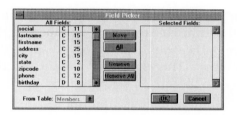

You can click a desired field in the All Fields list box, then click the Move button, to move the desired field into the Selected Fields list box. (Or, as a shortcut, you can simply double-click any field in the All Fields box to move it over.) Once you have the desired fields visible in the Selected Fields list box, click OK. When you later click OK from the Quick Report dialog box, the selected fields will be the only ones included in the report.

The other way in which you can obtain a quick report with only selected fields is by using the SET FIELDS command before you create the report. Briefly, the syntax of this command is

SET FIELDS TO *field1*, *field2*, *field3*,...*fieldx*

This command makes the database appear to contain only the fields you specify in the field list. Therefore, if you wanted a quick report of the

MEMBERS database, including only the name, city, state, and expiration date fields, you could first open the database and use the command

```
SET FIELDS TO LASTNAME, FIRSTNAME, CITY, STATE,
EXPIREDATE
```

and then proceed to create and save the report; the report would contain only the fields named in the command. After you have created the report, you can make the rest of the fields available again by closing and reopening the database, or by entering the command **SET FIELDS TO ALL**

The Report Dialog Box

When you choose the Report option on the Database menu to print a report, the default selections that appear in the Report dialog box (shown in Figure 7-1) cause the data to be displayed on the screen only, in Page Preview mode. (This is indicated by the fact that Page Preview is checked

FIGURE
7-1

Report dialog box

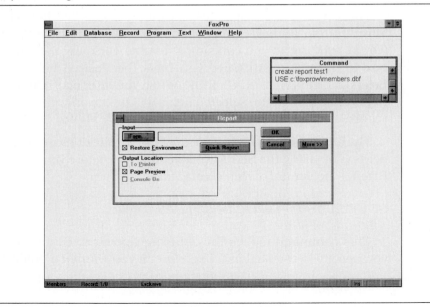

by default.) You can choose instead to direct the output of a report to the printer, or to a disk file in the ASCII (American Standard Code for Information Interchange) text format.

In the text box beside the Form button, you can enter the name of a report that was created and saved earlier with the Report Writer. (Or, you can click the Form button, and then pick the report by name from the list box that appears.) The Restore Environment check box tells FoxPro to use any environmental settings that were in effect while the report was being designed. When you create and save a report, FoxPro automatically saves the environment settings to a view file with the same name as the report (see Chapter 5 for more on view files).

The Output Location portion of the dialog box determines whether the output of the report will be directed to the screen, to the printer, or to a file. The Page Preview option in this area, which is checked by default, causes a representation of the report to appear onscreen. This is useful for checking the appearance of a report before you begin printing. Click the To Printer check box if you want the report to be printed.

Additional options that control a report's display or printing can be viewed if you click the More button within the Report dialog box. When you click More, the dialog box opens further to reveal the options shown in Figure 7-2.

In the Criteria area, the Scope, For, and While buttons let you limit the records that appear in the report. Scope can be used to limit the number of records that will be included. If the scope is omitted, FoxPro assumes that you want to use all the records in the database. (You can also enter ALL, if you want to to specify this explicitly.) You can enter NEXT and then enter a number, which specifies a group of records starting with the current pointer position; for example, entering NEXT 10 as the scope tells FoxPro to include only the next ten records. Or you can enter REST, which limits the operation to all records from the current pointer position to the end of the file.

The For and While options can be used to further limit your records, as described in Chapter 5. The While option works best with an index, but the For option can easily be used on any field, whether an index exists or not. When you choose For from the dialog box, the Expression Builder (discussed in Chapter 5) appears. Using the Expression Builder, you can

FIGURE 7-2   Expanded Report dialog box

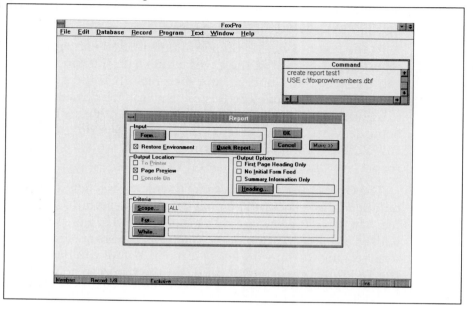

enter an expression that limits the records available to the report. Using the While option will also display a similar Expression Builder, which can be used in the same manner.

In the Output Options area, checking the First Page Heading Only box produces a report with headings on only the first page. The No Initial Form Feed option tells FoxPro not to send a page-eject code before printing the report. The Summary Information Only option tells FoxPro to produce a summary report only. In this case, individual records do not appear in the report; only summary totals appear. (This option makes sense when you have included summary fields in your report, a subject covered later in the chapter.)

The Heading option, when chosen, causes the Expression Builder to appear, this time containing a window for a heading, as shown in Figure 7-3. You can use this window to enter a custom heading of your choice, or you can build an expression that results in a desired heading. Any literal text that you want to place in your heading should be surrounded

FIGURE
7-3

Expression Builder containing report heading window

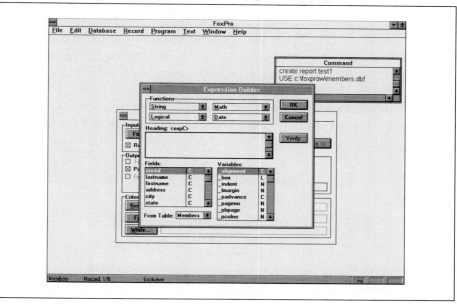

by quotes. Fields are normally used as headings in reports that use multiple groupings, a topic covered later in the chapter.

After entering the name of the report form in the Report dialog box, check the desired options and click the OK button. The report will be produced in accordance with your chosen options.

Producing Selective Reports with Ease

If you want maximum results in a minimum amount of time, keep in mind the flexibility that FoxPro provides through the use of queries. You can use the Report/Labels menu option in the RQBE window to produce reports based on a selected query, as described in Chapter 6. Or, you can use the SET FIELDS, INDEX ON...FOR, and SET FILTER commands to provide selective views of data.

You can use the SET FILTER command, described in Chapter 5, or you can add a FOR clause to the REPORT FORM command, to limit the records included in your reports. (An alternative way to do this is to produce the report using menu options rather than commands. When you use the File/New/Report menu options, the Report dialog box appears, and you can click More, then use the For button in the expanded dialog box to specify which records will appear in the report.) With large databases, you may find it less time-consuming to build a query, as described in Chapter 6, or to limit available records by building a selective index with the INDEX ON...FOR command. Details of this technique are found in Chapter 4.

In many cases, you can solve formatting problems by including selected fields and omitting unwanted fields. You can do so by clicking the Fields button in the Quick Report dialog box, or by using the the SET FIELDS command.

Consider the quick report produced if you use the MEMBERS file, create a report, and choose the Quick Report option from the Report menu. Obviously, there are far too many fields to fit on a standard sheet of paper. Perhaps all you are really interested in are the Lastname, Firstname, City, and Tapelimit fields, and you know that these *will* comfortably fit on one sheet. To try creating a Quick Report with only these fields, first enter **USE MEMBERS** if the file is not already open, then enter the following SET FIELDS command:

```
SET FIELDS TO LASTNAME, FIRSTNAME, CITY, TAPELIMIT
```

Next, create a new report by entering the command

```
CREATE REPORT SAMPLE
```

to get into the Report Writer. Open the Report menu, and choose Quick Report. Select OK, and notice that the report design that is produced contains only those fields listed with the SET FIELDS command, as shown in Figure 7-4.

Save the report with CTRL+S (answer Yes to the prompt to save environment information), close the report's window with CTRL+F4, and enter the command

```
REPORT FORM SAMPLE
```

Report design resulting from SET FIELDS

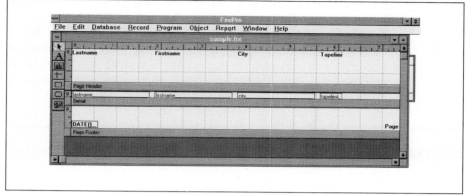

to display the report on the screen. The resulting report should contain all of the records from the MEMBERS database, but only the desired fields, as shown here:

```
LASTNAME     FIRSTNAME     CITY            TAPELIMIT
Miller       Karen         Chevy Chase     6
Martin       William       Silver Spring   4
Robinson     Carol         Falls Church    6
Kramer       Harry         Arlington       4
Moore        Ellen         Takoma Park     6
Zachman      David         Falls Church    4
Robinson     Benjamin      Washington      6
Hart         Wendy         Fairfax         2
```

Before proceeding, be sure to enter

```
SET FIELDS TO ALL
```

to restore access to all fields in the database for subsequent operations.

If you wanted to restrict the report's contents to specific records, you could use the methods described in Chapters 5 and 6 to impose any desired restrictions. (See the end of this chapter for a specific example of how you can use a stored report within a RQBE Window.) Also, if you wanted to see the records within the Quick Report in some specific order, you could use the indexing or sorting techniques covered in Chapter 4, apply any desired filter conditions, and print the report. Using these techniques, you can generate detailed reports based on complex conditions, with little or no custom report designing.

 Tip   If you are using the RQBE window to design a query that will produce a report, be sure to design and save the report first, before designing or implementing the query. (You will need to enter the report's name in the query dialog box during the query design process.)

Generating Reports with Commands

From the Command window, the LIST command is useful for printing data as well as for examining data on the screen. To direct output to the printer, use the TO PRINT option with the LIST command. This avoids having all your command instructions print on the page along with the desired data. The normal format of the command with this option is

LIST [*field1, field2...fieldx*] TO PRINT

To try this command, enter

```
LIST LASTNAME, CITY, STATE TO PRINT
```

to print the Name, City, and State fields for each record in the database. If you are using a laser printer, you may also need to enter an EJECT command to cause the printed sheet to feed out of the printer.

You can be selective by specifying a FOR condition with the LIST command, and still send output to the printer with TO PRINT. For example,

```
LIST LASTNAME, FIRSTNAME, CITY FOR LASTNAME =
"Robinson" TO PRINT
```

prints the last names, first names, and cities of both members named Robinson. The command

```
LIST LASTNAME, CITY, STATE, TAPELIMIT FOR TAPELIMIT < 6
```

provides a printed listing like the one shown here, with the last names, cities, states, and tape limits for all members with a tape limit of less than 6.

```
Record#     LASTNAME     CITY            STATE     TAPELIMIT
2           Martin       Silver Spring   MD        4
4           Kramer       Arlington       VA        4
6           Zachman      Falls Church    VA        4
7           Robinson     Washington      DC        2
8           Hart         Fairfax         VA        2
```

You can use curly braces surrounding a date to tell FoxPro that the enclosed set of characters should be read as a date value. The date value can then be used to form a conditional command for printing a report. This is a very handy tool for printing reports that indicate activity within a certain time period. For example, the command

```
REPORT FORM SAMPLE FOR EXPIREDATE <= {10/01/93} TO PRINT
```

produces a report of all records with expiration dates earlier than October 2, 1993. A report of all members with expiration dates within a particular month could be produced with a command like this one:

```
REPORT FORM SAMPLE FOR EXPIREDATE > {09/30/93} .AND.
EXPIREDATE < {11/01/93} TO PRINT
```

You can also generate stored reports with commands. The REPORT FORM command uses the following syntax:

REPORT FORM *filename* [*scope*]
[FOR *expression*]
[WHILE *expression*]
[TO PRINT / TO FILE *filename*]
[PLAIN] [SUMMARY] [NOEJECT]
[HEADING *character-expression*]
[ENVIRONMENT]

The SCOPE, FOR, and WHILE options work as discussed earlier in this book; see Chapter 5 for a full discussion of these options. If the TO PRINT clause is added to the command, the report is routed both to the printer and to the screen. If TO PRINT is omitted, the report is displayed only on the screen.

If the TO FILE option is included, the report is sent to a file in ASCII text format. You can use either TO PRINT or TO FILE, but you cannot use both options in the same REPORT FORM command.

The PLAIN option prints a plain report without the standard headings. The SUMMARY option prints a report with summary fields only. The NOEJECT option suppresses the normal page ejects (form-feed codes) that are sent to the printer. The HEADING option lets you add a custom heading; remember that straight text must be enclosed in quotes.

The ENVIRONMENT option can be used to specify a view file that will control which records are available for processing, which fields will appear, and whether any relationships will be maintained between the active database and other files. When you save a report, FoxPro automatically saves the current environment to a view file with the same name as the report. Referencing this environment file in the REPORT FORM command can therefore save you the trouble of explicitly opening a database and index file. For example, you could load FoxPro and enter a single command such as

```
REPORT FORM MYFILE ENVIRONMENT
```

to open the database and any index files, and to produce the report.

Designing Custom Columnar Reports

If you want to place fields in specific locations, add custom headers and footers, and change formatting attributes, you can design a custom report. Depending on how complex your needs are, the precise steps involved in the report's design will vary in complexity. The description that follows illustrates the basic process for creating a custom report, in columnar layout.

To start the process, open the database in question, then enter **CREATE REPORT** *filename* (or choose New from the File menu and select Report). In a moment, the design window of the Report Writer will appear, as shown in Figure 7-5. This window includes a new menu bar heading, entitled Report, and the layout of the report.

Report layout in Report Writer window

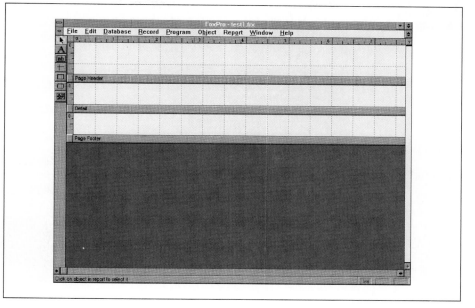

The Report Layout

The report's layout is made up of several parts, as illustrated in Figure 7-6. FoxPro views each layer of the report as a *report band.* Every report contains a Page Header band, a Page Footer band, and a Detail band. There can also be an optional Title or Summary band, and optional Group bands. (In the figure, the band containing only the name of a field, State, preceded by the heading "For State", is a Group band.)

The Page Header band appears once for each page of the report. In many cases, you'll use this area to print such information as the date or time of the report, or a report title. The Page Footer band at the bottom of the report layout has the same purpose as the header but is for footers, the information that typically appears at the bottom of each page.

Title bands, when used, contain any information that should appear only at the start of the report (rather than at the start of each page). Summary bands, when used, contain information that should appear at

FIGURE
7-6

Parts of a report layout

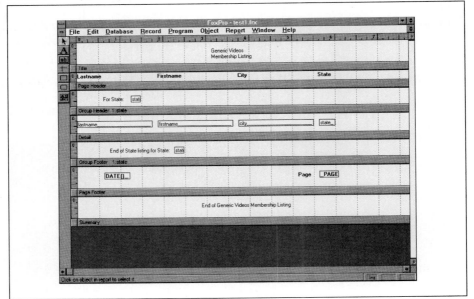

the end of the report. You'll usually use Summary bands for totals of numeric fields.

The Detail band is used to define the actual information that will appear in the body of the report. (While fields are the most common contents, expressions can also be used; such expressions might contain a function representing the current date, or a calculated value based on a numeric field.) The contents of the Detail band are represented by rectangular frames containing the name of each field or expression.

Group bands, which are optional, are printed once for each group of records in a report. Group bands provide a means of grouping the records; such grouping often includes some type of header identifying the group, along with subtotals of numeric data. You may or may not want to group records in a report; as an example of grouping, you might decide to print a list of members of the video store by state. If you decide to include groups, FoxPro lets you add an unlimited number of groups to a single report.

Making Changes to the Report's Design

Once the report layout appears on the screen, you can use the mouse and various options on the Report menu to add, rearrange, or remove fields; to add lines, text, or graphics; to increase or decrease spacing between bands; and to change the layout or format of the report in general. If you click the Report menu (or press ALT+O), the Report menu opens, as shown here.

About Page Layout

The Page Layout option on this menu lets you change specifications that affect the layout of the printed page. When you choose this option, you will see the Page Layout dialog box, as shown in Figure 7-7. You can use this dialog box to determine the width of columns in the report, the width of the left margin, the space between columns, and whether the report uses a report-oriented layout (data running top to bottom, column by column), or a label-oriented layout (data running left to right, row by row). The options in the Page Layout dialog box are detailed in the following paragraphs.

☐ *Left Margin* This value determines the left margin, or offset from the left side of the page. Type the desired value in the text box, or click the arrows in the Spinner to increase or decrease the value.

☐ *Columns* This value determines the number of columns in the report. Type the desired value in the text box, or click the arrows in the Spinner to increase or decrease the value. You can have from one to 50 columns in a report.

Page Layout dialog box

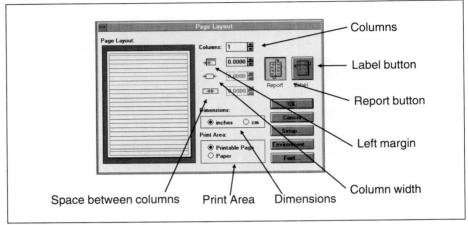

- *Column Width* This value determines the width of the columns. (If the report has only one column, this option is dimmed and unavailable.) Type the desired value in the text box, or click the arrows in the Spinner to increase or decrease the value.

- *Space Between Columns* This value determines the spacing between columns. (If the report has only one column, this option is dimmed and unavailable.) Type the desired value in the text box, or click the arrows in the Spinner to increase or decrease the value.

- *Dimensions* This option determines whether the values in the text boxes are measured in inches, or centimeters. Click inches or centimeters, as desired.

- *Print Area* Turn on the Printable Page option here to permit margins within the report, or turn on the Paper option to force the report to completely fill the page. (Note that using the Paper option may not be a wise idea with most laser printers, as most require at least a quarter-inch margin on all sides of the page.)

☐   *Report* clicking the Report button gives your report a "report-oriented" layout; columns are filled from top to bottom, beginning at the left side of the page.

☐   *Label* clicking the Label button gives your report a "label-oriented" layout; rows are filled from left to right, beginning at the top of the page.

☐   *Setup* clicking this button causes the Windows Print Setup dialog box to be displayed. You can then use it to change your printer's setup (see your Windows documentation for details on this).

☐   *Environment* clicking this button opens an Environment dialog box containing four buttons: Save, Restore, Clear, and Cancel. You can use these buttons to save the environment information along with the report, or to clear environment information that was loaded with a previously-saved report.

☐   *Font* clicking this button opens a Font dialog box. From this dialog box, you can change the font, font size, and font style used in the report.

About Page Preview

The Page Preview option on the Report menu lets you see what a report will look like, before you save the report and exit the Report Writer. After laying out the desired fields and other data, choose Page Preview from the Report menu, and a visual representation of the printed report, like the one in Figure 7-8, appears on the screen. This option is quite useful for checking your design; you can go back into the report layout, make changes to the report, and try Page Preview again until you are satisfied with the report's design.

To zoom in and view a full-scale representation of the report, move the mouse pointer over any desired area of the report, until it changes into the shape of a magnifying glass; then click. You can click again to zoom back out to the normal Page Preview scale. (An alternate way of zooming in and out between full-scale view and reduced size is to click the Zoom In and Zoom Out buttons at the upper-right side of the Page Preview window.)

FIGURE
7-8
Report preview

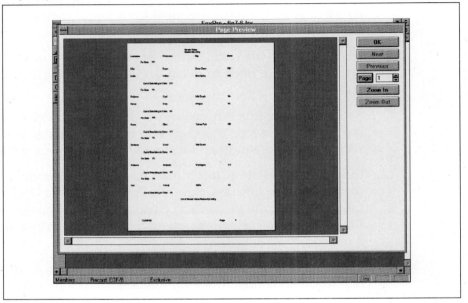

You can use the Next and Previous buttons in the window to move to the next or previous pages of a report (assuming the report spans multiple pages). (An alternate way to do this is to use the PGUP and PGDN keys; PGUP moves you to the previous page, while PGDN moves you to the next page.) You can also click the arrows within the Spinner to display a page number, or you can type in a value; then, click the Page button to move to a preview of that page of the report.

When you are done previewing a report, click the OK button within the window, and you will be returned to the report layout window.

About the Title/Summary Option

The Data Grouping option on the Report menu lets you add groups to a report. This topic is covered later in this chapter. The Title/Summary option lets you add Title bands or Summary bands to a report. When you choose this option, the Title/Summary dialog box appears on the screen, as shown in Figure 7-9. You can check the boxes that add the Title band,

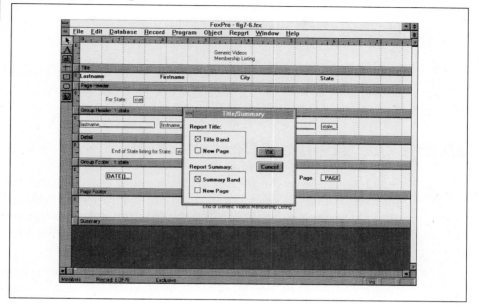

FIGURE 7-9 Title/Summary dialog box

the Summary band, or both. The bands, once added, are empty; you must then add any desired text or fields to the bands. The New Page option tells FoxPro to start the band on a new page. Once you check the desired boxes and choose OK, you are returned to the report layout.

The Variables option on the Report menu lets you add memory variables to a report. This is an advanced programming technique that is not covered in this chapter.

Moving and Sizing Fields

To move fields within a report, first click on the desired field. When you do so, the field will be surrounded by handles.

When the field is surrounded by the handles, you can click on the field itself, hold down the mouse button, and drag the field to the desired new location. To size a field, click the field to select it, then click and drag any of the *handles*.

Tip You can delete a field at any time by clicking to select it, and pressing DEL.

Using the Toolbox Design Tools

The left edge of the Report Writer window contains the *Toolbox*. The Toolbox displays a set of tools that are specific to the task of designing reports. You can use these tools to place various objects on a report, such as fields, lines, boxes, ovals, or graphics. Figure 7-10 identifies the various parts of the Toolbox.

To place an object in the report, first click the desired tool in the Toolbox, then click and drag in the Report Writer window to create the

Parts of the Toolbox

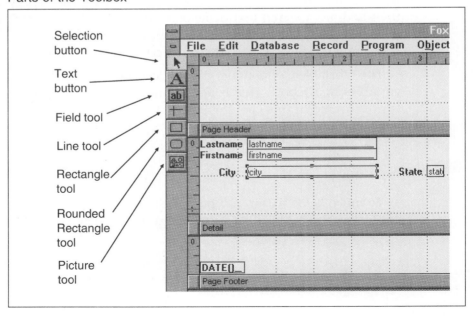

desired object. To include more than one object of the same type, double-click the tool in the Toolbox; then you can add multiple objects without needing to click the tool multiple times. Techniques for placing different objects (such as fields, lines, ovals, and graphics) are described in the following paragraphs.

Selecting Objects

To select an existing object in the Report Writer window, click the Selection tool, then click the desired object. You can select multiple objects by SHIFT+clicking on each desired object. To select all objects contained in a particular band, double-click the band marker.

Placing New Fields

To place a new field in the report, first click the Field tool, then click where you want to place the field in the Report Writer window. The Report Expression dialog box appears, and you can click the Expression button to bring up the Expression Builder, double-click the desired field by name in the Fields List, then click OK.

Adding Text

To add text to a report, first click on the Text tool in the Toolbox. Then, to place the insertion pointer at the desired location click in the Report Writer design window. When you release the mouse button, start typing the text. You can move the text frame at any time, by first clicking the text frame to select it, then dragging the frame to the desired new location.

Drawing Lines, Rectangles, or Rounded Rectangles

The Toolbox provides three commonly-used drawing tools: lines, rectangles, and rounded rectangles. You can add visual emphasis to your forms by placing these objects in appropriate locations. To add a line, rectangle, or rounded rectangle, first click on the desired tool in the Toolbox (the line tool, the rectangle tool, or the rounded rectangle tool).

Then click at the desired starting location in the report, and drag until the line, rectangle, or rounded rectangle reaches the desired size.

To choose how rounded a rounded rectangle should be, double-click the rounded rectangle. A dialog box will appear, containing different shapes for rounded rectangles (from completely oval to very rounded), and you can click the desired shape.

Adding Pictures to a Report

You can add a picture to a report, using the Picture tool of the Toolbox. In Figure 7-11, you see an example of a report which uses a graphic pasted in from a Windows bitmap file.

To add a graphic, first click on the Picture tool in the Toolbox. Then, in the Report Writer window, click at the desired location for one corner of the picture; this will start to display an outline box that represents the picture. Drag this corner until the outline box reaches the desired size.

When you release the mouse, a Report Picture dialog box will open.

FIGURE 7-11   Report using Windows bitmap as a picture

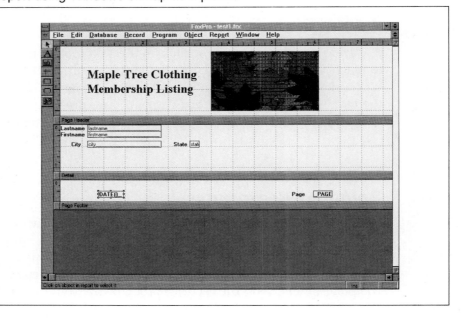

In the Report Picture dialog box, you can choose to insert a bitmap picture in the report by clicking the File button, then choosing the bitmap file from the Files list box which will appear. Or, you can insert a picture that is stored in a General field of the current record of the database by turning on the Field option, clicking the Field button, and choosing the field by name from the list of fields that appears. Chapter 8 provides more details on using pictures in FoxPro reports and in a database.

Saving and Running the Report

Once you have made your desired changes to the report design, press CTRL+S, or choose Save from the File menu (and enter a name, if prompted for one, in the dialog box that will appear). To run a report from the menus, choose Report from the Database menu, and enter the report's name in the dialog box that appears. You can also run a report from the Command window by entering the command

REPORT FORM *filename* TO PRINT

where *filename* is the name with which you saved the report. Omit the TO PRINT designation if you simply wish to view the report on the screen.

Practice Designing a Custom Report

As an example of the steps involved in creating a custom report, consider the case of the Generic Videos membership file. The company needs a report with the name and city of each member. To the right of this data, the report should list the comments in the Preferences field of this member's record. The company also wants the current date printed on the report. For now, the report will contain a single group of data; later, the report will be broken into separate groupings of members by state.

To begin designing the report, enter

```
USE MEMBERS
CREATE REPORT MEMBERS
```

The report layout will appear within a Report Writer window. You may want to maximize the window's size (click the Maximize button to do so) in order to see more of the work area. Let's begin with the headings. The date needs to appear in the upper-right corner of the first page, so this item needs to be placed in the Page Header band.

First, open the Report menu, and make sure that the Snap To Grid option is turned on. (This ensures that fields and other objects you place in the report can be easily sized and aligned, because they will always align with one of the imaginary lines formed by the dots of the grid.)

Click the Field tool in the Toolbox; then click in the Page Header band (remember, it's the top band) at roughly the 5-inch mark horizontally, and 1/4 inch down vertically. (Use the rulers at the top and left edges of the window to gauge these distances. If you want to be precise about these locations, you can open the Report menu and choose the Show Position option; with this option turned on, the mouse pointer's location always appears in the Status Bar.) Click and drag until the box (outlined by the dotted line) is approximately 1/4 inch in height, and one inch in width.

When you release the mouse, a Report Expression dialog box appears. (When adding fields or expressions to a report manually, you must use this dialog box to tell FoxPro what field or expression you want to place in the report.) Click the Expression button. In a moment, the Expression Builder appears. Here you can select field names, functions, and math, string, or logical symbols, to build the desired expression.

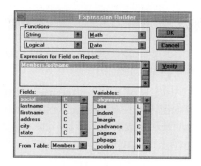

In this case, all that's needed is the appropriate function for the current date. Click the arrow to the right of the Date function (it's near the top of the dialog box). From the drop-down list that opens, choose Date by clicking it. When you do so, the expression DATE appears in the Expression for Field on Report portion of the dialog box.

Click OK, then click OK in the Report Expression dialog box to put it away. A field containing the DATE expression appears in the Page Header band.

Next, some additional room is needed in the Detail band, to provide sufficient room for the fields. Click the square to the left of the Detail band within the ruler, and while holding the mouse button, drag the square down approximately one inch.

Click the Field tool in the Toolbox, and place the mouse pointer in the Detail band, directly beneath the bottom of the Page Header band, and one inch to the right of the left edge (or at the one-inch mark on the horizontal ruler). Click and drag until the box formed by the dotted line is roughly 1/4 inch high and 1.5 inches in width.

When the Report Expression dialog box appears, click Expression to bring up the Expression Builder. In the Fields list box of the Expression Builder, double-click the Lastname field, then click OK. In the Report Expression dialog box, click OK again to close the dialog box and place the Lastname field into the report.

Click the Field tool in the Toolbox, and place the mouse pointer one grid space beneath the lower-left corner of the field you just placed. Click and drag until the box formed by the dotted line is roughly 1/4 inch high and 1.5 inches in width.

When the Report Expression dialog box appears, click Expression to bring up the Expression Builder. In the Fields list box of the Expression Builder, double-click the Firstname field, then click OK. In the Report Expression dialog box, click OK again to close the dialog box and place the Firstname field.

Click the Field tool in the Toolbox, and place the mouse pointer one grid space beneath the lower-left corner of the field you just placed. Click and drag until the box formed by the dotted line is roughly 1/4 inch high and 1.5 inches in width.

When the Report Expression dialog box appears, click Expression to bring up the Expression Builder. In the Fields list box of the Expression Builder, double-click the City field, then click OK. In the Report Expression dialog box, click OK again to close the dialog box and place the City field.

Click the Field tool in the Toolbox, and place the mouse pointer in the Detail band, directly beneath the bottom of the Page Header band, and four inches to the right of the left edge (or at the 4-inch mark on the horizontal ruler). Click and drag until the box formed by the dotted line is roughly one inch high and 2.5 inches in width.

When the Report Expression dialog box appears, click Expression to bring up the Expression Builder. In the Fields list box of the Expression Builder, double-click the Preference field, then click OK. In the Report Expression dialog box, click OK again to close the dialog box and place the Preference field.

Double-click the Text tool. Click approximately one inch to the left of the Lastname field, and type the word **Last**, followed by a colon (:). Click approximately one inch to the left of the Firstname field, and type the word **First**, followed by a colon (:). Click approximately one inch to the left of the City field, and type the word **City**, followed by a colon (:). Then, click the Selection tool (to deselect the Text tool).

Open the Report menu and choose Snap To Grid, to turn this option off. Then, click and drag each text object until the top of each one is flush with the top of the adjacent field. When done, your screen should resemble the example shown in Figure 7–12.

The staff has decided that a summary field showing the number of members in the video club would be a nice addition; for this, you need a summary field based on a count of records (members) in the database.

FIGURE
7-12

Report layout with fields added

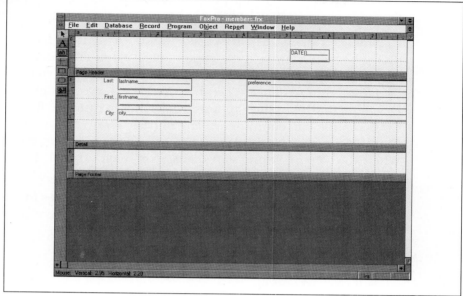

Open the Report menu and choose Title/Summary. From the dialog box that appears, turn on the Summary Band by clicking its check box. Then click OK in the dialog box.

This step adds the Summary band at the bottom of the report layout; you must still add any desired text or fields in the Summary band. Click the Text tool. Next, click roughly one inch from the left edge of the Summary band, about 1/4 inch down from the top of the band, and type the heading

```
Number of Members:
```

then click the Field tool. Click just to the right of the heading you just typed, and drag until the box formed by the dotted line measures roughly 1/4 inch high by one inch wide.

When you release the mouse, the Report Expression dialog box opens. Click the Expression button to bring up the Expression Builder. Because you will request a count of the total number of records, you could use any field that would always have an entry. Since the Social field will always contain an entry for each record, try double-clicking SOCIAL in the Fields list box, then clicking OK. When the Report Expression dialog box reappears, click the Calculate check box.

Your screen should now look like the one in Figure 7-13. The Calculate dialog box lets you base the contents of a summary field on a count of records, a numeric sum, an average, a lowest or highest value, a standard deviation, or a variance. The Sum, Average, Lowest, Highest, Standard Deviation, and Variance options apply only to numeric fields, while the Count option can count non-blank entries in any type of field. Click the Count button to select this option, then click OK within the dialog box. When the Report Expression dialog box reappears, click OK from the dialog box to complete placement of the field.

Save the report by pressing CTRL+S (and answering Yes to the Environment prompt which appears). Press CTRL+F4 to close the Report Writer window. In the Command window, enter the command

```
REPORT FORM MEMBERS
```

FIGURE 7-13

Calculate dialog box

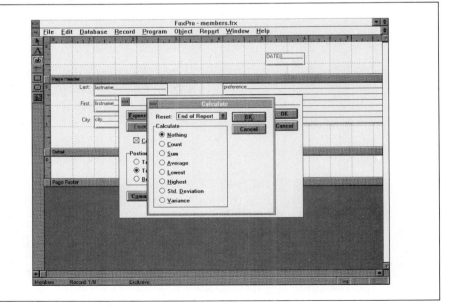

or, if your printer is connected and turned on, you might want to try the following command to print the report:

```
REPORT FORM MEMBERS TO PRINT
```

Adding Grouping to a Report

You can use the Data Grouping option on the Report menu to work with groupings of records within a report. You will probably need to arrange reports broken down by groups. For example, you might need to see all members divided into groups by state of residence. Using the Data Grouping option on the Report menu, you can define multiple levels of grouping.

While using more than two or three levels of groups may seem like overkill to some, it is nice to know that FoxPro is accommodating when you must base a complex report on a large number of subgroups. Multiple groupings can be quite common in business applications. In something as simple as a national mailing list, for example, you might need to see records by groups of states, and within each state group by city, and within each city group by ZIP code. That represents three levels of grouping alone. Cut the data in the table more specifically—by other categories like income levels, for example—and you can quickly come to appreciate FoxPro's ability to perform effective grouping.

When you choose the Data Grouping option from the Report menu while designing a report, the Data Grouping dialog box shown in Figure 7-14 is displayed.

You use the Add, Change, or Delete buttons to add, change, or delete Group bands from a report. When you choose Add, you see the Group Info dialog box shown in Figure 7-15. You can use this dialog box to enter or choose a field name (or other expression) to base your group on.

If you want to define the group by a field (as in groups of records from the same state, or with the same assignment), you enter the name of that field in the text box. (You can click the Group button, and then select a field name from the list of fields in the Expression Builder which appears.)

By clicking the Group button to display the Expression Builder, you can also group records based upon a valid FoxPro expression. For

FIGURE
7-14
Data Grouping dialog box

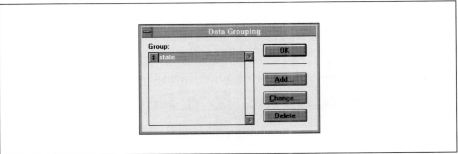

example, if you were using an index based on a combination of Lastname + Firstname to control the order of the records, you could enter the expression LASTNAME + FIRSTNAME to define the grouping. Once you add a Group band, you can then enter text or fields into that band within the report layout. After selecting the desired type of grouping, FoxPro inserts a new starting Group band and a new ending Group band for the group. Group bands always fall outside of the Detail bands.

The options in the panel labeled "When Group Changes, Begin" can be used to specify whether a new column or page should start printing whenever the group changes. If you turn on the Reprint Header check box, the header is reprinted whenever the group changes.

Once you've placed the desired group, you can check to see if the results are what you desire by opening the Report menu and choosing Page Preview. The resulting report will be divided by group. Note that the file must be sorted or indexed on the field by which you are grouping, to get the records in the proper group order; you may need to save the report, index or sort the file from the menus or Command window, and then run

FIGURE
7-15
Group Info dialog box

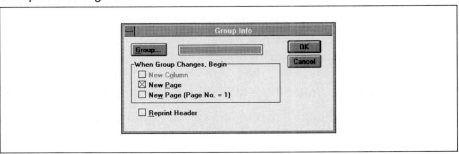

the report. Or you can create a query, set an order for that query, and generate the report from the RQBE window. When you are satisfied with the results, save the report layout by pressing CTRL+S.

Adding Grouping by State to the Membership Report

Try adding state-by-state groupings to the existing membership report you created earlier in the chapter. From the Command window, you can enter **MODIFY REPORT MEMBERS**. The report layout for the report you designed earlier will appear.

To add the group to the report, first open the Report menu, and choose Data Grouping to insert a new group. The Data Grouping dialog box appears. There are no existing groups in the report, so the list box is empty. Click the Add option in the dialog box to add a group. Doing so will reveal the Group Info dialog box (shown earlier in Figure 7-15.)

In the Data Grouping box (shown earlier in Figure 7-14), you enter the field name or expression that will control the grouping. (When you can't remember the name of a field, you can click the Group button and use the Expression Builder to select field names or parts of expressions.) In this case, click in the text box to the right of the Group button, and enter

STATE

in the text box, and then click OK. When you choose OK, you again see the Data Grouping dialog box; note that it now contains the designation

state

in the list box, showing that there is one level of grouping, based on the State field. Again, click OK from the dialog box. The new Group bands will appear in the report layout, as shown in Figure 7-16.

Click the Field tool, then click in the Group band, approximately two inches to the right of the left edge (or, aligned with the 2-inch mark on the horizontal ruler). Click and drag, until the box formed by the dotted line is roughly 1/4 inch high and 1/2 inch wide. When you release the

FIGURE
7-16 Group bands added to report layout

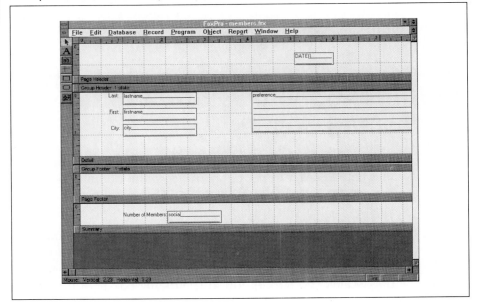

mouse and the Report Expression dialog box appears, click Expression. In the Fields list box within the Expression Builder that next appears, double-click State, then click OK. Click OK again to close the Report Expression dialog box and place the field.

Click the Text tool, then click approximately one inch to the left of the summary field you just placed. Type the heading **State** followed by a colon (:).

Click and drag the text object you just placed, until the top of the text object is even with the top of the adjacent field.

Save the report by pressing CTRL+S, and close the window with CTRL+F4. Then create an index file that will control the order of the grouping by entering the following command:

```
INDEX ON STATE TO STATES
```

The file will be indexed in the order needed to provide the groups within the report. Next, turn on your printer and enter the command

```
REPORT FORM MEMBERS TO PRINT
```

The report will be printed.

 Remember   You must create or activate an index, or sort the file, before a report containing groups will print properly.

Generating Reports from the RQBE Window

When you need reports based on specific data, you can generate your reports from within the RQBE window, whose operation is detailed in Chapter 6. This is generally the most efficient way to obtain selective groups of data in the form of a report.

Simply design your desired report, using the techniques that have been covered in this chapter, and save the report. Then design your selective query, using the techniques covered in Chapter 6. Then, open the query (if it is not already open) with the MODIFY QUERY command, or with the Open option on the File menu. Once you are in the RQBE window, use the menu in the Output To area to select Report/Labels, and then choose the Options button. When the next dialog box appears, select Report in the Formatting Options area, enter the name of your stored report, and choose your output options (you will usually direct output to the printer).

To see how this works, you can combine a query from the RQBE window with the membership report you designed earlier in this chapter, which is called MEMBERS.

First, enter the command **CREATE QUERY** in the Command window. (If asked for a database name, enter **MEMBERS**.) The RQBE window will appear. In the Output text box at the right side of the dialog box, choose Report/Label from the menu if it is not already chosen. Then click the Options button. In a moment, the RQBE Display Options dialog box will appear.

Under Formatting Options, choose Report (by clicking the button). Click anywhere in the Form Name text box to place the insertion pointer there, and enter **MEMBERS**. Turn off the Page Preview option, then turn on the To Printer option under Output Destinations. Finally, click OK in the dialog box.

When the RQBE window reappears, click anywhere in the Field Name box to open the list of fields, and choose State as the field to search on. In the example box, enter **VA**. Finally, make sure your printer is ready, then choose Do Query from the RQBE window. The results will be printed; in this case, you print a selective query (only those members living in Virginia), using the custom report you designed. For this example, you can exit the query without saving, by pressing ESC and answering No to the Save prompt. Remember, any time you want to save a query for repeated use with reports, you can do so by choosing Save As from the File menu.

Report Design

Before you start to design a custom report, you should plan the report's design. This may mean asking the other users of the database what information will actually be needed from the report. In the case of Generic Videos, you would consider what information the managers need from the report, and how the report should look.

In many cases, you'll find it advantageous to outline the report contents and format on paper. Once the report has been designed on paper, your outline should resemble the actual report that is produced by FoxPro. Also, when designing a report, you may find it helpful to print out the list of fields in the database structure—particularly if you are designing a report that contains a large number of fields. This can be done with the LIST STRUCTURE TO PRINT command.

CHAPTER

Using Pictures and Other Windows Objects in Databases

*I*n discussing database creation, Chapter 3 introduced the topic of *general fields.* A general field is basically a type of field that can be used in a FoxPro database to store different kinds of data. General fields can contain any type of data, including pictures, sound, cells of a spreadsheet, or text from a word processing document. Data from other Windows applications (such as pictures, spreadsheets, or word processing documents) are pasted into FoxPro by means of Windows' DDE or OLE capabilities. DDE is an abbreviation for *Dynamic Data Exchange,* and is supported in Windows versions 3.0 and above. OLE is an abbreviation for *Object Linking and Embedding,* a technique that Windows uses to share data between applications. It is supported in Windows version 3.1. Some Windows applications support DDE, some support OLE, and some support both.

Any data from another Windows package that supports DDE or OLE can be inserted into a general field of a FoxPro database. You insert the data using the Windows Clipboard, and Windows' built-in cut-and-paste capabilities. In a nutshell, you do this by first selecting the data in its source application, using the normal selection techniques for that application. You then choose Edit/Copy from the application's menus; this causes a copy of the selected data to be copied into the Windows Clipboard. Finally, back in FoxPro, you double-click in the general field of the desired record, then choose Edit/Paste or Edit/Paste Special (from the menus) to paste the data into the field.

If the source application supports DDE but not OLE, choosing Edit/Paste will paste a copy of the data into the general field, but any further changes to the data in the source application will not appear in the copied data within FoxPro. Choosing Edit/Paste Special will paste a "DDE link" back to the source data, and any further changes in the source application will appear in the copied data within FoxPro.

If the application supports OLE, choosing Edit/Paste will *embed* a copy of the data in the general field, and you can double-click the general field at any time to open the source application and make changes to the copy of the data that is embedded in FoxPro; however, the original data will not be affected by your changes. Choosing Edit/Paste Special will paste an "OLE link" back to the source data, and you can double-click the general field to change the original data through the source application. (See the next subheading for more details on the differences between linking and embedding.) Figure 8-1 shows an external object (in this case, a picture from Windows Paintbrush) pasted into a general field of a FoxPro database.

About Linking and Embedding

FoxPro's use of OLE capabilities is significant, so OLE is worth considering in detail. When you paste OLE data from another Windows application into a general field, FoxPro treats that data as an object. You can either define a link to the original object (hence, the term *object linking*) or you can *embed* a copy of the object in the FoxPro database. As an example, an entire word processing document created in a Windows word processor could be placed in a general field in a FoxPro database, either as a link to the original document, or as an embedded copy of the original document. In FoxPro, the menu options Edit/Paste and Edit/Insert Object can be used to embed an object in a general field of a database, while the menu option Edit/Paste Special is used to define a link to the original object.

Database containing picture in a general field

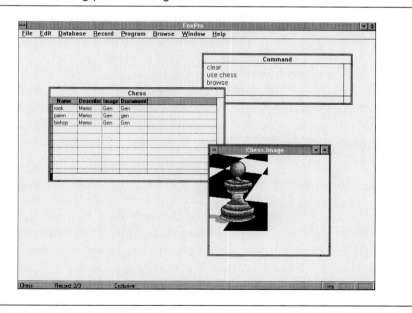

When you *link* an object (with the Edit/Paste Special menu option), you are creating a link to the original information (or, the source document). If you later make changes to the original information, those changes will be reflected in the linked object which is stored in the FoxPro database. On the other hand, when you *embed* an object (with the Edit/Paste or Edit/Insert Object menu options), you are placing a *copy* of the original information into the FoxPro database. You can later make changes to that copy, by double-clicking the field in FoxPro to launch the source application. However, any changes will be made to the embedded copy in FoxPro, and not to the original information.

In learning the distinction between linking and embedding, it may help to remember that the primary difference lies in where the information is stored. With object linking, the information is stored in the original, or source document. With object embedding, the information is stored in FoxPro, as a copy of the original.

Figure 8-2 shows another database containing OLE objects pasted into a general field; in this example, the objects are word-processing documents from Microsoft Word.

Which To Use: Linking or Embedding?

The distinction between OLE's two alternative methods—linking versus embedding—is important to remember, because each has advantages and disadvantages. If many users are going to be updating the same information stored in general fields, you should use object linking, so updates to the original documents can be easily made by many users. On the other hand, if you are going to be moving databases around between computers, you should use object embedding, so that all needed data stays with the FoxPro database, no matter where you copy the files to.

Available disk space is another important consideration to keep in mind when considering using object embedding. Because you are embedding a complete copy of the original information, in some cases you may quickly use up very large amounts of hard disk space. For example, if you decide to use object embedding to store copies of word-processing

FIGURE
8-2

Database containing word processing document in a general field

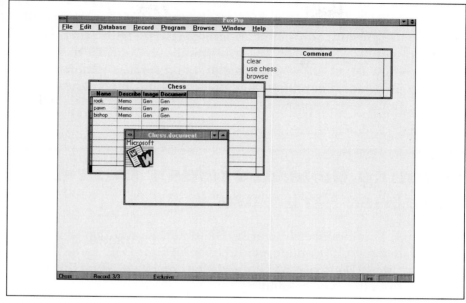

documents in the general fields of a database, the embedded copies will take up just as much disk space as the original documents do. If you are embedding objects that take up significant amounts of disk space, you may want to keep a close eye on remaining disk space.

About OLE Servers and Clients

If you make extensive use of OLE capabilities under Windows, you should note that FoxPro is an OLE *client*. Under Windows, an *OLE client* is an application that receives data, using the rules of object linking and embedding. An *OLE server* is an application that sends data, using OLE rules. Some applications are OLE clients, some are OLE servers, and some are both. Since FoxPro is an OLE client (but not an OLE server), it can receive OLE data from other applications, but it cannot provide OLE data to another Windows program.

This means that you could not copy part or all of a FoxPro database into an OLE container in another Windows application (such as a word processor). This limitation should not present a major problem, as there are effective ways of sharing FoxPro data with other applications. You could, for example, use the Database/Copy To menu option, or the equivalent COPY TO command, to create files that can be used in other programs. For additional details on using FoxPro data in other applications, see Chapter 19.

Defining General Fields within a Database Structure

You can specify, during the database creation process, that certain fields are to contain pictures, or DDE or OLE data. You do this in the Create Database Structure dialog box by choosing the general field type from the Type column.

Here's how to do this when creating a new database from scratch. From the menus, choose File/New, then click Table/DBF in the dialog box that appears, and click New to begin creating the database. (Or, in the Command window, enter the CREATE command.) At this point, the Table Structure dialog box appears. (See Chapter 3 for additional details about this dialog box, and the overall process of creating databases.)

After entering this field's name in the Field Name column, you can click the arrow in the Type column. This displays a drop-down list of available field types, as shown in Figure 8-3.

Choose General from the list to define a general field. (When you do so, the Width for this field will default to 10 characters. In reality, there is no size limit to a general field; the value of 10 characters is simply used as a marker by FoxPro to keep track of the general field's location.) When you are finished defining the remaining fields of the database, click OK to save the new database. If the Save As dialog box appears, use it to give the database a name.

FIGURE
8-3
Table Structure dialog box with menu of field types

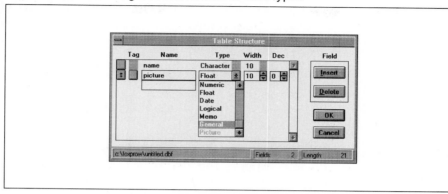

Adding Pictures to a Database

FoxPro lets you insert pictures into a database by means of the Windows Clipboard. To paste a picture from the Windows Clipboard, use the following steps:

1. Open the file containing the picture, using the Windows source application that created it. (The source application must be an application that has the capability to cut and paste data into the Windows Clipboard.)

2. Select the entire picture, or the desired portion of picture, and use Edit/Cut or Edit/Copy to cut or copy the picture to the Windows Clipboard. As an example, Figure 8-4 shows a picture image selected in Windows Paintbrush. If Edit/Cut is chosen from the Paintbrush menus, the selected image will be cut from its present location, and copied into the Windows Clipboard. If Edit/Copy is chosen from the Paintbrush menus, the selected image will be copied into the Windows Clipboard, while the original will remain where it is.

3. Assuming FoxPro is up and running, switch to FoxPro, using either the mouse or the keyboard. From the keyboard, you can switch applications through the Windows Task List (accessed by pressing CTRL+ESC), or by simply pressing ALT+ESC.

4. Once in FoxPro, open the database into which you want to insert the picture.

5. Find the desired record, and double-click a general field to open a window into that field.

6. Choose Edit/Paste, or choose Edit/Paste Special. (Some applications do not support the use of Edit/Paste Special; if it is not supported, the option will be dimmed. The difference between the two is explained earlier in this chapter.) FoxPro places the picture in the field of the database.

In Figure 8-5, the image previously pasted into the Clipboard has been inserted into a general field of a FoxPro database.

FIGURE 8-4

Selected image in Paintbrush

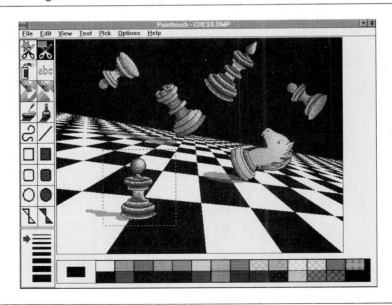

Database containing general field with picture pasted in from Clipboard

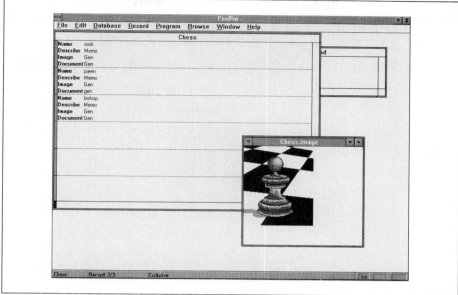

Adding OLE Data to a Database with the Clipboard

To place OLE data (such as a word processing document or a spreadsheet) in a general field, you must first open the source application that is the *OLE server*. (In Windows, any OLE-compatible application which can provide OLE data to another application is referred to as an OLE server.) Use the following steps to place OLE data in a field:

1. Open the source application containing the desired data. (The source application must have OLE server capability.)

2. Select the desired data in the source application, and use Edit/Cut or Edit/Copy to cut or copy the data to the Windows Clipboard. As an example, Figure 8-6 shows a selection from a spreadsheet in Microsoft Works for Windows. If Edit/Copy is chosen from the Works for Windows menus, the selected portion of the spreadsheet will be

FIGURE
8-6

Selected portion of spreadsheet in Works for Windows

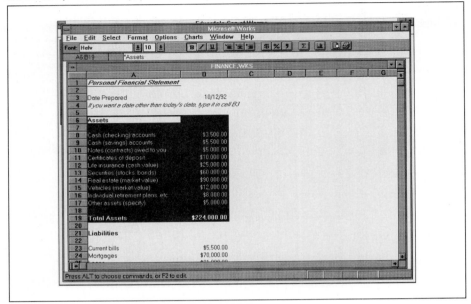

copied into memory, ready for pasting into a general field as an OLE object.

3. Assuming FoxPro is up and running, use the mouse or the Windows Task Switcher (accessed by pressing CTRL+ESC) to switch to FoxPro. (Note that you can also use ALT+ESC to switch between applications.)

4. Once in FoxPro, open the database into which you want to insert the data.

5. Find the desired record, and double-click a general field to open a window into that field.

6. Choose Edit/Paste, or Edit/Paste Special. (Remember, as explained earlier, Edit/Paste causes a copy of the original data to be embedded in the field, while Edit/Paste Special inserts a link to the original document.) FoxPro places the OLE object in the field. In Figure 8-7, a copy of the Works for Windows spreadsheet data appears in the general field of the FoxPro database, as an embedded OLE object.

FIGURE
8-7

Database containing general field with Works for Windows spreadsheet data inserted

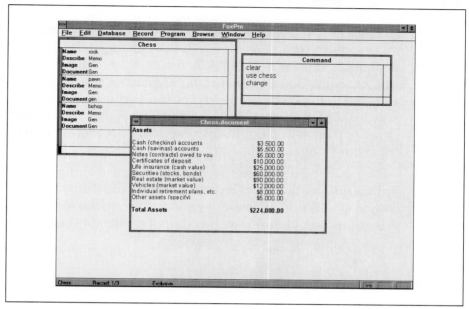

Adding OLE Data with Edit/Insert Object

You can also embed an object that is not stored in the Clipboard, or that has not yet been created, by using the Edit/Insert Object menu option. From the list box which then appears, choose the desired type of object (such as Microsoft Paintbrush picture, Microsoft Excel worksheet, or sound). Click OK, and the appropriate application will be launched. (What applications are available depends on what OLE-compatible Windows applications are installed on your computer.) Once you have created the desired object, exit this application, using the usual techniques and the object will be automatically embedded into the general field in FoxPro.

Editing OLE Data

Since OLE represents either a direct link to the source application, or an embedded copy of its data, you can edit any data in a general field by double-clicking on the field. When you do so, the data will appear in a window of the source application. Figure 8-8 shows the result of doing this with the general field containing our Works for Windows spreadsheet. Note that the title bar in the source application shows the name of the OLE object; in this case, the spreadsheet in Works is titled "Sheet in FoxPro[1001]."

You can then proceed to use the usual techniques of the source application to change the data, as required. If the object is stored by means of a link, changes are stored to the original file; if the object is an embedded one, changes are stored to the embedded copy of the original.

FIGURE
8-8

Double-clicking on general field causes application to open, with window containing OLE object

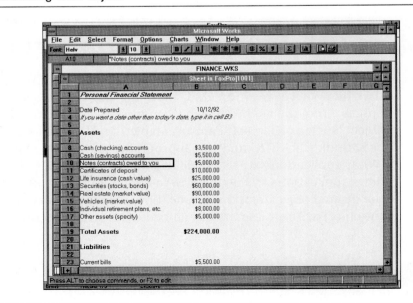

Working Examples with General Fields

The following section provides examples of how to use general fields to store external objects. To follow the examples that use pictures, all you need is a copy of the Windows Paintbrush program that is provided with Windows. The other examples require a Windows word processor, and a Windows spreadsheet program that support Windows DDE or OLE. You can use WordPerfect for Windows, Microsoft Word for Windows, Microsoft Excel, Borland's Quattro Pro for Windows, Lotus 1-2-3 for Windows, or the spreadsheet in Microsoft Works for Windows, if you have any of these products.

The first step is to create a database that will contain the objects from other Windows software. To create the file, enter the command:

```
CREATE OBJECTS
```

When the Table Structure window appears, enter the following field information.

Field	Field Name	Type	Width
1	Name	Character	15
2	Picture	General	
3	Document	General	

Once the fields have been entered in the structure, save the new database structure by clicking OK. When the "Input Data records now?" message appears, click Yes to begin adding new records to the file. With the first blank record visible in Append mode, enter **ARCHES** in its Name field.

Next, double-click anywhere in the Picture field, to open a window into that field. With the window open, you are ready to paste in an entry from the Windows Clipboard; but first, you must have something in the Clipboard to paste. For this example, a graphic image is desired, so the following paragraph will show you how to copy one into the Clipboard from Windows Paintbrush.

Press CTRL+ESC to open the Windows Task List. Choose Program Manager from the list to switch to the Windows Program Manager. Once the Program Manager appears, open the Accessories window (if it is not already open), and double-click the Paintbrush icon to start Windows

Paintbrush. When Paintbrush appears in its own window, choose File/Open from its menu bar. In the list of files which appears, double-click the filename ARCHES.BMP to open the file. (Note that this image is one of the sample illustrations provided with Windows Paintbrush; if you have images of your own, you may want to try using your images in these examples.)

Click the Selection tool in Paintbrush (it's the pair of scissors beneath the dotted-line rectangle). Then, place the insertion pointer at the upper-left corner of the image until it assumes the shape of a crosshair, and click and drag down to the lower-right corner of the image to enclose the image in a dotted line. From the Paintbrush menus, choose Edit/Copy. This action causes a copy of the image to be pasted into the Windows Clipboard.

To switch back to FoxPro, Press CTRL+ESC to bring up the Windows Task List, and choose FoxPro from the list. When FoxPro's desktop reappears, find the window for the Picture field and click anywhere inside it. Then choose Edit/Paste Special from the menus. In a moment, the portion of the image that you just selected in Paintbrush appears in the FoxPro general field, as shown in Figure 8-9. Because you chose Edit/Paste Special, the object is a link to the original Paintbrush file. If you like, try making a change to the original picture in Windows Paintbrush; you will see that the linked object in FoxPro changes accordingly.

Press CTRL+F4 to close the Picture field's window. Then double-click the next field, Document, to open a window into that field. In this field, you will paste objects from other Windows software that supports object linking and embedding.

Press CTRL+ESC to open the Windows Task List. Choose Program Manager from the list. Once the Program Manager appears, start your Windows word processor in the usual manner. When your word processor appears in its own window, choose File/Open from its menu, and open any document that contains three or more paragraphs. (If you don't have any documents of your own, you can type one now by choosing the New option from the word processor's File Open dialog box, or from its File menu. If you do create a new file, remember to save it by choosing File/Save and supplying a filename.)

Select the first paragraph of the document, by clicking and holding the mouse button at the start of the paragraph, then dragging to the end of the paragraph. From the menus, choose Edit/Copy. This action causes a copy of the paragraph to be placed in the Windows Clipboard.

General field containing image

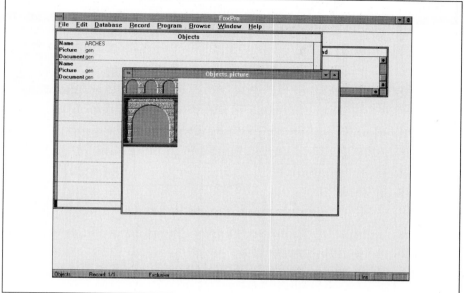

Press CTRL+ESC to bring up the Windows Task List, and choose FoxPro from the list. When FoxPro's desktop reappears, click anywhere in the window for the Document field, and choose Edit/Paste from the menus. (Note that if Edit/Paste is dimmed, it means your Windows word processor does not support DDE or OLE, and you cannot complete this exercise.) In a moment, one of two things happens: either a portion of the text you just selected in the word processor appears in the FoxPro general field (this happens if your application supports only DDE), or else an icon representing the text appears in the general field's window, as shown in Figure 8-10. (The icon will appear if your application supports OLE.) Press CTRL+F4 to close the window into the document field.

TAB to the first field of the second record, and enter **LEAVES** as a name. Double-click anywhere in the Picture field to open a window into the field, then press CTRL+ESC to bring up the Windows Task List. Choose Paintbrush from the Task List, to switch to Windows Paintbrush.

General field containing icon representing text of document

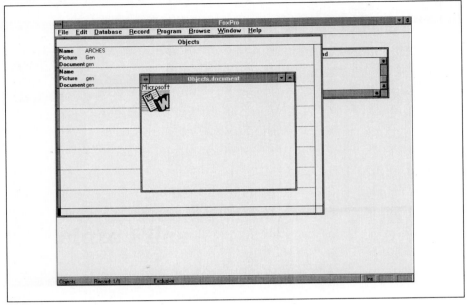

When Paintbrush appears in its own window, choose File/Open from its menu. In the list of files which appears, double-click the filename LEAVES.BMP to open that file.

Click the Selection tool in Paintbrush (rememebr, it's the pair of scissors beneath the dotted-line rectangle). Then, click and hold the mouse button at the upper-left corner of the image, and drag down to the lower-right corner of the image to enclose the image in a dotted line. From the menus, choose Edit/Copy, to copy the image into the Windows Clipboard.

Press CTRL+ESC to bring up the Windows Task List, and choose FoxPro from the list. When FoxPro reappears, click anywhere in the window for the Picture field, and choose Edit/Paste from the menus. In a moment, the portion of the image you just selected in Paintbrush appears in the FoxPro general field. In this case, because you used Edit/Paste, the object is an embedded copy of the original picture. If you try making changes to the original picture in Windows Paintbrush, you will see that the changes do not appear in the copy that is stored in FoxPro; however, you can separately make changes to the copy stored in FoxPro, by double-clicking the general field.

Press CTRL+F4 to close the Picture field. Double-click the next field, Document, to open a window into that field. Press CTRL+ESC to bring up the Windows Task List, and choose Program Manager. Once you are in the Program Manager, start your Windows spreadsheet program in the usual manner. (If you don't have a spreadsheet program, you can skip the step of placing data in this final field; however, you may want to read along to see how the overall processs works.)

Once you have started your spreadsheet program, open one of your spreadsheet files in the usual manner. Select a portion of the data in the spreadsheet, by clicking and dragging from the upper-left corner of the desired portion to the lower-right corner. Then, choose Edit/Copy from the menus, to copy the spreadsheet data to the Windows Clipboard.

Press CTRL+ESC to bring up the Windows Task List, and choose FoxPro from the list. When FoxPro reappears, click anywhere in the window for the Document field, and choose Edit/Paste from the menus. In a moment, the portion of the spreadsheet you just selected appears in the FoxPro general field. In Figure 8-11, an example is shown using a spreadsheet from Microsoft Works for Windows.

You can use procedures similar to those outlined in these examples, to copy data from your other Windows applications into general fields in FoxPro. Just remember that your Windows application must support the data-sharing techniques of DDE (Dynamic Data Exchange), or OLE (Object Linking and Embedding), or both. Some early Windows applications do not support DDE or OLE. Remember, the advantage of OLE over DDE is that with OLE, you can double-click the item in the general field of the FoxPro database, and immediately begin editing the item in its original application.

Displaying General Fields Alongside Other Data

You may often want to view the object embedded in a general field, while simultaneously viewing the data contained in the rest of your

FIGURE
8-11

Data from Works for Windows spreadsheet in FoxPro

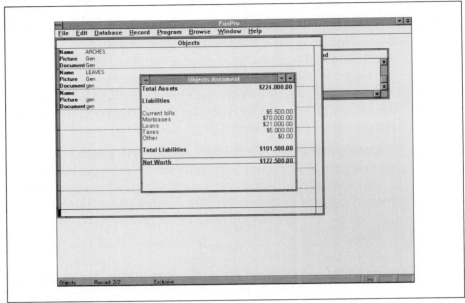

database. This is a particularly attractive option when you've used a general field to store a graphic image.

With the windowing capabilities built into FoxPro, this is easy to do. Simply open the database in a Browse window, double-click the desired general field to open a window into that field, and move and size both windows so that you can view the Browse window separately. If you click in the Browse window to make it the active window, you can then move from record to record, and the other window (containing the general field) will display its contents for each record that you select in the Browse window.

**FIGURE
8-12**
Simultaneous view of Browse window and general field

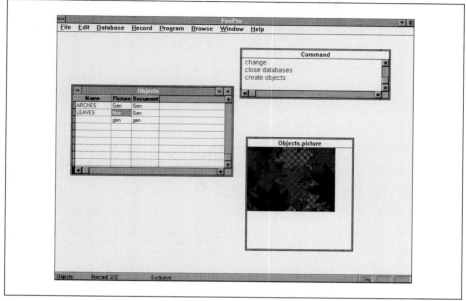

Figure 8-12 shows such an example; here, the sample database just created in this chapter is in use. After selecting Browse from the Browse menu and double-clicking in the Picture field to open the general field containing the picture, the general field is moved and resized so both it and the Browse window can be viewed simultaneously. Once this is done, if you move around in the database (within the Browse window), then for each record, the contents of the field named Picture will appear in the adjacent window.

CHAPTER

Managing Your Files

*T*his chapter's topic is file operations—copying, renaming, and erasing files, and using more than one database file at a time. Although some file operations usually are performed from the Windows File Manager or at the DOS prompt, these operations can also be performed without leaving FoxPro.

In addition to performing file operations without returning to the operating system, you can also transfer information between database files. You can transfer all the data in a file, or selected data. You can also open and work with more than one file at once. The use of using multiple files is common in a relational database manager like FoxPro, and you will find it a virtual necessity for performing some types of tasks, such as inventory systems and complex accounting functions.

Using the Filer

Various options for managing files are available through the Filer option on the Help menu. If you open the Help menu and choose Filer, the Filer window appears, as shown in Figure 9-1. Its list box shows all files in the current directory. Also, at the bottom of the Filer are buttons for file operations such as Find, Copy, and Move. You can perform these operations by clicking the corresponding buttons.

At the upper-right side of the Filer are two drop-down lists for your disk drives and directories. You can click the arrows at the right to display a list of either available disk drives, or available directories. Using these lists, you can navigate within other drives and directories.

 Note   FoxPro's Filer lets you perform many of the tasks you can perform from the Windows File Manager, although the two differ somewhat in operation.

Underneath the Drive and Directories lists is the Files Like text box. You can enter filenames or DOS wildcards here to restrict the types of files displayed in the list box. For example, entering ***.DBF** in the Files Like box would restrict the files shown to database files only.

FIGURE
9-1

FoxPro Filer

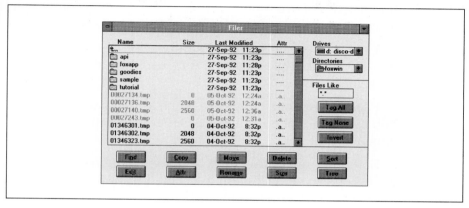

The list box is divided into four columns: Name, Size, Last Modified, and Attr (for Attribute). The Name column shows the file name and extension (if any) of the file. Directories and subdirectories display a "file folder" icon beside the directory name. At the top of the list, the symbol of an arrow followed by two periods [..] represents the parent directory.

The Size column shows the size of each file in bytes, and the Last Modified column shows the DOS date and time stamp on the file. The Attr column shows the attributes of the file, as determined by your operating system. Up to four letters can appear in this column: A, for archive; H, for hidden; R, for read-only; and S, for system. More information about file attributes can be found in your DOS manual.

Moving Around the Files List

You can click on the arrows in the scroll bar, or use the UP ARROW and DOWN ARROW keys and the PGUP and PGDN keys, to move the cursor within the files list. Try your PGDN and DOWN ARROW keys now to see the effect, then try scrolling both downwards and upwards with the scroll bar. As you highlight a particular file, you can press ENTER to *tag* the file (a tagged file appears in reverse video). Once a file has been tagged, you can use the options at the bottom of the Filer to perform a desired operation (such as copying or erasing) on the tagged file.

You can also tag individual files by clicking the desired file in the List box. To tag multiple files with a mouse, hold down the SHIFT key while dragging the mouse.

Files that are currently open, such as database files, appear dimmed. You cannot select open files for file-level operations (such as copying or erasing).

Note the Tag All, Tag None, and Invert options at the right side of the Filer. You can select Tag All to tag all files, and you can select Tag None to remove tags from all files. Selecting Invert reverses the status of existing tags; all tagged files are untagged, and all untagged files are tagged. You may find that using the Tag All option along with the Files Like entry box is useful for selecting groups of files of the same type. For example, you could delete all backup (.BAK) files by entering *.**BAK** the Files Like box, selecting Tag All, and then selecting Delete.

You are not limited to working within the current directory. By opening the Directories drop-down list box at the right side of the Filer, you can display directories at a higher level than the current one. Double-click the desired directory to switch to that directory, or click the symbol at the top of the list box to switch to the root directory. You can also double-click any lower-level directory that appears as an icon within the list of files.

When you take any of these actions, the Files list box will show the contents of the directory you have switched to. All subdirectories will appear in the Filer's list of files, and you can double-click any directory within the list to switch to that directory. Similarly, you can open the Drives drop-down list box and choose a drive identifier, to switch to that disk drive.

After experimenting with moving around, be sure to get back to the subdirectory that contains your working files (it is probably C:\FOXPROW, unless you set up your hard disk differently from the default when you installed FoxPro). You can get back into the subdirectory by double-clicking the subdirectory name within the files list in the Filer. When done using the Filer, you can exit it by pressing CTRL+F4, or by double-clicking the Filer window's Control menu icon.

Deleting Files

You can delete files through a two-step process. First, tag the file or files by clicking on their names; then click the Delete button. When you do this, a dialog box will warn you that the file will be deleted, and will ask you to confirm the deletion.

You must then choose Delete from the dialog box to actually delete the file. When multiple files have been tagged, the dialog box will contain two useful options: Skip, and Delete All. You can choose Skip when you decide *not* to confirm a deletion, and instead want to skip to the next tagged file. Or, you can choose Delete All, if you want to delete all tagged files without any further confirmation.

Caution   Exercise care when deleting files. FoxPro does not prevent you from deleting its own program files, or program files needed for Windows or other applications.

Renaming Files

You can rename a file by tagging the file and clicking the Rename button. When you do this, a dialog box displays the old name and asks you for the new name. Enter the new name, and click Rename in the dialog box.

Finding Files

The Find option lets you find files based on a name or extension, and tag those files. When you choose Find, the Find Files Like dialog box appears, as shown in Figure 9-2.

In the text box, you can enter the name and/or extension for the type of file that you want to find and tag. For example, entering ***.TXT** would cause the Filer to find and tag all files with a .TXT extension. Note that you can enter more than one file extension at a time, by separating the

FIGURE 9-2

Find Files dialog box

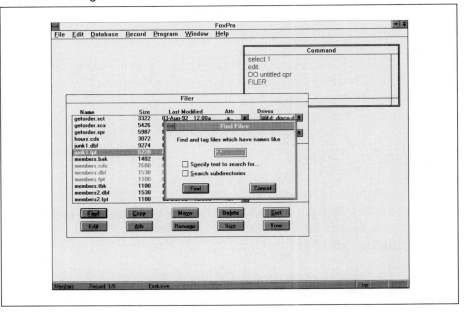

extensions with semicolons. As an example, you could enter *.**TXT**; *.**COM**; *.**EXE** in the text box.

Note that the Find Files Like dialog box also contains two options that add to its power; they are the check boxes labeled Specify text to search for and Search subdirectories. If you select Specify text to search for, another dialog box appears, and you can enter up to three text strings (of a maximum of 256 characters). If you use this option, the Filer tags only the files that it finds to contain this text string or strings.

The Search subdirectories option tells Filer to search all subdirectories in the current directory. Hence, if you start at the root directory, the Find option will search the entire drive. (This may take some time if you have a lot of files on your hard disk.)

When the Filer completes its search, you are placed back in the Files list, and all files matching your file name or extension are tagged. If you chose the Search subdirectory option, any directories containing a file that matched the specification are also tagged. You can then use the other Filer buttons to perform an operation on the tagged files. If you are performing a destructive operation such as a Delete, it might be a wise idea to check the names of the tagged files before performing the operation.

Editing Files

You can edit a file with the Edit option. (This should only be attempted with text files, such as programs you write in FoxPro; you should not attempt to load nontext files, such as databases or indexes, into the Editor.) To edit a file, click the desired file in the list box to select it, then click Edit. The uses of the Editor are covered in more detail in Chapter 14.

Copying and Moving Files

You can copy files with the Copy option. To copy a file, tag the desired file or files, and choose Copy. A Copy Files dialog box appears, asking for the target directory into which the file should be copied.

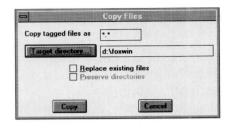

Enter the directory name, choose Copy from the dialog box, and the tagged file or files are copied to the specified directory. (Note that you can click the Target Directory button to open another dialog box containing a scroll box, and pick a different directory from that scroll box by name.) Two options in the Copy Files dialog box, Replace Existing Files and Preserve Directories, let you specify whether any existing files at the destination having the same name should be overwritten, and whether the directory structure should be copied as well as the files.

The Move option lets you move a file or files from one location to another. It operates just like the Copy option, with one difference: when the tagged file or files have been copied to the new location, they are removed from the old location.

Changing File Attributes

You can change the DOS attributes of a file with the Attr option. When you tag a file and then select Attr, a dialog box appears, with the four attribute choices: Read-Only, Archived, Hidden File, and System.

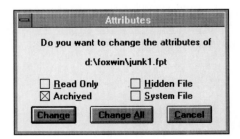

The check boxes for the choices will already be either selected or unselected, depending on the file's current status; for example, if you have tagged a file as read-only, the Read-Only check box will contain an X. You can click the check boxes with the mouse to change any file attributes as desired. The Change All button at the bottom of the dialog box can be used to tell FoxPro to change the attributes for all tagged files in the same way, without stopping to display the dialog box for each file you have tagged.

 Caution   You should not change file attributes without being aware of possible consequences, particularly in the case of files that are part of the FoxPro program, the DOS operating system, or the Windows package. If you were to change the attributes of one of these files, the results could be disastrous. Your computer could fail to operate normally.

Using Size and Tree

Use the Size option to display statistics on the size of a file. To do so, select the desired file in the list box and click Size. A dialog box containing information on the size of the file will appear.

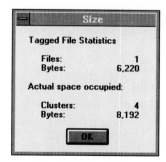

The Tree option can be used to display a Tree Panel (a visual representation of the layout of files within your directories). You can perform operations on entire directory structures from the Tree Panel. Click Tree, and FoxPro takes a few moments to scan your entire hard disk. When this is done, a Tree Panel appears displaying the files and directories on your disk, as shown in Figure 9-3.

To navigate within the Tree Panel, use the scroll bars and the mouse, the UP ARROW and DOWN ARROW keys, or the PGUP and PGDN keys. You can click the Drives drop-down list to display and select from all available disk drives. For your information, the right side of the Tree Panel shows the number of files on the disk, the disk space used, and the remaining free disk space.

Tree Panel

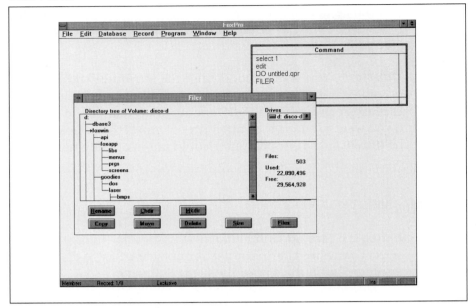

You can use the buttons shown at the bottom of the Tree Panel to rename directories, make directories, and change directories. You can also copy or move directories, delete directories, and determine the size (disk space used) for a particular directory.

Keep in mind that when you are working in the Tree Panel, you are working with entire directories, so the potential for accidental damage is great. It is a wise idea to back up files before performing any deletions of entire directories.

Also, you should not casually rename directories without first considering what effect this could have on other programs on your system. If, for example, you casually rename certain directories using FoxPro's Filer, you could wreak havoc when Windows later looks for directories that no longer exist. Note that you can get out of the Tree Panel and back to the Filer's normal display at any time, by clicking the Files button that appears at the lower-right corner of the dialog box. (If you are examining the Tree Panel now, click this button to exit the Tree Panel before examining the next topic.)

Using Sort

Use the Sort option to sort the files in the files list. When you choose the Sort option, the Sort Files dialog box appears to help you select the sort criteria.

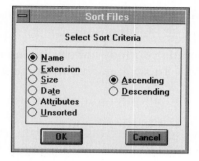

You can choose to sort by name, extension, size, date, or file attributes. You can also choose whether the list will be sorted in ascending or descending order. After choosing the desired options from the dialog box, click OK, and the files in the list box will be sorted. This in no way affects the order or arrangement of the files on the disk—only the way they are displayed in the list box.

Commands for Managing Files

If you prefer to stick with the Command window, you can use a number of different commands for file management. You can also selectively copy records from one database file to another file. You can even run a DOS command from the Command level within FoxPro.

The RUN Command

To exit FoxPro temporarily and run a DOS command, use the RUN command. The syntax for this command is

RUN *DOS command or program name*

It causes FoxPro to suspend itself in memory, and temporarily exit to DOS. Note that a substantial portion of FoxPro remains in memory when you do this. Because Windows is a complex environment and FoxPro is running under Windows, it is probably not a wise idea to attempt to run other large programs through FoxPro. It would be better to run such programs through Windows itself (see your Windows documentation for details on running several programs simultaneously from Windows).

The RUN command is primarily useful for executing relatively simple DOS commands you may already be familiar with, such as COPY, DIR, and RENAME. To see how this works, enter the following command:

```
RUN DIR/P
```

You see a window open, displaying the current directory just as if you had entered **DIR/P** at the DOS prompt. When the DOS command has executed, press ALT+SPACE to open the window's Control menu, then choose Close. You will be returned to the Command window within FoxPro. (You cannot close a DOS window from FoxPro with the usual CTRL+F4 combination.)

Note that you should never attempt to use the RUN command to run a program that will modify your PC's memory. (All memory-resident programs fall into this category, as does the PRINT command in DOS.) Running one of these programs may cause Windows to crash with an unrecoverable error.

The COPY FILE Command

You can use the COPY FILE command as an equivalent to the COPY command in DOS (or the Windows File Manager's File/Copy menu option). It lets you make copies of entire files. The format for this command is

COPY FILE *source-filename* TO *destination-filename*

You must include any extensions when using this command. As an example, if you wanted to make a copy of a file named LETTER1.TXT and the copy was to be named MYFILE.TXT, you could use the following command:

```
COPY FILE LETTER1.TXT TO MYFILE.TXT
```

Drive identifiers and path names can be included before the file names, if you want to copy into a different directory.

Note that if you use this method to copy a database file, be sure to also copy any .FPT (memo field) file that may accompany the database. Remember, whenever a database contains memo fields, it is made up of two files, one with a .DBF extension and another with a .FPT extension.

 Note   With very large fields, using COPY at the DOS level is much faster than using COPY FILE within FoxPro.

The COPY Command

The COPY command copies all or parts of a database file. The format for the COPY command is

COPY TO *filename*

where *filename* is the name of the new file that you want the records copied to. Before giving this command, you must first issue the USE command (or use the Database/Setup menu option) to open the database file that you want to copy from. For example, try the following commands now:

```
USE MEMBERS
COPY TO FILE1
USE FILE1
LIST
```

All of the records in the MEMBERS database will be copied to the new file, FILE1.

One advantage of the COPY command is that you need not worry about copying the memo field (.FPT) file; it is copied automatically. A disadvantage of COPY is that with large databases, it is much slower than the COPY FILE command.

This command can be quite useful for quickly backing up small or moderately-sized databases to a floppy disk. For example, you could copy the entire MEMBERS database to a floppy disk in drive A, with commands like these:

```
USE MEMBERS
COPY TO A:MYFILE
```

This approach to backing up a database file has one important disadvantage: the database (and any associated memo-field file) cannot be larger than the available disk space on a single floppy disk.

The COPY command offers significant flexibility when you want to copy only specific fields. To select the fields to be copied, use the format

COPY TO *filename* FIELDS *fieldlist*

By adding the word FIELDS after the file name and then adding a list of fields, you tell FoxPro to copy only the fields in this list to the new database. As an example, try copying just the Lastname, Firstname, City, and State fields in FILE1 by entering

```
COPY TO FILE2 FIELDS LASTNAME, FIRSTNAME, CITY, STATE
USE FILE2
LIST
```

And the results should resemble those shown below.

```
Record#   lastname          firstname          city               state
      1   Miller            Karen              Chevy Chase        MD
      2   Martin            William            Silver Spring      MD
      3   Robinson          Carol              Falls Church       VA
      4   Kramer            Harry              Arlington          VA
      5   Moore             Ellen              Takoma Park        MD
      6   Zachman           David              Falls Church       VA
      7   Robinson          Benjamin           Washington         DC
      8   Hart              Wendy              Fairfax            VA
```

The listing shows that only the fields you specified by name in FILE1 are copied to FILE2.

You can also use a FOR clause to copy only specific data from a database. When used with the COPY command, the optional FOR clause limits the records that are copied to the new file; only the records meeting the condition specified by the FOR clause are copied. The format for the COPY command, when used with the FOR clause, is

COPY TO *filename* FIELDS *fieldlist* FOR *condition*

Using the FOR clause as part of the COPY command, you could copy only the Lastname and Tapelimit fields from FILE1, only for records in which the Tapelimit field contains a value greater than three. To do this, enter

```
USE FILE1
COPY TO FILE3 FIELDS LASTNAME, TAPELIMIT FOR TAPELIMIT
> 3
```

(Note that the "COPY TO..." command should be typed on a single line.)

The FOR condition specified before the Tapelimit field means that the new file, FILE3, will contain only those members with a tape limit of more than three. To see the results, enter

```
USE FILE3
LIST
```

And the results should resemble those shown here:

```
Record#   lastname          tapelimit
      1   Miller                    6
      2   Martin                    4
      3   Robinson                  6
      4   Kramer                    4
      5   Moore                     6
      6   Zachman                   4
```

You can also perform this type of copy from the menus, if desired. Choose the Copy To option on the Database menu. A dialog box will appear, giving you a variety of options: you can specify a For or a While condition to limit the records that will be copied to the new database; you can also specify a scope of records, or a restricted list of fields.

Work Areas and Active Files

FoxPro can access any database file that is open, up to a limit of 225 database files at one time. Opening a database file is equivalent to telling

FoxPro, "I am ready to work with a database file that is stored on disk; now go get it." FoxPro can read any information from a database file once the file is open. However, if you want to change, add, or delete any of the information, the database file must be not only open, but active as well. Commands like CHANGE or EDIT, APPEND, and DELETE normally operate on active database files. FoxPro allows only one active database at a time, so out of a possible 225 open files, only one can be active.

Opening multiple database files from disk requires that each file be assigned to a *work area*. As you might have guessed, there are 225 work areas in FoxPro, numbered from 1 to 225. Assigning a database file to a work area, or opening a database file, is a two-step process. You tell FoxPro what work area you want to place the file in, and then you open the file in that work area. The SELECT command enables you to choose the work area, and the USE command opens the file. For example, if you wanted to open the MEMBERS file in work area 2, you could first select the work area by entering

```
SELECT 2
```

To load the MEMBERS file into the current work area, you would then enter

```
USE MEMBERS
```

As an alternative, you could perform both steps—specifying the work area and opening the file—on a single command line, by using the IN clause along with the USE command. For example, the following command tells FoxPro to open MEMBERS in work area 2:

```
USE MEMBERS IN 2
```

If you had specified a different file name—for example, RENTALS instead of MEMBERS—that file (RENTALS) would have been loaded into work area 2. In fact, for the rest of this FoxPro session, any database file that you now load with the USE command will be loaded in work area 2, unless you use the SELECT command to choose a different work area.

Note that the USE *filename* IN *work-area* syntax of the USE command does *not* select a work area; it only loads the file in the named work area. If the current work area happened to be work area 1, and you entered **USE MEMBERS IN 2**, the MEMBERS file would be loaded in work area 2, but you would still be using work area 1.

The current work area will always be the last area you chose with the SELECT command. The active database file will always be the last database file you loaded into the current work area. For an example, open the RENTALS file in work area 1 and the MEMBERS file in work area 2 by entering the following commands:

```
SELECT 1
USE RENTALS
SELECT 2
USE MEMBERS
```

MEMBERS is now the active database, because work area 2 was the last work area selected; thus, FoxPro is pointed to MEMBERS. FoxPro can now access information from either the MEMBERS or the RENTALS file, but can only change information in the MEMBERS file. If you wanted RENTALS to be the active file, then after opening both databases, you would enter **SELECT 1**. The active database would switch from MEMBERS to RENTALS, although MEMBERS would remain open.

You can see the effects of having multiple work areas open if you now enter the following commands:

```
SELECT 1
LIST TITLE, DAYRENTED
```

```
Record#    TITLE                              DAYRENTED
      1    Star Trek VI                       03/05/93
      2    Lethal Weapon III                  03/02/93
      3    Who Framed Roger Rabbit            03/06/93
      4    Doc Hollywood                      03/04/93
      5    Fried Green Tomatoes               03/01/93
      6    Wayne's World                      03/04/93
      7    Prince of Tides                    03/06/93
      8    Lethal Weapon III                  03/07/93
      9    Friday 13th Part XXVII             03/14/93
     10    Mambo Kings                        03/15/93
     11    Prince of Tides                    03/17/93
     12    Coming to America                  03/14/93
     13    Prince of Tides                    03/16/93
     14    Star Trek VI                       03/18/93
     15    Wayne's World                      03/19/93
     16    Mambo Kings                        03/16/93
```

```
SELECT 2
LIST LASTNAME,FIRSTNAME
```

Record#	LASTNAME	FIRSTNAME	EXPIREDATE
1	Miller	Karen	07/25/93
2	Martin	William	07/04/93
3	Robinson	Carol	09/05/94
4	Kramer	Harry	12/22/93
5	Moore	Ellen	11/17/95
6	Zachman	David	09/19/93
7	Robinson	Benjamin	09/17/94
8	Hart	Wendy	10/19/94

You can see, from this example, that with two database files open simultaneously in different work areas, you can use commands to obtain information from both of the databases. This technique for working with multiple databases will prove useful in Chapter 12.

The CLOSE DATABASES Command

Another command that you will use often is the CLOSE DATABASES command. It closes all open database and index files, and returns FoxPro to work area 1. Enter

```
CLOSE DATABASES
```

to close both of the database files that you opened earlier.

Combining Files

FoxPro lets you transfer records from one database file to another, by using a variation of the APPEND command. You have already used APPEND to add records to a database; however, the format of this command is somewhat different when it is used for transferring records from another database. Instead of simply entering **APPEND**, you must enter

APPEND FROM *filename*

where *filename* is the name of the file from which you wish to copy records. When you use the APPEND FROM command, FoxPro copies records from a source file to a destination file (the destination file is the currently active file). In a sense, APPEND FROM is the reverse of the COPY TO command. The file to which you are adding the records must be the active database file.

As an example, to transfer records from the newly created FILE3 database to the FILE2 database, you should first activate FILE2. Enter

```
USE FILE2
```

You can append the records to FILE2 with

```
APPEND FROM FILE3
```

When you list the database to see the appended records, your display should resemble this:

Record#	Lastname	Firstname	City	State
1	Miller	Karen	Chevy Chase	MD
2	Martin	William	Silver Spring	MD
3	Robinson	Carol	Falls Church	VA
4	Kramer	Harry	Arlington	VA
5	Moore	Ellen	Takoma Park	MD
6	Zachman	David	Falls Church	VA
7	Robinson	Benjamin	Washington	DC
8	Hart	Wendy	Fairfax	VA
9	Miller			
10	Martin			
11	Robinson			
12	Kramer			
13	Moore			
14	Zachman			

One characteristic of the APPEND FROM command becomes apparent when you examine the list: only fields having the same names in both databases are appended. Remember, you gave different structures to these files, by using a selective form of the COPY command. FILE2 contains the Lastname, Firstname, City, and State fields, while FILE3 contains the Lastname and Tapelimit fields. When you appended from FILE3 to FILE2, FoxPro found just one field in common between the two files: Lastname.

Even if the field name is the same, FoxPro may or may not append the field if the *data type* is different. FoxPro will only append the data if it can make sense of the transfer. For example, contents of a numeric field *will* be transfered to a character field in another database; the data will appear in the character field as numerals. A character field, if it contains *only* numbers, *will* transfer to a numeric field. A memo field will *not* transfer to any other type of field.

Also, if the source field has a larger size than the destination field in the target record, then character data will be truncated, and asterisks will be entered for any numeric data that does not fit within the smaller field.

The file from which you append data does not have to be a FoxPro database file. The APPEND FROM command is also commonly used to transfer data from other programs, like spreadsheets or word processors. This aspect of using FoxPro is discussed in more detail in Chapter 18.

Copying a Database Structure

Another helpful FoxPro command, COPY STRUCTURE, lets you make an identical copy of the active database's structure (in effect, an empty database with the same field structure). For example, you could use COPY STRUCTURE to create empty copies of a database on multiple floppy disks; others could then use these files on their machines (provided they have FoxPro) to add records. Later, the records from all these copies could be combined into one file, with the APPEND FROM command.

To use the COPY STRUCTURE command, first open the database whose structure you want to copy, by issuing the USE command. Then use the command

COPY STRUCTURE TO *filename*

where *filename* is the desired name for the file that will hold the empty copy. You can precede the file name with a path or a drive identifier, if desired. As an example, the command

```
USE MEMBERS
COPY STRUCTURE TO A:REMOTE
```

creates an empty database file called REMOTE.DBF, on the disk in drive A, with a structure identical to that of MEMBERS. If the source file contains memo fields, then both a .DBF and an .FPT file will be created under the new name.

CHAPTER

Automating Your Work with Macros

*F*oxPro provides the capability to create *macros,* which are combinations of keystrokes that can automate many of the tasks you frequently perform within FoxPro. Macros are created by recording a sequence of characters and commands to a single key combination. You can save the macro, and later press the same single key combination to play back the whole sequence. When the macro is played back, FoxPro performs as if you had manually performed the actions contained within the macro.

When you use macros, a single key combination can hold a complex series of menu choices or commands. You can also store frequently used phrases, names, or complete paragraphs of text in a macro. And you are not limited to one key combination; you can use various combinations of letter and function keys for macros. If you must print daily reports or perform similar repetitive tasks, you can save many keystrokes by using macros.

You should note one significant limitation of FoxPro macros: they cannot be used to record many mouse actions. Some mouse actions (such as selecting menu options and clicking the OK or Cancel buttons in dialog boxes) are recorded, but many mouse actions (such as clicking arrows in scroll bars) are not recorded. To be on the safe side, unless you are selecting menu options or dialog box buttons, you should avoid the use of the mouse when recording macros in FoxPro.

Creating Macros

To create a macro, follow these four steps:

1. Press SHIFT+F10 to display the Macro Key Definition dialog box. (An alternate method for this step is to choose the Macros option of the Program menu and then click New in the dialog box that appears.)

2. Hold down the CTRL or ALT key, and press and release the letter key or function key that is to be assigned to the macro. You can use CTRL or ALT plus any of the 26 letters or the 10 function keys with or without the SHIFT key. (Note that if you use ALT with a letter key that normally opens a menu, the macro key combination overrides the menu choice. For example, if you assign ALT+F to a macro, then while

that macro is loaded you will not be able to use ALT+F to open the File menu.)

3. Enter the keystrokes that will make up the macro. If you make an error, press SHIFT+F10, choose Discard from the dialog box to end the recording, and start again.

4. Once all the keystrokes have been entered, press SHIFT+F10, and then select OK to stop the macro recording.

Once the macro has been recorded, you can press the CTRL+*key* or ALT+*key* combination to play back the macro at any time.

For a quick example of what macros can do for you, consider editing within the MEMBERS database. Perhaps you regularly update records by splitting a Browse window just past the three leftmost fields, and then search the Lastname field for a desired last name. A macro would automate much of this process.

Press SHIFT+F10 and then press CTRL+A to designate that key combination for the macro. Click OK. In the lower left corner of the Status Bar, you will see

Recording CTRL_A. SHIFT+F10 stops.

indicating that FoxPro is now recording each of your keystrokes in the form of a macro. Enter **USE MEMBERS** to open the file, and enter **BROWSE** to enter Browse mode. Press ALT+B to open the Browse menu, and press R to choose the Resize Partitions option. Press the RIGHT ARROW key repeatedly until the window is split just past the Firstname field. Then press ENTER to complete the resizing. Press ALT+B to open the Browse menu, and press **c** to choose Change. Press CTRL+H to move the cursor to the left partition of the Browse window. Press CTRL+F10 to zoom the Browse window to full size.

Open the Record menu with ALT+R and choose Locate. From the dialog box that appears, choose For by pressing ALT+F. In the Locate Record For text box, enter the following (note the pair of quotes):

LASTNAME = " "

Then press the LEFT ARROW key once so the cursor is between the quotes. Press SHIFT+F10, and click OK from the dialog box to stop recording the macro.

To try the macro, first press ESC and click Yes from the dialog box. Then press ESC twice to exit the menus and exit Browse mode (because you haven't made any changes to the field, it's OK to use ESC to exit Browse). Assuming that you now want to open the file, to enter Browse mode, to split the window past the first three fields, and to search for a particular name, you could use the macro to carry out all steps except the final ones of entering the name to search for, choosing OK from the dialog box, and choosing Locate. Press CTRL+A now to play back the macro. All the keystrokes are entered from the macro, and you are presented with the incomplete LASTNAME = " " expression.

Go ahead and enter any last name that is in the database. Then click OK and click Locate in the next dialog box. When the Locate is complete, press CTRL+F4 to exit Browse mode.

Saving Macros

Macros that you create are saved in temporary memory, not permanently on the disk. If you want to keep a permanent record of your macros, you must use the Save option, which appears in the Macros dialog box when you choose Macros from the Program menu. Open the Program menu now and choose Macros. In the dialog box that appears, click Save. In the Save Macros dialog box which appears, FoxPro asks you to name the macro file; enter **MYMACROS** as the file name. Then click Save from the dialog box. Click OK in the Macros dialog box to put it away.

Once the file has been saved, you can exit FoxPro. When you return to the program, you can reload the macros you saved by choosing Macros from the Program menu. Then select Restore from the Keyboard Macros dialog box, click the desired macro filename in the list box which appears, and click Open.

While recording this macro, the ALT key shortcuts for menu choices were used on purpose. You could have used the cursor keys and the ENTER key to choose menu options, but when you are building macros it is a good idea to get into the habit of avoiding the cursor keys whenever possible. Not only does this use fewer overall keystrokes in the macro, but there is also less chance of an error occurring during playback if a list of available options is in a different state than it was during recording. This can be a particular problem when choosing file names from a pick list, because the alphabetical list changes as files are added to or deleted from your directory.

Command-Level Use and Macros

Macros can also be used to repeat a series of commands. You could start a macro with SHIFT+F10, assign a key to the macro, enter a series of commands in the Command window, and then stop the recording and save the macro. When you played back the macro, all of those commands would be repeated just as if you had typed them. However, this is not the speediest way to carry out a series of commands. FoxPro executes such a series much faster if they are stored in a command file or program. Details on creating programs begin with Chapter 14.

Macro Menu Options

When you choose the Macros option of the Program menu, a dialog box called Macros appears. At the left side of this dialog box is a list box containing all macros currently in memory and the keys assigned to those macros. If you use the scroll bar to scroll down the list, the lower portion shows any macros that are assigned to the function keys, and to SHIFT+ number key combinations.

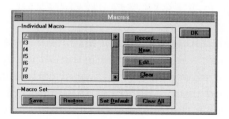

The Save and Restore buttons let you load a set of macros into memory or save the current macros in memory to a macro file. The command-level equivalents for these buttons are RESTORE MACROS FROM *macro-filename,* which loads the macro file, and SAVE MACROS TO *macro-filename,* which saves the current macros to the named file. The Set Default button stores the macros currently in memory to a startup macro file. The macros stored in this file are loaded automatically into memory whenever FoxPro is started.

The New button begins the creation of a new macro; selecting this option is equivalent to pressing SHIFT+F10, and it opens the dialog box requesting a key combination for the new macro. To record a macro, press the combination of ALT or CTRL and the function or letter key you want to assign to the macro. (If that key was used earlier, FoxPro asks for confirmation before overwriting the old macro in memory.) After pressing the desired key, you can perform the actions that you want to assign to the macro. When you are done, press SHIFT+F10, and then choose OK to stop the recording.

The Clear button clears a macro from memory. To clear a macro, first click the unwanted macro in the list box to select it. Then choose Clear to remove the macro. The Clear All button clears all existing macros from memory.

The Record button lets you begin recording a macro (the equivalent of pressing SHIFT+F10). The Edit button lets you edit an existing macro.

Since you can save different sets of macros under different file names, you can have an unlimited number of macros. One helpful hint in keeping track of your macro files is to give them the same name as the associated database file. Macros are saved to a file with an extension of .FKY.

Adding to Existing Macros

You can add to the end of an existing macro by pressing SHIFT+F10 to start a macro and then pressing the same key combination as the existing macro. For example, if you have already defined CTRL+A as a macro and want to add more keystrokes to the end of it, you can press SHIFT+F10, which reveals the Macro Key Definition box. Press CTRL+A as the key to define, and choose OK, and you will see the Overwrite Macro dialog box.

The dialog box presents you with three buttons: Overwrite, Append keystrokes, and Cancel. You can now click Append keystrokes to add your keystrokes to the end of the existing macro. Selecting Overwrite would clear the old macro and assign its key combination to a new macro; Cancel would exit the macro definition without adding any changes.

Adding Pauses to Macros

FoxPro lets you add pauses to a macro. This is useful for allowing a user to enter an item that changes from day to day. A good example is the macro you created earlier, which searches for a record based on a last name. A pause could be added to let the user enter a last name in the dialog box; then the macro could perform the final steps of selecting OK from the dialog box and selecting Locate from the next dialog box. To try this now, you need to be at the spot where the search process ends; you can easily get there by replaying the macro. Press CTRL+A to replay the macro. When the macro ends, you should be in the text box for the search expression, with the cursor flashing between the double quotes.

Press SHIFT+F10. When the Macro Key Definition box appears, press CTRL+A to add to the existing macro. Next, click OK in the dialog box. From the next dialog box to appear, choose Append keystrokes. You will see the message "Recording Ctrl+A" in the lower-left corner of the screen.

Press SHIFT+F10 again to display the Stop Recording dialog box. Click the Insert Pause button and this dialog box will vanish, leaving the Expression Builder still visible underneath. Click OK in the Expression Builder dialog box. In the next dialog box, click Locate. Then press SHIFT+F10 and choose OK from the next dialog box to stop recording the macro. Press CTRL+F4 to exit Browse mode.

Try playing the macro by pressing CTRL+A. When the macro pauses, enter any last name in the database, and then press SHIFT+F10 to continue the macro. This time the macro will complete the search process by locating the record.

Rules and Limitations of Macros

A macro should never be made a part of itself. (For example, if a macro can be called with the Macro menu's Play option followed by the ALT+J key, you cannot call up the Macros menu, choose Play, and enter the ALT+J key combination within the macro.) Such a technique would set up an anomaly known in programming as a *recursive loop,* where the macro chases its own tail. FoxPro lets you get away with this, but only to a point. The macro repeats itself until an internal limit is reached, and an error message then results.

Allowable key combinations that can be assigned to macros are ALT or CTRL, plus the function keys F1 through F9, or the 26 letter keys. Any attempt to assign a macro to other keys is ignored.

CHAPTER

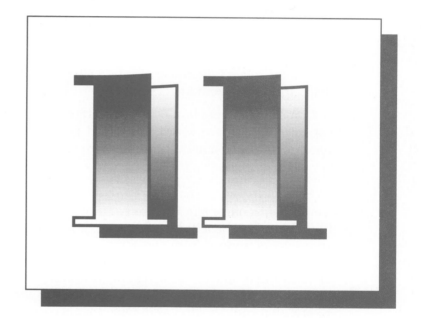

Advanced Report Topics

*I*n Chapter 7, you learned that FoxPro allows you to create quick reports and customized reports. This chapter continues to explore how FoxPro can meet your reporting needs, describing the use of form letters, labels, pictures, and other report topics in detail.

Using Expressions and Functions in Reports

You can coax much flexibility out of your reports and labels by using various expressions within the entry window of the Expression Builder. You usually enter a field in this window, but you can use any valid expression, including memory variables, field names, fields with alias names for related database files (see Chapter 12), and combinations of fields with or without spaces added.

Combinations of character fields are routinely used; as an example, consider a database with fields called Lastname, Firstname, and Midname (containing a middle initial). With such a database, the expression

```
TRIM(FIRSTNAME)+" "+LEFT(MIDNAME,1)+". "+TRIM(LASTNAME)
```

would yield a name like Thomas A. Harris. This expression uses the LEFT function to get the leftmost character of a field and the TRIM function to trim excess spaces from the Firstname and Lastname fields. (In this example, if there were no entry in the middle initial field, you would get an unwanted space and a period. However, this can be prevented by including the IIF function in the Expression for Field text box of the Expression Builder window, a topic that is covered in the next section in this chapter.) Combine names like this to save space in the report.

You can also combine various expressions of different types by converting the noncharacter portions of the expressions to characters. This is done with string functions (discussed in detail in Chapter 14). For example, you could enter an expression like

```
STR(AMOUNT) + " " + DTOC(DATESOLD)
```

to combine a numeric amount and a date field in a single column. This example uses the STR function, which converts a numeric value into a string of characters, along with the DTOC function, which converts a valid date into a string of characters.

Using the IIF Function in Expressions

The Immediate IF function, IIF, is also quite useful as part of an expression within reports or labels: Use it when you want to display one set of data when a condition is true and another set when a condition is false. In a personnel report, for example, you may want to indicate the number of weeks of vacation that an employee gets; the company gives two weeks to employees with fewer than five years employment, and three weeks to all others. Assuming five years is equivalent to 365 days multiplied by 5, plus 1 for at least one leap year, any employee whose hire date is at least 1826 days earlier than the date on the computer's clock gets three weeks' vacation. This is simple enough to calculate; for a given record in the personnel database with a date field called Hire_Date, the expression

```
IIF((DATE()-HIRE_DATE) < 1826, "two weeks", "three weeks")
```

would return the character string "two weeks" if fewer than 1826 days have passed since the date of hire, and "three weeks" if 1826 or more days have passed since the date of hire. You could place the entire expression into the Expression Builder window for a field within the report, and the report would display the appropriate number of weeks of vacation for that employee.

As an example of another use of the IIF function, recall the first example in this chapter. That report expression produces an unwanted period if no initial is entered in the middle-initial field. To solve this problem, you could use an expression like the following:

```
TRIM(FIRSTNAME) +" " + IIF(LEFT(MIDNAME) <> " ",
LEFT(MIDNAME,1))+". ","") + TRIM(LASTNAME)
```

If the leftmost character of the Midname field is a space (indicating no middle initial), a space appears instead of a middle initial and period.

Yet another common use for the IIF function within a report is to blank out numeric amounts that are equivalent to zero. For example, to display hyphens in place of zero if a numeric field called Balance in a sales database contains a zero, you could use the following expression:

```
IIF(BALANCE=0,"   ---",STR(BALANCE,7,2))
```

The results are shown in this sample report:

```
                   Credit Sales
                   Account Report
Customer Name      Cust.    High       Account
                   Number   Credit     Balance
Smith, A.          1001     2000.00     788.50
Johnson, L.        1002     1200.00     675.00
Jones, C.          1003      900.00     350.00
Jones, J.L.        1004     2000.00    1850.00
Allen, L.          1005     2000.00     312.00
Walker, B.         1006     1300.00    1167.00
Keemis, M.         1007     2000.00     ---
Artis, K.          1008     1200.00     ---
Smith, A.M.        1009     2000.00     220.00
Williams, E.       1010     2000.00     ---
Jones, J.          1011     2000.00     875.00
```

Again, if the precise syntax for these functions is unfamiliar, consult Chapter 14 for more information.

Other Useful Functions

A few additional functions and one system variable that may come in handy with reports and labels are shown here; see Chapter 14 if you need more detailed information.

_PAGENO   This is a special system memory variable that FoxPro interprets as the current page number. To add page numbering to a report, use it at the top or bottom of each page. Simply click the Field tool in the Toolbox, and click and drag to size and place the new field where desired in the Page Header band (for page numbers at the top of the page) or in the Page Footer band (for page numbers at the bottom of the page). Then click the Expression button in the dialog box to open the Expression Builder, and double-click _PAGENO in the Variables list box of the window. Select OK twice to close both dialog boxes and place the page numbers in the report.

DATE
TIME
These functions place the current date or the current time, respectively. You can place them anywhere within a report or label by clicking the Expression button to bring up the Expression Builder, and then choosing DATE() or TIME() from the Date list box in the Expression Builder.

CMONTH
DAY
YEAR
These functions can be combined with the DATE function to produce the current month, day, or year as determined by the PC's clock. For example, the expression

```
CMONTH(DATE())
```

produces the spelled-out name of the current month, while the expression

```
YEAR(DATE())
```

results in the current year. (Note that the YEAR function yields a number; to combine it with character data, you must use it with the STR function.) You can place these functions as expressions within text in a report to produce the full current date.

Designing Form Letters

Designing a report as a form letter lets you generate form letters for names and addresses within a database. You can do this by exporting a file for use with a word processor, but the following method has the advantage of letting you create the form letters without leaving FoxPro.

To design a report that will serve as a form letter, increase the size of the Detail band and place the text of the form letter, along with the necessary fields for the name and address, within this band. Add fields as desired at appropriate locations within the letter. Add a Summary band at the bottom of the report and turn on the New Page option for the Summary band, so that each record in the report prints on a separate page.

To see how this works, create a form letter for the MEMBERS database. Open the database with USE MEMBERS, and create a new report by entering CREATE REPORT LETTER. Maximize the window so you will be able to see more of your work area. Click the rectangle just to the left of the Page Header band, and drag it upwards to the top of the window. Then, click the rectangle just to the left of the Page Footer band and drag it downwards to the bottom of the window. (These rectangles are identified in Figure 11-1.) In the resulting report, all visible space is used by the detail band, as shown in Figure 11-1.

Click the Text tool in the Toolbox, then click at the gridline that is 1 inch down from the top of the window, at a point roughly 1/2 inch in from the left margin. Enter

September 1, 1993

FIGURE 11-1   Report with expanded Detail band

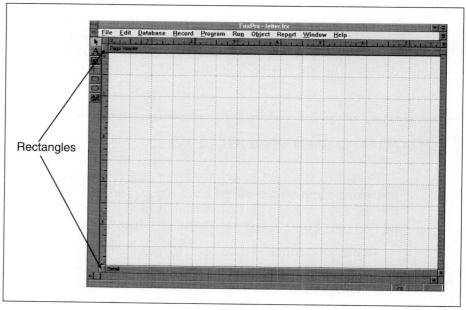

Rectangles

and click anywhere outside the text to deselect it. Then select the Field tool and click and drag just below the date until the box formed by the dotted line is roughly 1/4 inch high and 1 inch long (exact size and placement do not matter for now). When you release the mouse, the Report Expression dialog box appears.

Click the Expression button to open the Expression Builder. In the Expression for Field on Report text box, enter

```
TRIM(FIRSTNAME) + " " + LASTNAME
```

This expression causes the contents of the Firstname field (trimmed of extra blanks) to appear, followed by one space and the contents of the Lastname field. Click OK twice to close both dialog boxes. Click and drag the new field until it is aligned with the typed text, roughly 1/4 inch below the typed text. (You can judge distances by examining the horizontal and vertical rulers that appear at the top and left edges of the window.)

Next, you need to place the Address field in the report. Select the Field tool, then click and drag just below the name fields until the box formed by the dotted line is roughly 1/4 inch high and 2 inches long (again, exact size and placement do not matter for now). When you release the mouse, the Report Expression dialog box appears. Click the Expression button to open the Expression Builder, then double-click the Address field in the Fields list box to place it in the Expression for Field text box. Click OK twice to close the dialog boxes. After the new field appears, click and drag the field until it is directly under the name fields.

To place the city, state, and ZIP-code fields, you'll use an expression much like that used earlier to combine the first and last names on a single line. Select the Field tool in the Toolbox, then click and drag below the address field to place a field roughly 1/4 inch high and 2 inches in length. When you release the mouse, the Report Expression dialog box appears. Click the Expression button to open the Expression Builder. In the Expression for Field on Report text box, enter

```
TRIM(CITY) + ", " + STATE + " " + ZIPCODE
```

This expression causes the contents of the City field (trimmed of extra blanks) to appear, followed by a comma and space, the State field, a space, and the Zipcode field. Click CK twice to close both dialog boxes, then click and drag the new field until it is directly underneath the Address field.

To fill in the rest of the Detail band, you use the Text tool to place a text cursor below the existing name and address, and then you simply type the text of the form letter. The Report Writer does not have the automatic word-wrap capabilities of a word processor, so you must press ENTER at the end of each line. Click the Text tool now (remember, it's the icon containing the letter A), then click roughly 1/2 inch below the left edge of the last field you placed. Type the text shown, pressing ENTER after each line.

```
Dear Member:

We have been pleased to have you as a member of Generic
Videos movie club during the past year. Because you are a
valued member, we would like to extend to you the chance to
renew your membership now at a special reduced rate.
```

Due to an internal memory limit, FoxPro will not let you place more than roughly 255 characters in a single text object. To complete the text of our sample letter, you need to place the second paragraph of text in another text object.

Click anywhere outside of the existing text, then select the Text tool in the Toolbox again. Click roughly 1/2 inch below the existing paragraph, at the left edge. Then, type the second paragraph:

```
If you return the enclosed form within 30 days, you will
save an additional 33% off the regular membership rate.
```

Keep in mind that you can intermix fields within the text of the form letter. Although it is not necessary in this case, you might find such a technique helpful in your own applications. For example, if you had a database with a numeric field containing a customer's past-due amounts, you could have the past-due amount appear within a sentence in the letter. To do this, you would use the Field tool of the Toolbox to add a new field at the point in the letter where the data is to appear. Then, you would enter the field name in the Expression text box or click the Expression button to bring up the Expression Builder and choose the desired name from the list, and finally click OK to place the field.

If you insert numeric fields into the body of your form letters, you will want to get rid of any leading blanks. You can do this by converting the numeric value into a character string, and then using the LTRIM function to trim leading blanks. For example, if you wanted to insert the Tapelimit field into the text of the letter and trim the leading blanks, you could use the Field tool of the Toolbox to add a new field at the desired location, click the Expression button to bring up the Expression Builder, and enter an expression like

```
LTRIM(STR(TAPELIMIT))
```

to accomplish such a task.

One item is still needed: A Group band containing a New Page option must be added, so that each record will print on a separate page. Open the Report menu and choose the Data Grouping option. Click Add, then click Group. Double-click the Social field in the scroll box, then click OK to close the Expression Builder dialog box. Turn on the New Page option by clicking it. Finally, click OK in the dialog box to place the Group band in the report. Choose OK from the resulting dialog box. At this point, your screen should resemble the example shown in Figure 11-2.

Save the completed report by choosing File/Save. When prompted to save the environment information, answer Yes. Then, close the report design window by pressing CTRL+F4.

You can now use the command

```
REPORT FORM LETTER TO PRINT
```

to print a letter for every record in the database. Or, in the interest of saving paper, you may want to limit the scope of your printing by using a command such as

```
REPORT FORM LETTER NEXT 3 TO PRINT
```

FIGURE
11-2

Report layout for form letters

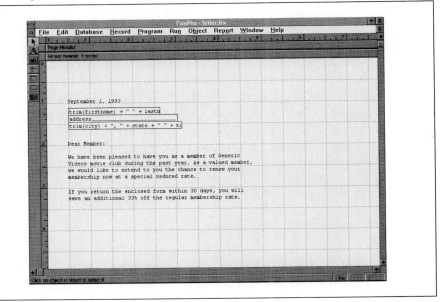

In either case, the result should resemble this sample:

```
September 1, 1993

Carol Robinson
4102 Valley Lane
Falls Church, VA   22043-1234

Dear Member:

We have been pleased to have you as a member of Generic
Videos movie club during the past year. Because you are a
valued member, we would like to extend to you the chance to
renew your video membership now at a special reduced rate.

If you return the enclosed form within 30 days, you will
save an additional 33% off the regular membership rate.
```

You can add more text by placing additional Detail lines as needed; in this example, a closing salutation could have been added in the lines following the last paragraph. Window size does not limit the number of Detail bands you can place in the report; as you reach the bottom of the window, use the scroll bars or drag the box in the vertical ruler down to cause the top of the report's layout to scroll off the screen as more of the bottom comes into view.

You can also change the size of the text used in your reports. If you click a text object you've placed in a report to select it and then choose Object/Font from the menus, the Font dialog box appears.

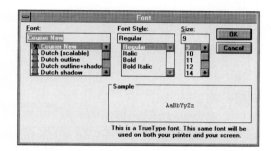

Choose the desired font, font style, and font size from the dialog box, then click OK. Keep in mind that you may want to apply the same kind of font and style changes to the fields used in your report; if you change the fonts for text but not for the field used, the result may be a report with a bizarre combination of character sizes and styles.

Adding Pictures to a Report

You can add pictures to a report, using the Picture tool in the Toolbox. Figure 11-3 shows a report with pictures that are stored in a general field of a FoxPro database. (See Chapter 8 for details on storing pictures in general fields.)

To add pictures contained in a general field to a report, begin designing the report in the manner outlined in Chapter 7. When you are ready to add the general field, click the Picture tool in the Toolbox. Then, click at the desired starting location in the report and drag until the frame that is to contain the picture reaches the desired size. When you release the mouse, the Report Picture dialog box appears on the screen, as shown in Figure 11-4.

FIGURE
11-3

Report using contents of general fields as pictures

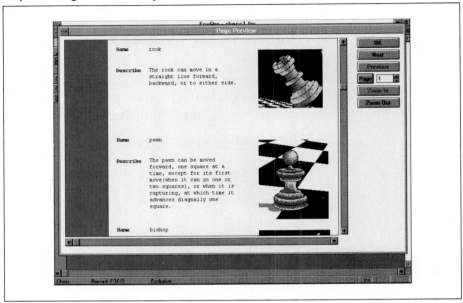

FIGURE
11-4

Report Picture dialog box

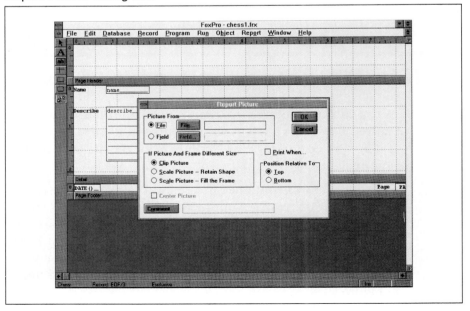

You can use the options within this dialog box to identify the source of the picture (the picture can come from a database field, or from a graphics file), and to tell FoxPro how to handle the display of the picture if the picture and the frame you've placed in the report are of different sizes.

If you want to use the contents of a general field as a picture, click the round Field button and enter the name of the field in the Field text box, or click the rectangular Field button and choose the desired field name from the scroll box (only general-type fields will be visible in the scroll box, since they are the only fields that can contain pictures). Click OK and the picture will appear as a shaded rectangle within the report, as seen in Figure 11-5.

If you want to use a graphics file as the source of the picture, click the round File button and enter the name of the file in the File text box, or click the rectangular File button and choose the file name from the scroll box. Choose OK and the picture appears as a shaded rectangle, again like the one shown in Figure 11-5. If you choose Report/Page Preview or you print the report, the result contains the actual pictures, similar to the example shown in Figure 11-3.

FIGURE 11-5

Report layout with picture added

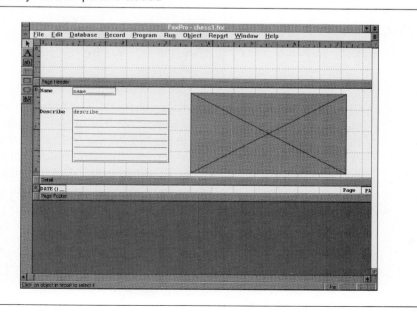

Creating and Printing Mailing Labels

FoxPro provides a feature for designing mailing labels. You can print labels in the common three-across or four-across formats, where the labels are printed in rows of three or four labels each, or you can enter various dimension parameters that allow you to use different label sizes. Label designs are stored on the disk with an .LBX extension.

Creating the Label

To create a mailing label, you choose New from the File menu, select Label from the dialog box that appears, and then click the New button. From the command level, you can enter

```
CREATE LABEL filename
```

where *filename* is the name assigned to the label file. The New Label dialog box appears, asking you to choose a layout.

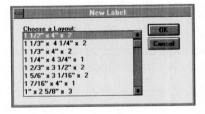

Click the desired label size, then click OK. The layout matching the label size you chose appears in a Report Writer design window, as shown in Figure 11-6. FoxPro uses the Report Writer (introduced in Chapter 7) to design labels, automatically setting the dimensions of the design area and the placement of headers and footers to match the label size you chose in the New Label dialog box. All you need to do is add any desired fields, text, or graphics to the label.

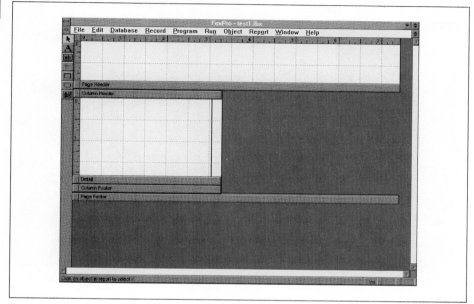

FIGURE 11-6 Report Writer window containing label layout

Adding Fields to the Design Area

To add fields to the design area of the screen, click the Field tool in the Toolbox, then click and drag to place a new field at the desired location. Click the Expression button in the dialog box that appears when you release the mouse. The Expression Builder appears, as shown in Figure 11-7.

Enter the desired field name or an expression (such as a combination of field names) in the window. You can combine two name fields with an expression as you do with reports; for example, an expression such as

```
TRIM(FIRSTNAME) + " " + LASTNAME
```

FIGURE
11-7

Expression Builder dialog box

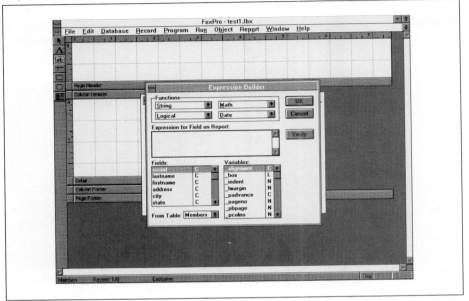

causes the first name to be printed without any blank spaces at the end, followed by a space, followed by the last name. You can also use calculations based on field values. With a numeric field called Salescost, you could enter the expression

```
SALESCOST * .06
```

to calculate a charge that is six percent of the amount contained in the Salescost field. And you can use functions, such as DATE(), to produce the current date.

Tip In many cases, you can save time by using the Quick Report option of the Report menu to automatically place fields in the design. The example that follows shows how you can do this.

You can check the design of the label as you go along by opening the Report menu and choosing Page Preview. When you choose this option, a visual representation of the label appears, as shown in Figure

11-8. Click Next to see additional labels, or click OK to return to the design area.

Saving the Label Design

Once you have placed the desired fields or expressions in the label, you can save the label by choosing Save from the File menu and answering Yes to any environment prompts. If you did not enter a name when you started the process, you are prompted for a file name for the label; then you are returned to the command level.

Printing Labels

Once the label design has been saved, you can print labels by choosing Label from the Database menu or by using the LABEL FORM command.

Use of Page Preview

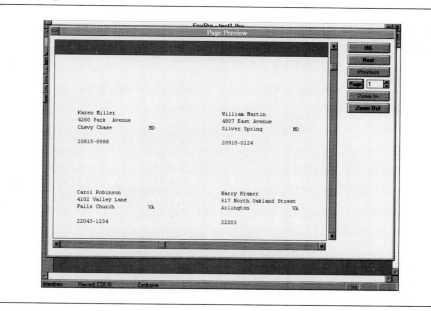

If you choose Label from the Database menu, the Label dialog box shown in Figure 11-9 appears.

Enter the name of the label in the Form text box, or click the Form button and choose the label name from the scroll box. You can select Scope, For, or While to limit the number of records that appear as labels; see Chapter 5 for a discussion of these options. Select the Sample option if you want to print a sample label (containing rows of *X*s) before printing actual data; this is often helpful for aligning labels in your printer. Select the To Printer option to route the labels to the printer; otherwise, they appear only on the screen.

When you are done selecting the options, click OK to begin producing the labels. The Console On option determines whether you will see the labels on the screen as they are printed.

To print labels from the command level, you use the command

LABEL FORM filename [SCOPE] [FOR condition] [WHILE condition] [SAMPLE] [TO PRINT]

FIGURE 11-9

Label dialog box

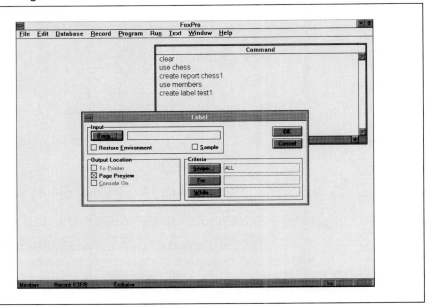

As with other commands, all clauses within the brackets are optional. The SCOPE, FOR, and WHILE clauses are used to limit the records printed, as detailed in Chapter 5. Add the SAMPLE clause to print a sample label (composed of rows of Xs) before you print the data. Add the TO PRINT clause to route the output to the printer.

If you want the labels printed in a certain order, simply index or sort the database first and then use the LABEL FORM command (or the Label option of the Database menu). It is usually wise to print a test run of labels on plain paper first and to visually align the printout with a sheet of blank labels. When the alignment looks correct, you can proceed to print on the labels themselves.

To print labels selectively, you can build a query (detailed in Chapter 6), use the SET FILTER or INDEX ON...FOR commands, or apply view files (as detailed in Chapter 5) that will specify a group of records for which you want to print labels. From the command level, you can combine conditional FOR clauses to print labels for specific records, just as you did with reports. For example, assuming the use of a label file based on the MEMBERS database, the command

```
LABEL FORM MEMBER1 FOR STATE = "VA" TO PRINT
```

prints mailing labels for members in Virginia. The command

```
LABEL FORM MEMBER1 FOR YEAR(EXPIREDATE) = 1993 TO
PRINT
```

prints mailing labels for only those members whose memberships expire in 1993.

A Sample Label

Create a label for use with the MEMBERS database by entering the commands

```
USE MEMBERS
CREATE LABEL MEMBERS1
```

When the New Label dialog box appears, click 1 5/16 by 3 1/16 by 2, and then click OK. The Report Writer appears, containing a layout customized for the desired label. Click the window's Maximize button, so you can see the entire window.

As mentioned earlier, you can manually place fields using the same methods used to place fields in a report. You could place the fields one at a time by using the Field tool, but to save time in this example, you will use the Quick Report option of the Report menu. (As you may recall from Chapter 7, this option automatically places fields in a report's layout.)

Choose Report/Quick Report from the menus now. When the Quick Report dialog box appears, click the row-oriented Field Layout button (remember, it is the button on the right).

Click the Fields check box to turn on this option; the Field Picker dialog box appears. Since not all fields are needed in the label, you will use the Field Picker to choose the desired fields. Double-click the Address, City, State, and Zipcode fields to add these to the Selected Fields portion of the dialog box. (Note that the Lastname and Firstname fields have been intentionally omitted here; later, you will manually add a single field that is a combination of the data in the first-name and last-name fields.) Click OK. Then, in the Quick Report dialog box, click OK again. The chosen fields appear within the new label's layout, as shown in Figure 11-10.

Click the State field to select it, and drag it until it is just to the right of the City field. Click the Zipcode field to select it, then drag it directly upwards until it is immediately below the City field. Finally, with the Zipcode field still selected (or still surrounded by handles), press and hold the SHIFT key and click the Address, City, and State fields. This causes all the fields to be selected at the same time.

Click and hold the mouse button anywhere in any one of the selected fields, and drag the collection about 1/2 inch downwards and 1/4 inch to the right. (Remember, you can use the rulers that appear at the edges of the layout as a guide in measuring distances.) Then, click anywhere outside of the collection to deselect the fields.

Click the Field tool in the Toolbox. Now, click and drag from a point roughly 1/4 inch above the start of the existing address field until you have a new field about 1/4 inch high and 2 inches in length (exact size does not matter for now). When you release the mouse button, the Report

FIGURE
11-10

Initial fields added to label's layout

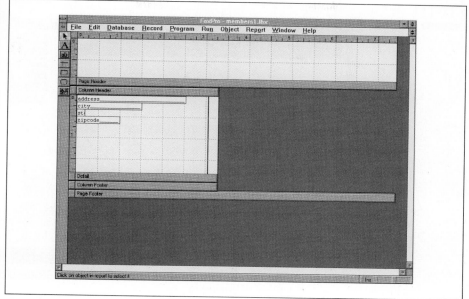

Expression dialog box appears. Click the Expression button to open the Expression Builder. In the Expression for Field on Report text box, enter

```
TRIM(FIRSTNAME) + " " + LASTNAME
```

As with the example used earlier in this chapter, this expression causes the contents of the Firstname field (trimmed of extra blanks) to appear, followed by a space and the contents of the Lastname field.

Click OK twice to close both dialog boxes. Then, click and drag the new field until it is positioned directly above the existing Address field, with the left edge aligned with the left edge of the Address field.

To get an idea of what the mailing labels will look like, you use the Page Preview option of the Report menu. Choose Report/Page Preview now. If you click the Zoom In button after the page preview appears, your screen should resemble the example shown in Figure 11-11.

Use of Page Preview

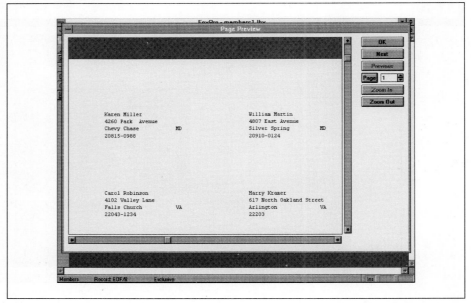

The labels do have one problem: There is a large amount of space between the City and State fields, because there is more space alloted to the City field than there are characters to fill it. You can solve this problem by turning on the Trim option for the field's format.

Click OK to exit the Page Preview mode and return to the design process. Double-click the City field to open the Report Expression dialog box for that field. Click the Format button; the Format dialog box, discussed in Chapter 7, appears. Select the Trim check box, and then click OK to close the Format dialog box. Click OK again to close the Report Expression dialog box.

Save the label by choosing File/Save. (Answer Yes to the environment prompt that appears.)

Try the labels by entering the command

```
LABEL FORM MEMBERS1
```

If you want to see a printed version, add the TO PRINT option at the end of the command. Your results should resemble those shown here:

```
Karen Miller
4260 Park Avenue
Chevy Chase MD 20815-0988


William Martin
4807 East Avenue
Silver Spring MD 20911-0124


Carol Robinson
4102 Valley Lane
Falls Church VA 22043-1234


Harry Kramer
617 North Oakland Street
Arlington VA 22203
```

Modifying Existing Labels

To change an existing label, use

MODIFY LABEL filename

at the command level, where *filename* is the name of the label you wish to change. Or, you can choose Open from the File menu, Label from the Type menu in the resulting dialog box, and the desired label name from the list box. With either method, the Report Design window appears, containing a label layout, as shown earlier in Figure 11-6.

Keep in mind that you can make changes to existing fields by double-clicking the desired field to display the Expression Builder. When the changes are completed, choose Save from the File menu to save the changes.

CHAPTER

Using FoxPro's Relational Powers

FoxPro is a relational database manager, which means that it offers you the ability to use more than one database file at a time, and to define relationships between them. This chapter describes a number of ways you can take advantage of the relational capabilities of FoxPro. For example, with the SET RELATION command, you can link multiple database files through a field that that is common to all of them. You can also establish relationships using FoxPro's Query-by-Example facility.

Ways to Relate Databases in FoxPro

FoxPro is quite flexible in the ways it lets you draw relationships between database files. Some products (like the original dBASE III PLUS) let you relate files at the Command level through the use of the SET RELATION command. Other products (like Borland's Paradox and dBASE IV) let you relate files by building queries within a Query-by-Example design screen. Still other database products (particularly some in the Macintosh environment) let you relate files by drawing a link between the files in some type of a "view" window.

FoxPro is unique in that it lets you use all three of these methods. You can relate files through the RQBE window, detailed in Chapter 6 in the section entitled, "Creating Queries with RQBE"; you can use the SET RELATION command, popular with those who have programmed in the dBASE or the FoxBASE+ programming language; or you can use FoxPro's View window to relate the files.

If you are new to all three methods, you are likely to find the RQBE window to be the easiest; its use is covered towards the end of this chapter. The View window will primarily appeal to those who have used FoxPro for DOS, prior to version 2. If you compare the use of the View window to the use of Query-by-Example, you will find that any relationship that can be established in the View window can be established with more flexibility through the RQBE window. However, for those who are familiar with the older versions of FoxPro for DOS, the View window will be covered in this chapter.

 Tip   If you are working with large databases, there is an inherent speed advantage in using the RQBE window to relate your files. As mentioned in Chapter 6, the RQBE window produces SQL SELECT commands, which automatically make use of FoxPro's Rushmore technology for optimizing queries. From the Command window, you can utilize Rushmore by opening index files to support any FOR statements used after the SET RELATION command. However, you must take the time to ensure that this step is performed. With the RQBE window, the optimization is done automatically.

The examples in this chapter make extensive use of the MEMBERS and RENTALS databases created in Chapters 2 and 3. If you did not create those database files as outlined earlier, do so now before proceeding.

Consider the MEMBERS and RENTALS files. The RENTALS file contains records of the videotapes rented by each member. However, it does not contain the names of the members. The MEMBERS file, on the other hand, contains the full name of each member but no record of the tapes that were rented.

The purchasing manager at Generic Videos needs a report in a format illustrated by Figure 12-1. A report with this kind of information is a *relational report* because it draws its information from more than one file. The MEMBERS file contains the Lastname and Firstname fields. The RENTALS file contains the Title, Dayrented, and Returned fields. In order to produce a report based on these fields, you can establish a relationship that permits the retrieval of data from both files. The data provided through the link can then be used to produce the desired report.

The key to retrieving data from a relational database is to link the desired records on some sort of matching, or common, field. In this context, the term *common field* is used to indicate a field that is present in both database files. Consider an example of two files: one contains records of computer parts, and the other contains purchasers who have ordered certain parts. These files (in this example, called PARTS and

FIGURE 12-1

Desired relational report

Last Name	First Name	Title	Day Rented	Day Returned
Miller	Karen	Star Trek VI	3/5/93	3/6/93
Martin	William	Lethal Weapon III	3/2/93	3/6/93
Robinson	Carol	Who Framed Roger Rabbit?	3/6/93	3/9/93

ORDERS) are typical examples of database files that benefit from the use of relational commands.

The PARTS file contains part numbers, descriptions, and the cost of each part:

Field Name	Type
Partno	Numeric
Descript	Character
Cost	Numeric

The ORDERS file, on the other hand, contains the names and customer numbers of the customers who order computer parts, as well as the part numbers and quantities of the parts that have been ordered:

Field Name	Type
Custno	Numeric
Custname	Character
Partno	Numeric
Quantity	Numeric

If you had a single database file with all of the fields present in these two files, each time one customer ordered a part number that had been previously ordered by another customer, you would have to enter the part description and part cost in the database, even though the same part description and part cost had been entered earlier. To avoid such duplication, you can use two files and link the files together, based upon the contents of the common Partno field, as illustrated in Figure 12-2.

With all relational databases, establishing a link between common fields allows you to match a particular record in one file with a corresponding record in another file. Take Generic Videos' problem of the rental tapes again. If you needed to know which tapes Carol Robinson rented, you could do this visually by looking at the data from the two files, shown in Figure 12-3. To find the answer manually, you would first look at the listing from the MEMBERS file and find the social security number for Ms. Robinson, which is 232-55-1234. You would then refer to the listing of the RENTALS file and look for all the records with a matching social security number. The process of matching on social

FIGURE 12-2

Concept of relational database

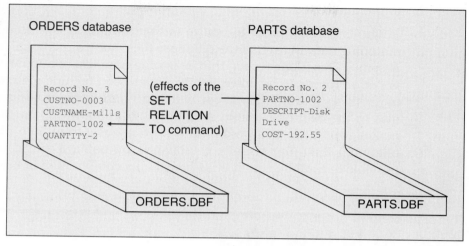

FIGURE 12-3

RENTALS and MEMBERS database files

Record#	SOCIAL	LASTNAME	FIRSTNAME	CITY	STATE
1	123-44-8976	Miller	Karen	Chevy Chase	MD
2	121-33-9876	Martin	William	Silver Spring	MD
3	232-55-1234	Robinson	Carol	Falls Church	VA
4	901-77-3456	Kramer	Harry	Arlington	VA
5	121-90-5432	Moore	Ellen	Takoma Park	MD
6	495-00-3456	Zachman	David	Falls Church	VA
7	343-55-9821	Robinson	Benjamin	Washington	DC
8	876-54-3210	Hart	Wendy	Fairfax	VA

Record#	SOCIAL	TITLE	DAYRENTED	RETURNED
1	123-44-8976	Star Trek VI	03/05/93	03/06/93
2	121-33-9876	Lethal Weapon III	03/02/93	03/06/93
3	232-55-1234	Who Framed Roger Rabbit?	03/06/93	03/09/93
4	901-77-3456	Doc Hollywood	03/04/93	03/05/93
5	121-90-5432	Fried Green Tomatoes	03/01/93	03/06/93
6	495-00-3456	Wayne's World	03/04/91	03/09/93
7	343-55-9821	Prince of Tides	03/06/93	03/12/93
8	876-54-3210	Lethal Weapon III	03/07/93	03/08/93
9	123-44-8976	Friday 13th Part XXVII	03/14/93	03/16/93
10	121-33-9876	Mambo Kings	03/15/93	03/17/93
11	232-55-1234	Prince of Tides	03/17/93	03/19/93
12	901-77-3456	Coming to America	03/14/93	03/18/93
13	121-90-5432	Prince of Tides	03/16/93	03/17/93
14	495-00-3456	Star Trek VI	03/18/93	03/19/93
15	343-55-9821	Wayne's World	03/19/93	03/20/93
16	876-54-3210	Mambo Kings	03/16/91	03/18/93

security numbers between the files could be repeated for every member in the database.

The important point to realize is that without a field that contains matching data in each of the database files, such a relational link is not possible. This is one reason that designing complex, relational databases is not a process to be taken lightly. Unless you include matching fields in the files you want to link, you will find it impossible to access multiple files in the desired manner. As Figure 12-3 illustrates, the Social field makes it possible to access data simultaneously from both files. While relational links are usually established by using a single field, it is possible to establish such links based on a combination of fields.

How to Relate Files

The relational powers provided by FoxPro are easily implemented from inside the Command window. You can link databases together with the SET RELATION command, which links the files through a matching field in the manner just described. In our example, you will draw a relation between the RENTALS database and the MEMBERS database by linking the common Social field. Then, whenever you move to a record in the RENTALS database, the record pointer in the MEMBERS database will move to the record that contains the same social security number as the record in RENTALS. As you will see shortly, this link allows you to display matching data from two files with a LIST command. You can also take advantage of a relational link within the reports or labels you create.

The format of the SET RELATION command is

SET RELATION TO (*key-expression*) INTO (*alias*)
[ADDITIVE]

The *key-expression* is the common field present in both databases. The *alias* is usually the name of the other database that the active database is to be linked to. Note that ADDITIVE is an optional clause, needed only when you are setting a relation in more than one file at a time.

The overall process of linking two databases using a common field involves the following steps:

1. Open the file from which you want to establish the relation in one work area.

2. In another work area, open the file you wish to link to the first file.

3. Activate an index file based on the field (or expression) that is common to both files.

4. Use the SET RELATION command to establish the link.

Once the link has been established, any movement of the record pointer in the active file (also known as the parent file) will cause FoxPro to seek the corresponding record in the related file (also known as the child file.) The nature of such a relationship can be seen in the example shown in the following paragraphs.

One important requirement of the SET RELATION command is that you must index the related file on the common field. In our case, the MEMBERS database must be indexed on the Social field. Enter the following commands now to create an index file for the MEMBERS database, based on the social security field:

```
USE MEMBERS
INDEX ON SOCIAL TO SOCIALS
```

To work with multiple database files, you need to open more than one database file at a time. As mentioned in Chapter 9, you do this by using different work areas in which to hold the database files. You choose the work area with the SELECT command; for example, entering SELECT 2 at the Command level chooses work area 2. (If no SELECT command is used, work area 1 is chosen by default.)

Open the RENTALS and MEMBERS database files by using the following commands:

```
CLOSE DATABASES
SELECT 1
USE RENTALS
USE MEMBERS IN 2 INDEX SOCIALS
```

An explanation of the last command is in order. The USE MEMBERS IN 2 portion of the command line tells FoxPro to open the database file MEMBERS, but to open it in work area 2 without actually switching work areas (hence the "IN 2" designation). The INDEX SOCIALS option tells FoxPro to open, and apply, the SOCIALS index file you just created.

It is now possible to link the files, using the Social field, with the SET RELATION TO command. The RENTALS database is the active database, so you will link the MEMBERS database to the RENTALS database. Enter

```
SET RELATION TO SOCIAL INTO MEMBERS
```

No changes are immediately visible, but FoxPro has linked the files. To see the effects, enter the commands

```
GO 3
DISPLAY
```

and you see the third record in the RENTALS database. The record indicates that a member having the social security number of 232-55-1234 rented *Who Framed Roger Rabbit?* To see just who this member is, enter these commands:

```
SELECT 2
DISPLAY
```

The MEMBERS database (open in work area 2) becomes the active database. The record pointer will be at record 3 (the record containing the social security number 232-55-1234), showing that the member in question is Carol Robinson.

Get back to the RENTALS database with these commands:

```
SELECT 1
GO 2
DISPLAY
```

Again, because of the relation, FoxPro will have automatically found a matching social security number in the MEMBERS database. You can verify this by entering these commands:

```
SELECT 2
DISPLAY
```

Wherever you move in the RENTALS database, FoxPro will try to move the record pointer to a record with a matching social security number in the MEMBERS database. If FoxPro cannot find a match according to the relation that you have specified, the record pointer will be positioned at the end of the database. (At the end of a file, all fields are blank. You can use this fact to test for failures to find a match by listing key fields from both databases and seeing whether they are blank.)

You can retrieve data in the related file by including the alias name and pointer (that is, the file name followed by a period) along with the field name. In the expression

```
MEMBERS.FIRSTNAME
```

the file name MEMBERS is the alias, while FIRSTNAME is the field name. The period is used as a pointer. To see how this works, try the following commands:

```
SELECT 1
LIST MEMBERS.LASTNAME, TITLE, DAYRENTED, RETURNED
```

the results are shown here:

SOCIAL	TITLE	DAYRENTED	RETURNED
123-44-8976	Star Trek VI	03/05/93	03/06/93
121-33-9876	Lethal Weapon III	03/02/93	03/06/93
232-55-1234	Who Framed Roger Rabbit	03/06/93	03/09/93
901-77-3456	Doc Hollywood	03/04/93	03/05/93
121-90-5432	Fried Green Tomatoes	03/01/93	03/06/93
495-00-3456	Wayne's World	03/04/93	03/09/93
343-55-9821	Prince of Tides	03/06/93	03/12/93
876-54-3210	Lethal Weapon III	03/07/93	03/08/93
123-44-8976	Friday 13th Part XXVII	03/14/93	03/16/93
121-33-9876	Mambo Kings	03/15/93	03/17/93
232-55-1234	Prince of Tides	03/17/93	03/19/93
901-77-3456	Coming to America	03/14/93	03/18/93
121-90-5432	Prince of Tides	03/16/93	03/17/93
495-00-3456	Star Trek VI	03/18/93	03/19/93
343-55-9821	Wayne's World	03/19/93	03/20/93
876-54-3210	Mambo Kings	03/16/93	03/18/93

This shows that using the SET RELATION command to establish a relational link, combined with the use of an alias and pointer, can provide a powerful tool for obtaining data from multiple, related files. You could add the TO PRINT option at the end of the LIST command to generate a printed list like this one.

When working with related files in this manner, keep in mind that you can test for mismatched records (such as an entry in the RENTALS file with no matching social security number) by listing the common field from each of the related files. For example, the command

```
LIST RENTALS.SOCIAL, MEMBERS.SOCIAL,
MEMBERS.LASTNAME
```

should produce a listing that includes a matching MEMBERS record for each entry in the RENTALS file. If a member name and social security number turn up blank next to an entry in the RENTALS listing, it is clear that a mismatch exists. Such a mismatch could be caused by a social security number entered incorrectly in the RENTALS file.

A Warning About Index Files

When you are working with related files, it is completely up to you to make sure that any indexes used in a SET RELATION command are kept updated. If you or other users open a database without using an accompanying index file, and add or edit records, the resulting incomplete index files can cause incorrect results when you are trying to establish relationships or generate relational reports. If in doubt, use REINDEX to rebuild any indexes you are using.

Using View Files to Store Relations

If you are going to establish relationships from the Command window (as opposed to creating them by running a program), keep in mind the CREATE VIEW FROM ENVIRONMENT command. This command, introduced in Chapter 5, stores to disk a record of all open databases and index files and any existing relationships. You can save much repetitive typing by saving the relationship as part of such a view file and then using the SET VIEW command to open the database files and index files and re-establish the relationship at the same time. You save the environment, including the relational link, by entering the command

CREATE VIEW *filename* FROM ENVIRONMENT

where *filename* is the name you assign to the view file. Later, you open the databases, index files, and the relational link by entering the command

SET VIEW TO *filename*

where *filename* is the name that you gave to the view file earlier. If you followed the prior example in establishing a relational link between MEMBERS and RENTALS, you can save that information in a view file now. Enter the following command:

```
CREATE VIEW RELATE1 FROM ENVIRONMENT
```

Then enter **CLOSE DATABASES** to close all the open files. If you now enter the commands

```
USE RENTALS
LIST MEMBERS.LASTNAME, TITLE, DAYRENTED
```

you get an "Alias MEMBERS not found" error message because the MEMBERS file is not open and no relationship exists. Enter **CLOSE DATABASES** again to close the open file and start from scratch. (This is not a requirement, but doing so makes it clear that the SET VIEW command will be all you need to open all files and re-establish the link.) Enter the command

```
SET VIEW TO RELATE1
```

Then retry the earlier command:

```
LIST MEMBERS.LASTNAME, TITLE, DAYRENTED, RETURNED
```

The results show that the files are open and the relationship has been re-established. You can verify this in another way with the DISPLAY STATUS command. Enter **DISPLAY STATUS** now. The first portion of the display you see should resemble the following:

```
Processor is INTEL 80386
Currently Selected Table:
Select area:  1, Table in Use: C:\FOXPROW\RENTALS.DBF
```

```
        Alias: RENTALS
Structural CDX file:    C:\FOXPROW\RENTALS.CDX
          Index tag:    SOCIAL    Key: SOCIAL
          Index tag:    TITLE    Key: TITLE
          Index tag:    DAYRENTED    Key: DAYRENTED
          Index tag:    RETURNED    Key: RETURNED
       Lock(s): Exclusive USE
   Related into:    Members
       Relation:    social
```

The first lines of the listing show the names of the open databases, the index files in use, and the relationship between the files.

Creating Relational Reports

As shown earlier, you can use the LIST...TO PRINT command to generate simple listings of relational data; you must include the alias (file name) and pointer (period) when you are retrieving data from the related file. The same technique can be used for designing relational reports. When you enter a field name or an expression into the Expression window during the creation of the report, you must again include the alias and pointer symbols to indicate a field that is in a related database.

As an example, consider a report similar to the one shown in Figure 12-1, but using a form-oriented layout. You could quickly construct such a report by opening the files, establishing the relationship, creating a new report, and adding the Lastname and Firstname fields to the report design, along with the file name and pointer.

To try this, first make sure the relationship described in the prior example is still in effect. (If not, use the SET VIEW TO RELATE1 command). Then enter

```
CREATE REPORT RELATE1
```

to start a new report. Maximize the Report Writer window by clicking the Maximize button. Open the Report menu and choose Quick Report. Click the Form Layout button (it's the one on the right side of the dialog box), and then click OK in the dialog box. The report appearing onscreen should resemble the one shown in Figure 12-4.

Quick Report based on RENTALS file

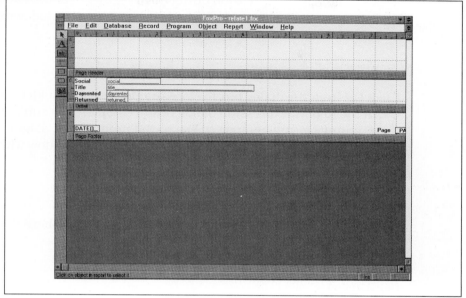

Because the RENTALS file is the active database, the quick report automatically placed all fields from that database into the report layout. Using the file name and pointer combination, you can replace the rather ambiguous social security number identifier with the actual name of the member from the related MEMBERS file. Click the word "social" and press the DEL key to delete it; then click the Social field and press DEL to remove the field.

Click the text tool in the Toolbox, then click just above the Title heading, and type **NAME**. Then click the Selection tool in the Toolbox, click the word you just typed (to select the entire word), and choose Object/Font from the menus. Click Bold in the dialog box that appears and then click OK. These steps result in a heading, Name, which appears in the same style as the other headings.

Click the Field tool in the Toolbox. Next, click just below the bottom of the Page Header at the same horizontal position at which the remaining fields begin, and drag the mouse until you have a new field of roughly the same length and width as the Title field.

When you release the mouse, the Report Expression dialog box appears. Click the Expression button to bring up the Expression Builder. With the cursor flashing within the text box, enter the following expression:

```
TRIM(MEMBERS.FIRSTNAME) + " " + MEMBERS.LASTNAME
```

Click OK from the dialog box to close the Expression Builder. Then, click OK in the Report Expression dialog box to complete the entry. Next, save the report with CTRL+S (answer Yes to the prompt that asks if you want to save the environment information), and close the window with CTRL+F4. Finally, enter the command

```
REPORT FORM RELATE1
```

to see the results. They should resemble those shown here:

```
Member      Karen Miller
Title       Star Trek VI
Day rented  03/05/93
Returned    03/06/93

Member      William Martin
Title       Lethal Weapon III
Day rented  03/02/93
Returned    03/06/93

Member      Carol Robinson
Title       Who Framed Roger Rabbit?
Day rented  03/06/93
Returned    03/09/93

Member      Harry Kramer
Title       Doc Hollywood
Day rented  03/04/93
Returned    03/05/93

Member      Ellen Moore
Title       Fried Green Tomatoes
Day rented  03/01/93
Returned    03/06/93

Member      David Zachman
Title       Wayne's World
Day rented  03/04/93
```

```
Returned     03/09/93

Member      Benjamin Robinson
Title       Prince of Tides
Day rented  03/06/93
Returned    03/12/93

Member      Wendy Hart
Title       Lethal Weapon III
Day rented  03/07/93
Returned    03/08/93

Member      Karen Miller
Title       Friday 13th Part XXVII
Day rented  03/14/93
Returned    03/16/93

Member      William Martin
Title       Mambo Kings
Day rented  03/15/93
Returned    03/17/93

Member      Carol Robinson
Title       Prince of Tides
Day rented  03/17/93
Returned    03/19/93

Member      Harry Kramer
Title       Coming to America
Day rented  03/14/93
Returned    03/18/93

Member      Ellen Moore
Title       Prince of Tides
Day rented  03/16/93
Returned    03/17/93

Member      David Zachman
Title       Star Trek VI
Day rented  03/18/93
Returned    03/19/93

Member      Benjamin Robinson
Title       Wayne's World
Day rented  03/19/93
Returned    03/20/93
```

```
Member      Wendy Hart
Title       Mambo Kings
Day rented  03/16/93
Returned    03/18/93
```

If desired, you could improve a report like this one by adding grouping to the report, as described in Chapter 7. You could index the RENTALS file on the Social field and then group the report on that field, using the member name in the group heading. You can use this same technique with labels, if desired. Just include the file name and pointer whenever you are referencing a field that is not in the active database.

Remember that all needed files must be open, and the relationship established, before you can produce a relational report or label. If, for example, you now enter **CLOSE DATABASES**, then open just one database, such as MEMBERS, and try to print this same report, you will get an "Alias not found" error message. This indicates that because the related file has not been opened and the relationship re-established, FoxPro cannot get at the external fields specified in the report design and therefore cannot retrieve the requested data.

The use of SET VIEW, combined with stored reports, provides you with a powerful capability for generating relational reports when needed. You can continue to add and edit data within the databases; whenever a relational report is needed, you can use commands like

```
SET VIEW TO RELATE1
REPORT FORM RELATE1 TO PRINT
```

to generate the needed data. Note that there is no need to name your view files and your reports with the same name, but it is often helpful in keeping track of which files are used with which reports. Also, when you save your report, a view file with the same name as the report is automatically created. This lets you use the ENVIRONMENT clause along with the REPORT FORM command to automatically re-establish needed file relationships before producing the report. For example, if you enter

```
REPORT FORM RELATE1 TO PRINT ENVIRONMENT
```

the ENVIRONMENT clause at the end of the command tells FoxPro to look for the view file with the same name as the report. That view file is put into effect automatically before the report is generated.

Because a view file is automatically created when you save the report, you should make sure any desired relationships exist *before* you create a relational report. It is possible to create and save a relational report without having established the relationships by manually entering the file names and pointers in your expressions. But if you do this, the saved view file won't contain the relationships, and the REPORT FORM...ENVIRONMENT command will result in an error message.

A Warning About SET FIELDS and dBASE

Those who are familiar with Ashton-Tate's dBASE products may be aware that they let you use the SET FIELDS command as a substitute for specifying external file names and pointers. In dBASE III PLUS or dBASE IV, you can use SET FIELDS to establish fields from related files once; from then on, you can drop the file name and pointer prefix from the field name, and dBASE will still find the data. As a brief example, using the same databases that have been used throughout this text, you could enter the following commands in dBASE IV:

```
SELECT 1
USE RENTALS
USE MEMBERS IN 2 INDEX SOCIAL
SET RELATION TO SOCIAL INTO MEMBERS
SET FIELDS TO MEMBERS.LASTNAME,
MEMBERS.FIRSTNAME, TITLE, DAYRENTED
```

From that point on, you could reference the Lastname and Firstname fields without repeating their file name and pointer prefixes. You could also create reports based on expressions that use such abbreviated references.

What's important to note is that FoxPro for Windows and its predecessors, FoxPro for DOS and FoxBase Plus, do *not* support this relational use of the SET FIELDS command. You can enter the SET FIELDS command in FoxPro just as shown for dBASE, and you will not get an error message. However, if you try to access the external fields without the file name and pointer prefix, it will not work. If you plan to use dBASE programs that use the SET FIELD command in this way, you will need to make changes to those programs so that they instead use the file name and pointer method of reference.

Getting Selective Data from Related Files

You can use the same techniques covered in Chapters 5 and 6—the SET FILTER, FOR, and WHILE clauses, the INDEX ON...FOR command, and queries—to retrieve selective data from multiple files. One of the biggest challenges in working with multiple files at the same time is in keeping track of where you are. This is particularly true when you want to retrieve specific data, because the commands you use will apply to the active file unless you include file names and pointers as a prefix to the field names. If, for example, you use the commands

```
SELECT 1
USE RENTALS
USE MEMBERS IN 2 INDEX SOCIALS
SET RELATION TO SOCIAL INTO MEMBERS
```

to establish a relationship, and you then apply a filter with a command like

```
SET FILTER TO TITLE = "Fried Green Tomatoes"
```

you can then LIST or report out selective data, based on the condition you just applied to the active file (RENTALS).

If you wanted to instead apply a filter to the MEMBERS file, you would need to do things a little differently. You would have to apply a filter condition within that work area. To do this, you would have to include a file name and pointer in the filter condition. For example, while the RENTALS file is active, you could enter the commands

```
SET FILTER TO MEMBERS.LASTNAME = "Kramer"
GO TOP
```

followed by a LIST command, to limit retrieved rentals to only those for Mr. Kramer.

Keep in mind that a filter condition is only saved along with a view if it was established from the active work area. If you establish a filter condition with SET FILTER, switch work areas, and then save the environment to a view file, the filter condition will not be saved in the view.

Relating More Than Two Database Files

FoxPro lets you link as many database files as you need (up to its limit of 225 possible open database files) to obtain the results you require. One common example of an application requiring more than two files is a system that tracks customers, sales, and product inventory. A complete sales-tracking system is commonly built around at least three database files: one containing customer data such as names and addresses, a second containing product data such as descriptions and prices, and a third containing a record of each item purchased by a customer. The three database structures shown here contain the fields that are required, at a minimum, to accomplish such a task:

ITEMS.DBF	ORDERS.DBF	CUSTOMER.DBF
Stockno	Custno	Custno
Descript	Stockno	Name
Cost	Quantity	Address
	Date	City
		State
		Zip

Such a database system, properly designed, could meet a variety of needs. Inventory could be tracked using the ITEMS file; reports summarizing total sales could be generated using the ITEMS and ORDERS files; and mass mailings to customers could be handled with the CUSTOMER file. The task of generating customer invoices is a prime example of a relational application demanding the use of three files; the data listed in an invoice would need to come from three different databases, as illustrated in Figure 12-5.

An example of the needed relationships can be demonstrated if you duplicate the following database structures and the sample data contained in the files. (If you decide to duplicate this example, enter a CLEAR ALL command first, to clear the previous view file and its relations from memory.) The structure of ITEMS.DBF is as follows:

FIGURE
12-5

Invoice and supporting databases

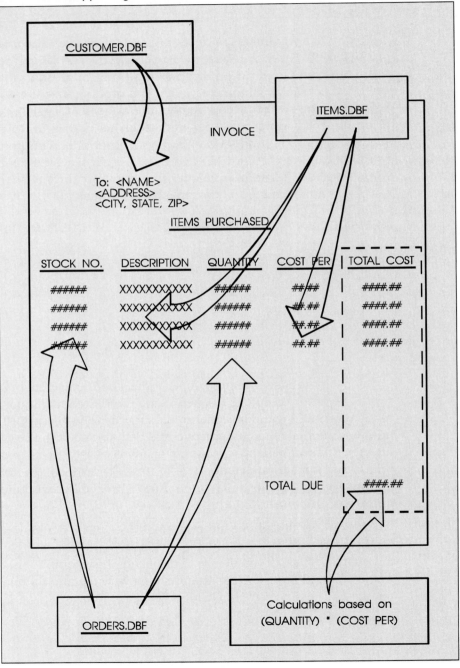

Field Name	Type	Width	Decimals
Stockno	character	4	
Descript	character	25	
Cost	numeric	7	2

Add this data to it:

Stockno	Descript	Cost
2001	leather handbag, black	89.95
2002	attache case	139.95
2003	suitcase, overnighter	159.95
2004	carry-on bag, leather	69.95

The structure of ORDERS.DBF is shown here:

Field Name	Type	Width	Decimals
Custno	character	4	
Stockno	character	4	
Quantity	numeric	2	0
Date	date		

Add this data to it:

Custno	Stockno	Quantity	Date
9001	2001	1	03/05/93
9001	2004	1	03/05/93
9002	2002	2	03/06/93
9004	2004	1	03/04/93
9003	2001	1	03/05/93
9001	2002	1	03/05/93
9003	2003	1	03/04/93
9005	2002	1	03/06/93
9002	2004	2	03/06/93

CUSTOMER.DBF has this structure (see the next paragraph for hints on creating this file):

Field Name	Type	Width
Lastname	character	15
Firstname	character	15
Address	character	25
City	character	15
State	character	2
Zipcode	character	10
Custno	character	4

To quickly duplicate the example CUSTOMER.DBF file, you can copy existing data from the MEMBERS file with the following commands:

```
CLOSE DATABASES
USE MEMBERS
COPY TO CUSTOMER NEXT 5 FIELDS LASTNAME, FIRSTNAME,
ADDRESS, CITY, STATE, ZIPCODE
USE CUSTOMER
MODIFY STRUCTURE
```

When the Database Structure dialog box appears, add a new field:

```
CUSTNO          character     4
```

and then save the structure. Then enter

```
BROWSE FIELDS CUSTNO, LASTNAME, FIRSTNAME FREEZE
CUSTNO
```

to add customer numbers to the existing records, as shown here:

```
Custno   Name
9001     Miller, Karen
9002     Martin, William
9003     Robinson, Carol
9004     Kramer, Harry
9005     Moore, Ellen
```

Once you have created databases similar to these, the entry of day-to-day sales, new customers, and changes to inventory can be performed on each file individually. Applications can be created, as detailed in Chapter 13, for adding and editing data. The ability of FoxPro to display data in multiple windows can come in handy here. If, for example, you enter

```
SELECT 1
USE ITEMS
BROWSE
```

and then click anywhere in the Command window (or just press CTRL+F2 to switch back to the Command window), you can next enter

```
SELECT 2
USE ORDERS
CHANGE
```

You can then move the windows until you have a clear view of both, and add new orders while viewing the descriptions in the inventory database, as shown in Figure 12-6. When done, remember that you can close a window by selecting it by name from the Window menu to make it active and then pressing ESC.

Display of data in multiple windows

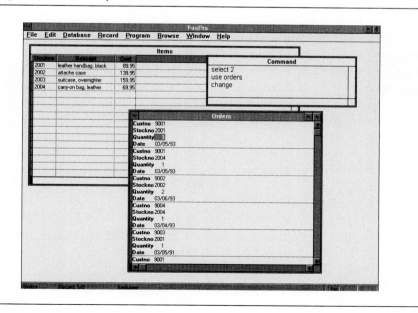

Most reports generated from this type of database will be of a relational nature. A visual representation of the needed links appears in Figure 12-7.

Assuming you are retrieving order data for reports or invoices, you could establish the relational links with these commands:

```
CLOSE DATABASES
SELECT 1
USE ITEMS
INDEX ON STOCKNO TO BYSTOCK
SELECT 2
USE ORDERS
INDEX ON CUSTNO TO BYCUST
SELECT 3
USE CUSTOMER
INDEX ON CUSTNO TO CUSTOM
SELECT 2
SET RELATION TO CUSTNO INTO CUSTOMER
SET RELATION TO STOCKNO INTO ITEMS ADDITIVE
```

Note the use of the ADDITIVE clause in the second SET RELATION command. Once a relation exists from an active file, the ADDITIVE clause must be used to establish a second relation. Without this clause, the second SET RELATION command would simply override the first.

Map of relationships

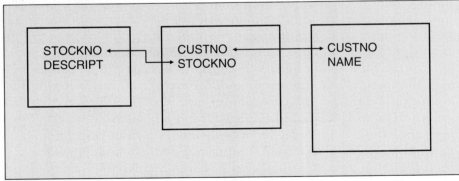

FIGURE 12-7

At this point, the ORDERS file is the active file. For any record located in the ORDERS file, the corresponding customer name and address can be retrieved from the CUSTOMER file, and the corresponding item cost and description can be retrieved from the ITEMS file. You can obtain a columnar listing of sales with a command like the one shown here. The OFF option turns off the record numbers, so each record will still fit on one line.

```
LIST CUSTOMER.LASTNAME, DATE, QUANTITY, ITEMS.DESCRIPT, ITEMS.COST OFF
CUSTOMER.LASTNAME       DATE       QUANTITY ITEMS.DESCRIPT           ITEMS.COST
Miller              03/05/93       1 leather handbag, black             89.95
Miller              03/05/93       1 carry-on bag, leather              69.95
Miller              03/05/93       1 attache case                      139.95
Martin              03/06/93       2 attache case                      139.95
Martin              03/06/93       2 carry-on bag, leather              69.95
Robinson            03/05/93       1 leather handbag, black             89.95
Robinson            03/04/93       1 suitcase, overnighter             159.95
Kramer              03/04/93       1 carry-on bag, leather              69.95
Moore               03/06/93       1 attache case                      139.95
```

An alternative is to lay out all desired fields in a report resembling an invoice, including file names and pointers (where necessary) to refer to the related files. Since the ORDERS database is the active file, any report would include one group of orders for each customer (unless you applied some type of filter first).

One significant point is the overall complexity involved in day-to-day management of a system of this nature. Adding and updating all three files, as needed, from the Command window will require all users of such a system to be familiar with FoxPro commands. With the staff turnover typical in today's workplace, this could be a problem.

Also, there is virtually no referential integrity in a relational system maintained entirely from the Command level. In a nutshell, this means that there is nothing to protect users from entering corrupt data, such as an incorrect social security number, that will not match up with the related records in other files. The same problem applies to edits of existing data. For example, if a user of the system deletes a customer from the CUSTOMER file while orders still exist for that customer in the ORDERS file, later invoices will contain orders for which no matching customer name can be found.

The answer to these problems lies in programming, the subject of the chapters to follow. With programming techniques, you can build applications that guard against mistakes such as inadvertantly deleting customers who have existing orders. Such applications can also present menu choices to novice users, shielding them from the complexity of the FoxPro command language.

Querying from Multiple Databases with RQBE

You can easily design a query based on multiple databases using the RQBE window, discussed at length in Chapter 6. The following paragraphs describe the overall process; after the description is an example you can follow, using the MEMBERS and RENTALS database files.

To query from two databases, first bring up the RQBE window, either by entering CREATE QUERY or by choosing New from the File menu, selecting Query in the dialog box that appears, and choosing New. If you are asked to select a database, choose the first database that you will be working with. If a database is already open, you will not be asked this question.

Once you choose the database, the RQBE window appears. The first database you have selected appears by name in the Tables box in the upper-left corner of the RQBE window. To add a second database to form a relational query, click on the Add button. The Open File dialog box will again appear, and you can choose the next desired database from the list box of databases in the dialog box. Once you click Open, a new dialog box appears, asking you for the RQBE Join Condition, as shown in Figure 12-8. In this dialog box, you must specify the condition that will be used to link the files together—that is, the basis of the relationship.

Click on the first drop-down list box, and a list of fields from the first database will appear. Click the field that will be used to establish the

FIGURE 12-8 RQBE Join dialog box

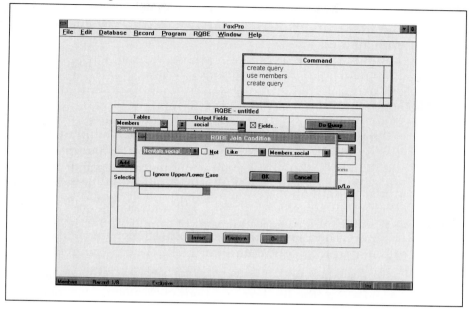

link. The list box in the center assumes that the "Like" condition is desired. Unless you are linking files based on a very unusual relationship, this default will be what you desire. Click on the drop-down list at the far right, to display a list of fields from the second database. Choose the field that you wish to link to its matching field in the first database. Then click the OK button.

At this point, you can select the fields that you want to place in the query. By default, all fields from the first database you opened will appear in the query. However, when working with relational queries, you will often want to pick and choose fields from both databases. To do so, click the Fields check box. When the RQBE Select Fields dialog box appears, use the list box of field names, along with the Move, Remove, and Remove All options, to place the desired fields in the Selected Output area. When the desired set of fields is visible in that area, choose OK.

At this point, you can choose any other desired options in the RQBE window, and then choose the Do Query option to produce the query results. Remember that you can specify where the query appears using the Output To option in the RQBE window. (See Chapters 6, "Creating Queries with RQBE," and 7, "Introducing Reports," for specifics on using the Output To options and for details on designing reports to be used with your queries.)

A Sample Relational Query

Returning to our Generic Videos scenario, suppose you want to get a listing of each member's name, along with the names of all the tapes this member has rented. You can generate this report from both the MEMBERS and RENTALS databases simultaneously by linking them through their common (Social) field. To do so, try the following steps: In the Command window, enter **CLEAR ALL** to close any databases that may be open. Then, enter **USE MEMBERS** to open the membership database. Enter **CREATE QUERY** to open the RQBE window and begin a new query.

Click Add. When the Open File dialog box appears, click RENTALS.DBF in the list box and then click Open. In a moment, the RQBE Join Condition dialog box appears, as shown earlier in Figure 12-8. In this case, FoxPro assumes that the Social field should be used to establish the relationship, since this is the common field.

Next, click OK. The complete expression needed, "Rentals.social Like Members.social," appears in the Select Criteria area at the bottom of the RQBE window, as shown in Figure 12-9.

Click the Fields check box. When the RQBE Select Fields dialog box appears, click Remove All. Doing so will remove all fields from the Selected Output area.

In the Fields in Table list box (at the left side of the dialog box), select the following fields, one by one, and move them into the Selected Output area: MEMBERS.LASTNAME, MEMBERS.FIRSTNAME, RENTALS.TITLE, RENTALS.DAYRENTED, and RENTALS.RETURNED. (You move each field name by clicking on it and then clicking the Move button.) When all these fields are visible in the Selected Output area at the right side of the dialog box, click OK.

Click the Do Query option. The results of the relational query will appear in a Browse window, assuming that the Output Options area is

FIGURE
12-9

An RQBE window containing criteria needed to relate files

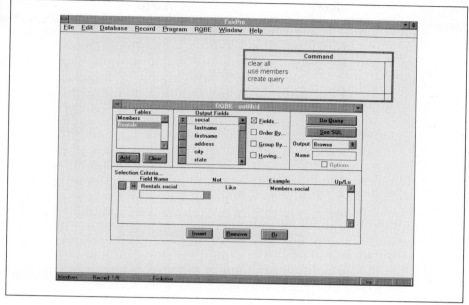

set to Browse. Your results should resemble those shown in the example in Figure 12-10.

Keep in mind that you can use any of the techniques discussed in Chapter 6 to further refine your relational queries. You can specify conditions for which records are to appear in the query results, and you can specify a sort order. Refer to Chapter 6 for more details on these techniques. See Chapter 7 for details on designing reports that can be used with the Output option of the RQBE window.

Using the View Window

Another way you can relate files is by using the View window. This method is not quite as simple as using the RQBE window to build a query because with the View window, your files must be indexed on the fields that are the basis of the relationship. (The RQBE window takes care of

FIGURE
12-10

The results of a sample relational query

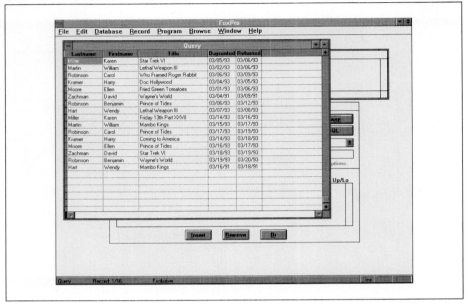

this indexing requirement automatically.) Nevertheless, you may prefer to link files using the View window, especially if you have used it with earlier versions of FoxPro for DOS. If you are going to duplicate the examples that follow, first close (without saving) any open queries by pressing ESC and then enter **CLEAR ALL** in the Command window to close any open files.

To relate databases using the View window, first open the View window by choosing View from the Window menu. The View window appears:

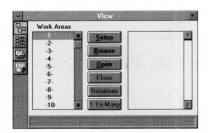

In the View window, you see multiple work areas, numbered from 1 to 225. A database file can be opened in each of these work areas. The option buttons that appear at the left side of the View window are, from top to bottom, the View, Options On/Off, Files, and Miscellaneous Values buttons. The View button is used to get back to displaying View information in this window after using one of the other buttons. The Options On/Off button displays a window of environment settings that can be turned on or off, such as the bell, and the use of the ESC key to interrupt programs. The Files button displays a Files window that you can use to set the default drive and path. The Miscellaneous Values button displays a window where you can change assorted settings in FoxPro, such as the symbol used for currency and the tone used for the bell.

When the View options are visible, the buttons in the center of the window—Setup, Browse, Open, and Close—relate to files you are using through the View window. Use Setup to display the Setup dialog box. From here, you can decide which index files should be used with a database, or you can change the structure of a database. Use the Browse button to display the currently selected database in a Browse window. Use Open to display the Open File dialog box, from which you can open a particular database file in the chosen work area. The Close button, when available, is used to close the database that is open in the currently selected work area.

Setting Relations Through the View Window

Once the View window is visible, you must open all needed files in their own work areas. To open a file, first click on the desired work area; then click Open to display the Open File dialog box. From this dialog box, click the desired file name, then click OK. If you have duplicated the sample databases in this book, click on work area 1, then click Open to display the Open File dialog box, click RENTALS.DBF in the Select a Table list box, click Open, and then finally click OK in the next dialog box to appear. In a similar manner, click on work area 2, then click Open to display the Open File dialog box, click MEMBERS.DBF in the list box, click Open and then click OK.

At this point, the View window will show both files open in work areas 1 and 2. The fact that MEMBERS is highlighted indicates that it is the active file. You can make any file the active one by clicking on it.

If you are following the example, the MEMBERS file is currently the active file in the Work Areas list box. Since the file that is to be the child database must be indexed, click RENTALS to select it. Then, click Setup. At the right side of the dialog box that appears (in the Index area), choose Add to add an index. Click New, and in the Output Area portion of the dialog box which now appears, click Single File IDX. Then, double-click the Social field in the list box. Click OK to accept the index, and click OK again to return to the View window.

The next step is to select the database that will be the parent database. Remember, with relationships, one database is the parent database, and the other is the child database. The parent database controls the child, so that whenever you move the record pointer in the parent database, the record pointer in the child database moves accordingly. Once you have highlighted the parent database in the Work Areas list box, you will then choose the Relations pushbutton at the top of the View window. The name of the parent database will appear in the Relations list (at the right side of the View window), and an arrow will be pointing from it.

If you are following the example, click the MEMBERS file in the list box to make that file the active file. Next, click on Relations. The name MEMBERS will appear in the list box at the right side of the View window, and a line will appear pointing below and to the right of the MEMBERS name.

Next, you must choose (in the Work Areas list box) the child database that will be related to the parent database. The child database must be indexed on the basis of the relation. Whenever the child database is already indexed (as in this case), the Expression Builder appears, and if the indexed field matches a field in the parent database, FoxPro uses this field name as the default in the Expression Builder. (You can change it to anything you want.)

If the child database is indexed but the order has not been set, a Set Index Order dialog appears, so you can choose the desired order. Note that if the child database has not been indexed, FoxPro assumes that you want to establish a relationship based on record numbers. This is rarely desirable, so you'll probably want to index your files before establishing relationships through the View window.

If you are following the example, click RENTALS in the Work Areas list box. When you do this, the Expression Builder appears. Double-click the Social field in the Fields list box and then click OK. At this point, the line coming out of the MEMBERS filename points into the RENTALS filename in the View window.

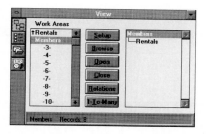

With MEMBERS still chosen in the Work Areas list box, you can click the Browse button to display a Browse window for the MEMBERS file. Then press CTRL+F1 until the View window is again active (or just click anywhere in the View window), click RENTALS in the Work Areas list box, and then click Browse. Another Browse window will appear for the RENTALS file. If you use one of the usual sizing methods to move and size the windows so that you can see both at the same time and you then click anywhere in the MEMBERS window to make it the active window, you will see that the relationship has been established. As you move the cursor within the MEMBERS file, you will see that there is a corresponding movement to the appropriate list of tapes in the RENTALS file, as illustrated by Figure 12-11.

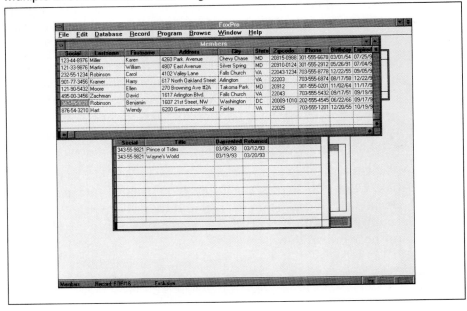

FIGURE 12-11

Multiple Browse windows showing effects of relationship

Analyzing Types of Relationships

Before you delve deeply into establishing relationships between multiple files, you may find it necessary to do some analysis on paper to determine the relationships that need to be drawn between the fields. The different possible types of relationships mean that you may want to establish your links in different ways.

Relationships can be one-to-one, one-to-many, or many-to-many. When one field in one record of a database relates in a unique manner to a field in another record in a different database, you have a one-to-one relationship. For example, consider a personnel system that contains medical and benefit information in one file and salary information in another file. Each database contains one record per employee, meaning that for every record in the medical file there is one corresponding record for the same employee in the salary file. The relationship between the files is, therefore, a one-to-one relationship.

Figure 12-12 shows two such databases and the type of relationship between them. In such a case, things are relatively simple: you use the SET RELATION command to link the two databases on their common field (in this example, a unique employee ID number).

When relating files, it is often advantageous to have a field that will always contain unique data for each record. The employee ID field is such a field; unless an incorrect entry is made, no two employees will ever have the same employee ID number. Customer numbers, social security numbers, and stock numbers are other types of data that are often used as unique identifiers.

In some cases, a single field with unique data may not be available; for example, you may have a list of customers, but your company may not assign customer numbers as a general practice. If you can't convince management to change the way it tracks customers, you have the alternative of creating a link based on more than one field. In the case of customers, you could index on a combination of Lastname + Firstname + Address and establish the relation on the basis of this compound expression using a command like

```
SET RELATION TO (LASTNAME+FIRSTNAME+ADDRESS) INTO
MYFILE
```

This would work, assuming you never have two customers with the same name living at the same address.

FIGURE 12-12

One-to-one relationship

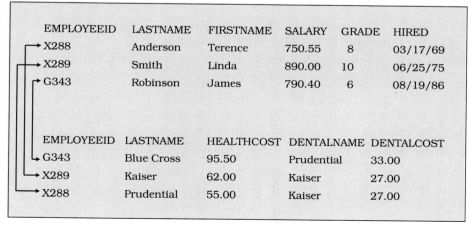

EMPLOYEEID	LASTNAME	FIRSTNAME	SALARY	GRADE	HIRED
X288	Anderson	Terence	750.55	8	03/17/69
X289	Smith	Linda	890.00	10	06/25/75
G343	Robinson	James	790.40	6	08/19/86

EMPLOYEEID	LASTNAME	HEALTHCOST	DENTALNAME	DENTALCOST
G343	Blue Cross	95.50	Prudential	33.00
X289	Kaiser	62.00	Kaiser	27.00
X288	Prudential	55.00	Kaiser	27.00

One-To-Many Relationships

A one-to-many relationship exists if one field of one record in the first file relates to a field in one or more records in the second file. An example is the relationship between the Generic Videos MEMBERS and RENTALS database files, as illustrated in Figure 12-13. For every member in the MEMBERS file there are a number of records in the RENTALS file, corresponding to rentals of different videotapes by that member. Again, SET RELATION is used to establish the link, as was demonstrated earlier in the chapter with the videos databases. However, things do get more complex with one-to-many relationships because you must keep track of where you are when performing data retrieval operations.

In this example, the MEMBERS file is the "one" file, and the RENTALS file is the "many" file. When a listing of all video rentals was needed, the RENTALS file had to be the active file, and the relation had to be set out

One-to-many relationship

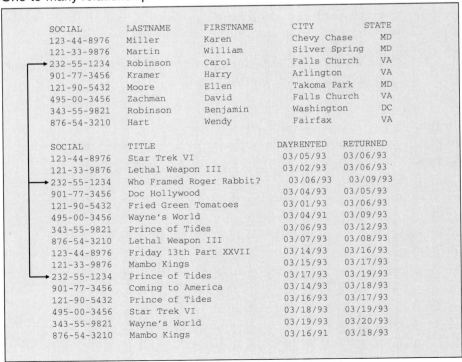

SOCIAL	LASTNAME	FIRSTNAME	CITY	STATE
123-44-8976	Miller	Karen	Chevy Chase	MD
121-33-9876	Martin	William	Silver Spring	MD
232-55-1234	Robinson	Carol	Falls Church	VA
901-77-3456	Kramer	Harry	Arlington	VA
121-90-5432	Moore	Ellen	Takoma Park	MD
495-00-3456	Zachman	David	Falls Church	VA
343-55-9821	Robinson	Benjamin	Washington	DC
876-54-3210	Hart	Wendy	Fairfax	VA

SOCIAL	TITLE	DAYRENTED	RETURNED
123-44-8976	Star Trek VI	03/05/93	03/06/93
121-33-9876	Lethal Weapon III	03/02/93	03/06/93
232-55-1234	Who Framed Roger Rabbit?	03/06/93	03/09/93
901-77-3456	Doc Hollywood	03/04/93	03/05/93
121-90-5432	Fried Green Tomatoes	03/01/93	03/06/93
495-00-3456	Wayne's World	03/04/91	03/09/93
343-55-9821	Prince of Tides	03/06/93	03/12/93
876-54-3210	Lethal Weapon III	03/07/93	03/08/93
123-44-8976	Friday 13th Part XXVII	03/14/93	03/16/93
121-33-9876	Mambo Kings	03/15/93	03/17/93
232-55-1234	Prince of Tides	03/17/93	03/19/93
901-77-3456	Coming to America	03/14/93	03/18/93
121-90-5432	Prince of Tides	03/16/93	03/17/93
495-00-3456	Star Trek VI	03/18/93	03/19/93
343-55-9821	Wayne's World	03/19/93	03/20/93
876-54-3210	Mambo Kings	03/16/91	03/18/93

FIGURE 12-13

of that file because it contained the "many" data. If the MEMBERS file had been the active file and a relation had been set out of MEMBERS into RENTALS, you could have retrieved only those rentals associated with a particular member. Depending on your needs at the time, this might have been exactly what you wanted. The point is to keep in mind the nature of the one-to-many relationship, and plan your relationships accordingly.

Many-To-Many Relationships

Finally, a type of relationship that is not as common as the first two but occasionally arises is the many-to-many relationship. This relationship exists when a field in several records of one database will relate to a field in several records of another database. A classic example of a many-to-many relationship is that of student tracking at a high school or college, where many students are assigned to many different classes. To set up this, or any, many-to-many relationship under FoxPro, you need at least three database files. The third file serves as an intermediate or "linking" file between the other two files, which contain the "many" data.

Using the example of students and classes, a student file can be created with the name of each student, along with a unique student ID number (for simplicity's sake, social security numbers are used in this example). A database containing a unique class ID number for each class, the class name, the room number, and the teacher name is also created. Finally, a schedule file containing a record for each student's enrollment in a class is also created. Figure 12-14 shows the databases and illustrates the relationships between the files. You can duplicate the files and the data shown if you want to try the examples that follow. If you decide to duplicate the example, you can easily create the STUDENTS database by copying the first five records from the MEMBERS file, including only the Social, Lastname, and Firstname fields in the copy.

Once the databases are created, you can use the SET RELATION command to link the SCHEDULE file to both the STUDENTS file and the CLASSES file. Depending on the data you need, you could use various

FIGURE
12-14

Many-to-many relationship

Record#	SOCIAL	LASTNAME	FIRSTNAME
1	123-44-8976	Miller	Karen
2	121-33-9876	Martin	William
3	232-55-1234	Robinson	Carol
4	901-77-3456	Kramer	Harry
5	121-90-5432	Moore	Ellen

Record#	SOCIAL	TITLE
1	123-44-8976	S100
2	123-44-8976	S102
3	123-44-8976	H101
4	123-44-8976	T101
5	121-33-9876	S102
6	121-33-9876	H100
7	121-33-9876	T100
8	232-55-1234	S101
9	232-55-1234	S102
10	232-55-1234	T100
11	232-55-1234	H100
12	901-77-3456	S100
13	901-77-3456	H100
14	901-77-3456	T101
15	121-90-5432	S102
16	121-90-5432	T101

Record#	CLASSID	TITLE	ROOM	TEACHER
1	S100	Earth Science	204	Williams, R.
2	S101	Biology	210	Sanders, B.
3	S102	Chemistry	205	Roberts, C.
4	H100	World History	114	Askew, N.
5	H101	Amer. History	121	Jones, R.
6	T100	Auto Repair	B14	Johnson, I.
7	T101	Microcomputers	B12	Jones, E.

LIST commands, or design different reports, to produce the desired results. If you duplicated the preceding files, you could try these commands:

```
SELECT 1
USE STUDENTS
INDEX ON SOCIAL TO STUDENTS
SELECT 2
USE SCHEDULE
SELECT 3
USE CLASSES
INDEX ON CLASSID TO CLASSES
SELECT 2
SET RELATION TO SOCIAL INTO STUDENTS
SET RELATION TO CLASSID INTO CLASSES ADDITIVE
```

If you wanted to use this relationship at a later date, it would be wise to save it with a command like

```
CREATE VIEW SCHOOL FROM ENVIRONMENT
```

You could then proceed to retrieve the needed data. As an example, a cross-list of student names and instructor names could be produced with a command like

```
LIST CLASSES.TEACHER, STUDENTS.LASTNAME,
STUDENTS.FIRSTNAME
```

The results would resemble this:

Record#	CLASSES.TEACHER	STUDENTS.LASTNAME	STUDENTS.FIRSTNAME
1	Williams, R.	Miller	Karen
2	Roberts, C.	Miller	Karen
3	Jones, R.	Miller	Karen
4	Jones, E.	Miller	Karen
5	Roberts, C.	Martin	William
6	Askew, N.	Martin	William
7	Johnson, I.	Martin	William
8	Sanders, B.	Robinson	Carol
9	Roberts, C.	Robinson	Carol
10	Johnson, I.	Robinson	Carol
11	Askew, N.	Robinson	Carol
12	Williams, R.	Kramer	Harry
13	Askew, N.	Kramer	Harry
14	Jones, E.	Kramer	Harry
15	Roberts, C.	Moore	Ellen
16	Jones, E.	Moore	Ellen

If you needed a course list for all students, you could use a command like

LIST STUDENTS.LASTNAME, STUDENTS.FIRSTNAME, CLASSID, CLASSES.TITLE

and the results would resemble this:

```
Record#  STUDENTS.LASTNAME  STUDENTS.FIRSTNAME CLASSID  CLASSES.TITLE
      1  Miller             Karen              S100     Earth Science
      2  Miller             Karen              S102     Chemistry
      3  Miller             Karen              H101     Amer. History
      4  Miller             Karen              T101     Microcomputers
      5  Martin             William            S102     Chemistry
      6  Martin             William            H100     World History
      7  Martin             William            T100     Auto Repair
      8  Robinson           Carol              S101     Biology
      9  Robinson           Carol              S102     Chemistry
     10  Robinson           Carol              T100     Auto Repair
     11  Robinson           Carol              H100     World History
     12  Kramer             Harry              S100     Earth Science
     13  Kramer             Harry              H100     World History
     14  Kramer             Harry              T101     Microcomputers
     15  Moore              Ellen              S102     Chemistry
     16  Moore              Ellen              T101     Microcomputers
```

If you wanted a list of classes for a single student, you could include a FOR clause, as in the following example:

```
LIST STUDENTS.LASTNAME, STUDENTS.FIRSTNAME, CLASSID,
CLASSES.TITLE FOR STUDENTS.LASTNAME = "Kramer"
```

The results would include only the classes for the named student:

```
Record#  STUDENTS.LASTNAME  STUDENTS.FIRSTNAME  CLASSID   CLASSES.TITLE
     12  Kramer             Harry               S100      Earth Science
     13  Kramer             Harry               H100      World History
     14  Kramer             Harry               T101      Microcomputers
```

You could use similar techniques to obtain listings of all students for a given teacher, as shown in this example:

```
LIST STUDENTS.LASTNAME, STUDENTS.FIRSTNAME, CLASSID,
CLASSES.TITLE FOR CLASSES.TEACHER = "Roberts, C."
```

Record#	STUDENTS.LASTNAME	STUDENTS.FIRSTNAME	CLASSID	CLASSES.TITLE
2	Miller	Karen	S102	Chemistry
5	Martin	William	S102	Chemistry
9	Robinson	Carol	S102	Chemistry
15	Moore	Ellen	S102	Chemistry

While managing a many-to-many application like this gets fairly complex, it also demonstrates the power and usefulness of a well-planned relational database system. To manage this data in a single database file would call for an enormous amount of redundant data entry; student names and teacher names would be repeated needlessly, dozens or hundreds of times, in such a file. In spite of this, database users all too often create single files to manage tasks like this, doing so either because of an aversion to learning the necessary relational commands or because student labor for data entry is cheap.

Creating Applications with FoxApp

*I*f you've closely followed this text, you should have a knowledge of how you can put FoxPro to work. You have created different database files, used menu options or commands for getting information from those database files, designed custom reports, and used macros to automate your work. This chapter shows how you can use an additional tool, FoxApp, to create menu-driven applications.

Applications Defined

First, why are applications so important to database users? In a nutshell, an application makes things easier for the average user by combining a series of "building blocks," such as database files, reports, and labels into a complete system. An application is what makes an accounts receivable *system* different from just a database containing accounts receivable information. Both deal with the same kinds of information—dollar amounts. But the accounts receivable database can only store the data, while the accounts receivable system includes the database plus any other other necessary files (indexes, reports, mailing labels, and programs) for solving a particular business problem, such as turning those dollar amounts into bills addressed to recipients.

Besides helping you meet the needs of a specific task, an application binds together the building blocks of a database system. If you consider the parts of a database system—the database file or files, the indexes, the labels, and the reports—to be building blocks of a sort, the application can be thought of as a kind of glue that binds these building blocks into a complete operating unit.

Applications are nothing new in the computer world, and there is a good chance that you have already used some kinds of specialized applications built around a database. Programs to handle mailing lists, inventory, sales tracking, and accounting are all specialized applications that make use of databases. But to use these types of applications you probably had to buy a software package designed only for that application, or pay a programmer to write it; and then you may have been stuck with something that did most—but not all—of what you wanted. By using programming skills (which are developed in the chapters to follow), along with tools such as FoxApp, you can build custom applications designed to do precisely what you want.

To further illustrate how an application can make things easier, consider the work you've done if you have followed the examples throughout this book to create a usable system for Generic Videos. You have database files for tracking both members and rental tapes checked out by members, and you have custom reports for printing the contents of those databases. Given your familiarity with FoxPro, if you want to add or edit data or generate reports, you can load FoxPro and use various menu options or commands to accomplish the desired results.

But what happens when you want to show someone else in the office how to add or edit data, or how to produce reports containing certain records? That person must go through the same learning curve, getting sufficiently familiar with the FoxPro menus or commands until she or he can accomplish the same results that you can manage. If your office has the usual moderate-to-high staff turnover common in today's business world, you could be faced with constantly having to show others how to use FoxPro for the same tasks.

The answer to this sort of dilemma, as proven by thousands of programmers year after year, is to build custom applications incorporating very simple menu choices, which casual users need no specialized training to understand.

Starting FoxApp

The FoxApp utility is actually a program written in the FoxPro programming language. As you will learn in the chapters to follow, you can run a program under FoxPro by using the DO command, or by choosing the DO option from the Program menu.

Open the Program menu now, and choose DO. The Do Program File dialog box appears as shown in Figure 13-1.

You may not see any programs in your list box; the contents of the list box depend on whether any programs have been stored in your current directory. If FOXAPP.APP appears in your list box, click FOXAPP.APP to select it, and then click Do from the dialog box to start FoxApp. If you do not see FOXAPP.APP in the list box, double-click in the Directory list box to choose the same directory that contains your FoxPro program files

FIGURE 13-1

Do Program File dialog box

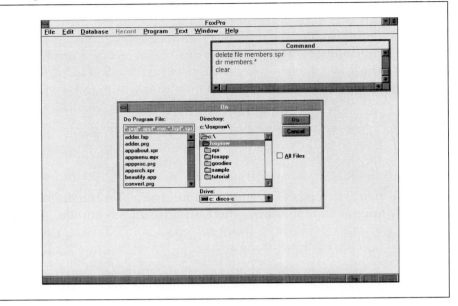

(usually FOXPROW, unless you named it something else during the installation process).

Once you have chosen the directory that contains your FoxPro program files, you should be able to scroll down in the list box and find FOXAPP.APP. Click the file to select it, and choose Do from the dialog box to start FoxApp.

When FoxApp is started, the FoxPro Application Generator dialog box appears, as seen in Figure 13-2.

FoxApp needs only two items to build the simplest of applications: the name of the database to use, and the name of a "screen." (The screen controls how the data appears when it is added to the database, or edited.) For this example, you can use the MEMBERS database that was created in earlier chapters. You will need to create a screen that controls how the data appears; however, this can be done within FoxApp.

The cursor should be highlighting the Database name entry box. Here, FoxApp needs to know the name of the database file that the application

FIGURE
13-2

FoxPro Application Generator dialog box

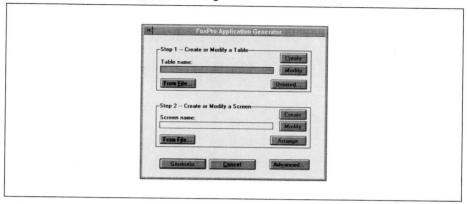

will use. You can either type in the file name (including the directory path name), or you can click the File List button and pick the name from a list of files. Because you may be running FoxApp from a different directory (the FoxPro program directory), you should use the File List button to find the proper location of the MEMBERS database.

Click the From File option under Table name. If MEMBERS.DBF is in the list box that appears, click it to select the file, then click Open. If it is not visible in the list box, double-click the name of your data directory in the list box to switch to that directory; then, click MEMBERS.DBF and click Open from the dialog box.

You may notice that once a database file name has been chosen, it appears in the Table name entry field of the FoxPro Application Generator dialog box, and a corresponding screen name appears in the Screen name entry field, as shown in Figure 13-3. FoxApp assumes that the screen to be used by the application will be given the same basic name as the database. (Note, however, that the screen file will have the extension .SCX, instead of .DBF.) In this example, the database name will do fine, although keep in mind that you can change the screen name to any name you desire.

Application Generator dialog box with filled-in names

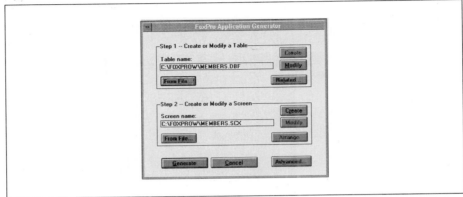

Relating A File

A major improvement of this FoxPro Application Generator over earlier versions is that it allows you to create applications that make use of relationships between two files. In the Application Generator, you can click the Related button, and use the options in the dialog box which next appears, to create applications that will use related files.

With relationships, one database is the *parent database*, and the other is the *child database.* The parent database controls the child, so that whenever you move the record pointer in the parent database, the record pointer in the child database moves accordingly. (Refer to Chapter 12 for further details about working with related database files.) When you are creating a relational application with the FoxPro Application Generator, the important point to remember is that the *parent database* must be the database whose name you enter in the Database Name entry box. When you add or edit records through the completed application, a record in the parent database will appear within a Change window. At the same time, all related records for the child database will appear in a separate Browse window. (In the next step, you will see how to tell the Application Generator which file to use for the child database.)

Note   If you were building an application that had no relations (that is, the application used only a single database file), you could skip the entire step outlined below, and continue under the heading "Creating A Screen."

Click the Related button in the dialog box now. In a moment, the Related Databases dialog box appears.

The parent database (in this case, MEMBERS.DBF) appears in the list box. Click the Add button to add a related database. When you do so, the familiar Open File dialog box appears. Since RENTALS.DBF is the file to be defined as the child database, click RENTALS.DBF in the file list, then click Open. This causes the Options dialog box, shown here, to appear.

In this dialog box, FoxPro is asking how the RENTALS file should be related to the MEMBERS file. Note that the SOCIAL field appears in both Fields text boxes. Because this is the only common field found in both files, FoxPro assumes that this field should be used to establish the relationship.

In this case, FoxPro's assumption is correct, so click OK. Then click OK in the Related Databases dialog box, to close it. This completes the process of establishing the relationship between the files, so you are now ready to create a data-entry screen for the application.

Creating a Screen

You may notice that because a screen does not exist for this database, the Create button is available as an option in the Screen name area of the Application Generator dialog box. Before proceeding, you should have an idea of just what a screen is.

A screen is simply a means of controlling how database fields will appear when data is appended and edited. You can create a screen either during the application design process (i.e., from within FoxApp) or from elsewhere in FoxPro (specifically, by choosing File New from the menus, and then selecting Screen from the dialog box that appears).

With the name MEMBERS.SCX already in the Screen name entry field, click the Create button in the panel labeled Create or Modify a screen. FoxApp automatically creates a screen for editing data, and you see a confirmation message reading, "Screen has been created" in the upper-right corner.

Generating the Application

With the database name and the screen name both entered in the dialog box, you are ready to generate the application. Click the Generate button at the bottom of the dialog box. As soon as you select this button, you see a Save As dialog box, asking for a name for your application. By default, FoxPro assumes that you want to use the same name as the database, so the name MEMBERS.APP appears in the Name text box. (All applications created by FoxApp are assigned a default extension of .APP.) Again, this name will do for this example; keep in mind that you can give your application any file name you prefer.

With MEMBERS.APP as the application name, click Save in the dialog box. In a moment, a message appears in the upper-right corner of the screen indicating that the application is being generated. While the application is being generated, various messages will flash near the center of the screen. When this process is complete, the message, "Press any key to start your application", appears in the upper-right corner of the screen. Press a key, and the application loads. It displays its own menu bar, along with a data-entry form window and a "Control Panel," as shown in Figure 13-4. (In the figure, the windows have been rearranged so all the windows are visible.)

Using the Application

The completed application provides an easy way for you or others to access the data in the MEMBERS and RENTALS files. The six option buttons that appear in the Control Panel window (near the bottom of the screen) can be used to quickly move throughout the database. You can select one of these options by clicking its button with the mouse. The options perform as indicated:

☐ **Top** This option moves you to the first record in the database. If the database is indexed, you are moved to the first record according to the index.

FIGURE 13-4

Completed Application

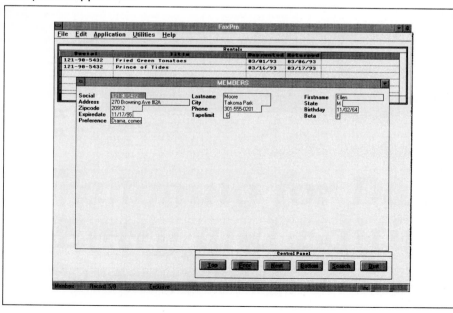

☐   *Prior*   This option moves you to the previous record. If you are already at the first record, a warning message appears to tell you so.

☐   *Next*   This option moves you to the next record. If you are already at the last record, a warning message appears to tell you so.

☐   *Bottom*   This option moves you to the last record in the database. If the database is indexed, you are moved to the last record according to the index.

☐   *Search*   This option lets you find a record in the database, using any of the fields as the basis for the search. When you choose Search, the "Search for" dialog box will appear on the screen, as shown in Figure 13-5.

In the "Find:" entry box, enter the term you want to search for. Then, from the "in:" drop-down list, choose the field in which you want to search. For example, if you wanted to find a video club member who lived in Silver Spring, you would enter **SILVER SPRING** in the "Find:" entry

FIGURE
13-5

Search for dialog box

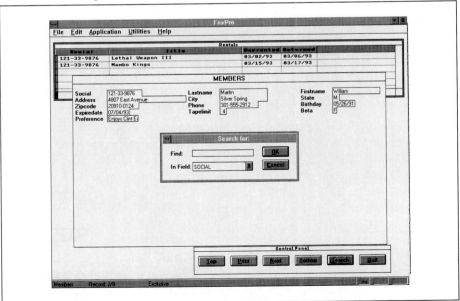

box. Then, in the drop-down list, you would choose CITY as the field to be searched. Finally, choose OK from the dialog box, and the desired record will be displayed (assuming it exists). If a record containing your search term cannot be found, the application displays a warning message to that effect.

☐   **Quit**   This option lets you exit the application, and return to the Command window.

Making Changes to Records

Within FoxPro applications, you can also add records, edit records, browse among records, or generate reports using the various options on the Application menu. This menu appears in any application created by FoxApp.

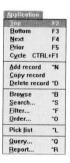

For example, if you wanted to change a record, you could first find the desired record with the search techniques described previously. Then, you could open the Application menu and choose Browse. From the Browse window that appears you could change the record as desired. (Remember, once a Browse window is visible, you can choose Browse or Change from the Browse menu to switch between a Browse-style display and an Edit-style display.) When you are done making changes, press CTRL+F4 (or double-click the Control menu icon) to exit the Browse display and return to the application.

Generating Reports

To display or print reports from an application, open the Application menu and choose Report. The dialog box that appears has choices labeled Print Report, Printer Setup, Create Report, and Modify Report.

The Create Report option creates a quick report (see Chapter 7 for an explanation of quick reports). The Modify Report option displays an Open File dialog box, showing names of previously-stored reports. Choose a report, and it will appear within the Report Writer's layout window, as detailed in Chapters 7 and 10. The Printer Setup option, when chosen, reveals a dialog box that lets you change the print device and the print margins.

If you choose Print Report, another dialog box appears showing the names of all stored reports. Pick the desired report by name, and from the next dialog box that appears choose the desired destination (screen, printer, or text file). Then choose OK, and the report will be produced.

If you want to produce a report based on selected records (which is often the case), there are two ways you can do this from within an application. One method is to specify a filter condition, and the other is to build a query that produces a report.

To specify a filter, open the Application menu and choose Filter. This will cause the Expression Builder to appear. As detailed in Chapter 5, the Expression Builder lets you enter an expression that limits the records available to the application. Enter the expression and click OK. From this point on, the only records available for editing, or for generating reports, will be those meeting the conditions you specified in the filter expression.

If your selective reports will be drawn from large databases, you will probably get faster results with the second method, which is to build a query. Design a query using the techniques outlined in Chapter 6, and specify Reports/Labels as the output choice during the query design. Once the query has been saved, you can use it from inside the application. Choose Query from the Application menu; then, in the dialog box that appears, enter the name of the previously-saved query. Any filter conditions that you specified in the query design take effect, and the report specified in the query design is printed.

Other Menu Options

The remaining options on the Application menu can be used for various database management tasks. The Top, Bottom, Next, and Prior options move you around in the database; they operate in the same manner as the Top, Bottom, Next, and Prior buttons in the Control Panel. The Cycle option (or its CTRL+F1 shortcut key) cycles you between windows. The Add Record option appends a blank record to the database, and you can then fill in the data for that record. The Copy Record option makes a copy of the current record, and you can then make any desired changes to the resulting new record. The Delete Record option deletes the current record.

The Search option performs the same functions as the Search button in the Control Panel; use it to search for a specific record, based on the contents of any field. As described earlier, the Filter option brings up the Expression Builder, which will let you enter a filter expression to limit the available records. The Order option brings up an Index Order dialog box; from this box, you can choose any existing index and make it active. The records will then appear in the order of that index.

The Help menu contains menu options that allow you to access the desktop tools described in Chapter 1, such as the Calendar/Diary, the Puzzle, and the Calculator. You can exit from the application by choosing the Quit option on the File menu. One point worth noting is that the Quit option of the File menu does not quit FoxPro entirely; it merely quits the application, and leaves you back in FoxPro.

The Utilities menu provides three options: Refresh screen, Construct index, and Pack. The Refresh Screen option simply redraws the screen. The Construct Index option rebuilds all index tags used by the application. The Pack option permanently removes all records that have been marked for deletion.

Running a Saved Application

To run an application that you have saved earlier, choose Program/Do from the menus, and choose the application by name from the dialog box that appears. Or, in the Command window, enter the command

```
DO filename.APP
```

where *filename* is the name you gave the application when you saved it.

 Note   Remember that, by default, applications are saved with an extension of .APP.

Quitting the Application

To exit the application, select Quit from the File menu. After a moment you will be returned to the FoxPro desktop and its Command window.

Just the Beginning

This chapter has given you an idea of the power and ease of use available through a professional application written with the FoxPro Application Generator. If creating an application can make your task easier, then take the time to explore all of the features that FoxApp provides. You might want to try creating a database that matches your own needs, then designing some reports and queries for that database, and finally building an application to tie them all together. The resulting ease of use will be well worth the time you spent.

CHAPTER

Introduction to FoxPro Programming

Although you may not have purchased FoxPro with the intent of becoming a computer programmer, you'll find that programming with FoxPro is not as difficult as you might expect. You may also find that the convenience of using programs that automate the way FoxPro works for you is well worth the effort spent in designing and writing those programs.

As you will see in this chapter, you program in FoxPro through the use of command files. For the most part, FoxPro is command compatible with dBASE IV and with dBASE III PLUS, so you can use programs written for these packages with FoxPro. dBASE IV users should note that there are a few dBASE IV commands and functions, such as SET SQL, that are not supported by FoxPro. If in doubt, compare the command listing from your dBASE IV documentation with the command listing in this book (or in your FoxPro documentation).

Any computer *program* is simply a series of instructions to a computer. These instructions are commands that cause the computer to perform specific tasks. The commands are written in a file stored on disk, and they are performed each time the file is retrieved from the disk.

A FoxPro *command file* is made up of FoxPro commands. Each time you use a command file, FoxPro executes the list of commands in sequential order, unless you request otherwise.

Tip   If you repeat the same commands over and over in your work, command files will save you considerable effort.

Let's look at an example using the Generic Videos database. If a Generic Videos manager wanted a printed listing of members' last names, cities, states, and expiration dates, that manager could enter commands, like those you have learned to use, to produce the listing. This may not seem like a complex task; in fact, it could be done with the following two commands:

```
USE MEMBERS
LIST LASTNAME, FIRSTNAME, CITY, STATE, EXPIREDATE TO PRINT
```

If, however, the manager needed to reprint this list frequently, typing the same commands over and over would be a waste of time. Instead, he could place them inside a command file and then type only one short command to execute all the commands in the file.

Two characteristics of command files make them a powerful feature of FoxPro:

☐   Any series of FoxPro commands entered from the Command window can be stored in a command file. When the command file is run, the FoxPro commands present in the file are executed just as if they had been entered from the keyboard.

☐   One command file can call and execute another command file. Information can be transferred between command files. This means that complex systems can be designed efficiently, through creating a series of smaller command files for individual tasks.

Using command files, you can create a system that provides the user with one or more menus of options. An example of a menu screen is shown in Figure 14-1. Rather than using individual commands, the user simply makes choices from the menu to retrieve and manipulate information in the database. Such a menu-driven system can easily be used by people unfamiliar with FoxPro commands.

FIGURE
14-1

Sample menu for Generic Videos

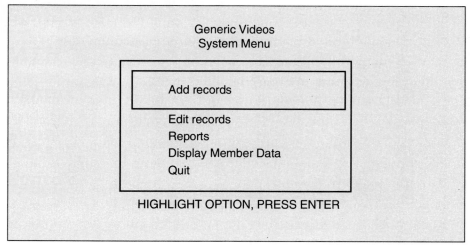

Generic Videos
System Menu

Add records

Edit records
Reports
Display Member Data
Quit

HIGHLIGHT OPTION, PRESS ENTER

Creating Command Files

You create command files with the MODIFY COMMAND command, using the form

MODIFY COMMAND *filename*

Entering **MODIFY COMMAND** along with a file name brings up a window containing the FoxPro Editor. You then use the Editor to type the commands that will be stored as a command file. When you use MODIFY COMMAND, the file you create will automatically be given an extension of .PRG (for Program) unless you enter a different extension. If the file name you enter already exists on the disk, it is recalled in the Editor window. If a file by this name does not already exist, a blank Editor window is displayed. You can also create command files from the menus by opening the File menu, choosing New, then clicking Program, and then New in the dialog box that appears.

To try a simple example of a command file now, enter

```
MODIFY COMMAND TEST
```

The FoxPro Editor appears within a window. (Like all windows, this one can be resized if you wish, to let you see more of the program you are typing.) At this point, the screen is like a blank sheet of paper. You type the commands that you wish to place in your command file, pressing ENTER as you complete each line. If you make any mistakes, you can correct them with the arrow keys and the BACKSPACE or DEL key. The editing keys available in the Editor are listed in Table 14-1.

When you use the Editor to edit existing text, any characters that you type will push existing characters over to the right, rather than replacing them. This is true unless you are in overwrite mode, in which new characters replace existing ones. You can get out of insert mode and into overwrite by pressing INS. If you're not sure which mode you're in, look at the Status Bar: if you are in insert mode, the letters INS will appear there.

One feature of the Editor that comes in handy for programming is its ability to delete, move, and copy blocks of text. You can mark a block of text for deletion in the Editor by clicking at the start of the desired text,

TABLE 14-1	Editing keys in the FoxPro Editor

Key	Action
UP ARROW	Moves cursor up one line
DOWN ARROW	Moves cursor down one line
LEFT ARROW	Moves cursor left one character
RIGHT ARROW	Moves cursor right one character
ENTER	Inserts a new line
INS	Turns insert mode on or off
DEL	Deletes character at cursor position
BACKSPACE	Deletes character to left of cursor
PGUP	Scrolls screen upwards
PGDN	Scrolls screen downwards
CTRL+S	Saves file on disk
ESC	Exits Editor without saving

and dragging to the end of the desired text. The marked text appears in a different shade. You can then delete the marked text by pressing the DEL key.

To move or copy text, you mark the block of text in the same manner, but you then use the Cut, Copy, or Paste option of the Edit menu. To copy a block of text to another location, first click and drag from the start of the desired text to the end of the text. Next, open the Edit menu and choose Copy. Move the mouse pointer to where the copied text should appear, and click once to place the insertion pointer there. Then open the Edit menu, and choose Paste. The copied text appears in the new location.

To move a block of text to another location, first click and drag from the start of the text to the end of the text. Open the Edit menu and choose Cut. Move the mouse pointer to where the text is to be placed, and click once to place the insertion pointer there. Then, open the Edit menu and choose Paste. The moved text appears in the new location.

Type the following series of commands now, pressing ENTER after you complete each line. Only one command should appear on each line. (If you don't have a printer on your system, omit the SET PRINT ON, SET PRINT OFF, and EJECT commands.)

```
USE MEMBERS
SET PRINT ON
LIST LASTNAME, FIRSTNAME, CITY, TAPELIMIT FOR STATE = "MD"
LIST LASTNAME, FIRSTNAME, CITY, TAPELIMIT FOR STATE = "VA"
LIST LASTNAME, FIRSTNAME, CITY, TAPELIMIT FOR STATE = "DC"
SET PRINT OFF
EJECT
```

Whenever you want to save a command file from the FoxPro Editor, you can choose Save from the File menu (or press CTRL+S). If you're all done working in the Editor, you can close the Editor window by pressing ESC. (If you want to leave the Editor without saving the file, you can press ESC and then answer No in the dialog box that appears.)

The simple command file that you have created prints a listing of each member, grouped by state, including member names, city names, and salary amounts. Make sure that your printer is turned on; then, to see the results of your work, open the Command window and enter

```
DO TEST
```

The commands in the file are carried out in sequential order, just as if you had entered them individually:

Record#	LASTNAME	FIRSTNAME	CITY	TAPELIMIT
1	Miller	Karen	Chevy Chase	6
2	Martin	William	Silver Spring	4
5	Moore	Ellen	Takoma Park	6
Record#	LASTNAME	FIRSTNAME	CITY	TAPELIMIT
3	Robinson	Carol	Falls Church	6
4	Kramer	Harry	Arlington	4
6	Zachman	David	Falls Church	4
8	Hart	Wendy	Fairfax	2
Record#	LASTNAME	FIRSTNAME	CITY	TAPELIMIT
7	Robinson	Benjamin	Washington	6

Tip   You can also run programs from the menus, by choosing Do from the Program menu and entering the name of the program.

You can also create a command file using other word processing programs. Although the FoxPro Editor is convenient and quite powerful, you may prefer to use your favorite word processing program. (If you do use your own editor, be sure to see the section on "Compiling," following this paragraph.) Any word processor that can save files in ASCII text format (i.e., as text without any formatting codes) can be used to create a FoxPro command file. This includes the programs WordPerfect for Windows and Word for Windows, as well as the Write and Notepad programs that are included with Microsoft Windows.

The important points to remember here are to save the file in ASCII text format (see your word processor's documentation for details) and to use the .PRG extension when naming the file. If you do not add a .PRG extension to the filename, FoxPro won't recognize the file as a command file unless you include the extension when calling the program with the DO command.

Compiling

FoxPro runs programs on a compiled basis, rather than an interpreted basis. (*Interpreters* convert each line of a program from words into machine language each time the program runs. *Compilers* translate the entire program into what is known as object code once; then each time the program is run, the compiler simply executes the more efficient object code.) A compiler offers significant speed over an interpreter. Earlier versions of Ashton-Tate's dBASE, including dBASE II, dBASE III, and dBASE III PLUS, were based on interpreters. By comparison, FoxPro for Windows, FoxPro for DOS, FoxBase Plus, and dBASE IV all use compilers.

When you run a FoxPro command file with the DO *filename* command, FoxPro looks for a compiled object-code file with the same name, but with an extension of .FXP. If FoxPro finds that file, it runs the program using the already compiled object code. If FoxPro can't find the file, it looks for a "source file"—an ASCII text file of commands with a .PRG extension. FoxPro compiles this file, creating an object-code file of the same name, and then runs the program.

It is important to know this if you use your own editor to modify existing programs. When you change an existing program with the

FoxPro Editor, FoxPro recompiles to a new object file when you run the program. If you use your own editor to change a program and the existing object-code file is not erased, using DO *filename* will cause the old version of the program to be run.

When making changes with your editor, you must erase the old object-code (.FXP) version of the program, or you must use the SET DEVELOPMENT ON command when you start your FoxPro session. Entering **SET DEVELOPMENT ON** tells FoxPro to compare creation dates and times between source (.PRG) and object (.FXP) files; if they differ, FoxPro recompiles the program before running it.

There are various concepts associated with programming that you should know about before delving into the topic of FoxPro command files: constants, variables, expressions, operators, and functions.

Constants

A *constant* is an item of fixed data, or data that does not change. Unlike fields (whose values change, depending on the position of the record pointer), a constant's value is dependent on nothing; once established, the constant remains the same. There are numeric, character, date, and logical constants. For example, 5.05 might be a numeric constant, while the letter "a" might be a character constant. To help FoxPro know what kinds of constants it's dealing with, all character constants used in FoxPro programs must be surrounded by quotes; date constants must be surrounded by curly braces, and logical constants must be surrounded by periods.

Memory Variables

A *memory variable* (or simply *variable*, for short) is a memory location within the computer that is used to store data. Memory variables are referred to by their assigned names. A variable name must be ten or fewer characters. It must consist only of letters, numbers, and underscores, and it must start with a letter. You cannot use the names of commands as variable names, and it is best not to use field names. Because the contents of a memory variable are stored apart from the contents of a database, memory variables are useful for the temporary processing of values and data within a FoxPro program. Data can be stored in the form of memory variables and then be recalled for use by the program at a later time.

Tip   Think of a memory variable as a temporary place to put a piece of information that will be needed later in the program.

The STORE command is commonly used to assign data to a variable. The format is

STORE *expression* TO *variable-name*

An alternate way of assigning data to a variable is to use the "variable = X" format, as shown here:

variable-name = *expression*

FoxPro allows four types of variables: character, numeric, date, and logical. Character variables store strings of characters, which can be letters, numbers, or a combination of both. Numbers stored to a character variable are treated as characters. Numeric variables contain whole or decimal numbers. Date variables contain dates written in date format (for example, 12/16/84). Logical variables contain a logical value of T (true) or F (false), or Y (yes) or N (no).

You do not have to designate the type when creating a variable—just assign the value you will be using. Give each variable a descriptive name that will help you remember what is stored in it. For example, the following STORE command assigns a numeric value of 18 to the variable LEGALAGE:

```
STORE 18 TO LEGALAGE
```

If you prefer the alternate format, you could accomplish the same result with the statement

```
LEGALAGE = 18
```

You can change the variable's value by using the STORE command again:

```
STORE 21 TO LEGALAGE
```

The contents of a field can be stored to a memory variable. As an example, the command STORE LASTNAME TO ROSTER would store the contents of the Lastname field to a memory variable named ROSTER. When a list of characters is stored in a variable, the list of characters, known as *character string,* must be surrounded by single or double quotation marks. For example, the command

```
STORE "BILL ROBERTS" TO NAME
```

would store the character string BILL ROBERTS in the variable NAME.

Surround the logical variables T, F, Y, and N with periods to distinguish them from regular characters: while .T. has a logical value of true, T is simply the letter T. Logical values can also be stored in variables with the STORE command. The following command would assign a logical value of false to the variable CHOICE:

```
STORE .F. TO CHOICE
```

To assign a value to a date variable, surround the date value with curly braces. As an example, the statement

```
STORE {11/01/91} TO MYDAY
```

would store the date 11/01/91 in a date variable named MYDAY.

Each memory variable is assigned a different name. You can view the contents of memory variables by entering statements like the following:

```
STORE 25 TO QUANTITY
STORE "Jefferson" TO NAMES
STORE TIME() TO CLOCK
? QUANTITY, NAMES, CLOCK
```

The "?" statement in the previous example displayed the specific values that had been stored in memory with the STORE commands. However, you can use the DISPLAY MEMORY command to take a look at all variables that have been defined in memory. Enter the following:

```
DISPLAY MEMORY
```

to display a listing of each variable's name, contents, and type (as designated by a single letter). The letter C indicates a character variable, N a numeric variable, D a date variable, and L a logical variable. The designation "Pub" beside each variable indicates that these are public variables, available to all parts of FoxPro. Variables can be public or private. For now, you needn't be concerned about this designation. Along with the memory variables you created, you will see information on some print system memory variables that FoxPro uses; you can also ignore these for now.

You should keep two guidelines in mind. First, it's a good idea to avoid giving variables the same names as fields. If a program encounters a name that can be either a variable or a field, the field name takes precedence over the memory variable. If you must give a variable the same name as a field, use the M-> prefix ahead of the variable name, so that FoxPro knows when you are referring to the variable. For example, if MEMBERS were in use, LASTNAME would refer to the Lastname field, while M->LASTNAME would refer to a variable called LASTNAME.

Second, note that you must store a value to a memory variable before you start using that variable in a program. This must be done because of FoxPro's firm rule that some type of value, even if it is a worthless one, must be stored to a FoxPro variable before you can begin using the variable. If you attempt to use variables in a program before defining them, FoxPro responds with a "Variable not found" error message.

You can use memory variables in direct commands and in command files. However, memory variables are only temporary: as soon as you exit FoxPro or turn off the computer, they vanish. You can make a memory variable permanent by storing the variable to a memory file on disk. As you might expect, when the values are stored on disk, they can be recalled by a FoxPro program.

To save variables on disk, use the SAVE TO command. The format of this command is

SAVE TO *filename*

where *filename* is the name of the file that you want the variables saved under. The .MEM extension is automatically added to the file name.

Right now, you have at least three memory variables defined from the previous examples—QUANTITY, NAMES, and CLOCK. (You may also have other variables created from prior examples.) To save the variables currently in memory to disk, enter the following:

```
SAVE TO FASTFILE
```

Once the variables have been stored to disk, you can clear the variables out of memory with the RELEASE ALL command. Enter the following:

```
RELEASE ALL
DISPLAY MEMORY
```

You'll see that the variables no longer exist in memory. To get the memory variables back from FASTFILE, use the command RESTORE FROM *filename*. This command restores variables from the file to memory. You do not have to include the file extension .MEM. Enter

```
RESTORE FROM FASTFILE
```

Then enter **DISPLAY MEMORY**. The variables are again in your computer's memory, ready for further use.

When you use the RESTORE FROM *filename* command, all variables currently in memory are removed to accommodate variables from the file. If you want to keep existing variables in memory while loading additional variables that were saved to a disk file, use the RESTORE FROM *filename* ADDITIVE variation of the command.

The RELEASE ALL command also lets you select specific variables to remove from memory, by including either the EXCEPT or the LIKE option. RELEASE ALL with EXCEPT eliminates all variables except those that you list after EXCEPT. RELEASE ALL with LIKE, on the other hand, removes only the variables that you list after LIKE, the opposite of EXCEPT. As an example, the command

```
RELEASE ALL LIKE N*
```

causes all memory variables starting with the letter N to be erased from memory.

You can use LIKE to erase some memory variables while leaving other variables untouched. Try this:

```
RESTORE FROM FASTFILE
RELEASE ALL LIKE Q*
DISPLAY MEMORY
```

This causes all memory variables beginning with the letter Q, including the memory variable QUANTITY, to be erased from memory (the others will be untouched). Note that you can use the same LIKE and ALL options in a similar manner with the SAVE TO command. For example, you could enter the command

```
SAVE ALL LIKE Q* TO QFILE
```

to save all memory variables starting with the letter Q to a file called QFILE.

Expressions

An *expression* can be a combination of one or more fields, functions, operators, memory variables, or constants. Figure 14-2 shows a statement combining a field, a memory variable, and a constant to form a single expression. This statement calculates total rent over a period of months, deducting 5% for estimated utilities (water, garbage, and so on). Each part of an expression, whether that part is a constant, a field, or a memory variable, is considered an element of the expression. All elements

FIGURE 14-2

An example of an expression

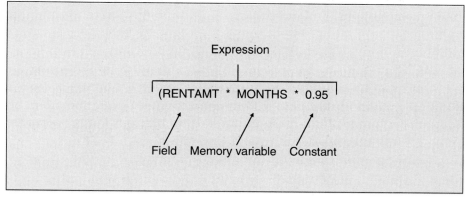

of an expression must be of the same type. You cannot, for example, mix character and date fields within the same expression, unless you use functions to convert the dates to characters. If you try to mix different types of elements within an expression, FoxPro displays an "Operator/operand type mismatch" error message.

The most common type of expression found in FoxPro programs is a math expression. Math expressions contain elements like constants, fields, memory variables, and/or functions, usually linked by one or more math operators (+, −, *, /). Examples of math expressions include

```
HOURLYRATE - SALARY

COST + (COST * .05)

HOURLYRATE * 4

637.5/HOURLYRATE

82
```

Character expressions are also quite common in FoxPro programs. Character expressions are used to manipulate character strings or groups of characters. Examples of character expressions include the following:

```
"Bob Smith"

"Mr." + FIRSTNAME + " " + LASTNAME + " is behind in payments."
```

Operators

Operators, which are represented by symbols, work on related values to produce a single value. Operators that work on two values are called *binary operators;* operators that work on one value are called *unary operators*. Most of FoxPro's operators are binary operators, but there are a couple of unary operators. FoxPro has four kinds of operators: mathematical, relational, logical, and string.

Mathematical Operators

Mathematical operators are used to produce numeric results. Besides addition, subtraction, multiplication, and division, FoxPro has operators for exponentiation and a unary minus (assigning a negative value to a number, as in –47). The symbols for math operators are as follows:

Operation	Symbol
Unary minus	–
Exponentiation	** or ^
Division	/
Multiplication	*
Subtraction	–
Addition	+

If an expression contains more than one math operator, FoxPro executes the operations in a prescribed order, known as the *order of precedence.* Unary minus is performed first, followed by exponentiation; then multiplication or division is calculated, and then addition or subtraction. In the case of operators with equal precedence—division and multiplication, or subtraction and addition—calculation will be from left to right. In the case of logical operators, the order is .NOT., then .AND., and then .OR. When different types of operators are present in a single expression, any math or string operators are handled first, and then any relational operators, then any logical operators.

You can alter the precedence of operations by grouping them with matched pairs of parentheses. For example, the parentheses in (3 + 6) * 5 force FoxPro to add 3 + 6 first, and then multiply the sum by 5. You can group operations within operations with nested parentheses. FoxPro begins with the innermost group and calculates outward, as in the case of ((3 + 5) * 6) ^ 3, where 3 + 5 is added first, then multiplied by 6, and then raised to the third power.

Relational Operators

Relational operators are used to compare character strings with character strings, date values with date values, and numbers with numbers. The values you compare can be constants or variables. The relational operators are as follows:

Operation	Symbol
Less than	<
Greater than	>
Equal to	=
Not equal to	< > or #
Less than or equal to	<=
Greater than or equal to	>=

Any comparison of values results in a logical value of true or false. The simple comparison 6 < 7 would result in .T. The result of 6 < NUMBER depends on the value of NUMBER.

You can also compare character strings, in expressions such as "canine" < "feline", because FoxPro orders letters and words as in a dictionary. However, all uppercase letters come before all lowercase letters, so Z < a (even though "a" comes before Z in the alphabet).

Logical Operators

Logical operators compare values of the same type to produce a logical true, false, yes, or no. The logical operators are .AND., .OR., and .NOT. Table 14-2 lists all possible values produced by the three logical operators. .AND. and .OR. are binary operators, and .NOT. is a unary operator.

String Operators

The string operator you will most commonly use in FoxPro is the plus sign (+). It is used to combine two or more character strings, which is

TABLE 14-2	Truth Table for Logical Operators .AND., .OR., and .NOT.			
First Value	**Operator**	**Second Value**	**Result**	
.T.	.AND.	.T.	.T.	
.T.	.AND.	.F.	.F.	
.F.	.AND.	.T.	.F.	
.F.	.AND.	.F.	.F.	
.T.	.OR.	.T.	.T.	
.T.	.OR.	.F.	.T.	
.F.	.OR.	.T.	.T.	
.F.	.OR.	.F.	.F.	
.T.	.NOT.	N.A.	.F.	
.F.	.NOT.	N.A.	.T.	

known as concatenation. For example, "Orange" + "Fox" would be combined as "OrangeFox" (remember, a blank is a character). Strings inside variables can also be concatenated; for example, if ANIMAL = "Fox" and COLOR = "Orange", then COLOR+ANIMAL would result in "OrangeFox".

Functions

Functions are used in FoxPro to perform special operations that supplement the normal FoxPro commands. FoxPro has a number of different functions that perform operations ranging from calculating the square root of a number, to finding the time.

Every function statement contains the function's name, followed by a set of parentheses. Most functions require one or more arguments inside the parentheses. A complete list of functions can be found in Appendix B. For now, it will help to know about some functions that are commonly used in command files.

EOF

The EOF function indicates when the FoxPro record pointer has reached the end of a database file. The normal format of the function is simply EOF(). To see how EOF() is set to true when the pointer is past the last record, enter

```
GO BOTTOM
```

This moves the pointer to the last record. Now enter

```
DISPLAY
```

and you will see that you are at record 8, the final record in the database. Next, enter

```
? EOF()
```

to display the value of the EOF function. FoxPro returns .F. (false), meaning that the value of the EOF function is false because you are not yet at the end of the file.

The SKIP command, discussed shortly, can be used to move the FoxPro record pointer. Enter

```
SKIP
```

to move the pointer past the last record. Next, enter

```
? EOF()
```

The .T. (true) value shows that the pointer is now at the end of the file.

BOF

The BOF function is the opposite of the EOF function. The value of BOF is set to true when the beginning of a database file is reached. The format is "BOF()." To see how BOF operates, enter

```
GO TOP
```

The pointer moves to the first record. Now enter

```
DISPLAY
```

and the first record in the database is displayed. Next, enter

```
? BOF()
```

to display the value of the BOF function, which is .F. (false) because the pointer is at the first record and not at the beginning of the file. Enter

```
SKIP -1
```

to move the pointer above record 1. Then enter

```
? BOF()
```

The .T. (true) value shows that the pointer is at the beginning of the file.

DATE and TIME

The DATE and TIME functions are used to provide the current date and time, respectively. FoxPro looks up the date and time by means of a clock built into your computer. For this reason, if the date and time you set through your computer's operating system are incorrect, the date and time functions of FoxPro will also be incorrect.

The format for DATE is DATE(), and it provides the current date in the format *MM/DD/YY*. Dates follow the American date format, month followed by day followed by year, unless you use the PICTURE option (Chapter 15) or the SET DATE command to tell FoxPro otherwise. The TIME form of the function is TIME(), and it provides the current time in HH:MM:SS format. Note that for either function you do not need to supply anything between the parentheses, since they serve only to identify TIME and DATE as functions.

From the Command window, you could display the current date and time by entering

```
? DATE()
? TIME()
```

The output of the DATE and TIME functions can be stored as a variable for use within a program, as in the example shown here:

```
? "Today's date is: "
?? DATE()
STORE TIME() TO BEGIN
?
LIST LASTNAME, FIRSTNAME, TAPELIMIT, EXPIREDATE
?
? "Starting time was: "
?? BEGIN
? "Ending time is: "
?? TIME()
```

UPPER

The UPPER function converts lowercase letters to uppercase letters. This function is especially useful when you want to search for a character string and you are not sure whether it was entered in all capital letters, or just in initial caps. UPPER can thus be used to display text and variables in a uniform format if consistency is desired. It may be used with a character field, a character string, a constant, or a memory variable that contains a character string. Here is an example:

```
? UPPER ("This is not really uppercase")
THIS IS NOT REALLY UPPERCASE
STORE "not uppercase" TO WORDS
? UPPER(WORDS)
NOT UPPERCASE

? WORDS
not uppercase
```

As shown in the example, the UPPER function displays characters in the uppercase/lowercase format, but does not actually alter the data.

You can use the UPPER function to compare data when you are not sure whether the data was entered as all uppercase, or with initial caps only. For example, a command like

```
LIST FOR UPPER(LASTNAME) = "SMITH"
```

finds a record whether the last name was entered as Smith or SMITH.

LOWER

The LOWER function is the reverse of UPPER; it converts uppercase characters to lowercase characters, as in the following example. As with the UPPER function, the LOWER function does not convert the actual data; it changes only the appearance of the data.

```
STORE "NOT CAPS" TO WORDS
? LOWER(WORDS)
not caps
```

CTOD and DTOC

CTOD and DTOC are the Character-To-Date and Date-To-Character functions, respectively. CTOD converts a string of characters to a value that is recognized as a date by FoxPro. DTOC performs the opposite function, converting a date into a string of characters.

Acceptable characters that can be converted to dates range from 1/1/100 to 12/31/9999. The full century is optional. Usually, you only specify the last two digits of the year, unless the date falls in a century other than the current one. Any character strings having values that fall outside of these values produce an empty date value if the CTOD function is used.

As an example of the CTOD function, the following command might be used within a program to convert a string of characters to a value that could be stored within a date field:

```
MYEAR = YEAR(DATE())
STORE CTOD("01/01/" + LTRIM(STR(MYEAR))) TO JAN1
```

As an example of the DTOC function, the following command combines a text string along with a date converted to a text string:

```
? "The expiration date is: " + DTOC(EXPIREDATE)
```

DTOS

The DTOS function converts a date to a character string that follows the *YYYYMMDD* format. For example, the DTOS function would convert a date of 12/03/1986 to the character string 19861203. This function is very useful when building indexes based on dates, because it ensures that the dates will be sorted chronologically by year and then by month, rather than just by month. (If you were to instead use the DTOC function to build the index, dates would appear in true chronological order only if they all occurred within a single year.) As an example, the command

```
INDEX ON DTOS(EXPIREDATE) TO BYDAYS
```

creates an index in chronological order, with records arranged by order of the expiration date.

SPACE

The SPACE function creates a string of blank spaces, up to a maximum length of 254 spaces. As an example, the following commands make use of a variable called BLANKS, which contains ten spaces (the variable is created with the SPACE function):

```
STORE SPACE(10) TO BLANKS
LIST LASTNAME + BLANKS + CITY + BLANKS + STATE
```

TRIM

The TRIM function removes trailing blanks, or spaces that follow characters, from a character string. You have already used this function in expressions for reports and labels. The expression

```
TRIM(CITY) + ". " + STATE + " " + ZIPCODE
```

for example, was used to print the contents of the City and State fields, separated by one space.

The TRIM function can be used to close large gaps between fields in an expression, when you will be displaying information with the LIST or DISPLAY command. For example, the following listing:

```
USE MEMBERS
GO 2
SET PRINT ON
? FIRSTNAME, LASTNAME, ADDRESS
```

will result in an unattractive printout that looks like this:

```
William        Martin        4807 East Avenue
```

With the TRIM function, the large gaps between the fields can be eliminated, as shown here:

```
USE MEMBERS
GO 2
SET PRINT ON
? TRIM(FIRSTNAME), TRIM(LASTNAME), ADDRESS

William Martin 4807 East Avenue
```

Note that you should *not* use the TRIM function as part of an indexing expression, such as INDEX ON TRIM(LASTNAME) + FIRSTNAME TO NAMES. Such an index would result in variable-length index entries, which can cause problems in searching for data.

LTRIM

The LTRIM function performs an operation similar to that of the TRIM function, but it trims leading spaces (spaces at the start of the expression or field name) rather than trailing spaces. The following example shows the effect of the LTRIM function:

```
STORE "          ten leading spaces here." TO TEXT
? TEXT
          ten leading spaces here.
? LTRIM(TEXT)
ten leading spaces here.
```

STR

The STR function is used to convert a numeric value into a character string. This type of conversion lets you mix numeric values with characters within displays and reports. As an example of the STR function, the command

```
? "Name is " + LASTNAME + " and limit is " + TAPELIMIT
```

produces an "Operator/operand type mismatch" error message because Tapelimit is a numeric field and the rest of the expression contains character values. The STR function can convert the numeric value into a character value as follows:

```
? "Name is " + LASTNAME + " and limit is " + STR(TAPELIMIT)
```

Commands Used in Command Files

Some FoxPro commands are often used within command files but are rarely used elsewhere. You will be using command files with increasing regularity through the rest of this book, so these commands deserve a closer look. At the end of this chapter, you will begin using the commands to design a program.

SET TALK

SET TALK ON allows onscreen display of the commands inside a command file as they execute. Conversely, when a SET TALK OFF statement is executed, visual responses to the FoxPro commands and prompts will halt until a SET TALK ON command is encountered. You can use SET TALK OFF to stop the display of messages such as the "% of file indexed" message during indexing or the record number displayed after a GO TO or LOCATE command. When you begin a FoxPro session SET TALK is on.

SKIP

The SKIP command moves the record pointer forward or backward. The format of the command is

SKIP [+/-*integer*]

The integer specified with SKIP moves the pointer forward or backward by the indicated number of records. For example, entering **SKIP 4** moves the record pointer forward by four records. Entering **SKIP 2** moves the record pointer backward by two records. Entering **SKIP** without an integer moves the pointer one record forward.

The values can be stored in a memory variable, which can then be used as part of SKIP. For example, entering **STORE 4 TO JUMP** assigns 4 to JUMP; then the SKIP JUMP command moves the record pointer forward by four records. If you attempt to move the record pointer beyond the end of the file or above the beginning of the file, an "End of file encountered" or a "Beginning of file encountered" error message results.

RETURN

The RETURN command halts the execution of a command file. When a RETURN command is encountered, FoxPro leaves the program and returns to the Command window. If the RETURN command is encountered from within a command file that has been called by another command file, FoxPro returns to the command file that called the file containing the RETURN command.

ACCEPT and INPUT

Two FoxPro commands display a string of characters and wait for the user to enter a response that is then stored in a variable. These commands are ACCEPT and INPUT. The ACCEPT command stores only characters; the INPUT command stores values of any data type. The format for ACCEPT is

ACCEPT "prompt" TO *variable-name*

For INPUT, the format is

INPUT "prompt" TO *variable-name*

The order of the terms is the same whether you are dealing with characters or numbers. You enter the command, followed by the question or message that is to appear on the screen (it must be enclosed in single or double quotes), followed by the word TO, followed by the memory variable you want to store the response in. For example, let's use this format with the ACCEPT statement to store a name in a memory variable. Enter the following:

```
ACCEPT "What is your last name? " TO LNAME
```

When you press ENTER, you see the message "What is your last name?" appear on the screen. FoxPro is waiting for your response, so enter your last name. When the cursor reappears in the Command window, enter the following:

```
? LNAME
```

(The "?" command, as you may recall, displays the contents of the expression following the question mark.) You'll see that FoxPro has indeed stored your last name as a character string within the memory variable LNAME.

The same operation is used for numbers, but you use the INPUT statement instead. For example, enter

```
INPUT "How old are you? " TO AGE
```

and in response to the prompt, enter your age. Next, enter

```
? AGE
```

You'll see that the memory variable AGE now contains your response.

Tip   ACCEPT works well when you want to ask for a character response, like a name. INPUT works well when you want to ask for a numeric response.

COUNT

The COUNT command counts the number of occurrences of a condition within a database. One condition to count might be the number of occurrences of the name Robinson in a file; another might be to find out how many members live in Washington. The general format is

COUNT FOR *condition* TO *variablename*

The condition is often an expression of the form *fieldname* = *value*. It can also take the form of *fieldname* > *value*, or *fieldname* > *value* .AND. *fieldname* < *value2*. Or, in the case of logical fields, the condition can simply take the form *fieldname*. The value to which you compare the field must be of the same data type as the field. The entire logical expression constitutes the condition. Every condition can eventually be evaluated as true or false.

The number of occurrences of the condition is stored in *variablename*. The variable can then be used in another part of the program, for calculations or for printing. For example, the command

```
COUNT FOR LASTNAME = "Robinson" TO NAMECOUNT
```

counts the occurrences of the last name Robinson in the Lastname field. That count is stored as a memory variable, NAMECOUNT. The FOR clause used in this example is optional. You could accomplish the same type of selective counting by setting a filter with the SET FILTER command, and then simply entering the COUNT command.

SUM

The SUM command calculates a total for any numeric field. The basic form of the command is

SUM [*scope*] [*fieldlist*] [FOR *condition*] [WHILE *condition*] TO [*variablelist*]

SUM can be used with or without conditions in a number of ways. The scope identifies the magnitude of the summation; that is, if *scope* is absent, all records are summed; if *scope* is NEXT followed by an integer, then only the specified number of records is summed, or if *scope* is ALL, all records are summed, which is the same as when no scope is specified.

The record pointer is considered to be at the beginning of the current record, so a command like SUM NEXT 5 sums the current record plus the next four records. If *scope* is REST, all records, from the current record onward are summed. If the clause RECORD <*n*> is used as a scope only the single record designated by <*n*> is summed (which is rather ridiculous, since there is nothing to add together).

The *fieldlist* parameter is a list of the numeric fields to be summed by the SUM command. Entering **SUM** without a field list causes FoxPro to add and display the totals of all the numeric fields within the database. Note that SUM always displays its results unless SET TALK is off. You may also want to store the results in memory variables, so you can redisplay them later, or use them in calculations.

The memory variable list (*variablelist*) defines the memory variables to which the values produced by SUM will be stored. The command SUM TAPELIMIT TO TOTAL stores the total of the Tapelimit field in a memory variable called TOTAL. The command SUM TAPELIMIT, HOURLYRATE TO C,D stores the total of the Tapelimit field in variable C and the total of the Hourlyrate field in variable D. SUM TAPELIMIT FOR LASTNAME = "Robinson" TO E would store tape limit amounts for the name Robinson in variable E.

The WHILE clause, which is optional, is used with indexed files to sum the records while (or as long as) a particular condition is true. For example, in a file indexed by last names, you could find the first occurrence of the name Smith and then use a command like

```
SUM WHILE LASTNAME = "Smith"
```

to obtain the sum of any numeric fields for all the persons named Smith. You can use the FOR clause to accomplish the same task, but in a large database, using WHILE is considerably faster.

AVERAGE

The AVERAGE command calculates the average value of a numeric field. The basic format is

AVERAGE [FOR *fieldname*, ...] [WHILE *fieldname=condition*]
[TO *variable*, ...]

Here, *fieldname* must be a numeric field (there can be more than one field name). If you include a TO clause, the average of each field named will be stored in *variable*.

The command AVERAGE TAPELIMIT TO F stores the average value of the Tapelimit field in variable F.

@, ?, ??, and TEXT

Four commands are commonly used to display or print text: @, ?, ??, and TEXT. The ? and ?? commands display a single line of text at a time. If ? is used, a linefeed and carriage return occur before the display. A ?? command does not include a linefeed and carriage return before the display, so the subsequent value is displayed on the current line.

If the ? or ?? command is preceded by a SET PRINT ON command output is also routed to the printer. An example is shown in the following command file:

```
SET PRINT ON
? "The last name is: "
?? LASTNAME
?
? "The salary per 40-hour week is: "
?? SALARY * 40
SET PRINT OFF
```

You can also add the optional AT clause, and a column position, to the ? or ?? command to control where on the line the data will appear. For example, the command

```
? "Lastname:" AT 26
```

prints "Lastname:" starting at column 26 on the current line.

For more selective printing or display, the @ command moves the cursor to a specific location on the screen or page and, when combined with SAY, can display information or a prompt there. FoxPro divides the screen into 24 rows and 80 columns. The top left coordinate is 0,0, and the bottom right coordinate is 23,79. The general format of the @ command is

@ *row,column* [SAY *character-string*]

Omitting the SAY clause will clear (blank out) the designated row onscreen from the current column position to column 79.

To try the use of the @ command, enter

```
CLEAR
@ 12,20 SAY "This is a display"
```

Using the @ command with the SAY option, you can generate report headings or statements at any required location. Screen formatting with the @ command will be covered in greater detail in Chapter 15.

The TEXT command is useful for displaying large blocks of text onscreen. It is commonly used to display operator warnings, menus, and notes that appear during various operations of the program. The term TEXT is followed by the specific text to be displayed; then the whole process is ended with the term ENDTEXT. The text does not need to be surrounded by quotes. Everything between TEXT and ENDTEXT is displayed. The following example erases the screen with CLEAR, and then displays a copyright message:

```
CLEAR
TEXT
* * * * * * * * * * * * * * * * * * * * * * * * * * * * * * * * * * * * * * * * * * * * * * * * * * * * * * * * * * * *
              FoxPro Copyright (C) 1989-93 Microsoft Corp.
      Personnel Director Copyright (C) 1992 J Systems, Inc.
      For technical support, phone our offices at 555-5555
* * * * * * * * * * * * * * * * * * * * * * * * * * * * * * * * * * * * * * * * * * * * * * * * * * * * * * * * * * * *
ENDTEXT
WAIT
```

In this example, the WAIT command at the end of the program causes FoxPro to display a "press any key" message, and pause until the user presses a key.

The TEXT command must be used from within a command file. Any attempt to use TEXT as a direct command results in an error message.

Overview of a Program Design

How do you start to write a program, and after it is operational, how do you determine whether the program is efficient? Unfortunately, there is no one correct way to write a program or to determine when it is efficient or good. However, most programmers have a natural tendency to follow five steps in the design of a program:

1. Defining the problem

2. Designing the program

3. Writing the program

4. Verifying the program

5. Documenting the program

As these steps imply, the process of good programming is more than just writing a series of commands to be used in a particular command file. Programming requires careful planning of the code, and rigorous testing after it has been written.

If you are programming, you are probably building *applications,* which are groups of programs that perform a general task. Designing an application is somewhat similar to the process of designing a database (outlined in Chapter 1) in that careful planning is required. However, because you are designing an application and not a database, you must think about how the application will use information in the source database, how the application will produce reports, and how the application can be designed so that it is easy to use. Once these design steps have been clearly defined, you can proceed to design and create the programs that will make up the application.

Defining the Problem

The first step is to define the problem that the program is intended to solve. This step is too often skipped, even by professional programmers, in the rush to create a program. The problem may be as simple as wanting to automate a task; but in the process of defining it, you should query the people who will be using the program and find out what they expect the program to do. Even if you will be the only user, you should stop to outline what the program must provide before you begin writing it.

Output Requirements

Output, the information the application must produce, should be considered. Output is often useful in the form of a printed report, so defining what type of output is needed is often similar to the process of defining what is needed in a report. What types of output must the application produce? What responses to queries do the users expect? What must the reports look like? Sample screen displays or reports should be presented to the users for suggestions and approval. This may sound like a time-consuming process (and it often is), but the time saved by avoiding unnecessary rewrites of an inadequate program is worth the initial effort.

In the case of Generic Videos, asking the staff to list the kinds of reports they needed revealed two specific output needs. The first is a printed summary report that shows all outstanding rented tapes by state. The second is a way to find and display all of the information about a particular member. You want to be able to display information so that it appears organized, is easy to read, and is visually pleasing.

Input Requirements

Input, the ways in which the application will facilitate the collection of the data, also should be considered during the problem definition process. How will the information used by the application be entered and manipulated? A logical method for getting all of the information into the computer must be devised, and once the information is in the computer, you'll need efficient ways to change the data.

For example, someone must key in all of the information for an inventory that is being placed on the computer system for the first time. It's easy to think, "Why not just use the APPEND command to enter a record and let personnel type in all the data they might ever need?" Data integrity is the reason to avoid such an approach; if the data entry screens aren't easy to understand and logically designed, and if verification of the data isn't performed, chances are you'll have a database full of errors. Good design comes from using program control to make the data entry process clear and straightforward.

Most database applications must encompass two specific input needs. The first is a way to add new records to the database. You will do this using not only the APPEND command, but also other commands that make the screen display visually appealing and easy to read. The second is a way to select, and edit or delete, a particular record in the database. If you outline the output and input requirements of Generic Videos, the list might look like the one in Figure 14-3.

Designing the Program

Well-designed applications are collections of smaller programs, often referred to as *modules*, each performing a specific function. For example, a payroll accounting application is thought of as one program, but most such applications consist of at least three smaller modules. One module handles accounts receivable, the process of tracking incoming funds; the

FIGURE 14-3 Input and output operations for Generic Videos' database system

Generic Videos
Database System

Output Operations
1. Print summary report
2. Display member data

Input Operations
1. Add new records
2. Edit existing records

second module handles accounts payable, the process of paying the bills; and the third module handles the general ledger, a financial balance sheet that shows the funds on hand. This breakdown is shown in Figure 14-4.

Small modules help you tackle large programming tasks in small steps, which is an important principle of good program design. Many tasks worth performing with a database management system are too large in scope to be done in one simple operation. Moreover, dividing a program into modules makes it easier to find programming errors, since the problems can be isolated to the module(s) performing the specific tasks that are misbehaving.

An inventory system is an excellent example. At first glance, such a system may appear to be just a way of keeping track of the items on hand in a warehouse. Scratch the surface, though, and you'll find that there are numerous modules in such a system. The first module in the system adds items to the inventory as they are received; a second module subtracts inventory items as they are shipped; a third module monitors inventory levels; and if the quantity of an item falls below a specific point, a fourth module alerts the user by printing a message on the screen.

Modules of an accounting program

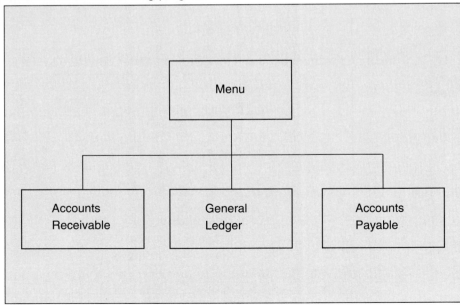

These modules interact and exchange information with other modules in the system, but they share one basic pool of information: the database itself.

It is during the design phase that the general and subsidiary functions of the program are outlined in detail.

 Remember any program worth writing is worth outlining on paper. The designer should resist the urge to begin writing programs at the keyboard without first outlining the steps of the program. The outline will help ensure that the intended program design is followed and that no steps are accidentally left out. Outlines are of great help in identifying the smaller tasks to be done by your system.

You'll find that it's best to list the general steps first and then break the general steps into smaller, more precise steps. Let's use the Generic Videos database system as an example. The system should perform these tasks:

1. Allow new members and new rentals to be added

2. Allow existing records to be changed (edited)

3. Display data from a record

4. Produce reports on all rentals or members

This simple outline shows what is basically required of the database management system. You then add more detail to the outline, as shown in Figure 14-5.

For purposes of simplicity, a specific requirement for the deleting of records has been omitted from this design. In a complete database system, you would also want to include a specific process for deleting records, as well as for performing file maintenance (such as rebuilding index files and performing a PACK from time to time).

With so much to think about during the process of designing a program you can easily overlook how the user will use it. Good program design, however, anticipates users' needs by including menus. Menus provide the user with a simple way of selecting what he or she would like to do. In a way, they are like a road map of the system; they guide the user through the steps involved in performing a task. For that reason,

FIGURE 14-5

Outline of database management system

> Outline of Program Design
>
> 1. Allow new entries to be added - APPEND
>
> 2. Change (edit) existing entries
>   –Show all record numbers and names on the screen
>   – Ask the user for the number of the record to edit
>   – Edit the selected record
>
> 3. Display data regarding a chosen entry
>   – Ask the user for the name of the member
>   – Search for that name in the database
>   – If name is found, print the information contained in all fields of the record
>
> 4. Produce reports of all rentals or all members
>   – Use the REPORT FORM *filename* command to produce a report

menus should be easy to follow, and there should always be a way out of a selection if the user changes his or her mind. In addition, the program should not operate abnormally or crash (stop running) in the event that the user makes an error when entering data.

Writing the Program

Now it's time to write the program. Most applications begin with a menu of choices, so the menu module should be written first. Each selection within the menu should then lead to the part of the program that performs the appropriate function. For example, a Run Report choice on a menu could result in a REPORT FORM command being issued to print a report. An Add New Entries choice could result in an APPEND command that adds data to the database. When you design your own systems, you'll find it helpful to design the menu first, and then use it as a starting point for the other modules in the program. In this example, however, you will not design the program's menu module until the next chapter because it uses various commands that are explained there.

It often helps, particularly if you are new to designing programs, to use pseudocode. Writing *pseudocode* means writing out all the steps of an operation in English. In other words, you write the program in pseudocode and then convert it into actual code. For instance, the process that would allow users to display a list of names and edit a particular name would look like this in pseudocode:

1. Open the MEMBERS database.

2. Clear screen.

3. List all names in the database.

4. Ask user for number of record to be edited, and store that number as a variable.

5. Edit specified record.

6. Return to main menu.

When you know what steps are needed to perform the task, you store the corresponding commands in a command file. As an example, enter

```
MODIFY COMMAND EDITMEMB
```

to create a new command file called EDITMEMB.PRG. When the Editor appears, enter the following commands and then choose File/Save (or press CTRL+S) to save the command file:

```
USE MEMBERS
CLEAR
LIST LASTNAME, FIRSTNAME
INPUT "Edit what record? " TO RECNO
CHANGE RECNO
RETURN
```

Verifying the Program

Any noticeable errors in the program should be corrected during this step. You should also examine the program to see if the needs of all the users have indeed been met; if not, you may need to make changes or additions to some modules. In addition, you should now make any improvements that can speed up the system or minimize user confusion.

The best way to find errors in a program is to use the program, so verify the program's operation by pressing ESC to close the Editor's window, and then entering this command in the Command window::

```
DO EDITMEMB
```

The program displays a list of all member names. The corresponding record numbers are shown to the left of the names:

```
Record#    LASTNAME       FIRSTNAME
       1   Miller         Karen
       2   Martin         William
       3   Robinson       Carol
       4   Kramer         Harry
       5   Moore          Ellen
       6   Zachman        David
       7   Robinson       Benjamin
       8   Hart           Wendy

Edit what record?
```

The program now asks for the number of the record that you wish to edit. In response to the prompt, enter **8** (for record 8). If the program works as designed, the Edit screen for record 8 should appear. Change the phone number for Wendy Hart to 555-3456, and save the change by pressing CTRL+F4. (Later, as a convenience for users unfamiliar with FoxPro, you may want to display a message explaining how to save changes.)

You should return to the Command window, and for now, that is all that is expected of the program. In later chapters, you'll add commands that use more attractive designs to view and edit data.

Documenting the Program

Documentation of a program takes one of two forms: written directions (like a manual) explaining how the program operates, and comments within the program itself about how the program is designed. The use of clear and simple menus and instructions within the program can help minimize the need for written documentation. A few sentences on how to start FoxPro and run the command file that displays the menu may be sufficient. As for directions and remarks within the program, FoxPro lets you put comments in the form of text at any location in a command file. Comments are preceded by an asterisk (*) or by the NOTE command. You can also use the double ampersand (&&) to add a comment to the right of a command on the same line. When FoxPro sees a line beginning with an asterisk or the word NOTE no action is taken by the program. And when FoxPro sees a double ampersand at the end of a command line FoxPro ignores everything that follows it on that line.

Comments are simply an aid to you and to any other person who modifies your command files. As an example, this short program file includes comment lines preceded with NOTE statements and asterisks (*):

```
CLEAR
NOTE Display the employees' names
LIST LASTNAME, FIRSTNAME
NOTE Ask for a record number and store it.
INPUT "Edit what record?" TO RECNO
*Edit the record.
EDIT RECNO
RETURN
```

This file may seem to have an overabundance of comments because it does not need elaboration. If a program file consists of dozens of commands, however, comments become more necessary. Not only do they make the program easier for you to understand, but if someone else must someday make changes to your program the comments will make it vastly easier for them to figure out your basic design.

CHAPTER

Program Control

When using command files to automate the storing and retrieving of records, you can achieve even greater flexibility by using conditional statements to control the flow of the command file. A program can prompt the user for input, and then let the user's response determine what the program does next.

To program a conditional statement, you need a way to evaluate user responses and, based on those responses, cause FoxPro to perform certain actions. Similarly, a program can read through a database file and perform different actions depending on the values stored in individual records. In this chapter you will use the IF, ELSE, ENDIF, DO WHILE, and ENDDO commands to perform these operations within a program. A number of other commands that control programs, such as CANCEL, EXIT, and WAIT, will also be covered.

Going in Circles

There will be many times when your program will need to perform the same task repeatedly. FoxPro has two commands, DO WHILE and ENDDO, that are used as a matched pair to repeat a series of commands as many times as necessary. The commands that you want to repeat are enclosed between the DO WHILE and the ENDDO commands.

The DO WHILE command always begins the loop, and the ENDDO command normally ends it. The commands inside the loop will continue to execute until the condition that you've specified, as part of the DO WHILE command, is no longer true. The condition that you specify will determine when the loop should stop; otherwise, the loop could go on indefinitely. The format is

DO WHILE *condition*
        [*commands...*]
ENDDO

As long as the condition within the DO WHILE command is true, the commands between the DO WHILE and the ENDDO commands are executed. Whenever ENDDO is reached, FoxPro returns to the top of the loop and reevaluates the condition. If the condition is still true, FoxPro executes the commands within the loop again; if the condition is not true,

FoxPro jumps to the command following the ENDDO command. If the condition is false when the DO WHILE command is first encountered, none of the commands in the loop will be executed, and the program proceeds to the first command that follows the ENDDO command.

Remember   ENDDO is a matching statement for DO WHILE. For every DO WHILE there must be an ENDDO, or your program will not behave as intended.

As an example, you could use the DO WHILE and ENDDO commands to create a command file that will print all the names and addresses in the Generic Videos database, with triple line-spacing between them. Go to the Command window and open a new command file named TRIPLE, by entering

```
MODIFY COMMAND TRIPLE
```

When the FoxPro Editor comes up, enter the following command file:

```
SET TALK OFF
USE MEMBERS
SET PRINT ON
DO WHILE .NOT. EOF()
  ? FIRSTNAME + LASTNAME
  ? ADDRESS
  ? CITY + STATE + " " + ZIPCODE
  ?
  ?
  ?
  SKIP
ENDDO
? "Triple report completed."
SET PRINT OFF
EJECT
```

Tip   After indenting lines with TAB, you can get back to the left margin by pressing the HOME key.

Before you save this command file, take a brief look at its design. After such preliminaries as activating the MEMBERS file and routing the output to the printer, the program begins the DO WHILE loop. The condition for DO WHILE is .NOT. EOF(), which simply means, "As long as the end of the file—EOF()—is NOT reached, continue the DO WHILE loop." The first three statements inside the loop print the name and address from the current record. Next, three question-mark symbols print three blank lines between each pair of records.

The SKIP command moves the pointer down one record, each time the body of the DO WHILE loop is executed. (If this command were absent, the pointer would never reach the end of the file, the condition would never become false, and the program would never leave the loop. It would, in fact, simply continue printing the same record over and over again!)

The ENDDO command is then reached, so FoxPro returns to the DO WHILE statement to re-evaluate the condition. If the pointer hasn't reached the end–of–file, the loop is repeated. Once the end-of-file has been reached, FoxPro proceeds past the ENDDO command. The final two commands in the program are executed, and control is returned to the Command window.

Indenting the commands between DO WHILE and ENDDO is a convention that can help you identify the body of the loop. This is especially helpful if you have *nested* DO WHILE loops—that is,placed a DO WHILE loop within a DO WHILE loop.

After typing the above commands, press CTRL+S to save the command file to disk, and close the window with CTRL+F4. Then make sure your printer is on, and enter the command **DO TRIPLE**. The command file will print the names and addresses on your printer, with three blank lines between each pair.

SCAN and ENDSCAN

Another set of commands you may encounter in working with FoxPro programs are the SCAN and ENDSCAN commands. These commands, like DO WHILE and ENDDO, are a matched pair. Also like DO WHILE and ENDDO, the SCAN and ENDSCAN commands let you create a repetitive loop in which operations are performed for a group of records in a database. The syntax for these commands is

SCAN [*scope*] [FOR *condition*] [WHILE *condition*]
        [*commands...*]
ENDSCAN

The SCAN and ENDSCAN commands are simpler alternatives to the DO WHILE and ENDDO commands. If you simply wish to use DO WHILE and ENDDO to perform repetitive processing, you can often use SCAN and ENDSCAN instead, and use slightly fewer lines of programming code.

As an example, perhaps you want to write a program that, using a DO WHILE loop, would print the name and tape limit for every person in the database who has a tape limit of more than three. You could accomplish the task with a program like this:

```
USE MEMBERS
SET PRINT ON
DO WHILE .NOT. EOF()
    IF TAPELIMIT > 3
        ? LASTNAME, FIRSTNAME
        ?? TAPELIMIT
    ENDIF
    SKIP
ENDDO
```

By comparison, you could use the SCAN and ENDSCAN commands to accomplish the same task. An example of the program code using SCAN and ENDSCAN is shown here:

```
USE MEMBERS
SET PRINT ON
SCAN FOR TAPELIMIT > 3
    ? LASTNAME, FIRSTNAME
    ?? TAPELIMIT
ENDSCAN
```

Because the SCAN command combined the WHILE and IF clauses to specify the condition (a tape limit greater than three), you can use fewer lines of program code to accomplish the same task.

FoxPro automatically skips to the next successive record when it encounters ENDSCAN, unless you are at the end of the file. Once the end of the file is reached, program control drops out of the loop and moves on to the next command. Note that program control may exit from the loop before the end of the file is reached if you include a WHILE clause as a part of the SCAN statement.

IF, ELSE, and ENDIF

In many command files, FoxPro needs to perform different operations depending on a user's response to an option, a previous calculation or operation, or different values encountered in a database. For example, if a program's main menu gives the user a choice of editing or printing a record, the program must be able to check which choice the user makes, and then start the appropriate operation.

FoxPro can use the IF, ELSE, and ENDIF commands to branch to the part of the program where the chosen operation is performed. Much like the DO WHILE-ENDDO loop, the IF and ENDIF commands are used as a matched pair, enclosing a number of commands. The ELSE command is optional, and is used within the body of IF-ENDIF as another decision step. The IF and ENDIF commands can be used to decide between actions in a program.

The format of the command is

IF *condition*
        [*commands...*]
ELSE
        [*commands...*]
ENDIF

This decision-making command must always start with IF and end with ENDIF. The commands that you place between the IF and ENDIF statements determine exactly what will occur if the condition is true. (Again, indenting the commands within the body of IF-ENDIF makes the flow of the program easier to understand.) The optional ELSE statement can be used to specify an alternate set of commands that will be carried out only if the condition in the IF statement is not true.

A good way to build IF and ELSE structures is to write them first in pseudocode, then in the FoxPro command language, and then compare them to make sure your commands specify what you originally intended. For example:

Pseudocode	FoxPro
If last name is Cooke, then display last name.	IF LASTNAME = "Cooke" ? LASTNAME ENDIF
If monthly rent is less than $300, then display "Reasonably priced."	IF RENTMONTH < 300 ? "Reasonably priced." ENDIF

Using IF and ENDIF alone works fine for making a single decision, but if you wish to add an alternative choice, you need the ELSE statement:

Pseudocode	FoxPro

If last name is Cooke, then print last name; or else print "There is no one by that name in this database."	IF LASTNAME = "Cooke"
	   ? LASTNAME
	 ELSE
	   ? "There is no one by that name in this database."
	 ENDIF

FoxPro evaluates the condition following the IF command to see if any action should be taken. If no action is necessary (that is, the condition is false), FoxPro looks for an ELSE statement. If it finds one, it executes the commands following the term ELSE; otherwise, control simply passes to the next command after the ENDIF command. In the following example, if SALARY is not 10 then the STORE command will not be executed, and FoxPro will proceed to the command following ENDIF:

```
IF SALARY = 10
    STORE SALARY TO MATCH
ENDIF
```

You can also use multiple IF-ENDIF commands if you need to have the program make more than one decision. Consider this example:

```
? "Enter 1 to print mailing labels or 2 to edit."
INPUT "What is your choice?" TO CHOICE
IF CHOICE = 1
```

```
        DO TRIPLE
ENDIF
IF CHOICE = 2
        DO CHANGES
ENDIF
```

The answer that the user types is stored in a memory variable called CHOICE. One of three things can happen then, depending on whether the user has typed a 1, a 2, or something else in response to the question. If CHOICE equals 1, the TRIPLE program is run from disk. If CHOICE equals 2, the CHANGES program is run. If CHOICE equals neither 1 or 2, then the program proceeds to the next command after the ENDIF command.

Nesting IF-ENDIFs

You can use nested IF-ENDIF statements, which are IF-ENDIF statements placed inside of other IF-ENDIF statements. For the innermost IF-ENDIF statement to be processed, the condition tested by the outermost IF-ENDIF statement must be true. The following is an example of a nested IF-ENDIF statement:

```
INPUT "Display report on (S)creen or (P)rinter?" TO ANS
IF UPPER(ANS) = "P"
        INPUT "Ready printer, press Enter, or type C then;
        press Enter to cancel report." TO ANS2
        IF UPPER(ANS2) = "C"
            *user canceled print run.
            RETURN
        ENDIF
        REPORT FORM MEMBERS TO PRINT
        EJECT
ENDIF
```

In this example, whether the innermost IF-ENDIF will ever be processed is determined by the response supplied to the outermost IF-ENDIF statement. If the user does not type P for printer, FoxPro skips ahead to the outermost ENDIF statement. If the user does respond with P for printer, FoxPro displays the "Ready printer" message, and the innermost IF-ENDIF tests for the user's response and takes appropriate action.

Tip If you are going to nest IF-ENDIF statements, then indenting your commands will help you keep track of whether you have matching statements (that is, an ENDIF for each IF). It is very important to make sure that nested IFs and ENDIFs match up, or else your program will incorporate serious (and often hard-to-find) errors.

The Immediate IF Function

Within programs, you may want to make use of the IIF (Immediate IF) function. The syntax for the function is

IIF(*condition, expression1, expression2*)

If the condition specified is true, FoxPro returns the first expression; if the condition is false, FoxPro returns the second expression. As an example, the statement

```
CREDITOK = IIF(INCOME>=15000, "yes", "no")
```

would, when processed in a program, store a character expression of "yes" to the CREDITOK variable if the amount in INCOME was equal to or greater than 15,000. Otherwise, it would store the character expression "no". In effect, this statement performs the same task as the following commands:

```
IF INCOME >= 15000
     CREDITOK = "yes"
ELSE
     CREDITOK = "no"
ENDIF
```

The advantage of the Immediate IF function is that it takes fewer lines of code to accomplish the same task, and it is executed slightly faster.

Using the IF-ENDIF Statement

You can use the IF-ENDIF statement in a command file to search for and display data from a specific record in your database. For example, if you want to find a member named Zachman, you can use the ACCEPT and IF-ENDIF commands to search for the record. (This operation can be done faster with SEEK, but for demonstration purposes, a combination of IF and DO WHILE is used here.)

First, let's use pseudocode to outline what needs to be done:

USE MEMBERS database.
ACCEPT the last name.
BEGIN the DO-WHILE loop.
IF the Lastname field = the ACCEPT variable,
PRINT (on the screen) name, address, tape limit, and expiration date.
END the IF test.
SKIP forward one record.
END the DO-WHILE loop.
RETURN to the Command window.

Now create a command file by entering

```
MODIFY COMMAND SHOWMEMB
```

When the FoxPro Editor appears in a window, enter the following:

```
*This program finds and shows data in the members file.
USE MEMBERS
SET TALK OFF
CLEAR
*Begin loop that contains commands to display record.
ACCEPT "Search for what last name? " TO SNAME
DO WHILE .NOT. EOF()
      IF LASTNAME = SNAME
          ? "Last name is: "
          ?? LASTNAME
          ? "First name is: "
          ?? FIRSTNAME
          ? "Address is: "
          ?? ADDRESS
          ? CITY + STATE + " " + ZIPCODE
          ?
          ? "Tape limit is: "
          ?? TAPELIMIT
          ? "Expiration Date is: "
          ?? EXPIREDATE
          ?
```

```
        ENDIF
        SKIP
ENDDO
WAIT
RETURN
```

After saving the file with CTRL+S, try running the program by entering **DO SHOWMEMB** in the Command window. In response to the lastname prompt that appears on the screen, enter **Zachman**, and FoxPro will search the database for the record containing this name. Run the program again, and enter **Robinson**. You will see the records for both Robinsons displayed.

In this search you used the ACCEPT, IF, and ENDIF commands. The ACCEPT command stored the name that you entered into the memory variable SNAME. The IF loop began a decision-making process that stated the condition, "If the memory variable SNAME contains the same name as the Lastname field, then execute the commands that follow the IF command."

There is no limit to the number of commands that you can place between IF and ENDIF in the loop. You can also link multiple IF-ENDIF and ELSE commands if multiple choices are needed within a program.

Using CASE to Evaluate Multiple Choices

Your program may need to make more than two or three decisions, based on a single response. A series of IF-ENDIF statements could do the job, but using more than three IF-ENDIFs to test the value of one field (or memory variable) is unwieldy. There is an easier way: use the CASE statement. With the CASE statement, the IF-ENDIF tests are made into alternative cases of one long conditional statement, and FoxPro then chooses the first case, the second case, or whichever other case matches the user's response.

The CASE statement is framed by a matched pair of terms: DO CASE and ENDCASE. All conditional choices are declared between DO CASE and ENDCASE. The OTHERWISE term functions exactly like the ELSE in an IF-ENDIF statement. The general format is

```
DO CASE
     CASE condition
     [commands...]
     [CASE condition...]
     [commands...]
     [OTHERWISE]
     [commands...]
ENDCASE
```

Whenever FoxPro encounters a DO CASE command, it examines each CASE term until it finds a condition that is true; then it executes the commands below that line, until it encounters either the next CASE term or the ENDCASE term (whichever comes first).

If you want to create a simple menu that offers a choice of displaying a record, printing labels, editing a record, or adding a record, you could write a command file like this:

```
CLEAR
? "1. Display a membership record"
?
? "2. Print the membership database"
?
? "3. Change a membership record"
?
INPUT "Choose a selection " TO SELECT
DO CASE
     CASE SELECT = 1
          DO SHOWMEMB
     CASE SELECT = 2
          DO TRIPLE
     CASE SELECT = 3
          DO EDITMEMB
ENDCASE
```

In this example, the INPUT statement queries the user for a selection. When the user's response has been entered, it is stored in the SELECT variable. Then, in the DO CASE series, FoxPro compares the value of the SELECT variable against the test value in each CASE. If it finds a match, it executes the command file named within that CASE statement, and no other CASE statement is evaluated. (Note that the SHOWMEMB command file for the first selection was created in the last chapter).

If no match is found, FoxPro proceeds to the next statement after the ENDCASE command. Like IF-ENDIF, the DO CASE and ENDCASE commands are used in pairs. You must always end a CASE series with an ENDCASE command.

You should use DO CASE to process menu selections if you have more than three choices. For example, if you wanted to offer the same three selections from the last program using IF-ENDIF and ELSE, the command file might look like this:

```
CLEAR
? "1. Display a membership record"
?
? "2. Print the membership database"
?
? "3. Change a membership record"
?
INPUT "Choose a selection" TO SELECT
IF SELECT = 1
     DO SHOWMEMB
ENDIF
IF SELECT = 2
     DO TRIPLE
ENDIF
IF SELECT = 3
     DO EDITMEMB
ENDIF
```

Using IF-ENDIF becomes more complex than DO CASE as the number of choices increases.

Let's use a CASE statement to create a main menu for the Generic Videos database. (Note that FoxPro provides much better and more attractive ways to create menus, but this technique is used here for the sake of simplicity.) In the Command window, enter the statement **MODIFY COMMAND MENU1**, and when the FoxPro Editor appears, enter the following command file:

```
USE MEMBERS
SET TALK OFF
STORE 0 TO CHOICE
DO WHILE CHOICE <> 5
CLEAR
 * Display the menu.
? "Generic Videos Membership System Menu"
```

```
?
? " 1. Add a new entry to the database."
? " 2. Change an existing entry."
? " 3. Produce the membership report."
? " 4. Display data regarding a particular member."
? " 5. Exit this program."
INPUT "Enter selection: " TO CHOICE
DO CASE
        CASE CHOICE=1
             APPEND
        CASE CHOICE=2
             DO EDITMEMB
        CASE CHOICE=3
             REPORT FORM SAMPLE
        CASE CHOICE=4
             DO SHOWMEMB
        CASE CHOICE=5
             CLOSE DATABASES
             SET TALK ON
             RETURN
        ENDCASE
ENDDO
```

The menu offers five choices, and the INPUT command stores the user's response in the CHOICE variable. If FoxPro finds a matching choice, it executes the command or commands that follow that choice.

Save this command file by pressing CTRL+S, and close the window with CTRL+F4. When the prompt reappears, enter DO MENU1. Try some of the menu choices on your own to see how the system operates.

The simple menu created by the above example does the job, but is not very appealing from a visual standpoint. In the next chapter, you will learn how you can create menus that resemble the menus used by FoxPro.

EXIT

The EXIT command can be used within a DO WHILE-ENDDO programming statement; it lets FoxPro exit from the DO WHILE-ENDDO loop to the first command below ENDDO. Note that an EXIT command arbitrarily placed within a DO WHILE loop will prevent FoxPro from ever reaching the commands between the terms EXIT and ENDDO; thus, EXIT makes sense only if it is executed conditionally. For this reason, you will frequently find EXIT commands inside IF-ENDIF and CASE statements.

Consider the following example, in a program that lists a name based on a desired address. The same task could be accomplished with a LOCATE command, but to demonstrate the EXIT command, this program uses a DO WHILE loop.

```
USE MEMBERS
SET TALK OFF
GO TOP
ACCEPT "What is the address- " TO CHOICE
DO WHILE .NOT. EOF()
       IF ADDRESS = CHOICE
              ? LASTNAME, FIRSTNAME
              EXIT
       ENDIF
       SKIP
ENDDO
```

If the contents of Address (a field) match CHOICE (a variable), the EXIT command will cause the DO WHILE loop to terminate. Otherwise, the SKIP command below the ENDIF statement will advance the pointer by one record, and the comparison will be repeated. If no match is found at all, control will finally pass out of the loop after the last record is read.

Use EXIT commands conservatively: a program that is always jumping out of loops—and around the program, for that matter—is difficult to follow and debug, and is contrary to good program design. Most DO WHILEs that have EXITs can be redesigned to omit them.

CANCEL

The CANCEL command halts execution of a FoxPro command file and returns you to the Command window. It can be useful when you are testing command files. However, using CANCEL in a completed FoxPro program may be unwise. CANCEL simply drops the user into the Command window, and the inexperienced user may not know how to restart the program or exit FoxPro. QUIT is an alternative command, which will exit both the command file and FoxPro, and return the user to the

Windows desktop. You can include an option on your command file's main menu that invokes the QUIT command.

WAIT

The WAIT command halts execution of a FoxPro program until a key is pressed. WAIT can also display a message or prompt and store the value of the pressed key to a character variable. The normal format of the command is

WAIT [*prompt*] [TO *memory-variable*]

Both *prompt* and *memory-variable* are optional. If a prompt is not specified, FoxPro supplies the message "Press any key to continue..." as a default prompt. As an example, to display a message, halt execution of a program until a key is pressed, and store that key as a variable named ANSWER, you could use the following command:

```
WAIT "Enter Y to begin processing transactions, any other key
to continue:" TO ANSWER
```

You could then use an IF-ELSE-ENDIF structure to test the value of ANSWER and take different actions depending on the result.

ZAP

The ZAP command is a one-step command for erasing all records from a database while leaving the structure of the database intact. Using ZAP is functionally equivalent to entering **DELETE ALL** and then entering **PACK**. However, ZAP operates considerably faster than a DELETE ALL command followed by a PACK command.

If you include the ZAP command in a program, you may want to place the SET SAFETY OFF command above it; this tells FoxPro not to ask for confirmation before erasing all records from the database. If so, make sure to SET SAFETY ON again afterwards. Also, since the ZAP command is destructive, be very careful in using it. If the database file which you are ZAPping is anything more important than a temporary scratch database, be sure to make a backup copy of the file before testing the ZAP command.

Using Programming Macros

FoxPro has a handy macro-substitution function. It is used specifically within programs and is not to be confused with the types of macros covered in Chapter 9. Macro substitution works like this: an ampersand (&) is placed in front of a memory variable name, and the combination of ampersand and variable name becomes the FoxPro macro. Then, whenever FoxPro sees the macro, it replaces it with the contents of the memory variable.

If, for example, you have a memory variable called NAME, you could store the names of different people in this variable at different times as a program runs. If an instruction in the program precedes the term NAME with an ampersand (&), then NAME becomes a macro. Each time FoxPro encounters &NAME, it will reference the current value of &NAME, instead of the name of the variable itself. Try a macro operation by entering the following commands from the Command window:

```
USE MEMBERS
INDEX ON LASTNAME TO NAME
STORE "Zachman" TO TEST
FIND &TEST
DISPLAY
```

Commands that take literal values as arguments require macros if they are to derive values from variables. One such command is FIND. With the FIND command, you are normally required to enter the literal value, or the actual characters, of the item to be found. With the macro function, however, you are able to substitute a variable for the actual name.

In the example just shown, you could easily have directly entered **FIND "Zachman"**, instead of using the variable "TEST" as a macro. But using macros saves time in programming, since a reference to one variable can take the place of several references to specific literal values.

You can use macro substitution, in response to a user's query, to search a database selectively for information; once you have found the item, you can edit or delete it. An example of these techniques is used in a routine for editing records, discussed in the following chapter.

CHAPTER

Programming for Data Entry and Editing

403

*F*oxPro can help you design screen displays that will help make your
database management system more understandable for the people
who use it. The appearance of screen displays may at first seem like a
point of minor importance, but if you were a new FoxPro system user,
consider which screen display in Figure 16-1 would be easier to use: the
top screen, or the bottom screen? Obviously, the bottom screen will make
more sense to the novice FoxPro user; it is clearer and less cluttered than
the top screen.

As you will see in this chapter, you can easily create well-designed
screens by storing various screen-display commands within a FoxPro
command file. You'll use the @ command and the SAY and GET options
to place prompts and information at selected locations on the screen, and
the READ option to allow responses to the prompts displayed by the
system. You can use the PROMPT and MENU TO commands to create,
with relative ease, pop-up menus similar to those used by FoxPro. You'll
also examine how the forms design screen can provide most of the
commands needed for the formatting of screens.

FIGURE
16-1   Two screen displays

Generic Video Membership System
1. Add new entries
2. Change an entry
3. Print reports
4. Display member data
5. Exit system

Generic Videos Membership Data System
Add members
Edit members
Print reports
Display member data
Exit system

Putting Information on the Screen

The @ command (commonly referred to as the "AT" command) tells FoxPro where to place the cursor on the screen. When using the @ command, think of the FoxPro screen as being divided into 25 lines and 80 columns, as shown in Figure 16-2. Rows are numbered from 0 to 24, and columns are numbered from 0 to 79. Row 0, column 0 is in the upper-left corner of the screen; row 24, column 79 is in the lower-right corner. The cursor can be placed in any screen position.

Once the cursor has been placed in the proper position with the @ command, you can display a message with the SAY option. The SAY option causes any text (or the contents of any string variable) that follows the command to appear on the screen. The SAY option can be used, along with the @ command, in one of these two possible ways:

@ *row,column* SAY *"message"*
@ *row,column* SAY *varname*

FIGURE
16-2

FoxPro screen

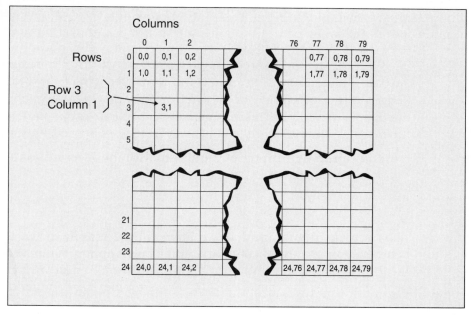

In the first format, SAY is followed by one or more characters, which must be enclosed by double or single quotes. (You should use double quotes whenever there is an apostrophe within the message itself.) The characters are displayed on the screen exactly as they appear between the quotes. In the second format, *varname* is the name of a string variable. Any value that your program has stored in that variable will be displayed.

To try the first format, let's display a message beginning at row 12, column 40, on the screen. Get to the Command window, and then enter

```
CLEAR
@ 12,40 SAY "Enter name."
```

This displays the prompt "Enter name." beginning at row 12, column 40, on the screen.

You can try the second format by entering

```
STORE 1200.57 TO AMOUNT
@ 6,30 SAY AMOUNT
```

This stores the string of text "1200.57" in the variable named AMOUNT, and then displays the value at row 6, column 30.

 Tip   When calculating screen locations, figure the possible length of an expression to be sure it will fit. Some trial and error may be required to get it right.

When designing a screen display using an "@...SAY..." statement with a pair of coordinates, keep in mind that specifying coordinates for the edges of the screen may or may not actually display visible characters at your screen's edges. This is because some monitors cut off the edges. So, to be safe, you may want to stay away from the outer edges of the screen.

You can erase any part of the screen with the @ command and CLEAR option. The format is

```
@ row,column CLEAR
```

The screen beginning at *row,column* will be erased to the lower-right corner. You use the @ command and CLEAR option in a manner similar to the @ command and SAY option, but don't enter any prompts or variables after the word "CLEAR." For example, the command

```
@ 9,7 CLEAR
```

erases the screen from the point at row 9, column 7, to the lower-right corner.

Using GET and READ with @ and SAY

Now that you know how to display information at selected places on the screen, you need a way to store users' responses to screen prompts. This is done with the GET and READ options. When used in combination, these commands can display existing variables or field names, can indicate the lengths of fields, and can store the user's replies. There are two formats:

@ *row,column* SAY "prompt" GET *varname*... READ
@ *row,column* SAY "prompt" GET *fieldname*... READ

The GET option tells FoxPro to get ready to accept information. The argument that follows the GET term (i.e., the destination for the information) can be either an existing memory variable, or a field in the active database. The READ option then tells FoxPro to enter Edit mode, which, much like Append mode, allows the user to move the cursor around a screen display that represents fields or variables with blanks. FoxPro will then accept responses from the keyboard for any of the preceding GET options, and will store the responses in memory. In addition, the READ option lets you edit the displayed information.

A READ command applies to all GET statements between the READ option and any previous use of the READ option, or the start of the program, whichever is closest.

A GET option does not have to be immediately followed by a READ option; it can be the last command in a series of GET statements. But if you use GET without READ, you cannot enter any responses from the keyboard. READ options are only used following GET options.

You could, for example, create a command file like this one:

```
@ 5,10 SAY "Enter name." GET LASTNAME
@ 7,10 SAY "Enter address." GET ADDRESS
@ 9,10 SAY "Enter city." GET CITY
```

```
@ 11,10 SAY "Enter state." GET STATE
READ
```

If you were to load the database containing these field names and run this command file, FoxPro would provide a screen display that prompted you for the desired information. The prompts would appear at the screen locations identified by the @-SAY commands. Once the READ option was encountered, FoxPro would enter full-screen Edit mode, and the cursor would be placed at the start of the first area identified by a GET option.

As data was entered, FoxPro would store all of the entries in memory under the field names (or variable names) indicated. The name would be stored in Lastname, the address in Address, the city in City, and so on. Once a READ occurs, data entered under the field names is stored by FoxPro.

You could also use the INPUT command (along with a prompt) to place information on the screen and store a response, but with INPUT, it is not easy to specify where on the screen the information appears. The example that follows uses the @ command in combination with the SAY, GET and READ options, and the PROMPT and MENU TO commands, to produce a clear, well-designed menu screen.

Working with Memo Fields

Although you can use the name of a memo field as an argument to @–SAY–GET commands like those just shown, you will probably want to take advantage of better ways to enter and edit data in memo fields. If you include a memo field in a command file, as in

```
@ 12, 5 SAY "Preferences? " GET PREFERENCE
```

the field appears in a small box containing the word "memo," and you will have to use the same editing techniques discussed earlier to enter and exit the memo field. If you instead make use of the MODIFY MEMO command, you will automatically open a window in which to edit the memo field. The syntax for the command is

MODIFY MEMO *field1* [, *field2*...] [NOWAIT]

When processed in a program, the command automatically opens a window for each of the named memo fields. The contents of the memo field for the current record appear in the window, and the window(s) remain open until closed. (You close these memo windows using the same methods you would use to close any other window.)

The MODIFY MEMO command can be issued from the Command window, or from a program; the NOWAIT option is used only within programs. Normally, a program halts while a memo editing window is open, and continues when the window is closed. You can add the NOWAIT option to tell FoxPro to open the window and continue execution of the program.

In the case of the MEMBERS database, a program specifically designed to edit the contents of the Preference field might resemble the following:

```
*EditMemo.PRG edits memo field.
USE MEMBERS
INPUT "Which record number? " TO FINDIT
GOTO FINDIT
CLEAR
@ 22, 5 SAY "Member: " + TRIM(FIRSTNAME) + " " + LASTNAME
MODIFY MEMO PREFERENCE
RETURN
```

Your programs will probably use a more detailed method to search for the desired record, but this simple example demonstrates the use of the MODIFY MEMO command. Once the desired record number has been entered, the member name appears near the bottom of the screen and the memo field opens within a window. You can edit the memo field, and you can move or resize the window as desired. In the example, the RETURN statement will exit this routine when the window is closed.

Customizing a Data Entry Screen

One area of the system that could stand improvement is data entry. Currently, the system relies on the APPEND command. With the @ command and the SAY, GET, and READ options, you can display the prompts more neatly than you can with the APPEND command, while still storing the data to the fields of the database.

Let's create a new command file called ADDER that will be used whenever you want to add a record to the database. Enter **MODIFY COMMAND ADDER**, and type the following instructions:

```
USE MEMBERS
CLEAR
@ 0,5,14,60 BOX
APPEND BLANK
@ 1,10 SAY "      Social Sec." GET SOCIAL
@ 2,10 SAY "        Lastname:" GET LASTNAME
@ 3,10 SAY "       Firstname:" GET FIRSTNAME
@ 4,10 SAY "         Address:" GET ADDRESS
@ 5,10 SAY "            City:" GET CITY
@ 6,10 SAY "           State:" GET STATE
@ 7,10 SAY "        ZIP Code:" GET ZIPCODE
@ 8,10 SAY "       Telephone:" GET PHONE
@ 9,10 SAY "      Birth date:" GET BIRTHDAY
@ 10,10 SAY " Expiration Date:" GET EXPIREDATE
@ 11,10 SAY "      Tape limit:" GET TAPELIMIT
@ 12,10 SAY "           Beta?:" GET BETA
READ
MODIFY MEMO PREFERENCE
RETURN
```

Examine this command file before saving it. After opening the file with USE, clearing the screen, and using the @...BOX command to draw a box, it then uses the BLANK option of the APPEND command. Whenever FoxPro sees APPEND BLANK as a command, it adds a blank record to the end of the database, and the record pointer is positioned at this new last record.

Each @–SAY command displays a query, such as "Birth Date:". The GET option not only displays the contents of each field listed, but it displays them in reverse video, in dimensions corresponding to the field's width. Since the record pointer is referencing the last record, which is empty, only the reverse video is displayed. The READ command toward the end of the command file activates the full-screen entry and editing specified by the GET statements. When data entry or editing has been completed for the last field, you will return to the main menu section of the program.

Press CTRL+S to save the command file, then close the window with CTRL+F4. Now you'll need to make one change in the main menu command file to integrate the new ADDER command file into the system. Enter

MODIFY COMMAND MENU1 to change the program. Delete the USE MEMBERS line directly underneath CASE CHOICE = 1, and change APPEND in the command file to **DO ADDER**. Then, press CTRL+S to save the file, and close the window with CTRL+F4.

Try out the new command file by entering **DO MENU1**. Choose the first option on the menu, and try entering a new member of your own choosing.

Using PICTURE

The PICTURE option is used with the @ command to format data. Using PICTURE, you can display dollar amounts with comma separators and decimal points, and you can display dates in American or European date formats. PICTURE can be used to restrict the way data can be entered into the system. You can create a statement that accepts numbers only (for dollar amounts), or a date only, rejecting any other characters.

The PICTURE option is divided into function and template symbols (see Table 16-1). The format is

@ *row,column* SAY *expression* PICTURE "*clause*"

You use the PICTURE option by adding the word PICTURE, and then the arguments that specify the function or template. The function or template symbols in the clause are surrounded by quotes. In the case of functions, the @ symbol must precede the letter or character that identifies the function.

Two examples of the PICTURE option are shown here:

```
@ 12,40 SAY "Enter effective date-" GET PICTURE "@E"
@ 14,20 SAY "Customer name is: " LASTNAME PICTURE "!!!!!!!!!!!!!!!!!"
```

In the first example, the @ symbol after the word PICTURE defines the argument as a function. The letter E defines the function as European date format. The second example uses a template. The exclamation points in this template will cause the field's contents to be displayed in upper-case letters, regardless of how the characters were stored in the database.

TABLE 16-1

Functions and templates used with PICTURE

Symbol	Meaning
	FUNCTIONS
A	Displays alphabetic characters only
B	Left-justifies numeric data
C	Displays CR for credit, after a positive number
D	Displays American date format
E	Displays European date format
X	Displays DB for debit, after a negative number
Z	Displays any zeros as blanks
!	Displays capital letters only
(	Surrounds negative numbers with parentheses
	TEMPLATES
9	Allows only digits for character data, or digits and signs for numeric data
#	Allows only digits, blanks, and signs
A	Allows only letters
L	Allows only logical data (.T. or .F.;.Y. or .N.)
N	Allows only letters and digits
X	Allows any character
!	Converts letters to uppercase
$	Displays dollar signs in place of leading zeros
*	Displays asterisks in place of leading zeros
.	Specifies a decimal position
,	Displays a comma if there are any numbers to the left of the comma

Some of the functions used with PICTURE apply only to certain kinds of data. The C, X, B, (, and Z functions apply only to numeric data. The @ and ! functions apply only to character data, but the D and E functions apply to date, character, and numeric data.

You can combine function symbols to apply multiple functions. For example, the function symbols BZ align numeric data at the left side of the field, and display any zero values as blanks.

You can get a better idea of how the PICTURE option is used if you try a few examples. First let's try the X and C functions. The X function will display DB, for debit, after a negative number, and the C function will display CR, for credit, after a positive number. Try the following commands to illustrate these functions:

```
CLEAR
STORE 1650.32 TO A
STORE 795 TO B
@5,0 SAY A PICTURE "@X"
@10,0 SAY B PICTURE "@C"
```

The results are as follows:

```
1650.32 DB

795 CR
```

This is useful in accounting.

The ! template is useful when you want characters to display in all uppercase letters. Try this:

```
CLEAR
STORE "small words" TO WORDS
@10,10 SAY WORDS PICTURE "@!"
```

The # template reserves space for digits, blanks, or signs, and the comma template specifies where the comma should appear in numeric data. Try these templates with the following example:

```
STORE 1234.56 TO A
@16,0 SAY A PICTURE "#,###.##"
```

```
1,234.56
```

When you are using templates, you must use a symbol to represent each character that is to be displayed with SAY or GET. To display a character field that is ten characters wide in uppercase, for example, you would need ten exclamation points in the template. The template would look like this:

```
@20,10 SAY "Name is—"+NAME PICTURE "!!!!!!!!!!"
```

Let's try using a PICTURE option in the command file for adding a record. Enter **MODIFY COMMAND ADDER**. Change the line of the program that reads

```
@ 1,10 SAY "Social Sec.: " GET SOCIAL
```

to this:

```
@ 1,10 SAY "Social Sec.: " GET SOCIAL PICTURE "999-99-9999"
```

Note the use of the hyphens in this example. Any characters that are not valid template symbols are displayed as literal data; hence, they are called literals. In this template, the hyphens are literals, while the 9s are valid template symbols.

Save the program with CTRL+S, then close the window with CTRL+F4 and run the system with **DO MENU1**. Choose the Add New Entries option and enter another record. You'll see the new format imposed by the PICTURE specification as you enter the social security number; the hyphens will automatically be added. You can get out of the system without making changes to the database by pressing the ESC key and then choosing the Exit System option to return to the Command window.

Note that when you use functions and templates along with a GET command, as you did in this example, the data is stored in the specified format, not just displayed that way (as with the SAY command). The use of functions and templates along with GET commands can be very useful for forcing data entries into uppercase.

Using Format Files

Let's say that you wanted to enter only last names, first names, and membership expiration dates without being required to step through all of the other fields that normally appear on the screen—addresses, phone numbers, birth dates, and so on. You can limit the amount of information shown on a screen in either Append mode or Change mode by using a *format file*. A format file is a special file with the extension .FMT, containing a set of @–SAY–GET statements; it displays messages and prompts according to your arrangements. Once you have created the format file, you can implement it with the SET FORMAT TO command. For an example, create a format file with the Editor by entering

```
MODIFY COMMAND QUICKIE.FMT
```

This creates a file called QUICKIE with the format extension .FMT. Now enter the following commands:

```
@ 10,10 SAY "The last name is: " GET LASTNAME
@ 12,10 SAY "The first name is: " GET FIRSTNAME
@ 14,10 SAY "The expiration date is: " GET EXPIREDATE
```

Press CTRL+S to save the format file, then close the window with CTRL+F4. Then, from the Command window, enter

```
USE MEMBERS
GO TOP
CHANGE
```

Notice that what you see is the normal editing screen with all of its fields. Press ESC to get back to the Command window.

To use the format file, you must use the command SET FORMAT TO *filename* (you don't have to supply the .FMT extension). Enter

```
SET FORMAT TO QUICKIE
```

Now enter **APPEND**. With the new format file in effect, only the specified fields will be displayed. Press ESC to leave Edit mode without saving any changes.

Now enter **GOTO 5**. This moves the pointer to record 5. Enter **CHANGE**. Instead of the normal editing screen, you see just those fields specified in the format file. Press ESC to get out of Edit mode without making any changes. To disable a format file when you finish using it, simply enter **CLOSE FORMAT**. (You need not specify the name of the format file, since only one format file may be opened at a time.) Enter **CLOSE FORMAT** now, before proceeding.

Remember   The PICTURE and FUNCTION templates, discussed earlier, can be used in format files.

Format files can come in handy when you want to use the same screen
format many times in different parts of a program. You can include SET
FORMAT TO *filename* anywhere in a FoxPro command file, and the
resulting format file will take effect for any appending or editing until you
use CLOSE FORMAT.

Using Windows

One of FoxPro's greatest assets, which you should not ignore when
designing programs, is its ability to display information within windows.
From your prior use of commands like BROWSE and EDIT, you know
that FoxPro lets you add and edit data within windows. It should also be
clear by now that you can open multiple windows at the same time, and
place them at various locations on the screen. What may not be obvious
is that you can use certain window-related commands within programs
to display or edit data inside of windows.

There are three often-used commands that relate to window management within FoxPro.

☐   DEFINE WINDOW *windowname* is used to define the screen coordinates (location) and the display attributes for a window.

☐   ACTIVATE WINDOW *windowname* [ALL] is used to activate a window that has already been defined. Once a window has been
activated, all screen output will appear in this window until another
window is activated, or until the current window is deactivated. The
ALL option, when used, activates all previously defined windows,
and causes current screen output to appear in the last window to
be defined.

☐   DEACTIVATE WINDOW *windowname* [ALL] is used to deactivate,
or turn off, an active window. The ALL option, when used, deactivates all open windows.

To use windows in your program, you first use the DEFINE WINDOW command to define as many windows as will be needed (one DEFINE WINDOW command is used for each window). Window names can be up to ten characters in length. Then, as you need to display data in a window, you use the ACTIVATE WINDOW command to make the window active. When you are done with the window, you use the DEACTIVATE WINDOW command to deactivate the window.

Defining the Window

A number of options can be used with the DEFINE WINDOW command to control the appearance of the window. All of the options are covered in detail in Appendix A; for now, some of them are detailed along with this command:

DEFINE WINDOW *windowname* FROM *row1,col1* TO *row2,col2*
[TITLE *character-expression*][DOUBLE/PANEL/NONE]
[SYSTEM *border-string*] [SHADOW/NOSHADOW][CLOSE/NOCLOSE]
[GROW/NOGROW]

The *row1,col1* coordinates indicate the row and column number for the upper-left corner of the window. The *row2,col2* coordinates indicate the row and column number of the lower-right corner of the window. The TITLE option, followed by a character expression, defines an optional title. If it is used, the expression will appear in a title bar at the top of the window.

SYSTEM provides a window that resembles the standard windows used by FoxPro for Windows. The DOUBLE, PANEL, and NONE options can be used to define a different border for the window. The default border, if none of these options is specified, is a single-line box. DOUBLE causes the window to have a double-line box. PANEL gives the window a border made up of thin panels, similar to the design of windows used by DOS versions of FoxPro. NONE specifies no border.

The SHADOW and NOSHADOW options specify whether or not a drop-shadow appears beneath the window. You must have used a SET SHADOWS ON command earlier in the program, if any shadows that you define are to take effect. The CLOSE/NOCLOSE option specifies whether or not a close box is provided (allowing a window to be closed with the mouse). The GROW/NOGROW option specifies whether a window can be sized.

You can use as many optional clauses as you need. Here is an example of a window definition:

```
DEFINE WINDOW members1 FROM 8,8 TO 22,75 SYSTEM CLOSE GROW
```

This defines a window that resembles the standard FoxPro windows, with its upper-left corner at row 8, column 8 of the screen. The window's lower-right corner is at row 22, column 75 of the screen. Once the window is activated, it can be resized on the screen, and it can be closed.

Activating and Using the Window

Once you have defined a window with the DEFINE WINDOW command, use the ACTIVATE WINDOW *windowname* command to activate, or turn on the window. When you activate a window, all screen output appears inside that window. When you use @-SAY commands to place data inside a window, it is important to realize that the coordinates are now *relative* to the window. This means that row column 0 is no longer the upper-left corner of the screen; it is now the upper-left corner of the window. It remains that way until you stop using the window with a DEACTIVATE WINDOW command. It is important to grasp this point to avoid errors in your program. If, for example, you activate a window that is only five rows deep and you then try to display data at row 15, your program will halt with the error message: "Position is off the screen," because the window you are using has no row 15.

Note If you use ACTIVATE WINDOW to activate a window, and later use ACTIVATE WINDOW to activate a different window, the previous window is automatically deactivated, since only one window can be active at a time.

You can use the LIST or DISPLAY command to display data without worrying about specific screen locations, and the data will be contained completely within the window. If the lines of data wrap around in an unattractive fashion, you can either change the size of the window to fit more data, or include fewer fields in the LIST or DISPLAY command. And you can activate a window and then use a BROWSE, CHANGE, or EDIT command to allow changes inside the window (although this is not generally necessary, since BROWSE, CHANGE, and EDIT cause windows to open on their own). You might find such a technique useful if, for some reason, you wanted a Browse or Edit window of a specific size to appear at a specific screen location.

Deactivating the Window

Once you are done with the window, use the DEACTIVATE WINDOW *windowname* command to turn off the window. Screen output is then restored to the normal screen. If you have activated a number of windows, you can use the ALL clause in place of a window name with the DEACTIVATE command, and all the windows will be deactivated.

An Example of Window Use

Assuming you've created the MEMBERS and RENTALS files in earlier chapters, you can try the following program to see how multiple windows can be used to visually highlight your application. Perhaps Generic Videos would like a program that asks for a user's name, displays the corresponding tape limit and membership expiration date, and then displays all tapes rented by that member. The program shown here presents the information inside of multiple windows, using shadows and different colors.

```
*windows.prg shows off window use.
STORE SPACE(15) TO MLAST
DEFINE WINDOW members1 FROM 5,5 TO 10,50 SYSTEM CLOSE GROW
DEFINE WINDOW rentals1 FROM 10,8 TO 22,75 SYSTEM CLOSE GROW
DEFINE WINDOW askthem FROM 3,15 TO 8,45 SYSTEM CLOSE GROW
USE MEMBERS INDEX NAME
ACTIVATE WINDOW askthem
@ 1,1 SAY "Last name? " GET MLAST
READ
SEEK MLAST
IF .NOT. FOUND()
    @ 1,1 SAY "NAME NOT FOUND IN DATABASE!"
    WAIT
```

```
        DEACTIVATE WINDOW askthem
        CLOSE DATABASES
        RETURN
ENDIF
STORE SOCIAL TO FINDER
ACTIVATE WINDOW members1
@ 1,2 SAY "Name: " + TRIM(FIRSTNAME) + " " + LASTNAME
@ 2,2 SAY "Exp. date:"
@ 2,15 SAY EXPIREDATE
@ 2,25 SAY "Tape limit:"
@ 2,38 SAY TAPELIMIT
WAIT "Press a key to see rentals..."
SET ESCAPE OFF
ACTIVATE WINDOW rentals1
SELECT 2
USE RENTALS
DISPLAY ALL OFF FOR SOCIAL = FINDER
WAIT "Press a key when done viewing..."
DEACTIVATE WINDOW ALL
CLOSE DATABASES
SET ESCAPE ON
RETURN
```

Early in the program, three DEFINE WINDOW commands are used to define three different windows for later use. After opening a database and index file, the program activates the window called Askthem and displays a prompt for a last name within that window.

Once the user responds with a last name, a SEEK command finds the name in the index, and the window called Members1 is activated. The tape limit and expiration date, along with the member's full name, are displayed in this window, and the user is asked to press a key to see the tape rentals. Once the user presses a key, the window called Rentals1 is activated, and all tapes rented by that member are shown in it. At the end of the program, all of the windows are deactivated and the files are closed.

You may have noticed the addition of the SET ESCAPE OFF command just before the final window is opened. This is used to prevent a user from halting the program in midstream by pressing the ESC key. You may prefer to use the SET ESCAPE OFF command early on in most of your programs so users cannot interrupt a program by accidentally pressing ESC.

Designing Light-bar Menus with @-PROMPT and MENU TO

You now have a main menu system for the Generic Videos database, but it uses "?" and INPUT commands that do not provide much flexibility when it comes to placing the information on the screen. You can replace these commands with the @-PROMPT and MENU TO commands. Using @-PROMPT and MENU TO, you can create light-bar menus similar to those used by FoxPro.

 Note The commands described below can provide relatively attractive menus with a minimum amount of programming. However, if you plan to perform extensive programming in FoxPro, you should familiarize yourself with FoxPro's Menu Builder, a built-in utility that can be used to create complex menus. The use of the Menu Builder is beyond the scope of this text, but you can learn more about it by referring to your FoxPro documentation.

First, a series of @-PROMPT commands will be used to display the desired menu options at specific positions on the screen. The format for this command is

@ *row,column* PROMPT "*expression*" [MESSAGE "*expression*"]

where the text *expression* that follows the PROMPT term will appear in a bar, at the specified *row* and *column* position. The MESSAGE clause is optional. If it is used, the *expression* that follows MESSAGE will appear in the message area of the screen whenever that particular menu option is highlighted.

A series of @-PROMPT commands are followed by a MENU TO command. The format of this command is

MENU TO *memory-variable*

It activates the menu choices defined with the PROMPT commands and waits for a user response. The user can highlight the desired menu option and press ENTER, at which time a numeric value representing the chosen menu option gets passed on to the memory variable specified in the

MENU TO command. For example, if the user highlights the first menu option and presses ENTER, 1 gets stored to the variable. If the user highlights the fourth menu option and presses ENTER, 4 gets stored to the variable.

To use these commands in the Generic Videos menu, you must get into the FoxPro Editor and edit the command file used to display the menu. Enter this:

```
MODIFY COMMAND MENU1
```

When the FoxPro Editor appears, the menu command file you developed in Chapter 14 will appear along with it. Change the file so it looks like the one shown next.

 Note You can delete a whole series of lines at once, by clicking and dragging from the start of the first unwanted line to the end of the last unwanted line. With all the unwanted lines highlighted, press the DEL key to remove them. You can use ENTER to add new blank lines between existing lines.

```
USE MEMBERS
SET TALK OFF
STORE 0 TO CHOICE
DO WHILE CHOICE < 5
    CLEAR
    *Display main menu.
    @  5, 5 SAY "Generic Videos Database System Menu"
    @  6, 4 SAY "Highlight selection, and press Enter:"
    @  8,10 PROMPT "Add Members    "
    @  9,10 PROMPT "Edit Members   "
    @ 10,10 PROMPT "Print Report   "
    @ 11,10 PROMPT "Display Member"
    @ 12,10 PROMPT "Exit System    "
    @  7, 8 TO 13,30
    * above line draws line box around menu.
    MENU TO CHOICE
    DO CASE
        CASE CHOICE = 1
            DO ADDER
        CASE CHOICE = 2
            DO EDITMEMB
        CASE CHOICE = 3
            REPORT FORM SAMPLE
        CASE CHOICE = 4
```

```
                 DO SHOWMEMB
        CASE CHOICE = 5
                 CLOSE DATABASES
                 SET TALK ON
                 CLEAR
                 RETURN
     ENDCASE
ENDDO
```

When you are finished changing the command file, press CTRL+S to save it, then close the window with CTRL+F4. You then might want to try using the system; start it by entering **DO MENU1**. Choose the menu choice for adding a record, and while you are watching the system's operation, you might want to think about ways to further improve on the system design. Perhaps you can modify the command files used by your system so that other choices from the menu provide easy-to-understand screen displays. When you are finished using the system, CTRL+S gets you out of any of the Edit or Append functions and back to the system menu.

Editing Records Under Program Control

You know that you can edit records with the CHANGE or EDIT command or by using @-SAY-GET and READ commands, but you must get to the record before you can change it. Let's use macro substitution for the editing functions of the Generic Videos database system. If you remember where you left that section of the system, the Editor program (EDITMEMB.PRG) displays all records in the database. The system then asks you for the record number to be edited, and the EDIT command is used to edit that record. If the database has grown beyond a screenful of members, however, you won't be able to see all of the records on the screen at once. Obviously, a better method of editing is needed.

The employees of Generic Videos have agreed that it would be best if they could enter the last name of a member to have FoxPro search for the record. When you think about what must be done to implement this, you might first draw up, on paper, a list like the following:

1. Ask for the last name of the member whose record is to be edited.

2. Store the name to a variable.

3. Using the macro function, find the name in the database.

4. Edit the record whose number corresponds to that name.

Let's change the EDITMEMB command file so that it does this task. Enter

```
MODIFY COMMAND EDITMEMB
```

Change the program so it looks like this:

```
CLEAR
STORE SPACE(15) TO TEST
USE MEMBERS
SET INDEX TO NAME
@ 5,10 SAY "Editing a record."
@ 7,10 SAY "Enter the last name of the member."
@ 10,10 SAY "Last name: " GET TEST
READ
IF TEST = " "
     RETURN
ENDIF
FIND &TEST
IF .NOT. FOUND()
     CLEAR
     @5,10 SAY "There is no such name in the database."
     WAIT
     *wait command causes a pause.
     RETURN
ENDIF
CHANGE
RETURN
```

Press CTRL+S to save the file, then close the window with CTRL+F4. Try the system again by entering **DO MENU1**, and choose the Edit menu selection. Try entering the name **Miller**. If all went well, the selected record will appear on the screen. The key to the solution is the command FIND &TEST; when this command is executed, then whatever name was entered with the ACCEPT command will be substituted for the macro. The SEEK command, which accepts a memory variable directly, could be used in place of FIND and a macro. In this example, FIND was used instead to demonstrate the use of the macro (&) function.

One obvious flaw in this program's design is that the search routine is based on the last name only. If two persons have the same last name, such a design may not find the name you want. However, you can apply the same logic to combinations of several fields, if you use an index file built on that same combination of fields to perform the search. You could, for example, build the NAME index file on a combination of Lastname and Firstname with commands like

```
USE MEMBERS
INDEX ON LASTNAME + TRIM(FIRSTNAME) TO NAME
```

and then the search routine could be rewritten to prompt for both the last and the first names. The responses could be combined with the plus symbol, which combines (concatenates) text strings. The combined expression could then be used as the search term. As an example, the modified search routine shown here would work if the NAME index was built on a combination of last and first names:

```
CLEAR
STORE SPACE(15) TO TESTLAST
STORE SPACE(15) TO TESTFIRST
USE MEMBERS
SET INDEX TO NAME
@ 5,10 SAY "Editing a record."
@ 7,10 SAY "Enter the last name of the member."
@ 8,10 SAY "Last name: " GET TESTLAST
@ 10,10 SAY "Enter the first name of the member."
@ 11,10 SAY "First name: " GET TESTFIRST
READ
STORE TESTLAST + TRIM(TESTFIRST) TO TEST
IF TEST = " "
      RETURN
ENDIF
FIND &TEST
IF .NOT. FOUND()
      CLEAR
      @5,10 SAY "There is no such name in the database."
      WAIT
      *wait command causes a pause.
      RETURN
ENDIF
CHANGE
RETURN
```

Data Entry and Editing with Memory Variables

Another common method of writing programs for data entry and editing makes use of memory variables for the temporary storage of data. This method has not been used for any of the examples in this book, up to this point. However, it is popular with many programmers, and you may want to consider it in designing your own programs. This programming approach moves data from memory variables to fields. If memory variables were used, our data entry routine might resemble the following:

```
*create memory variables.
CLEAR
MLAST = SPACE(15)
MFIRST = SPACE(15)
MADDRESS = SPACE(25)
MCITY  = SPACE(15)
MSTATE = SPACE(2)
MZIP = SPACE(10)
*display prompts, store data to variables.
@ 3,5 SAY "LAST NAME:" GET MLAST
@ 4,5 SAY "FIRST NAME:" GET MFIRST
@ 8,5 SAY "ADDRESS:" GET MADDRESS
@ 10,5 SAY "CITY:" GET MCITY
@ 10,35 SAY "STATE:" GET MSTATE
@ 10,45 SAY "ZIP CODE:" GET MZIP
READ
*open database, make new record, store variables.
USE NAMES INDEX NAMES
APPEND BLANK
REPLACE LASTNAME WITH MLAST, FIRSTNAME WITH MFIRST;
ADDRESS WITH MADDRESS, CITY WITH MCITY;
STATE WITH MSTATE, ZIP WITH MZIP
RETURN
```

Such a routine has three main parts. The first part consists of a series of commands that create memory variables; each memory variable precisely matches the type and length of its corresponding field. The second portion of the file uses @–SAY–GET commands to display prompts at the desired screen locations, along with data entry fields for the desired data, and stores the user's responses to the memory variables. The final portion of the file opens the database, uses an APPEND BLANK command to add one blank record to the end of the database, and uses the REPLACE command to move the data from the variables into the database fields.

Once all of the required records have been added, the database can be closed. The code just described is often enclosed within a DO WHILE .T. loop, with a conditional prompt added just before the ENDDO that matches the DO WHILE command, as in the following example:

```
(previous lines of program here)
WAIT "Add another record? Y/N:" TO ANSWER
IF UPPER(ANSWER) = "N"
    CLOSE DATABASES
    EXIT
ENDIF
ENDDO
```

If the data entry person presses "N" in response to the prompt, the program ends.

Given how popular this method is with programmers, it clearly must have advantages. One significant one is *database integrity*; with this approach, the database is open only during the append process, but not necessarily throughout the entire application. This minimizes the chances of damage.

Another advantage is ease of validation; since the data is being stored in memory variables and later moved to the fields of the actual database, you could insert other lines in the program to check whether the data was valid, before moving it to the database. And you can make it easier on the data entry operators by storing default values in the memory variables. As an example, if 80% of the addresses that get stored in an orders database are in San Diego, you could store the text string "San Diego", along with the required number of trailing spaces to fill the field in the memory variable for the City field. It will then appear by default in the entry screen, and the users can either accept it or overtype the entry to enter something else.

Now the disadvantages: This approach involves a lot of programming, like it or not. Anyone who has written an entry routine like this one for a 60-field database will tell you that it is no fun typing all the lines of program code; you'll spend two pages just creating the variables! The effort involved in writing such a program is enough to make you wonder whether database integrity is all that important, or whether you can get by with a format file and a CHANGE or EDIT command. Whether or not you want to take on the effort is a matter of programming preference.

Deleting Records Under Program Control

If you're going to be writing your own applications, you should add a routine for deleting unwanted records. This is too frequently left out of a system's design, as if programmers assume that users want to add, but never want to delete, records from a database. The logic is very similar to a search-and-edit program, because for both the editing and deleting you have to find the record first.

For deleting a record, your program-design pseudocode might look like this:

```
open database, index files
prompt user for variables to search by
FIND variable in index file
IF NOT FOUND
     show error message, exit routine
ELSE
     show record to user with @-SAY commands
     ask user for confirmation to delete record
     IF confirmation is given
             DELETE the record
      ELSE
             move to next record to see if it is same name
             ask user for confirmation to delete record
     ENDIF
ENDIF
```

The fastest way to build such a routine is probably to copy your "edit" routine, remove the lines of code that allow for changing the fields, add lines of code that ask for confirmation, and proceed to delete the record. Here is an example that uses a modified version of the program shown earlier for record editing, based on a last and first name:

```
CLEAR
STORE SPACE(15) TO TESTLAST
STORE SPACE(15) TO TESTFIRST
```

```
USE MEMBERS
SET INDEX TO NAME
*name.idx is indexed on lastname + firstname.
@ 5,10 SAY "DELETING a record."
@ 7,10 SAY "Enter the last name of the member."
@ 8,10 SAY "Last name: " GET TESTLAST
@ 10,10 SAY "Enter the first name of the member."
@ 11,10 SAY "First name: " GET TESTFIRST
READ
STORE TESTLAST + TESTFIRST TO TEST
FIND &TEST
IF .NOT. FOUND()
      CLEAR
      @5,10 SAY "There is no such name in the database."
      WAIT
      *wait command causes a pause.
      RETURN
ENDIF
DO WHILE .NOT. EOF()
      STORE "N" TO DOIT
      @ 5,5 SAY " Lastname:"
      @ 5,15 SAY LASTNAME
      @ 6,5 SAY "Firstname:"
      @ 6,15 SAY FIRSTNAME
      @ 7,5 SAY "  Address:"
      @ 7,15 SAY ADDRESS
      @ 8,15 SAY TRIM(CITY) + " " + STATE + " " + ZIPCODE
      @ 12,20 SAY "DELETE THIS MEMBER? Y/N or C to CANCEL: "
      @ 12,62 GET DOIT
      READ
      DO CASE
         CASE UPPER(DOIT) = "Y"
         DELETE
         RETURN
         CASE UPPER(DOIT) = "N"
         SKIP
         CASE UPPER(DOIT) = "C"
         RETURN
      ENDCASE
ENDDO
RETURN
```

Note that the commands that display the member's information, and request the user's confirmation, are placed in a DO–WHILE loop. The advantage of this approach is that if two members have the same last and first names, the user can press N (for No) to automatically view the next record according to the NAME index. Once the user views the desired member to delete and presses Y for Yes, the record is deleted.

Note also that this routine does not immediately perform a PACK, because packing a database can be time-consuming (particularly with larger databases). For this reason, most systems provide the user with an option to pack the file at a later point, rather than in the record-deletion loop. It probably isn't wise to pack the database all too often—nor is it necessary, since you can place a SET DELETED ON statement near the start of the program, to prevent the deleted records from being displayed. Given that a PACK is going to be time-consuming with all but the smallest of databases, this should be an option that is performed at the user's discretion.

Many systems provide a PACK option in the form of a question that the user sees just before exiting the system. This can be done with a program like the one shown here:

```
CLEAR
ACCEPT "  ==PACK database now? Y/N: " TO PACKANS
IF UPPER(PACKANS) = "Y"
     CLEAR
     @ 5,5 SAY "Please wait... do NOT interrupt!"
     SET TALK ON
     USE MEMBERS INDEX NAME
     PACK
     SET TALK OFF
ENDIF
QUIT
```

The user, who may not want to spend the time at that particular instant, now has the option of performing or not performing the PACK.

Helpful Hints on Screen Design

Think about these aspects of screen design when you are designing a FoxPro system:

☐ Use menus as often as necessary. They should clearly say what choices are available to the user.

☐ Avoid overly cluttered menus or data entry screens. Rather than trying to fit a large number of fields on one data entry screen, it may be better to break the entry screen in half; input half of the information, clear the screen with CLEAR, and then input the other half of the information. You can apply the same tactic to a menu, by placing a number of related choices in a second menu—a reports menu, for example—that can be reached by a single choice from the main menu.

☐ Give users a way out—that is, a way of changing their minds after making a choice from a menu or selecting a particular entry screen. Many application designers handle this need by making the last option on any menu serve as an "exit" back to the previous menu. (This is accomplished by using a RETURN statement.)

☐ Finally, never leave the screen blank for any noticeable period of time. Few things are as unnerving to a computer user as a blank screen. A simple message that states that the computer is doing something (sorting, indexing, or whatever) is reassuring to the user.

Programming for Data Retrieval

*T*his chapter covers ways to retrieve data in the form of reports from within your programs. You should already be familiar with the use of the Report Writer for designing reports, as detailed in Chapters 7 and 12. The stored reports created by the Report Writer can be called from within a program to produce the corresponding reports. You can also write programs that produce reports from scratch, although the flexibility of the Report Writer makes this task only rarely necessary.

Generating Reports from Stored Report Forms

If you have already designed your reports using the Report Writer, all that is needed to generate a report is to place the REPORT FORM command (detailed in Chapter 7) at the appropriate place in your program. You may also want to build selective indexes, or set some sort of filter, before generating the report, and it is a good idea to give users a way to cancel the report just before it starts.

A simple report-producing routine called from one of the options in the main menu might resemble the following:

```
*REPORTER.PRG produces the membership report.
CLEAR
TEXT
************************************************************
This menu option prints the membership report.
Make sure that the printer is turned on, and that
paper is loaded.

Press C to CANCEL, any other key to start printing.
************************************************************
ENDTEXT
WAIT TO DOIT
IF UPPER(DOIT) = "C"
     *user canceled option, so...
     RETURN
ENDIF
REPORT FORM MEMBERS TO PRINT
RETURN
```

Using stored reports, like the one called by this program is by far the easiest way to generate reports within a program. You can also add more lines to the program to limit the records that are printed; this can be accomplished by inserting an INDEX ON-FOR command, by placing a query into effect, or by using a SET FILTER command. You can construct a query using the RQBE window (detailed in Chapter 6) and set up the query to print the stored report (see Chapter 7 for details). To place that query into effect from within your program and to generate the report, use the command

DO *queryname*.QPR

where *queryname* is the file name under which you saved the query. For example, if you have a query that prints a report, stored under the name SAMPLE1, you could use the following line of code within your program:

```
DO SAMPLE1.QPR
```

When this line is executed, the query would be placed into effect and the report printed.

An alternate method for accomplishing the same task would be to use the SET FILTER command. (Note, however, that if an index doesn't exist to support the filter, the SET FILTER command will be slower than using a stored query.) With SET FILTER, you could offer various menu options that select different filter conditions and then print the same stored report.

As an example, one user might want to see the members in the video database restricted by a specific ZIP code, while another user might want to see all members who lived in a specific state. You could provide menu options to handle this task in a simple reporting program like the one shown here:

```
*REPORTER.PRG produces the membership report.
CLEAR
@ 5,5 PROMPT "All members      "
@ 6,5 PROMPT "By State        "
@ 7,5 PROMPT "By ZIP code range"
@ 4,4 TO 8,23 DOUBLE
MENU TO CHOICE
DO CASE
     CASE CHOICE = 1
```

```
          WAIT "All members chosen. Press a key."
          CASE CHOICE = 2
          STORE SPACE(2) TO MSTATE
          @ 12,10 SAY "For which state? " GET MSTATE
          READ
          SET FILTER TO UPPER(STATE) = UPPER(MSTATE)
          GO TOP
          CASE CHOICE = 3
          STORE SPACE(10) TO STARTZIPS
          STORE SPACE(10) TO ENDZIPS
          @ 12,10 SAY "Starting ZIP code? " GET STARTZIPS
          @ 13,10 SAY "  Ending ZIP code? " GET ENDZIPS
          @ 15,10 SAY "(enter same ZIP code for a single ZIP.)"
          READ
          SET FILTER TO ZIPCODE >= STARTZIPS .AND. ZIPCODE <= ENDZIPS
          GO TOP
ENDCASE
CLEAR
TEXT
**********************************************************
Ready to print the membership report. Make sure that
the printer is turned on, and that paper is loaded.
Press C to CANCEL, any other key to start printing.
**********************************************************
ENDTEXT
WAIT TO DOIT
IF UPPER(DOIT) = "C"
     *user canceled option, so...
     SET FILTER TO
     *above line needed to clear effects of filter.
     RETURN
ENDIF
REPORT FORM MEMBERS TO PRINT
SET FILTER TO
*above line needed to clear effects of filter.
RETURN
```

In this example, depending on the menu choice selected, one of two filters may be set to limit the records printed. Note the inclusion of the SET FILTER TO statement near the end of the program to clear any existing filter. If a filter is set and not cleared after the report is done, it may cause havoc in other parts of your program when records suddenly appear to be "missing" from the database.

Users' Choice: Reporting to the Screen or the Printer

Often, a program may need to display a report on the screen and optionally send the output to the printer. Anyone who has designed a single report to try to meet the two different needs of screen and printer has discovered that the two tasks are similar, but not identical. The screen limitation of 24 lines puts a severe constraint on the amount of information you can display at once; the program must prompt for each display, or the data scrolls by so fast as to be useless. With a printer, on the other hand, there is no need to stop every 24 lines, but page ejects must be taken into consideration.

One way to handle such a need is to use a program like the one shown here:

```
PRINANS = "S"
@ 5,5 SAY "Screen (S) or Printer (P)?" GET PRINANS
READ
IF UPPER(PRINANS) = "P"
     REPORT FORM MEMBERS TO PRINT
ELSE
     GO TOP
     CLEAR
     WAIT "Press C to CANCEL, any other key to view members."
     CLEAR
     DO WHILE .NOT. EOF( )
         REPORT FORM MEMBERS NEXT 20
         WAIT TO KEEPGOING
         IF UPPER(KEEPGOING) = "C"
             RETURN
         ENDIF
     ENDDO
ENDIF
RETURN
```

This lets the same stored report work for both the screen and the printer. If the user answers the prompt with S for screen, the DO WHILE loop causes the REPORT FORM MEMBERS NEXT 20 statement to repeat over and over until the end of the file is reached. The scope of NEXT 20 limits the report to 20 records (which will fit on one screen), and the WAIT command pauses the screen, allowing the user to view the records. In your application, you could change NEXT 20 to whatever number of records fit on your screen at one time.

Writing Reports with Program Code

Before proceeding, you should know that producing stored reports with the Report Writer is far easier than using the following methods of writing reports directly with program code. The methods are described here primarily because you may run into FoxPro applications written by other programmers who chose to use these methods. This choice was often due to the limitations in earlier versions of Fox Software products, particularly FoxBase and FoxBase Plus. The Report Writer in FoxBase did not let you create form-oriented reports with ease, so many programmers wrote report programs to accomplish the task.

It may help to be familiar with these methods of programming in case you ever want to modify another programmer's work, but if at all possible, you should avoid these techniques and instead write programs that employ stored reports created by the Report Writer.

There are about as many ways to design a reporting program as there are to build data entry screens. About the only thing such programs have in common is one or more repetitive (DO WHILE) loops, which print selected fields for each record within a group of records. Beyond this, the commands you need will vary with the complexity of the reports, with the levels of grouping, with whether or not the report is relational, and with numerous other factors. However, many reports written in program code do follow a common methodology, which in pseudocode would read something like this:

OPEN Database and Index files
FIND first record in desired group, or SET FILTER and go top
Initialize any memory variables for page and line counters
Route output to the printer
Print report headings
DO WHILE not at the end of the file or the desired data group
     Print the desired fields or expressions for one record
      Update counter for page position

```
     IF page position counter exceeds max lines per page
          Print footers, if any
          EJECT the paper
          Print headers, if any
     ENDIF
     SKIP to the next record in logical sequence
ENDDO
```

There are two ways to route the data to the printer: by using SET PRINT ON and a series of "?" statements, or by using SET DEVICE TO PRINT followed by a series of @-SAY statements. As an example, the two simple programs shown here illustrate both approaches within the design framework just shown:

```
*MEMLIST.PRG prints membership roster.
CLEAR
STORE 1 TO LINES
STORE 1 TO PAGES
USE MEMBERS INDEX NAMES
SET PRINT ON
? "*****************************************"
? " Membership Address and Phone Roster"
? "*****************************************"
DO WHILE .NOT. EOF( )
     ? "Name: " + TRIM(FIRSTNAME) + " " + LASTNAME
     ? "Phone: " + PHONE
     ?? "Expiration Date: " + DTOC(EXPIREDATE)
     ? "Home address: " + ADDRESS
     ? SPACE(15) + TRIM(CITY) + " " + STATE + " " + ZIPCODE
     ? "*******************************"
     STORE LINES+ 5 TO LINES
     IF LINES > 55
          ?
          ? SPACE(40) + "Page" + LTRIM(STR(PAGES))
          EJECT
          STORE 1 + PAGES TO PAGES
          STORE 1 TO LINES
          ? "*****************************************"
          ? " Membership Address and Phone Roster"
          ? "*****************************************"
     ENDIF
     SKIP
ENDDO
IF LINES > 1
     EJECT
```

```
ENDIF
SET PRINT OFF
RETURN
```

The SET PRINT ON and "?" statements get the job done, but they don't offer precise control over where the data appears in the report. For more precision, you can use the other method of programming a report, which is to use SET DEVICE TO PRINT to reroute screen output to the printer and then use a series of @-SAY commands to position the data in precise locations on the printed page. The following example of a printing program employs this approach to create a simple tabular report with custom headers and footers:

```
CLEAR
STORE 5 TO LINES
STORE 1 TO PAGES
USE MEMBERS INDEX NAMES
SET DEVICE TO PRINT
@ 2,15 SAY "MEMBERSHIP EXPIRATION DATES REPORT"
@ 3,10 SAY "****************************"
@ 4,10 SAY "Name          City"
@ 4,50 SAY "Tape Limit     Exp.Date"
DO WHILE .NOT. EOF( )
    @ LINES, 5 SAY TRIM(FIRSTNAME) + " " + LASTNAME
    @ LINES, 30 SAY CITY
    @ LINES, 50 SAY TAPELIMIT
    @ LINES, 60 SAY EXPIREDATE
    STORE LINES + 1 TO LINES
    IF LINES > 50
        @ LINES + 2,40 SAY "PAGE " + TRIM(STR(PAGES))
        EJECT
        STORE PAGES + 1 TO PAGES
        STORE 5 TO LINES
        @ 2,15 SAY "MEMBERSHIP EXPIRATION DATES REPORT"
        @ 3,10 SAY "**************************"
        @ 4,10 SAY "Name          City"
        @ 4,50 SAY "Tape Limit     Exp.Date"
    ENDIF
    SKIP
ENDDO
IF LINES > 5
    EJECT
ENDIF
SET DEVICE TO SCREEN
RETURN
```

Whichever approach best suits you can be modified to handle any complex reporting need. For example, it is quite simple to create a report based on multiple files: you do this by selecting appropriate work areas and including file names and pointers in the references to fields, as discussed in Chapter 12. In one-to-many relationships, where one record in the controlling database may have dozens or hundreds of records in a related file, you can add program code to monitor the page count and line count, and to eject pages and print new headings when appropriate.

Note that both of the examples of report code use memory variables, incremented by the program, to keep track of page numbers and line counts. This approach was also common in FoxBase Plus and other earlier dBASE-compatible languages. In FoxPro, however, *system* memory variables can be used to keep track of page numbers and line positions. These system memory variables work with the stored reports, and you may want to consider using them if you need reports that begin with a specific page number other than 1.

Controlling Your Printer

By changing the *printer memory variables,* you can control the various print settings that are used when a REPORT FORM command generates a stored report. Printer memory variables are special memory variables that FoxPro uses to interpret REPORT FORM commands into printer output. They can modify settings like the page length, the page offset from the left margin, the number of pages printed within a report, and the line spacing. You can change the values of these memory variables by storing different values to them before running the report with the REPORT FORM command.

If you perform a LIST MEMORY command, you will see the printer memory variables, similar to the example shown here. The names of printer memory variables start with P.

```
LIST MEMORY

    0 variables defined,      0 bytes used
  256 variables available, 6000 bytes available
```

```
Print System Memory Variables

ALIGNMENT      Pub   C    "LEFT"
BOX            Pub   L    .T.
INDENT         Pub   N            0 (          0.00000000)
LMARGIN        Pub   N            0 (          0.00000000)
PADVANCE       Pub   C    "FORMFEED"
PAGENO         Pub   N            1 (          1.00000000)
PBPAGE         Pub   N            1 (          1.00000000)
PCOLNO         Pub   N           55 (         55.00000000)
PCOPIES        Pub   N            1 (          1.00000000)
PDRIVER        Pub   C    " "
PECODE         Pub   C    " "
PEJECT         Pub   C    "BEFORE"
PEPAGE         Pub   N            1 (          1.00000000)
PFORM          Pub   C    " "
PLENGTH        Pub   N           66 (         66.00000000)
PLINENO        Pub   N           52 (         52.00000000)
PLOFFSET       Pub   N            0 (          0.00000000)
PPITCH         Pub   C    "DEFAULT"
PQUALITY       Pub   L    .F.
PSCODE         Pub   C    " "
PSPACING       Pub   N            1 (          1.00000000)
PWAIT          Pub   L    .F.
RMARGIN        Pub   N           80 (         80.00000000)
TABS           Pub   C    " "
WRAP           Pub   L    .F.
```

The variables have the following meanings:

PADVANCE is a character variable, containing either the expression LINEFEED or FORMFEED. Depending on which expression is present, new pages will be generated either with multiple linefeeds or with form feeds.

PAGENO indicates the page number to use on the first page of a report. The default is 1, but you can enter any value from 1 to 32,767.

PBPAGE indicates the beginning page of a report when you don't want to print the entire report.

PCOLNO indicates a new starting column position. This re-positions the printer at the specified cursor location before the report begins.

PCOPIES indicates the desired number of copies of a report; the default is 1.

PDRIVER contains a character expression that is the name of the printer driver in use, such as EPSONFX (for Epson FX series) or HPLAS1 (for Hewlett-Packard LaserJet 1). If no printer has been chosen with the Printer Setup option, the default is a null string ("").

PECODE contains any ending escape codes you may want to send to the printer after the report is completed.

PEJECT contains the character expression NONE, BEFORE, AFTER, or BOTH. NONE indicates no form feed is needed (other than those that naturally occur inside the report); BEFORE indicates a form feed should occur at the start of printing; AFTER indicates a form feed should occur at the end of printing; and BOTH indicates a form feed is needed both before and after printing.

PEPAGE indicates the ending page of a report, when you don't want to print the entire report.

PFORM contains a character expression that evaluates to the name of a stored report-form file.

PLENGTH indicates the page length for the printed page, in numbers of lines. The default of 66 matches standard 11-inch (U.S.) paper; you can store 84 to this value if you are using 14-inch (U.S. legal-size) paper.

PLINENO indicates a new starting line number. This re-positions the printer at the specifed row on the page, before the report begins.

PLOFFSET indicates the left offset (distance from left page edge) where printing will begin. Enter a desired numeric value, such as 15 for a left offset of 15 spaces.

PPITCH contains a character expression that selects the printing type style. Valid choices are PICA, ELITE, COMPRESSED, and DEFAULT. Note that a printer driver must be installed, and your printer must support the option, for the desired type style to be used successfully.

PQUALITY indicates whether quality printing mode will be used. A logical "False" stored to this variable turns off quality printing, and a logical "True" turns it on. Note that a printer driver must be installed, and your printer must support quality printing, for this variable to have any effect.

PSCODE contains any starting escape codes you want to send to the printer before the report begins printing.

PSPACING is a numeric variable, containing a value of 1, 2, or 3, indicating the line spacing to be used within a report. The default value for this is 1.

PWAIT indicates whether the printer should pause between pages. A logical value of "False" indicates no pause, and a logical value of "True" indicates a pause.

Most of these parameters can also be controlled in other ways, such as through the various selections you make when originally designing the report, or through entering other commands, such as SET MARGIN TO (the command equivalent of the left offset variable). However, these printer memory variables are quite useful if you want to offer your users multiple options for report printing, while under program control. Depending on the user's responses to various menu options, you could store different values to the various printer variables and then print the report with the REPORT FORM command.

Sending Escape Codes to the Printer

In its default mode, FoxPro treats the printer as a simple device capable of receiving ASCII-format files, and it sends a plain ASCII representation of your data to the Windows Print Manager. This saves you the worry of trying to get a particular printer to match the output of FoxPro, but it also means that FoxPro will not, by default, use any special effects that your printer may have to offer.

You can, however, take advantage of your printer's special effects by sending escape codes to the printer, using the CHR function to send the applicable code. As an example, the code for compressed print on Epson-compatible dot-matrix printers is the ASCII value of 27 (the escape code) followed by the ASCII value of 15. You can, therefore, switch an Epson-compatible printer into compressed mode with commands like

```
SET PRINT ON
??? CHR(27) + CHR(15)
SET PRINT OFF
```

The printer remains in this mode until you send another escape code that either clears the prior one or selects a different font, or until you manually reset the printer. (Note the use of the ??? command, which is ideal for sending data to the printer. Unlike the ? command, the ??? does not add a carriage return or linefeed code.)

Consult your printer manual for a listing of your escape codes. If you are using an HP-compatible laser printer, you may want to experiment with the various escape codes before using them in an application. Because FoxPro assumes a standard character width for each printed character, characters rendered in a proportionally-spaced font may or may not appear where you would like to see them. Experimentation will help you determine how to achieve satisfactory results with your particular printer.

Advanced Programming Topics

This chapter describes additional commands and programming techniques for creating more intricate command files to automate your work with FoxPro.

Hiding and Showing Variables

FoxPro offers two commands, PRIVATE and PUBLIC, that are used to classify memory variables. The terms *private* and *public* refer to how the individual programs within a large FoxPro program treat variables. Private variables are available only to the program in which they are created, and to all programs called by that program. Variables that you create in one program are considered private by default; if you do not use the PUBLIC command, FoxPro assumes that all variables you create are private variables. This means that if you create a variable in a program that is called by another program, and then transfer control back to the calling program with the RETURN command, the contents of that memory variable are lost. You may or may not want those contents to be discarded, so you can use the PRIVATE and PUBLIC commands to specifically tell FoxPro how to handle your variables.

The PUBLIC command tells FoxPro that a memory variable is to be made available to all programs, regardless of where the memory variable was created. The PRIVATE command tells FoxPro that the variable will be available only to the program that created the variable, and to programs that are called by that specific program.

Declaring a variable public requires two steps: using the PUBLIC command in the format: PUBLIC *variablename*, and declaring the actual variable with the STORE command, or with an assignment symbol (=). Here is an example:

```
STORE 0 to YearsRents
PUBLIC YearsRents
STORE rentamt * 12 to YearsRents
```

In this example, the variable YearsRents will be available to all parts of the program, even if program control returns from the portion of the program containing this set of commands to a higher-level (calling) program.

There is normally little need to declare a memory variable private, since FoxPro sets all memory variables to private by default. However, there may be times when you want to declare as private a variable that was previously declared public. To do this, you can use the PRIVATE command (in the format: PRIVATE *variablename*), much the same way as you used the PUBLIC command. An example is

```
PRIVATE Staffer
STORE LASTNAME + FIRSTNAME to Staffer
```

As an example of the problems that can occur if variables are not declared private or public, consider the following programs. The first program, FIRST.PRG, passes control to the second program, SECOND.PRG. The second program declares a variable (NAME) and then passes control back to the calling program, FIRST.PRG. The calling program then tries to display the contents of the memory variable NAME.

```
*FIRST.PRG is first program
CLEAR
? "This program will call the second program."
WAIT
DO SECOND
CLEAR
? "Control has returned to first program."
? "The name is: " + NAME
? "End of first program."

*SECOND.PRG is second program
CLEAR
STORE "Smith" to name
? "The name is: " + NAME
WAIT "Press any key to return to first program."
RETURN
```

When the program is run with DO FIRST, an error message appears after control returns from the second program to the first (calling) program. FoxPro considers this an error because the NAME variable was private to the second program. When control was passed back to the first program, the contents of this private variable were lost. This problem can be solved by declaring the variable public, as shown in the following example:

```
*SECOND.PRG is second program
CLEAR
PUBLIC NAME
STORE "Smith" to NAME
? "The name is: " + NAME
WAIT "Press any key to return to first program."
RETURN
```

When the FIRST program is run, after this change is made, the program completes successfully without an error.

You can use the ALL, LIKE, and EXCEPT options with PRIVATE, to declare the status of more than one variable at a time. Here are some examples of how to use these options with PRIVATE:

```
PRIVATE ALL EXCEPT YearsRents
PRIVATE ALL LIKE *rent
PRIVATE ALL EXCEPT ???names
```

You can use the accepted DOS wildcard characters—the asterisk (*) and question mark (?)—as a part of the variable-name string, to represent a group of variables whose names share a common set of characters. The asterisk represents any sequence of characters, and the question mark represents any single character.

Debugging Techniques

Debugging is the process of finding out why a program does not operate the way it was designed to. Debugging can range from correcting a spelling error to rewriting the entire program. Some program bugs are relatively easy to find and solve; for example, a misspelled command, which results in a "Syntax error" message displayed on the screen when the command is executed. Other program bugs may cause problems that don't surface until you reach a different part of the program, and these can be far more difficult to solve. But remember that it is truly a rare experience for a program of any complexity, written and run for the first time, to operate without any bugs.

FoxPro helps you find bugs by placing you at or near the source of the problem. When an error in a program causes the program to halt, the Editor automatically opens a window, and highlights the line where the program halted. This line often (but not always) contains the cause of the error.

The bugs that you are likely to see most often in FoxPro are as follows:

☐ *Misspelled variable names and commands* The message "Syntax error" is usually displayed for misspelled commands. The message "Variable not found" is usually displayed for misspelled variables.

☐ *Missing ENDIF, ENDDO, ENDCASE, or ENDSCAN commands* Every DO WHILE loop must end with an ENDDO statement; every IF statement must be matched by an ENDIF statement; every DO CASE statement must have a matching ENDCASE statement; and every SCAN statement must have a matching ENDSCAN statement. FoxPro will wander off in the wrong direction if you leave out an ending statement.

☐ *Errors in loops* To avoid this major cause of program bugs, verify on paper that your program loops are properly designed to begin with. An example of an improperly designed DO WHILE loop is

```
STORE 0 TO CHOICE
DO WHILE CHOICE < 3
        INPUT "Enter selection:" TO CHOICE
        IF CHOICE = 1
                IF .NOT. EOF( )
                    SKIP
                ENDIF
                DELETE
        ELSE
                IF .NOT. EOF( )
                    SKIP
                ENDIF
                ? NAME, CITY, STATE
ENDDO
STORE RECNO( ) TO LOCATION
ENDIF
(rest of program...)
```

The mistake in this example is that the IF statement begins within the DO WHILE loop, but ends outside of it. Whenever an IF-ENDIF statement is used inside a DO WHILE loop, the IF statement must terminate within the DO WHILE loop. The same is true for the other programming structures with matching statements—ENDSCAN,

ENDDO, and ENDCASE. In this example, the properly designed loop would look like this:

```
STORE 0 TO CHOICE
DO WHILE CHOICE < 3
      INPUT "Enter selection:" TO CHOICE
      IF CHOICE = 1
              SKIP
              DELETE
      ELSE
              IF .NOT. EOF( )
                      SKIP
              ENDIF
              ? NAME, CITY, STATE
      ENDIF
ENDDO
STORE RECNO( ) TO LOCATION
(rest of program...)
```

☐   *Improper mixing of data types, such as character strings mixed with numeric variables, or date strings mixed with logical expressions* If you tell FoxPro to store the value 3 to a variable and to store the character string "3" to another variable, the two items are interpreted in entirely different ways. FoxPro recognizes the first entry as a numeric value of 3. The second entry is stored as a string of characters—in this case, the character 3. If you apply a string option to the numeric variable or try to use the string variable in a numeric calculation, you will get all sorts of errors in your program. Different types of variables cannot be used interchangeably, unless you use functions (like ASC, DTOC, and VAL) to convert them to compatible types.

FoxPro provides you with debugging tools to help you track down hard-to-find bugs in your programs. These tools take the form of several SET commands: SET TALK, SET ECHO, and SET ALTERNATE.

Using SET TALK

You have routinely used the SET TALK command in previous examples. If SET TALK is activated (which is true by default), FoxPro displays responses to commands that perform calculations or display record numbers (like LOCATE). This extra information isn't all that necessary during daily operation of the program, but in debugging it is useful to display results as the command file is being executed. To see this "talk" on the screen, add the SET TALK ON command to the beginning of the command file. You can then watch the screen as the program is run for hints that will help you find the errors in the program. Entering SET TALK OFF turns off the screen display of processing results. Note that turning on either SET TALK or SET ECHO (detailed next) slows down program execution.

Using SET ECHO

SET ECHO is similar to SET TALK. The SET ECHO command opens a Trace window displaying each command line of the program as it is executed. This lets you follow the flow of the program's control. Since SET ECHO is normally deactivated enter a SET ECHO ON command before debugging a program. Entering a SET ECHO OFF command disables the display in the Trace window. (You can double-click the Trace window's control menu icon, or press CTRL+F4, to close it.)

Using SET ALTERNATE

For problems that occur only when you are not around and some one else is using the program, you can use the SET ALTERNATE commands to save a record of operations to a disk file. SET ALTERNATE TO *filename* creates a file that stores any keyboard entries, and most screen displays. The file will have the extension .TXT. When the SET ALTERNATE ON command is used, everything that appears on your screen, with the exception of full-screen editing operations, is stored in the specified text file in ASCII format. When you no longer want the information to be stored in the file, you use the SET ALTERNATE OFF command. You can continue to use SET ALTERNATE ON and SET ALTERNATE OFF as many times as desired to add more text to the file. When you are finished with the process altogether, you can close the file with the CLOSE ALTERNATE command.

You can later examine the contents of the text file to see what replies to the program were typed and what program responses occurred as a result. Obviously, using these commands may quickly consume disk space, so consider available disk space before using the SET ALTERNATE commands for an extended period of time.

 Tip   SET ALTERNATE can also generate text files for use with word processors. See Chapter 19 for details.

Customizing FoxPro with SET Commands

Other SET commands can be used to customize your program and take advantage of various FoxPro features. The list presented here is not complete, but it does include the most commonly used SET commands.

SET BELL

The SET BELL ON command activates the beep that sounds during data entry. The beep is normally on, and sounds when you fill a field with data or enter incorrect data into a field (such as character data into a numeric field). SET BELL OFF deactivates the beep.

SET CARRY

When you use APPEND, the record that appears on the screen is normally blank. Entering a SET CARRY ON command causes FoxPro to copy the entries from the fields of the previous record to the new record when you issue an APPEND command. SET CARRY OFF disables this feature.

SET CONSOLE

The SET CONSOLE command turns screen displays on or off. SET CONSOLE is normally on, but once a SET CONSOLE OFF command is encountered, no information is displayed on the screen, although commands will still be executed. Not until a SET CONSOLE ON command is executed will information again be displayed. Using SET CONSOLE is like turning the monitor screen on or off.

 Note The SET CONSOLE command has no effect on output produced with @...SAY commands; such commands will still cause screen display even after a SET CONSOLE OFF command has been entered.

SET DATE

The SET DATE command sets the desired format for date values and expressions. FoxPro offers you a choice of ten date formats: American (*MM/DD/YY*), ANSI (*YY.MM.DD*), British/French (*DD/MM/YY*), Italian (*DD-MM-YY*), Japan (*YY/MM/DD*), USA (*MM-DD-YY*), German (*DD.MM.YY*), MDY (*MM/DD/YY*), DMY (*DD/MM/YY*), and YMD (*YY/MM/DD*). Unless told otherwise, FoxPro sets the default value of the date format to American. The format of the command is SET DATE *format*, where *format* is American, ANSI, British, Italian, French, German, Japan, USA, MDY, DMY, or YMD.

SET DECIMALS

This command sets the number of decimal places that will be displayed during calculations. The format of the command is SET DECIMALS to *expression*, where *expression* is an integer value limiting the number of decimal places. Thus, if SET DECIMALS is set to 4, then 4 decimal places will be displayed until another SET DECIMAL command is executed. The default value is 2 digits. Numbers are rounded off as necessary to match the restriction imposed with SET DECIMALS.

SET ESCAPE

The SET ESCAPE command disables the ability of the ESC key to interrupt a program. To disable the ESC key, you enter the SET ESCAPE OFF command. SET ESCAPE ON turns the ESC key back on. In most cases, the use of SET ESCAPE OFF within a program is recommended. You probably do not want novice users pressing the ESC key and seeing the dialog box with the Cancel, Ignore, and Suspend choices. Most novice users would have no idea what to do at such a point. Simply add a SET ESCAPE OFF statement near the start of your program to disable the use of the ESC key.

SET EXACT

The SET EXACT command tells FoxPro to perform (or not to perform) exact comparisons between character strings. The format of the command is SET EXACT ON/OFF. The default for SET EXACT is off. For example, assuming that SET EXACT is off, the commands

```
USE MEMBERS
LIST FOR LASTNAME = "Rob"
```

will find all records with "Robinson" in the Lastname field, because when SET EXACT is off, FoxPro only compares as many characters as are contained in the target string (in this case, the three characters in "Rob"). By comparison, the commands

```
SET EXACT ON
USE MEMBERS
LIST FOR LASTNAME = "Rob"
```

will not find any records in the MEMBERS database, because "Rob" is not an exact match of "Robinson".

Tip   Use SET EXACT to add precision to your searches.

SET NEAR

The SET NEAR command tells FoxPro to position the record pointer at the nearest record if a FIND or SEEK operation is unsuccessful. If SET NEAR is off (which is the default) and you perform a FIND or SEEK command that is not successful, the record pointer is placed at the end of the database, and the EOF( ) function returns a logical "True". You can use the SET NEAR ON command to tell FoxPro to get as close as possible if a search of the index is not successful. This can be useful when you are searching for the beginning of a range of data.

SET FUNCTION

The SET FUNCTION command changes the performance of the function keys. Each function key is assigned, by default, to a FoxPro command. When pressed, the keys execute the commands shown in Table 18-1 (the semicolons following the commands produce carriage returns).

You can change the definitions of the function keys, except those of F1 and F10, to any character expression of 79 characters or fewer by entering

SET FUNCTION *integer-expression* TO "*character-string*"

TABLE 18-1

Function key assignments

Function Key	FoxPro Command
F1	HELP;
F2	SET;
F3	LIST;
F4	DIR;
F5	DISPLAY STRUCTURE;
F6	DISPLAY STATUS;
F7	DISPLAY MEMORY;
F8	DISPLAY;
F9	APPEND;

The F1 key is reserved for the Help function, and the F10 key is reserved for the FoxPro menus.

The character string must be enclosed in quotes. For example, to change F7 from DISPLAY MEMORY to BROWSE, enter

```
SET FUNCTION "7" TO "BROWSE;"
```

Remember to include the semicolon to produce a carriage return after the command, so that it will be interpreted at the Command level.

The SET FUNCTION command can be quite useful for reducing the number of repetitive steps during the data entry process. As an example, if you include the following SET FUNCTION commands within the MENU.PRG program for Generic Videos, the function keys are redefined to automatically enter the names of various cities:

```
SET FUNCTION "2" TO "Silver Spring"
SET FUNCTION "3" TO "Rockville"
SET FUNCTION "4" TO "Columbia"
SET FUNCTION "5" TO "Washington"
SET FUNCTION "6" TO "Alexandria"
SET FUNCTION "7" TO "Falls Church"
SET FUNCTION "8" TO "Arlington"
SET FUNCTION "9" TO "Springfield"
```

When the commands shown in this example have been executed, users can press the respective function keys during an APPEND or CHANGE operation to enter these names without typing the actual keystrokes. You can also assign a sequence of commands to a function key, providing you separate commands with semicolons, and do not exceed the 79-character limit. During large data entry jobs, reassigning the function keys in this manner can save hours of time in entering records.

 Tip You can use the CLEAR MACROS command to clear your function key assignments from memory.

SET MEMOWIDTH TO

The SET MEMOWIDTH TO command controls the width of a memo field when it is displayed with a LIST or DISPLAY command. The default value is 50 characters wide. (You can specify any width from 8 to 256 characters.) Using the SET MEMOWIDTH TO command can produce a narrower, more pleasing display of information. As an example, the commands

```
USE MEMBERS
LIST LASTNAME, FIRSTNAME, PREFERENCE
```

result in this display:

```
Record#      LASTNAME      FIRSTNAME      PREFERENCE
      1      Miller        Karen          Prefers science fiction,
horror movies. Fan of Star Trek films.


      2      Martin        William        Enjoys Clint Eastwood, John
Wayne films.


      3      Robinson      Carol          Likes comedy, drama
films.
      4      Kramer        Harry          Big fan of Eddie Murphy.
Also enjoys westerns.
```

The display is an unattractive one because the words in the memo field wrap around the screen at the right-hand margin. The commands

```
SET MEMOWIDTH TO 20
USE MEMBERS
LIST LASTNAME, FIRSTNAME, PREFERENCE
```

provide a much more attractive format for the display of the memo field, as shown here:

```
Record#      LASTNAME      FIRSTNAME      PREFERENCE
      1      Miller        Karen          Prefers science
                                          fiction, horror
                                          movies. Fan of Star
                                          Trek films.
      2      Martin        William        Enjoys Clint
                                          Eastwood, John Wayne
                                          films.
```

| 3 | Robinson | Carol | Likes comedy, drama films. |
| 4 | Kramer | Harry | Big fan of Eddie Murphy. Also enjoys westerns. |

SET SAFETY

The SET SAFETY command lets you specify whether a prompt will warn you when FoxPro is about to overwrite an existing file. When SET SAFETY is ON, any command that will result in overwriting an existing file (such as rebuilding an index, or sorting to a file with the same name as an existing file), will cause FoxPro to display a warning message within a dialog box. You will have to confirm that you want to overwrite the file by choosing the Overwrite option. SET SAFETY is normally ON with FoxPro; this can result in unwanted messages and interruptions within your programs when you want to intentionally overwrite a file. In such cases, you can include a SET SAFETY OFF command and FoxPro will not stop to ask for confirmation before overwriting a file. If you use SET SAFETY OFF in a program, it is a good idea to turn it on again before returning the user to the Command window.

User-defined Functions

User-defined functions (UDFs) are functions that you design, and like the standard FoxPro functions, they can be provided with values as arguments and they can return values. You can use UDFs to accomplish specialized tasks that are outside the range of the standard functions provided with FoxPro.

You can place user-defined functions at the end of your program files, along with any other procedures your program may be using. All UDFs start with the FUNCTION command, and they contain the commands and parameters needed to return the desired values. The names given to UDFs must be no more than eight characters in length. The syntax of a UDF is shown here:

FUNCTION *UDFname*
PARAMETERS *list-of-parameters*
 commands....
RETURN *value-or-variable*

where *list-of-parameters* is a list of one or more memory variable names representing the values you will supply to the function. As an example, perhaps you often need to convert temperature readings in Centigrade, stored in a scientific database, to Fahrenheit. You could define the following function for this purpose:

```
FUNCTION FARENHT
PARAMETERS ctemp
ftemp = 9/5 * (ctemp+32)
RETURN ftemp
```

Then, at any location in the program, you call the function just as you would any other function. If the database field containing the temperature readings were named TEMP, you could use a statement like

```
? FARENHT(TEMP)
```

and the FARENHT function would return the value contained in the Temp field, converted to Fahrenheit.

You can also specify that a UDF return a value of "True" or "False", depending on how the commands within your UDF evaluate a particular condition. An example of this technique appears in the sample UDF shown here, which checks to see if a two-letter code for a state entered by a user is actually a valid abbreviation:

```
FUNCTION ValState
PARAMETERS State
IF UPPER(state) $ "AK AL AR AZ CA CO CT DC DE FL GA + ;
HI IA ID IL IN KA KY LA MA MD ME MI MN MO MS MT NB + ;
NC ND NH NJ NM NY OH OK OR PA RI SC SD TN TX UT VA + ;
VT WA WI WV WY"
        RETURN .T.
ENDIF
RETURN .F.
```

A portion of a data entry program could use the function to check for proper entries, as shown here:

```
@ 7, 5 SAY "State: " GET MSTATE
READ
IF .NOT. ValState(MSTATE)
      WAIT "Error in State code."
      LOOP
ENDIF
<...rest of program...>
```

If the user's response did not match one of the two-letter codes defined in the function, the function would return a value of "False", causing the error message to appear.

Drawing Bar Graphs

Bar graphs can be drawn by using the CHR and REPLICATE functions to plot representative columns on the screen. If your printer supports the IBM PC extended character set, you can route the output to the printer and achieve similar results there. Given a database containing the data shown here,

Record#	SALESREP	REPNUMB	AMTSOLD
1	Jones, C.	1003	350.00
2	Artis, K.	1008	110.00
3	Johnson, L.	1002	675.00
4	Walker, B.	1006	1167.00
5	Keemis, M.	1007	47.00
6	Williams, E	1010	256.00
7	Smith, A.M.	1009	220.00
8	Allen, L.	1005	312.00
9	Smith, A.	1001	788.50
10	Jones, J.	1011	875.00
11	Shepard, F.	1004	1850.00
12	Robertson, C.	1013	985.50

plotting the data with the following program results in the display shown in Figure 18-1.

```
*Bars.PRG is bar graph program.
SET TALK OFF
Divisor = 30
*See note in text on calculating Divisor.
*AmtSold is field in database to be graphed.
```

FIGURE
18-1

Bar Graph

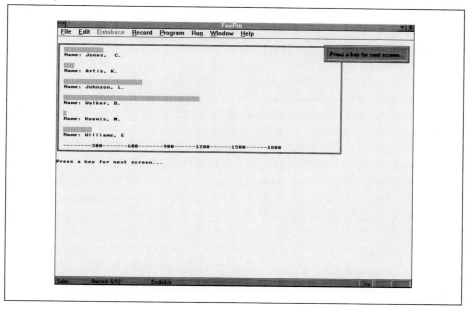

```
CLEAR
USE SALES
@ 2,1
*above line positions cursor at row 2, col 1.
DO WHILE .NOT. EOF( )
        BarLength = INT(AMTSOLD/DIVISOR)
        @ ROW( ), 2 SAY REPLICATE(CHR(177),BarLength)
        @ ROW( )+1,2 SAY "Name: " + SALESREP
        @ ROW( ) + 2,0
        IF ROW( ) > 18
                @ 20,2 SAY "--------300-------600-------900--" +;
                "----1200------1500------1800"
                @ 1,0 TO 21,79 DOUBLE
                WAIT "Press a key for next screen..."
                CLEAR
                @ 2,1
        ENDIF
        SKIP
ENDDO
IF ROW( ) > 2
        @ 20,2 SAY "--------300-------600-------900--" +;
```

```
                   "----1200------1500------1800"
                   @ 1,0 TO 21,79 DOUBLE
                   WAIT
     ENDIF
     RETURN
```

The program takes the contents of a field that is to be graphed (in this case, Amtsold), divides it by a set amount (Divisor), and uses the INT function to return an integer based on that figure. This number, stored to the memory variable BarLength, is then used as an argument in the REPLICATE function to determine the length of the bar. The ROW function, which returns the current row in which the cursor is located, is used at various locations in the program to place data on the screen.

The calculation of the best value for Divisor is a simple matter. Assuming you want to use nearly a complete screen width for the longest bar, the value of Divisor must be no less than the value of the highest amount to be graphed, divided by the available screen width. In this example, the highest sales amount ($1850) divided by a screen width of 76 (which leaves room for the starting position and the borders) suggests a value of no less than 24. The example used a value of 30, partly to make the scale simple to construct and partly to leave room for increased sales performance. You will need to adjust the scope of your scale accordingly.

Using Modular Programming

Don't get the impression that this section is going to take you through a textbook discussion of the benefits of system analysis and modular design. You can find that kind of a discussion in many basic programming textbooks. What this section does demonstrate are ways to design FoxPro applications in modular form, so you can easily utilize the same code repeatedly.

Assuming you write programs in FoxPro (and if you didn't, you probably wouldn't be reading this chapter), chances are you're spending time on the development of more than one program. If all your FoxPro work centers around a single application (like that monster of a sales-tracking system that keeps tabs on things at your office), then writing modular programs may not help you very much except as an aid in debugging and by providing a warm feeling for having developed efficient code. But if you have to develop or maintain a number of different applications at your work location or for others, you will save a lot of time by writing programs in modules and re-using the modules (with appropriate modifications) for different tasks.

The first step in adopting a system of modular FoxPro coding is to recognize that tasks in most FoxPro applications fall into the same common groups. Applications provide a main menu, leading to other choices stored as individual programs or as procedures. Among those other tasks typically handled within the submodules, or individual procedures of the FoxPro application, are the tasks of adding records, editing records, and deleting unwanted records. You can further break down many of the subtasks into common parts.

As an example, consider the task of editing records in a database. Well-written routines for editing records are faced with performing at least six tasks:

1. Find the desired record to edit.

2. Store the contents of the fields into memory variables.

3. Display the prompts and memory variables on the screen.

4. Allow editing of the memory variables with GET statements.

5. Perform any data validation desired, and allow corrections when necessary.

6. Move the validated data into the database.

Most programs written to perform a task like this one are written as one complete module that handles all these steps. But if you are going to use and re-use your code for multiple applications, strict adherence to the concepts behind modular programming suggests that you take it a step further and create individual modules for the individual steps. This may seem like a lot of work, but the first time you need to use the existing code in another application, you'll be glad that you chose this method of design.

A general approach that you can consider taking when designing highly modular code for a FoxPro application is to write the following routines for each database file and then enclose the routines within a procedure file that can be accessed through the command SET PROCE-

DURE TO *filename*. (For more information on procedures, see SET PROCE-
DURE in Appendix A.) Such a procedure file might contain the following:

- [ ] A "display" procedure for adding borders and graphic designs in a consistent format

- [ ] A "makevars" procedure for creating memory variables

- [ ] A "fillvars" routine for moving the contents of a field into a memory variable

- [ ] A "sayer" routine to display the prompts and memory variables

- [ ] A "getter" routine for getting memory variables

- [ ] A "validate" routine for performing any desired data validation

- [ ] A "movevars" routine to move the contents of the memory variables into the database fields

- [ ] A "finder" routine to locate records based on FIND or SEEK commands using available index files

As an example, consider the procedures described within a procedure file:

```
*Procedrs.PRG
Procedure Border
@ 0,0 TO 19,79 DOUBLE
@ 0,1 TO 4,78 DOUBLE
Draw = 1
Do While Draw < 4
        @ Draw, 2 SAY REPLICATE(chr(176),76)
        Draw = Draw + 1
Enddo
Return
*************************
Procedure Finder
DO MAKEVARS
@ 3,5 SAY "Enter BLANKS to EXIT."
@ 5,5 SAY "Last name? " GET M_LAST
@ 6,5 SAY "First name? " GET M_FIRST
READ
STORE M_LAST + M_FIRST TO FINDIT
SEEK FINDIT
RETURN
*************************
```

```
Procedure Sayer
@ 5,10 SAY "Last Name:"
@ 5,22 SAY M_LAST
@ 6,10 SAY "First name:"
@ 6,22 SAY M_FIRST
@ 7,10 SAY "Address:"
@ 7,22 SAY M_ADDRESS
@ 8,15 SAY "City:"
@ 8,22 SAY M_CITY
@ 9,15 SAY "State:"
@ 9,22 SAY M_STATE
@ 10,15 SAY "Zip:"
@ 10,22 SAY M_ZIP
RETURN
* * * * * * * * * * * * * * * * * * * * * * * * *
Procedure Getter
@ 5,22 GET M_LAST
@ 6,22 GET M_FIRST
@ 7,22 GET M_ADDRESS
@ 8,22 GET M_CITY
@ 9,22 GET M_STATE
@ 10,22 GET M_ZIP
RETURN
* * * * * * * * * * * * * * * * * * * * * * * * *
Procedure MakeVars
PUBLIC M_LAST, M_FIRST, M_ADDRESS, M_CITY,;
M_STATE, M_ZIP
M_LAST = space(15)
M_FIRST = space(15)
M_ADDRESS = space(25)
M_CITY = space(15)
M_STATE = space(2)
M_ZIP = space(10)
RETURN
* * * * * * * * * * * * * * * * * * * * * * * * *
Procedure FillVars
M_LAST = LASTNAME
M_FIRST = FIRSTNAME
M_ADDRESS = ADDRESS
M_CITY = CITY
M_STATE = STATE
M_ZIP = ZIPCODE
RETURN
* * * * * * * * * * * * * * * * * * * * * * * * *
```

```
Procedure MoveVars
REPLACE LASTNAME WITH M_LAST, FIRSTNAME WITH M_FIRST,;
ADDRESS WITH M_ADDRESS, CITY WITH M_CITY,;
STATE WITH M_STATE, ZIPCODE WITH M_ZIP
RETURN
**************************
Procedure Validate
IF M_LAST = SPACE(15)
   WAIT " Name required!"
   VALID = .F.
ENDIF
RETURN
```

By putting all of these tasks in a procedure file, and using DO commands
to call the procedures from your add, edit, and delete subroutines, you
can repeatedly use the same procedures in all of the routines. A program
using these procedures for adding records can be visually laid out in a
block diagram, as shown in Figure 18-2. The resultant code might be
used as follows:

```
*Adder.PRG adds records
VALID = .T.
DO WHILE .T.
     DO MAKEVARS
     CLEAR
     DO BORDER
     @ 3,10 SAY "DATA ENTRY SCREEN ADD NEW RECORDS"
     DO SAYER
     DO GETTER
     READ
     DO VALIDATE
     IF .NOT. VALID
          LOOP
     ENDIF
     APPEND BLANK
     DO MOVEVARS
     ACCEPT "Add another record? Y/N:" TO ANS
     IF UPPER(ANS) = "N"
          EXIT
     ENDIF
ENDDO
```

The beauty of taking program modularization down to this level is that
you can get away with the same code that is already in the procedures
for the edit and delete routines. An editing routine, assuming the

FIGURE
18-2 Block diagram of add routine

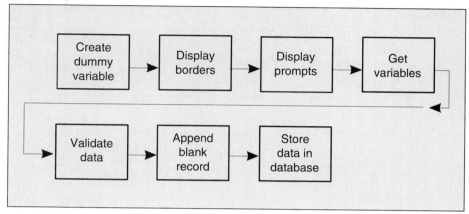

database is indexed on a combination of last and first names, is illustrated in the block diagram shown in Figure 18-3. The resultant code that might be used is shown here:

```
*Editor.PRG edits records
SET INDEX TO NAMES
DO WHILE .T.
        CLEAR
        DO MAKEVARS
        DO FINDER
        VALID = .T.
        IF FOUND( )
            CLEAR
            DO BORDER
            DO FILLVARS
            DO SAYER
            DO GETTER
            READ
            DO VALIDATE
            IF .NOT. VALID
                EXIT
            ENDIF
        ENDIF
        DO MOVEVARS
        CLEAR
        ACCEPT "Edit another? Y/N " TO ANS
        IF UPPER(ANS) = "N"
                EXIT
        ENDIF
```

Block diagram of edit routine

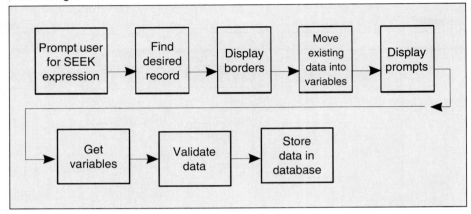

```
        ELSE
            CLEAR
            @ 5,5 SAY "No record by that name!"
            WAIT
            EXIT
        ENDIF
ENDDO
```

Your routine for deleting records would use much of the same code, as illustrated in Figure 18-4, and shown in this code:

```
*Eraser.PRG deletes records
SET INDEX TO NAMES
DO WHILE .T.
    CLEAR
    STORE "Y" TO ANS
    DO MAKEVARS
    DO FINDER
    IF FOUND( )
        CLEAR
        DO BORDER
        DO FILLVARS
        DO SAYER
        @ 20,5 SAY "Delete record, are you SURE? Y/N:"
        @ 20,40 GET ANS
        READ
        IF UPPER(ANS) = "Y"
```

FIGURE
18-4

Block diagram of delete routine

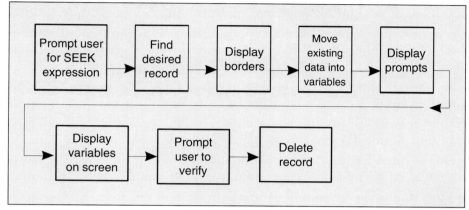

```
            DELETE
        ENDIF
    ELSE
        CLEAR
        @ 5,5 SAY "No record by that name!"
        WAIT
        EXIT
    ENDIF
ENDDO
```

Since the routines that perform the adding, editing, and deleting of records are generic routines (containing few or no statements specific to any particular application), you'll find that when you have to rewrite an application for a different database design, most of the necessary changes will be only in the procedure file.

When do you modularize? It's easy to get carried away and modularize virtually every task in an application, but this probably won't buy you visible benefits in every case. A major objective of the modular approach is to save you the time it takes to duplicate program code in more than one location. So a general rule to follow is obvious: If the task is likely to be repeated at more than one place in your application, code that task as a procedure, and call it from the procedure file. If the task will only be performed once, you may want to leave it as program code integral to that particular program, since calling it as a procedure won't provide you with any visible benefits.

Using FoxPro with Other Software

*T*he ability to exchange information with other programs enhances FoxPro's power. FoxPro allows you to transfer files to and from many popular software packages available for the PC. There is just one limitation on this capability: the other program must be able to transfer information in a format acceptable to FoxPro.

File Formats

The file formats in which FoxPro can transfer information include: Delimited format (a specialized form of ASCII text file, with fields separated by characters, blanks, or tabs); System Data format (SDF); and DBMEMO3/FOXPLUS format (a version of the dBASE III/IIIPLUS and FoxBase Plus format that supports memo fields).

Additionally, you can transfer files by using any of five Lotus 1-2-3 or Symphony worksheet formats (WK1, WK3, WKS, WR1, and WRK), or the Microsoft Excel worksheet format (XLS). You can also use the common Data Interchange Format (DIF), the Microsoft Symbolic Link format (SYLK), or the Microsoft Multiplan 4.0 format. And you can read Paradox version 3.5, Framework, or RapidFile databases into FoxPro. While you cannot write files in the Paradox, Framework, or RapidFile formats, you can write files in the dBASE III PLUS format, which can then be easily used by Paradox, Framework, or RapidFile.

ASCII Format

The term *ASCII format* refers to files that are composed of characters and spaces, not necessarily arranged in any particular order. ASCII stands for the American Standard Code for Information Interchange, an international standard for representing information in computers. Text files created by most word processors can be stored as ASCII text. You use ASCII files if you need to merge the contents of a database with a document created by a word processor. If, for example, your database contains a list of names, you can save those names to a text file in ASCII format. You can then use your word processor to call up the text file and use it as part of a document.

Delimited Format

Delimited-format ASCII files contain records in which fields *are delimited,* or separated, by a specific character or a space. If fields are separated by a comma, the format is called Character-Delimited. If the fields are separated by a single space, the format is called Blank-Delimited.

Character-delimited files can use any character as the delimiter; but the most commonly-used format surrounds the data in each character field with a pair of quotation marks, and separates each field from adjacent fields by a comma. Each record ends in a carriage return, so each record occupies a separate line. The following example shows a character-delimited file using this common format:

```
"Miller","Karen","4260 Park Avenue","Chevy Chase","MD",
   "20815-0988"
"Martin","William","4807 East Avenue","Silver Spring","MD",
   "20910-0124"
"Robinson","Carol","4102 Valley Lane","Falls Church","VA",
   "22043-1234"
"Kramer","Harry","617 North Oakland Street","Arlington","VA",
   "22203"
"Moore","Ellen","270 Browning Ave #2A","Takoma Park","MD",
   "20912"
"Zachman","David","1617 Arlington Blvd","Falls Church","VA",
   "22043"
"Robinson","Benjamin","1607 21st Street, NW","Washington","DC",
   "20009"
"Hart","Wendy","6200 Germantown Road","Fairfax","VA","22025"
```

SDF Format

Like delimited files, files in SDF format store each record as an individual line, so the records are separated from each other by carriage returns. However, each field in an SDF file is of a preset width, regardless of the data stored in that field for any particular record. All records are therefore identical in length. (The term SDF was popularized by Ashton-Tate, the original inventors of dBASE; many other vendors call the same type of file a "flat file," "fixed-length file," or "DOS text file.") FoxPro can store files in SDF format for use by other programs. Many spreadsheets can also store data in SDF format; FoxPro can then read those files, using an SDF option of the APPEND command (which is discussed shortly).

The following example shows a file in SDF format, created by FoxPro using the Lastname, City, Expiredate, and Tapelimit fields of the Generic Videos database. Note that in this format, dates are stored in a year-month-day arrangement.

```
Miller      Chevy Chase    19920725  6
Martin      Silver Spring  19920704  4
Robinson    Falls Church   19930905  6
Kramer      Arlington      19921222  4
Moore       Takoma Park    19941117  6
Zachman     Falls Church   19920919  4
Robinson    Washington     19930917  6
Hart        Fairfax        19921019  2
```

The SDF format uses a fixed number of spaces for each field, regardless of the actual size of the information in the field. Information that is too long to fit in an SDF file is truncated.

FOXPLUS or DBMEMO3 Format

The FOXPLUS/DBMEMO3 formats create files in dBASE III/III PLUS and FoxBase Plus file format. (This is actually a single format, with several names.) FoxPro provides these format options to aid in importing and exporting database files containing memo fields.

FoxPro stores memo field data in a manner that is more efficient than, but incompatible with most other dBASE-language products. As a result, trying to open a FoxPro database file containing memo fields causes error messages with products that normally accept dBASE files, such as Lotus 1-2-3, Excel, dBASE III PLUS, dBASE IV, and even FoxBase and Foxbase Plus.

To get around this problem, you can use the FOXPLUS or DBMEMO3 option to transfer files containing memo fields. Either option will create a file in the older FoxBase Plus/dBASE III PLUS format. That file can then be read by any other product that has the ability to read dBASE files. You need the FOXPLUS/DBMEMO3 format even when transferring data to dBASE IV, because FoxPro and dBASE IV use different methods of storing memo-field data.

 Note If you use menu options rather than commands to export files, note that FOXPLUS/DBMEMO3 does not appear in the dialog box as an available file type. Instead, the name "Database" appears as an available file type. Choose this choice to create files in the FOXPLUS/DBMEMO3 format.

Keep in mind that the DBMEMO3/FOXPLUS format is not needed if your database has no memo fields. (Using it won't hurt, but it won't provide any benefits, either.) FoxPro database files without memo fields can be used "as is" in any other product that can read the dBASE format.

Lotus File Formats

Programs made by the Lotus Development Corp. (such as the popular Lotus 1-2-3 spreadsheet) use a variety of Lotus file formats. FoxPro can write files in any of four Lotus formats, and can read files in any of five Lotus formats. You can write files using the WK1, WKS, WR1, and WRS type formats. You can read files in any of these formats, and in the WK3 format.

Lotus 1-2-3 version 2.x uses the WK1 format, Lotus 1-2-3 version 3.x uses the WK3 format, Lotus 1-2-3 version 1A uses the WKS format, Lotus Symphony version 1.0 uses the WRK format, and Lotus Symphony versions 1.1 and 1.2 use the WR1 format. When data is read from any of these spreadsheet files into a FoxPro database, the columns of the spreadsheet become fields in the database, and the rows of the spreadsheet become records in the database.

Note that Lotus 1-2-3 version 3.x, and Lotus 1-2-3 for Windows, can read all Lotus file formats; so if you are using either of these Lotus versions, you can transfer data from FoxPro through any of the available Lotus formats.

Note also that FoxPro cannot directly read files stored in the Lotus 1-2-3 for Windows spreadsheet format. If you want to export data from Lotus 1-2-3 for Windows into FoxPro, you will need to save the data in one of the earlier Lotus 1-2-3 formats. (See your 1-2-3 documentation for details on how to do this.)

Microsoft File Formats

FoxPro can read and write files in the MOD, SYLK, and XLS formats. MOD files are compatible with Microsoft's Multiplan, version 4.01. SYLK is an acronym for Symbolic Link, a file format used by some Microsoft programs (including Microsoft Chart and earlier versions of Microsoft Multiplan). The XLS format is used by Microsoft Excel, a popular spreadsheet package running under Windows and on the Macintosh.

Paradox, Framework, and RapidFile Formats

FoxPro can read files from the database packages Paradox 3.5, Framework, and RapidFile using (respectively) the PDOX, FW2, and RPD file formats. As noted previously, FoxPro cannot export files in these formats; but it can export in the dBASE III PLUS format, which all of these packages can read.

The DIF File Format

FoxPro can read and write files in the DIF format (DIF is an abbreviation for Document Interchange Format). DIF files can be used by a wide assortment of programs, including VisiCalc (an early spreadsheet package), and early versions of R:Base and PC–File III (two database managers). Internally, the DIF format is similar to the character-delimited ASCII format, but DIF files are not plain text files.

When transferring data out of FoxPro, you must decide what format you wish to use. A list of some of the better-known programs, and the types of data they can exchange, is shown in Table 19-1. As a general rule, most word processors can transfer in ASCII, Delimited, or SDF format. You generally use the Delimited format for mailmerge files. Many spreadsheets can transfer data in SDF format, and most database

<table>
<tr><td>TABLE
19-1</td><td colspan="3">File formats for other software</td></tr>
</table>

Brand	Type of Package	File type
WordPerfect	word processor	delimited, SDF, or DIF
Microsoft Word	word processor	delimited or SDF
Lotus 1-2-3	spreadsheet	WK1, WK3, or WKS
Excel	spreadsheet	XLS
Quattro Pro	spreadsheet	WK1, WK3, or WKS
dBASE III/IV	database manager	FOXPLUS/DBMEMO3
Paradox	database manager	FOXPLUS/DBMEMO3

managers can transfer data in Delimited format. All but the earliest versions of Lotus 1-2-3 and all versions of Symphony can read and write files in the dBASE file format. If it isn't obvious which format your software package uses, check the owner's manual.

Data Sharing with the APPEND and COPY Commands

Many data exchanges between FoxPro and other programs are accomplished by using certain TYPE options with the COPY and APPEND commands. Using COPY, you can copy data from FoxPro to another program; using APPEND, you can append, or transfer data from another program into a FoxPro database. (The menu equivalents for these commands are Database/Copy To, and Database/Append From.) The normal format for these commands, when used with a TYPE option, is as follows:

COPY TO *filename* [SCOPE] [FIELDS *fieldlist*] TYPE *type*

APPEND FROM *filename* [FIELDS *fieldlist*] TYPE *type*

In this case, *filename* is the name of the file to be transferred between FoxPro and the other program, and *type* is one of the acceptable file types.

The acceptable TYPE options are DELIMITED [WITH *character*], SDF, FOXPLUS or DBMEMO3, DIF, MOD, PDOX, SYLX, WK1, WKS, WR1, WRK, and XLS. Also, with the exception of Paradox (PDOX), Framework (FW2), and RapidFile (RPD), the FW2, RPD, and WK3 (Framework, RapidFile, and 1-2-3 version 3.*x*) TYPE options can be used with the APPEND FROM command, but not with the COPY TO command. The WITH parameter of the DELIMITED option lets you specify a character to use as the field delimiter, in place of the default quotation marks.

As a brief example, to copy the Generic Videos database into a file that could be read by Lotus 1-2-3 version 3.0, you might use this command:

```
COPY TO 123FILE TYPE WK3
```

You might use the following command to transfer a file from Microsoft Excel to FoxPro:

```
APPEND FROM SCFILE TYPE XLS
```

You can add other options to the COPY command when transferring data to other programs, such as a scope (ALL, NEXT, or a record number), or a list of fields. You can also use the FOR condition to specify records that will be transferred.

When using the APPEND command to import data from foreign files, note that you can include a FOR clause, but you cannot use a scope.

You can also use menu options to perform the equivalent of the COPY TO and APPEND FROM commands. To copy the contents of a database to a foreign file type, choose Database/Copy To. In the Copy To dialog box which appears, enter the desired file name in the Output/Save As text box, and use the File Type drop-down list box to specify the desired file format. Then, click the Copy button.

To append records from a foreign file, choose Database/Append From. In the Append From dialog box which appears, enter the desired file name in the Output/From text box (or click the From button, then choose a filename from the list box which appears). If you want to specify which fields will be appended, click the Fields button, and choose the desired fields from the dialog box which appears. Then, click the Append button in the Append From dialog box.

Examples of Transferring Files

The rest of this chapter provides working examples of transferring files. Since you may not be using the software packages described here, you may not be able to follow along with the examples. If you have the software package mentioned, or a similar software package with the ability to use the file formats acceptable to FoxPro, try using the examples with your software.

Transferring from FoxPro to WordStar and Other Word Processors

Most word processors work with ASCII format, so let's try it first. Suppose you needed to pull employee names and salary amounts from a database, to use in a memo to the company president. You can use the LIST command, with its TO FILE option, to help you perform this task. When you enter LIST (along with any preferred fields), followed by TO FILE and a file name, the data retrieved by the command will be stored as an ASCII text file with the name you specified.

Try using the TO FILE option of the LIST command by entering the following:

```
USE MEMBERS
LIST LASTNAME, FIRSTNAME, EXPIREDATE TO FILE PEOPLE.TXT
```

Now exit FoxPro and load your word processor. (For this example, you can use Windows Write if you don't have another Windows word processor.) Press CTRL+ESC to open the Windows Task List, choose Program Manager, and load your word processor (or Windows Write) from the Program Manager in the usual manner. Use your word processor's File/Open command to open the file. When your word processor asks you for the file name to load, enter the drive and path of your FoxPro data directory, followed by the file name **PEOPLE.TXT**. The file should then appear on your screen. Figure 19-1 shows an example of the file loaded into Windows Write.

FIGURE
19--1

File transfer from FoxPro to Windows Write

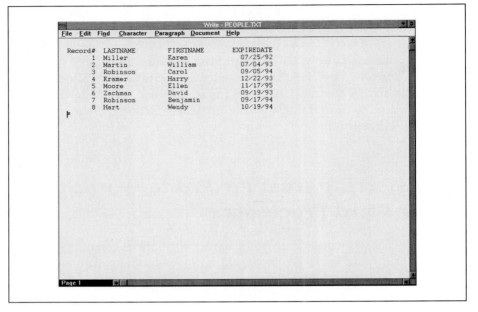

You can also run a report and store its output in a file, by adding the TO FILE option to the end of a REPORT FORM command. As an example, the command

```
REPORT FORM SAMPLE TO FILE REPS.TXT
```

creates an ASCII text file, named REPS.TXT, containing the data specified in the stored report SAMPLE.

At the bottom of the file that was transferred from FoxPro, there may be a left-pointing arrow or a similar graphics character (its presence or absence depends on what word processor you are using). This character represents an end-of-file marker that FoxPro produced when it was finished writing to the file. You can use the BACKSPACE key to erase the unwanted character. Different word processors interpret this end-of-file marker in different ways, so you may see a character other than a left-pointing arrow.

Switch back to FoxPro now, by bringing up the Windows Task List with CTRL+ESC, and choosing FoxPro from the task list.

Transferring from FoxPro to Merge Files and to Other Database Managers

Delimited formats are used by the merge-print options of many word processors, and by some older database managers. If you need to transfer data to another database manager, first check your documentation to see if the database manager can accept files in dBASE format. If it can, then either load the FoxPro file directly into the other program (if no memo fields are present), or else export it from FoxPro in the FOXPLUS/DBMEMO3 format.

If the other database manager cannot read files in dBASE format, you can export the data from FoxPro in Delimited format, using the DELIMITED option of the COPY command. Its format is

COPY TO *filename* [SCOPE] [FIELDS *fieldlist*] TYPE DELIMITED

where *filename* is the name of the delimited file you will export.

You can limit which records to copy by including a scope, specified by ALL, NEXT, or RECORD. You can also restrict which fields are exported by using the FIELDS *fieldlist* option. Also, note that when you specify the DELIMITED option, the .TXT extension will automatically be appended to *filename*, unless you specify otherwise.

As an example, let's say that you need to transfer a list of the names, addresses, and cities from MEMBERS to a file named DATAFILE, that will be used by another database manager. Enter the following commands:

```
USE MEMBERS
COPY TO DATAFILE FIELDS LASTNAME, FIRSTNAME, ADDRESS,
CITY, STATE TYPE DELIMITED
```

(Note that the "COPY TO..." command should be typed on a single line.)

The DATAFILE.TXT file created by COPY TO will contain one line for each record that was copied from MEMBERS. Each record includes the member's last name, first name, address, city, and state. Each field is enclosed by quotation marks, and fields are separated by commas.

You can use FoxPro's TYPE command to examine on-screen the contents of any text file. (Note that this is a command called "TYPE", not to be confused with the "TYPE" option that you've added to other commands in order to specify a file format.) Let's examine DATAFILE with the TYPE command, to see the Delimited file format. This command requires you to supply the file extension (in this case, .TXT), so enter the command

```
TYPE DATAFILE.TXT
```

and your display will resemble the following:

```
"Miller","Karen","4260 Park Avenue","Chevy Chase","MD"
"Martin","William","4807 East Avenue","Silver Spring","MD"
"Robinson","Carol","4102 Valley Lane","Falls Church","VA"
"Kramer","Harry","617 North Oakland Street","Arlington","VA"
"Moore","Ellen","270 Browning Ave #3C","Takoma Park","MD"
"Zachman","David","1617 Arlington Blvd","Falls Church","VA"
"Robinson","Benjamin","1607 21st Street, NW","Washington","DC"
"Hart","Wendy","6200 Germantown Road","Fairfax","VA"
```

This file can be used by many older database managers, or it can be used by the merge-print options of many word processors to create form letters. (More detailed explanations of how to use FoxPro data with Microsoft Word or WordPerfect to print form letters appear in the next section.) In such cases, you must use the appropriate commands of your particular database manager or word processor to import a file in the Delimited format.

Transferring from Merge Files and Other Database Managers to FoxPro

Remember that when you import data into FoxPro with the APPEND command, your FoxPro database structure must match the structure of the records in the file you're importing. In other words, the fields must be in the same order, and the fields in the FoxPro database should be wide enough to accommodate the incoming data. As an example, if you had a file of names and addresses in your word processor laid out in this format:

Lastname	(longest name: 12 characters)
Firstname	(longest name: 10 characters)
Salary	(dollar amounts not larger than 999.99)
Hired	(a date)

and you wanted to transfer data in such a format to a FoxPro database, you would need to create a database structure like the one shown here:

Field Name	Field Type	Width	Decimal
Lastname	Character	12	
Firstname	Character	10	
Salary	Numeric	6	2
Hired	Date	8	

In such a case, the field names would not matter. What is important is that the fields in the FoxPro database structure must be in the same order as in the incoming file.

Creating Files for Use With Mailmerge Options

If your word processor supports some type of mailmerge or merge-print operation, you may prefer to create a foreign file and use that file with your word processor to generate form letters. The precise approach differs from word processor to word processor, so several of the more popular approaches are covered in detail here.

Microsoft Word

With Microsoft Word, you can create a delimited file with the default delimiters of commas and quotation marks. Microsoft Word expects the field names to appear as the very first line of text in the foreign file, with the fields separated by commas (under Word for DOS) or separated by tabs or commas (under Word for Windows). The file would need to resemble the following:

```
last,first,address,city,state,zip
"Miller","Karen","4260 Park Avenue","Chevy Chase","MD",
  "20815-0988"
"Martin","William","4807 East Avenue","Silver Spring","MD",
  "20910-0124"
"Robinson","Carol","4102 Valley Lane","Falls Church","VA",
  "22043-1234"
"Kramer","Harry","617 North Oakland Street","Arlington","VA",
  "22203"
"Moore","Ellen","270 Browning Ave #2A","Takoma Park","MD",
  "20912"
```

To export such a file from FoxPro, you would use commands like the following:

```
USE MEMBERS
COPY NEXT 5 TO WFILE.TXT FIELDS LAST, FIRST, ADDRESS, ;
CITY, STATE, ZIPCODE TYPE DELIMITED
```

Then, in order to create the heading needed by Word, build a separate text file that contains the heading. Then use the FoxPro RUN command to combine the heading file with the delimited file, to produce a file ready for use by Microsoft Word. This can be done with commands like these:

```
SET TALK OFF
SET ALTERNATE TO HEADS
SET ALTERNATE ON
? "Last,First,Address,City,State,Zip"
?
CLOSE ALTERNATE
RUN COPY HEADS.TXT + WFILE.TXT WORDFILE.TXT
```

Note that if you are using Word for Windows, the TYPE DELIMITED option should be TYPE DELIMITED WITH TAB. The resultant file, called WORDFILE.TXT in this case, would resemble the delimited file shown earlier, with the addition of the field-name header as the first line.

When designing a form letter from within Microsoft Word (the DOS version), use CTRL+[to mark the start of each field, and CTRL+] to mark the end of each field. The CTRL+[key combination actually produces a symbol that resembles a double less-than sign, and pressing CTRL+] produces a symbol resembling a double greater-than sign.

In Word for Windows, first create a main merge document using the usual procedures (see your Word documentation for details). Then, while typing the document, use CTRL+F9 to produce a double-brace symbol for each field, then type the field's name between the double braces. Using these characters, you can create a form letter like this example:

```
<<data wordfile.txt>>



                    Johnson, Johnson
                    Fennerson & Smith
                    303 Broadway South
                    Norfolk, VA 56008


<<first>> <<last>>
<<address>>
<<city>>, <<state>> <<zip>>

Dear <<first>> <<last>>:


        In response to your letter received, we are
pleased to enclose a catalog of our latest products. If
we can answer any questions, please do not hesitate to
call.


Sincerely,



Mike Rowe
Sales Manager
```

You could generate the form letters within Microsoft Word, using Word's Print Merge command.(See your Microsoft Word documentation for details, if needed.)

An Export Program for WordPerfect

If you wish to use WordPerfect's mailmerge feature, you must do things a little differently than with most other software. WordPerfect expects to see data on individual lines, all flush left, with the ends of fields marked by a ^R followed by a carriage return. The end of a record is indicated by a ^E followed by a return. A data file formatted as a WordPerfect "secondary merge file" would resemble the following:

```
Jerry^R
Sampson^R
1412 Wyldewood Way^R
Phoenix^R
AZ^R
78009^R
^E
Paris^R
Williamson^R
P.O. Box 1834^R
Herndon^R
VA^R
22070^R
^E
Mary^R
Smith^R
37 Mill Way^R
Great Neck^R
NY^R
12134^R
^E
```

Unfortunately, you cannot create a file like this with something as simple as a COPY command. You can, however, write a short program to accomplish this task. To generate such a file, simply write each desired field out to a line of a file, and end that line with a ^R (ASCII 18). After the last field of the record, write a line containing only ^E (ASCII 5). You can use the SET ALTERNATE TO and SET ALTERNATE ON commands to direct the output to a text file, then write each line until all records have been written; then close the foreign file with the CLOSE ALTERNATE command.

As an example, the following program would accomplish this task. You can create the program file from inside FoxPro: In the Command window, type MODIFY COMMAND *filename* (where *filename* is the name you want to give the program). Then type the program listing as shown, saving it with CTRL+S. Substitute your database file name, and your field names, for the ones used in this example.

```
*CREATES Word Perfect MAIL MERGE FILES.
USE MEMBERS
SET TALK OFF
STORE CHR(18) TO ENDFIELD
STORE CHR(5) TO ENDREC
SET ALTERNATE TO PERFECT
SET ALTERNATE ON
GO TOP
DO WHILE .NOT. EOF( )
   ? TRIM(FIRSTNAME) + ENDFIELD
   ? TRIM(LASTNAME) + ENDFIELD
   ? TRIM(ADDRESS) + ENDFIELD
   ? TRIM(CITY) + ENDFIELD
   ? STATE + ENDFIELD
   ? ZIPCODE + ENDFIELD
   ? ENDREC
   SKIP
ENDDO
CLOSE ALTERNATE
RETURN
```

When you run the program with the command DO *filename* (where *filename* is the name you gave the program file), the result would be a text file similar to the one just shown, with each field on a separate line terminated by the ASCII character ^R, and with the end of each record marked by the character ^E on a line of its own.

To use the files in a WordPerfect secondary merge document, first make note of the order in which your program output the fields. Word-Perfect will recognize the first field of each record as field 1, the next as field 2, and so on.

Then, when creating the form letter document in WordPerfect, use the ALT+F9 key combination to insert placeholders for these fields, by number. For example, to indicate field #3, you would press ALT+F9, then type **F** followed by **3**, and then press ENTER. WordPerfect would then display a symbol (^F3^) that indicates that when the form letters are generated, the contents of each record's third field will appear in that position. Our WordPerfect form letter might resemble the following:

```
                          Johnson, Johnson
                          Fennerson & Smith
                          303 Broadway South
                          Norfolk, VA 56008

    ^F1^  ^F2^
    ^F3^
    ^F4^,  ^F5^  ^F6^


    Dear  ^F1^  ^F2^:


          In response to your letter received, we are
    pleased to enclose a catalog of our latest products. If
    we can answer any questions, please do not hesitate to
    call.


    Sincerely,



    Mike Rowe
    Sales Manager
```

Save the letter, using WordPerfect's usual save commands. To generate the form letters in WordPerfect, first import the data file from FoxPro: press CTRL+F5, select DOS Text File as the file type, then select Retrieve. Eliminate any blank lines at the top of the document, and press F10 to save the file under a new name. Use F7 to exit the document and get to an empty document window. Then press CTRL+F9, choose Merge, enter the name of the form letter document, and then enter the name you just gave to the imported data file. WordPerfect will proceed to create the letters, which can then be printed in the usual manner.

Transferring Between FoxPro and Lotus 1-2-3 or Symphony

Exchanging data between FoxPro and Lotus 1-2-3 or Symphony is a simple matter, as FoxPro can read and write files in most Lotus formats.

And all but the earliest versions of Lotus and Symphony can read and write data in the dBASE III file format.

To transfer data to Lotus 1-2-3 or Symphony, you use the COPY command with one of the Lotus file TYPE options (or, if memo fields exist, with the DBMEMO3/FOXPLUS file type) as shown here:

```
COPY TO LOTUSFIL TYPE WKS
```

This will produce a copy of the active database, in a file format that can be read by Lotus 1-2-3 or Symphony. To transfer spreadsheet data from Lotus 1-2-3 or Symphony into FoxPro, simply open an existing FoxPro database, then use the appropriate TYPE option of the APPEND command to append the contents of the Lotus worksheet.

If you have Lotus 1-2-3 (or Borland's Quattro Pro, which is 1-2-3 file compatible), try the following commands to create a file for conversion to a 1-2-3 spreadsheet:

```
USE RENTALS
COPY TO 123FILE
```

Press CTRL+ESC to bring up the Windows Task List, and choose Program Manager. From the Program Manager, get into Lotus 1-2-3 in the usual manner. You can now use the usual File/Load commands in 1-2-3 or Symphony to load the spreadsheet. In the example in Figure 19-2, the Set Column-Width command in Lotus 1-2-3 was used to widen the columns, to allow for a full display of the Social, Title, Dayrented, and Returned fields.

Spreadsheet users should keep in mind that nearly all spreadsheets are limited in size by the available memory of the computer, while FoxPro files are limited, in practice, only by available disk space. It is possible to export a FoxPro file so large that it cannot be loaded into your spreadsheet. When creating spreadsheet files from large databases, you may find it necessary to export small portions of the file. You can do this by using a FOR condition with the COPY command, or you can set a filter with the SET FILTER command before exporting the data.

Also, when transferring data out of a spreadsheet program to import into FoxPro, you should save a worksheet file containing only the database range of the larger worksheet (excluding any titles, macro references, or explanatory text).

FoxPro table in spreadsheet

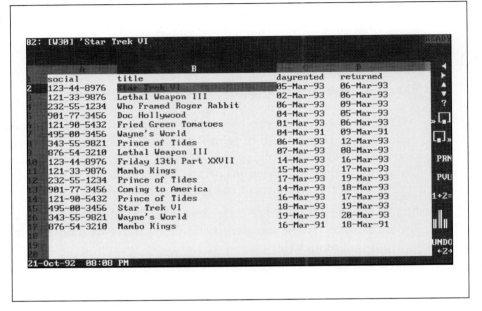

Note   When you translate logical fields from a FoxPro or dBASE file into Lotus 1-2-3, Lotus recognizes only the values T (true) and F (false). It does not recognize Y (yes) and N (no), even though these are acceptable logical values in FoxPro.

Transferring from FoxPro to Older Spreadsheets

The SDF format is used for transferring data from FoxPro to spreadsheet packages that cannot read dBASE or 1-2-3 files. (This format is also useful for exchanging data with mainframe computers, or with computers that are not IBM-compatible.)

To save a file in SDF format, you can use the COPY command with the TYPE SDF option. Try this variation of the COPY command to create an SDF file:

```
USE MEMBERS
COPY TO CALCFILE FIELDS LASTNAME, CITY, EXPIREDATE TYPE SDF
```

The CALCFILE.TXT file created by this command will contain one line for each record, and each line will contain the fields Lastname, City, and Expiredate. Instead of being surrounded by quotes and separated by commas, each field is allotted space according to its width. To see the file in SDF format, enter

```
TYPE CALCFILE.TXT
```

and the following is displayed on your screen:

```
Miller      Chevy Chase      19920725
Martin      Silver Spring    19920704
Robinson    Falls Church     19930905
Kramer      Arlington        19921222
Moore       Takoma Park      19941117
Zachman     Falls Church     19920919
Robinson    Washington       19930917
Hart        Fairfax          19921019
```

How you load the file into your spreadsheet package depends on what spreadsheet you are using. It would be impossible to explain the file loading commands for all spreadsheets, but in most cases you need to use an appropriate load command that lets your spreadsheet open files in the SDF format. Your spreadsheet documentation should contain details on how you can do this.

Transferring from Other Spreadsheets to FoxPro

When you need to get data from a spreadsheet into FoxPro, your first choice of format should be either one of the Lotus file types, or the XLS file type (used with Microsoft Excel). Many spreadsheets (even those made by companies other than Lotus and Microsoft) can read and write files in one of the Lotus or Excel file formats. When appending from a Lotus or Excel spreadsheet, you need to use the APPEND FROM command, which means you need to have a database file with the same structure as the spreadsheet.

If your intended database already exists, it is usually easiest to start in the spreadsheet package. Open the appropriate worksheet, and copy the desired range of data to a blank area of this worksheet. There, you can move the columns around until the structure of this data range matches the structure of the target FoxPro database. Then, save that range of the worksheet to a separate file (see your spreadsheet program's manual for details). Finally, load the new worksheet file into FoxPro with the APPEND FROM command, using the appropriate TYPE option.

Before transferring an SDF file into a database, be sure that the database field types and field widths match the SDF format precisely.

Note that you can't use a scope with the APPEND command when appending from non-FoxPro files. The APPEND FROM command with the TYPE SDF option operates exactly like APPEND FROM with the TYPE DELIMITED option.

Transferring from Other Word Processors to FoxPro

Transferring data from a word processor into a FoxPro database may take just a little more work than moving FoxPro data into a word processor. This is because files brought into a FoxPro database must follow a precise format, such as an SDF or Delimited format. Thus, before transferring the data, you must edit the word processor file until it matches the format of a delimited or an SDF file.

After your word processor creates a file in Delimited or SDF format, you can use FoxPro's APPEND command to copy in the data. At first glance, it may seem easier to use the SDF format instead of the Delimited format, because you don't have to type all the quotes and commas. But if you choose the SDF format, you must keep track of the size of each field; each field must have the same width as the database field to which you will be transferring its data. For this reason, it is sometimes easier to use the Delimited format.

When transferring files created by your word processor (or any other program) to FoxPro, you must also create or use a FoxPro database with a structure that matches the design of the files you wish to transfer. For purposes of simplicity, the following examples assume that the files created by other software match the structure of the Generic Videos database.

Let's try a transfer using a delimited file. Suppose you have created a mailing list in a word processor, and you now want to use that mailing list with FoxPro. If you have a word processor that can create files in ASCII text, follow along.

Use your word processor to create the following delimited file, and give it the name MAIL2.TXT. (Whatever word processor you are using, be sure to save the file as ASCII text.)

```
"123-80-7654","Johnson","Larry","4209 Vienna Way","Asheville","NC","27995"
"191-23-5566","Mills","Jeanette","13 Shannon Manor","Phoenix","AZ","87506"
"909-88-7654","Simpson","Charles","421 Park Avenue","New York","NY","10023"
```

Save the file as ASCII text, using the appropriate commands in your word processor. Now switch back to FoxPro (you can use CTRL+ESC to bring up the Windows Task List). You use the DELIMITED option of the APPEND FROM command to append the file to MEMBERS. The format of the APPEND command, when used to import a delimited file, is

APPEND FROM *filename* DELIMITED

To transfer MAIL2.TXT to FoxPro, enter the following commands:

```
USE MEMBERS
APPEND FROM MAIL2.TXT TYPE DELIMITED
```

FoxPro responds with the message "3 records added." To examine the database, enter **GO TOP** and then **LIST**, and at the bottom of the database you will see that the names and addresses from the mailing list have been added to the database.

In this example, the fields are stored in the following order: social security number, last name, first name, address, city, state, and ZIP code. By a marvelous coincidence, this is the same order as the fields in MEMBERS. In real life, though, things may not be as simple.

When the order of fields in the external program's data file does not match the field order in the FoxPro database, you will need to perform whatever work is necessary to make them match. You can do this in one of two ways: either change the order of the data in the other file, or design a new database in FoxPro that matches the order of the data in the other file.

In most cases, it is easiest to first create a matching file structure in FoxPro, and then append the data from the other file. After the data has been imported into FoxPro, you can play with the field order either by modifying this FoxPro file's structure, or by copying the data into a second FoxPro file that has the fields in the desired order (in which case FoxPro will match fields by the name).

Notes About FoxPro and Other dBASE Compatibles

Files from FoxBase, FoxBase Plus, and FoxPro for DOS can be used in FoxPro without any changes. You can also use FoxPro for Windows database files within FoxPro for DOS, FoxBase, and FoxBase Plus. However, because of differences in the way memo-field text is stored, neither FoxBase nor FoxBase Plus will open a FoxPro database that contains memo fields. You must convert the database to FOXPLUS/DBMEMO3 format, using the COPY TO *filename* command with either the TYPE FOXPLUS or the TYPE DBMEMO3 option. The copied file can then be opened by FoxBase or FoxBase Plus.

You should use the same TYPE FOXPLUS/DBMEMO3 option if you are exporting a file containing memo fields to other dBASE-compatible database managers. This includes dBASE III PLUS and dBASE IV. FoxPro files *not* containing memo fields can be used in these products without alteration.

APPENDIX

Glossary of FoxPro Commands

*T*his appendix contains a listing of FoxPro commands. Each command name is followed by the syntax of the command and a description of how the command works. Examples of applications are provided for some commands. You will recognize most commands from the tutorial section; others will be introduced here.

Because this is a beginning-to-intermediate-level text, some commands and options relating to advanced programming are not covered in detail here. Refer to your FoxPro documentation for additional information about these commands.

Glossary Symbols and Conventions

1. All commands are printed in UPPERCASE, although you can enter them in either upper- or lowercase letters.

2. All parameters of the command are listed in *italics*.

3. Any part of a command or parameter that is enclosed by [ ] (left and right brackets) is optional.

4. When a slash separates two choices in a command, as in ON/OFF, you specify one choice but not both.

5. An ellipsis (...) following a parameter or command mean that the parameter or command can be repeated "infinitely"—that is, until you exhaust the memory of the computer.

6. The *scope* parameter, which is always an option, can have four different meanings, depending on the command: ALL for all records, NEXT *n* for *n* number of records beginning at the current position of the record pointer, REST for all records from the pointer position to the end of the file, and RECORD *n* for record number *n*.

7. The term *expC* indicates a character expression, *expN* indicates a numeric expression, and *expL* indicates a logical expression. Where data type does not matter, the term *expr* is used.

List of Commands

\ or \\

Syntax

\ <<text line>>
\\ <<text line>>

The \ and \\ commands are used in implementing FoxPro's text-merge capability. The \ and \\ commands send a line of text to the current output device. If the \ command is used, a carriage return and linefeed are sent before the contents of the text line are evaluated. If the \\ command is used, a carriage return and linefeed are not sent.

Expressions (including field names), variables, and functions placed within delimiters in the text line will be evaluated if SET TEXTMERGE is ON (see SET TEXTMERGE). If SET TEXTMERGE is OFF, the expressions, variables, or functions appear as literal characters. For example, if SET TEXTMERGE were ON, the command

\ <<LASTNAME>>

which consists of the \ command followed by a field called Lastname, would output the contents of that field for the current record of the active database. If SET TEXTMERGE were OFF, the same command would output the name of the field enclosed by the double angle brackets (in this case, Lastname).

? or ??

Syntax

?/??[*expr*][PICTURE "*clause*"][FUNCTION "*functionlist*"]
[AT *expN*]

The ? command displays the value of a FoxPro expression. If a single question mark (?) is used, the cursor executes a carriage return and linefeed, and then the value of the expression is displayed. If the double question mark (??) is used, the cursor is not moved before the value of the expression is displayed. The PICTURE and FUNCTION options may be used to customize the appearance of the displayed information. The AT option may be used to place the expression at a specific column location.

???

Syntax

??? *expC*

The ??? command sends characters to the printer without changing the current row and column positions. Use this command to send control codes or escape sequences to the printer. To specify control codes, enclose the ASCII code in {} (curly braces).

@

Syntax

@ *row,col*[SAY *expr*][PICTURE *expr*][FUNCTION *list*][GET *variable*][PICTURE *expr*][FUNCTION *list*][RANGE *low,high*] [VALID *condition*][ERROR *expC*][COLOR *std/enhanced*][COLOR SCHEME *expN*][WHEN *expC*][DEFAULT *expC*][OPEN WINDOW name] [ENABLE/DISABLE][SIZE *nrows* x ncols]

The @ command places the cursor at a specific screen location, identified by *row,col.* The @ command can be used with one or more of the named options. The SAY option displays the value of the expression following the word "SAY." The GET option allows editing of the variable (which can be a field). Note that a READ command must follow the use of GET commands to achieve full-screen editing. The PICTURE option allows the use of templates, which specify the way data will be displayed or accepted in response to the GET option. The RANGE option is used with the GET option to specify a range of acceptable entries. The VALID option specifies acceptable entries for GET by using a condition. ERROR displays a custom error message if VALID is not met. COLOR defines new color settings for the @-SAY-GET command. COLOR SCHEME is a numeric value from 1 to 11, denoting colors based on the corresponding color scheme (see SET COLOR OF SCHEME). Note that in FoxPro for Windows, color commands and options change only the colors used by *user-defined* windows and menus; all other elements under Windows must be changed through the Windows color option in the Control Panel. WHEN is a logical expression that permits or prevents editing in the GET. DEFAULT provides a default value for the GET. OPEN WINDOW is used with memo fields, to open a predefined window for the field. DISABLE is used to disable editing in a GET field; the cursor skips the field. SIZE *nrows* x *ncols* can be used to define a size for the field other than the default.

Example

To place the message "Enter shareholder name:" at screen location 12,2 and to allow full-screen editing of the value contained in the variable SHN, enter

```
@ 12,2 SAY "Enter shareholder name:" GET SHN
```

Note that there are some additional options of the @...GET command that are not covered here, due to their advanced nature. These options create check boxes, radio buttons, list boxes, pop-ups, spinners, and push buttons within programs. Refer to your FoxPro documentation for further information on these options.

@-BOX

Syntax

@ *row1,col1,row2,col2* BOX *expC*

This command draws a box between the specified coordinates. (Note that this command is compatible with FoxBase Plus. If compatibility with dBASE IV is desired, use the @ *row,col* TO *row,col* variation of the command.) An optional character expression containing up to nine different characters may be specified, in which case those characters are used to construct the box. The first four characters define the four corners, starting from the upper-left corner and moving clockwise. The next four characters define the four sides, starting from the top and moving clockwise. The last character, if specified, is used as the background. If no character expression is provided, a single-line box is drawn.

Example

To draw a single-line box with the upper-left corner at row 4, column 1, and the lower-right corner at row 18, column 70, enter

```
@ 4,1,18,70 BOX
```

@-CLEAR TO

Syntax

@ *row,col* CLEAR/CLEAR TO *row,col*

This variation of the @ command clears a portion of the screen. If @ *row,col* CLEAR is used, the screen is cleared to the right of and below the coordinates provided. If @ *row,col* CLEAR TO *row,col* is used, the screen is cleared within a rectangular area, with the first coordinate indicating the upper-left corner and the second coordinate indicating the lower-right corner.

Example

To erase a rectangular area from row 4, column 5, to row 12, column 70, while leaving the remainder of the screen unchanged, enter

```
@ 4,5 CLEAR TO 12,70
```

@...EDIT

Syntax

@ *row,col* EDIT *variable*[FUNCTION *expC2*][DEFAULT *expr*]
SIZE *expN1*, *expN2*[,*expN3*][ENABLE/DISABLE][MESSAGE *expC3*]
[VALID *expL1* [ERROR *expC4*]][WHEN *expL2*][NOMODIFY][SCROLL]
[TAB/NOTAB][COLOR SCHEME *expN4*/COLOR *colorpairslist*]

The @...EDIT command allows editing of text in a rectangular area. The text to be edited can be a field (referenced by the field name), a memo field, a variable, or an array element. All standard FoxPro editing features are available, wordwrap occurs normally, and text can be scrolled vertically. Note that in FoxPro for Windows, color commands and options change only the colors used by *user-defined* windows and menus; all other elements under Windows must be changed through the Windows color option in the Control Panel. This command is used in advanced programming; for further details, refer to a more advanced programmer's text or to your FoxPro programmer's documentation.

@-FILL TO

Syntax

@ *row1,col1* FILL TO *row2,col2* [COLOR *std/enhanced*] [COLOR SCHEME *expN*]

The @-FILL TO command changes the color of the screen within the defined area. The *std/enhanced* is *x/y*, where *x* is the code for the standard color and *y* is the code for the enhanced color. If the COLOR option is omitted, the screen is cleared within the defined area. COLOR SCHEME is a numeric value from 1 to 11, denoting a color based on the corresponding color scheme (see SET COLOR OF SCHEME). Note that in FoxPro for Windows, color commands and options change only the colors used by *user-defined* windows and menus; all other elements under Windows must be changed through the Windows color option in the Control Panel.

Example

```
@ 5,5 FILL TO 10,40 COLOR B/R
```

@-MENU

Syntax

@ *row,col* MENU *array,expN1*[,*expN2*][TITLE *expC*]

This command creates a pop-up menu. Note that the DEFINE BAR and DEFINE POPUP commands can accomplish the same result; DEFINE BAR and DEFINE POPUP are compatible with dBASE IV programs, while @ *row,col* MENU is compatible with FoxBase Plus programs. The row and column locations specify the left corner location of the menu; *array* is a one-dimensional array that contains the menu items; *expN1* is the number of items in the menu; and *expN2*, which is optional, is the number of menu items to be displayed on the screen simultaneously, to a maximum of 17. TITLE is an optional menu title that appears at the top of the menu window.

@-PROMPT

Syntax

@ *row,col* PROMPT *expC*[MESSAGE *expC*]

This command, along with the MENU TO command, is used to create light-bar menus. (These commands for menu design are compatible with FoxBase Plus and Clipper; if compatibility with dBASE IV is desired, use the DEFINE POPUP and DEFINE BAR commands instead.) A series of PROMPT commands is used to display the options on the screen at the positions indicated by the *row,col* coordinates. The MENU TO command invokes the light-bar menu, and the user response is controlled by the cursor keys. A maximum of 128 prompts can be displayed on the screen at a time. If an optional message is included, the message appears at the row defined with the SET MESSAGE TO command when that particular option is highlighted in the menu.

Example

```
@ 5,5 PROMPT "1. Add records    "
@ 6,5 PROMPT "2. Edit records    "
@ 7,5 PROMPT "3. Delete records"
@ 8,5 PROMPT "4. Print records  "
@ 9,5 PROMPT "5. Quit System    "
MENU TO Mychoice
DO CASE
     CASE Mychoice = 1
          DO ADDER
     CASE Mychoice = 2
          DO EDITOR
     CASE Mychoice = 3
          DO ERASER
     CASE Mychoice = 4
          DO REPORTER
     CASE Mychoice = 5
          QUIT
ENDCASE
```

@-TO

Syntax

@ *row,col* TO *row,col*[DOUBLE/PANEL/*borderstring*][PATTERN *expN*][PEN *expN1*, *expN2*][STYLE *expC*]
[COLOR *standard*[,*enhanced*]][COLOR SCHEME *expN*]

This variation of the @ command draws lines, rectangular borders (boxes), circles, and ellipses on the screen. The first value represents the upper-left screen coordinate, and the second value represents the lower-right screen coordinate of the drawn object. If both coordinates share a horizontal or vertical coordinate, a line is drawn; otherwise, a rectangular border is drawn. When used with the DOUBLE options, the @ command draws double lines or borders (or a combination) on the screen. The PATTERN option accepts a numeric argument *expN* from 0 to 7 that specifies the fill pattern for the object (box, rounded-corner box, circle, or ellipse), as shown in the table below.

expN	Fill Pattern
0	None
1	Solid
2	***************
3	***************
4	\\\\\\\\\\\\\\\
5	///////////////
6	Upright crosshatch
7	Diagonal crosshatch

Include the PEN clause to identify an object's outline. The pen width is specified with *expN1*, and the pen type is specified with *expN2*. If you include both *expN1* and *expN2*, the pen type *expN2* overrides the pen width *expN1*.

The following tables contain values for *expN1* and *expN2* and the corresponding pen widths and types:

expN1	Pen Style
0	Hairline (the default)
1	1 Point
2	2 Point
3	3 Point
4	4 Point
5	5 Point
6	6 Point

expN2	Pen Type
0	None
1	Dotted
2	Dashed
3	Dash-Dot
4	Dash-Dot-Dot

Use the STYLE *expC* option to specify the type of object created (box, rounded-corner box, circle, or ellipse). Provide a number from 0 to 99 in *expC* to specify the corner curvature of the object. A 0 specifies no curvature and creates square corners, while 99 specifies the maximum curvature and creates circles and ellipses.

COLOR *standard[,enhanced]* denotes a color-pair combination for the foreground and background colors of the line or box. COLOR SCHEME is a numeric value from 1 to 11, denoting colors based on the corresponding color scheme (see SET COLOR OF SCHEME). Note that in FoxPro for Windows, color commands and options change only the colors used by *user-defined* windows and menus; all other elements under Windows must be changed through the Windows color option in the Control Panel.

Example

To draw a single line from row 3, column 5, to row 3, column 50, enter the following:

```
@ 3,5 TO 3,50
```

To draw a double-line box with the upper-left corner at row 4, column 1, and the lower-right corner at row 18, column 70, enter

```
@ 4,1 TO 18,70 DOUBLE
```

ACCEPT

Syntax

ACCEPT [*expC*] TO *memvar*

The ACCEPT command stores a character string to the memory variable *memvar*. ACCEPT can be followed by an optional character expression. If this expression is included, its contents will appear on the screen when the ACCEPT command is executed.

Example

To display the prompt "Enter owner name:" and store to the memory variable OWNER the character string that the user enters in response to the prompt, enter

```
ACCEPT "Enter owner name:" TO OWNER
```

ACTIVATE MENU

Syntax

ACTIVATE MENU *menuname* [PAD *padname*] [NOWAIT]

The ACTIVATE MENU command activates a predefined menu and displays that menu on the screen. If the PAD option is specified, the highlight bar appears at the named pad; otherwise, the first pad in the menu is highlighted. The NOWAIT clause forces program execution to continue after the menu is displayed.

Example

```
ACTIVATE MENU MainMenu PAD Add A Record
```

ACTIVATE POPUP

Syntax

ACTIVATE POPUP *popupname*
[AT *row,col*] [BAR *expN*] [NOWAIT][REST]

The ACTIVATE POPUP command activates a predefined pop-up menu and displays it on the screen. The AT clause defines the menu's location. BAR *expN* defines which bar of the menu is highlighted by default. The NOWAIT clause forces program execution to continue after the pop-up is displayed. The REST clause initially selects the pop-up option that corresponds to the record number of the current record in the active database.

Example

```
ACTIVATE POPUP Printer
```

ACTIVATE SCREEN

Syntax

ACTIVATE SCREEN

The ACTIVATE SCREEN command redirects output to the screen instead of to a predefined window.

Example

```
ACTIVATE SCREEN
```

ACTIVATE WINDOW

Syntax

ACTIVATE WINDOW *windownamelist*/ALL [BOTTOM/TOP/SAME] [NOSHOW]

The ACTIVATE WINDOW command activates a predefined window from memory. After the ACTIVATE WINDOW command is used, all screen output is directed to that window. If the ALL option is used, all defined windows in memory are displayed in the order in which they were defined. Use BOTTOM or TOP to place a window at the bottom or top of a stack of existing windows. The SAME option applies only to windows previously hidden with DEACTIVATE WINDOW or HIDE WINDOW. Use SAME to put the previously hidden window back in the position it occupied earlier.

Use the NOSHOW option to send output to a window without changing the window's status (a hidden window will receive output but remain hidden, for example).

Example

```
ACTIVATE WINDOW MyWindow
```

APPEND

Syntax

APPEND [BLANK]

The APPEND command appends records to a database. When the APPEND command is executed, a blank record is displayed, and FoxPro enters full-screen editing mode. If the BLANK option is used, a blank record is added to the end of the database, but full-screen editing mode is not entered.

APPEND FROM

Syntax

APPEND FROM *filename*[FIELDS *fieldlist*][FOR *condition*][TYPE *filetype*][DELIMITED[WITH *delimiter*/BLANK/TAB]]

APPEND FROM copies records from *filename* and appends them to the active database. The FOR/WHILE option specifies a condition that must be met before any records will be copied. If the file name containing the data to be copied is not a FoxPro database, an acceptable type option must be used. Valid type options are DELIMITED, DELIMITED WITH BLANK, DELIMITED WITH TAB, DELIMITED WITH "*specifiedcharacter*," or SDF, DIF, FW2, MOD, PDOX, RPD, SYLK, WK1, WK3, WKS, WR1, WRK, and XLS.

APPEND FROM ARRAY

Syntax

APPEND FROM ARRAY *arrayname* FOR *condition*[FIELDS *fieldlist*]

The APPEND FROM ARRAY command appends records to a database file from a named array. (Note that APPEND FROM ARRAY is compatible with dBASE IV; if you need compatibility with FoxBase Plus, use the GATHER FROM command instead.) The contents of each row in the array are transferred to a new record in the database file. The first column in the array becomes the first field, the second column in the array becomes the second field, and so on. If there are more elements in the array than fields in the database, the extra elements are ignored. If there are more fields in the database than there are elements in the array, the extra fields remain empty. The FOR clause, which is optional, lets you define a condition that must be met before data in the array will be added to a new record. An array must exist (defined with DECLARE and filled with data using STORE) before you can successfully use the APPEND FROM ARRAY command. If a FIELDS clause and a field list is included, only those fields named are updated.

Example

```
APPEND FROM ARRAY TempData FOR Dues = "paid"
```

APPEND GENERAL

Syntax

APPEND GENERAL *generalfield* FROM *file* [LINK] [CLASS *oleclass*]

The APPEND GENERAL command imports an OLE object from a field, and inserts the object into a general field. If the general field contains existing data, the existing data is overwritten by the OLE object. *Generalfield* represents the name of the general field, and *file* is the filename for the OLE object. If the file is in a directory other than the current one, you must include the entire filename and path, including any extension. Include the LINK option if you want to include a link between the OLE object and the file containing the object. The CLASS clause may be included to specify an OLE class other than the default class of OLE objects.

Example

```
APPEND GENERAL photos FROM c:\pictures\jaguar.bmp
```

APPEND MEMO

Syntax

APPEND MEMO *memofieldname* FROM *filename* [OVERWRITE]

The APPEND MEMO command imports a file into a memo field. The contents of the file are normally added to the end of any existing text in the memo field. If the OVERWRITE option is used, the contents of the file overwrite any existing text in the memo field. FoxPro assumes that the file has an extension of .TXT. If this is not the case, the extension must be specified along with the file name. If the file has no extension, include a period at the end of the file name.

Example

```
APPEND MEMO comments FROM letter.doc
```

AVERAGE

Syntax

AVERAGE *fieldlist*[*scope*][FOR *condition*][WHILE *condition*]
[TO *memvarlist*/TO ARRAY *arrayname*][NOOPTIMIZE]

The AVERAGE command computes an average of the specified numeric field listed in *fieldlist*. If the TO option is not used, the average is displayed on screen. If TO is used, the average of the first field is assigned to the first memory variable, the average of the second field to the second memory variable, and so on down the list; and the average is stored as the memory variable specified. If the *scope* option is not used, the quantifier of ALL is assumed, meaning all records in the database will be averaged unless you use the FOR or WHILE option. The FOR option can be used to specify a condition that must be met for the fields to be averaged. If you use the WHILE option, records will be averaged until the condition is no longer true. The NOOPTIMIZE clause turns off FoxPro's internal optimization techniques (also known as Rushmore).

BROWSE

Syntax

BROWSE FIELDS[*fieldlist*] [FOR *forclause*] [FORMAT] [FREEZE *field*] [LAST][NOAPPEND] [NOCLEAR][NODELETE][NOEDIT/ NOMODIFY] [NOMENU] [NOFOLLOW] [NORMAL] [NOWAIT] [SAVE] [WIDTH *expN*]
[WINDOW *windowname*] [PREFERENCE *expC*] [COLOR[*standard*] [,*enhanced*][,*border*]]/[COLOR SCHEME *expN*] [NOOPTIMIZE] [NOLINK] [NOLGRID] [NORGRID] [LEDIT] [LPARTITION] [PARTITION *n*] [REDIT] [TIMEOUT *n*]

The BROWSE command displays a number of records in a tubular format from a database on screen. If the database contains too many fields to fit on the screen, BROWSE displays only the fields that fit. You can view more fields by scrolling to the left or right with the mouse or the TAB key. The contents of any field can be edited while in Browse mode. To save changes made during Browse, press CTRL-F4 or CTRL-W; to exit Browse, press ESC. The FIELDS option displays only the fields listed in *fieldlist*. FORMAT tells the Browse window to assume any settings of an active format file. FREEZE *field* freezes the cursor within the named field. LAST tells FoxPro to use the most recent configuration (window size, column sizes) of Browse, as stored in the FoxUser configuration file. NORMAL causes the Browse window to assume normal color attributes rather than those of a previously defined window.

If NOFOLLOW is included, changes to a field that is part of an index expression will not cause the Browse display to follow the record to its new location in the database. The NOWAIT option is used within programs; when included, program control continues immediately after the Browse window is opened, rather than waiting for the user to exit Browse mode. The SAVE option is also used only in programs; it keeps both the Browse window and any memo-field window that is active open after editing is completed.

The NOAPPEND, NOEDIT, and NODELETE options restrict appending, editing, or deleting in Browse mode. The WIDTH option lets you adjust the width of columns. The WINDOW option causes the Browse display to appear in a previously defined window. PREFERENCE, when used initially, states the Browse settings under the name provided to the FoxUser file. When used with a previously stored name, PREFERENCE causes the Browse settings stored with that name to take effect. NOMENU prevents user access to the Browse menu. NOCLEAR leaves the Browse window visible on the screen after Browse mode is exited. The COLOR or COLOR SCHEME option may be used to specify colors for the Browse window. Note that in FoxPro for Windows, color commands and options change only the colors used by *user-defined* windows and menus; all other elements under Windows must be changed through the Windows color option in the Control Panel.

If the FOR clause is included, only records matching the logical expression specified in the FOR clause will be included in the Browse window. The LEDIT and REDIT clauses cause the Browse window to be split, with one side in the Change (or Edit) mode. Use LEDIT to place the left half of the window in Edit mode; use REDIT to place the right half of the window in Edit mode. The PARTITION n clause forces the Browse window to split into partitions; the numeric value n specifies the column where the window is split. Use LPARTITION along with the PARTITION clause; when LPARTITION is included, the cursor is placed in the first field of the left partition.

The NOLGRID and NORGRID clauses remove the field lines from the left or right partition of a split Browse window. Use NOLGRID to remove the field lines from the left partition, and use NORGRID to remove the field lines from the right partition. The NOLINK clause breaks the normal link between the two sides of a split Browse window, allowing independent movement in each side. The NOOPTIMIZE clause turns off FoxPro's internal optimization techniques (also known as Rushmore). The TIMEOUT n clause lets you specify how long a Browse window will wait for input; the value of n (in seconds) controls the length of time the window remains on the screen without any user input before the window closes. Note that the TIMEOUT clause can be used only in programs; it has no effect when used from the Command window.

BUILD APP

Syntax

BUILD APP *.fxp file* FROM *projectname*

The BUILD APP command converts information stored in a project file into a complete application. This command is typically used by advanced programmers in building applications for mass distribution; for further details, refer to a more advanced programmer's text or to your FoxPro programmer's documentation.

BUILD PROJECT

Syntax

BUILD PROJECT *projectfile* FROM
[program/menu/report/label/screen/library]

The BUILD PROJECT command creates a project database by opening and processing one or more database, program, screen, report, label, or library file. The project database can then be used along with the BUILD APP command to build a complete application. This command is typically used by advanced programmers in building applications for mass distribution; for further details, refer to a more advanced programmer's text or to your FoxPro programmer's documentation.

CALCULATE

Syntax

CALCULATE [*scope*]*options*[FOR *condition*][WHILE *condition*]
[TO *memvarlist*/TO ARRAY *arrayname*][NOOPTIMIZE]

The CALCULATE command calculates amounts, using standard financial and statistical functions. The functions are defined as part of the options list shown here. All records are processed until the scope is completed or the condition is no longer true. When used, the NOOPTIMIZE clause turns off FoxPro's internal optimization techniques (also known as Rushmore). The following financial and statistical functions can be used within the options list:

AVG(*expN*) calculates the numerical average of value *expN*.
CNT() counts the records in a database file. If a condition has been specified with the FOR clause, the condition must be met before the record will be counted.
MAX(*exp*) determines the maximum value in a field; *exp* is usually a field name or an expression that translates to a field name.
MIN(*exp*) determines the minimum value in a field; *exp* is usually a field name or an expression that translates to a field name.
NPV(*rate, flows, initial*) calculates the net present value where *rate* is the discount rate, *flows* is a series of signed periodic cash-flow values, and *initial* is the initial investment.
STD(*exp*) determines the standard deviation of values stored in a database field; *exp* is usually a field name or an expression that translates to a field name.
SUM(*exp*) determines the sum of the values in a database field; *exp* is usually a field name or an expression that translates to a field name.
VAR(*exp*) determines the variance of the values in a database field; *exp* is usually a field name or an expression that translates to a field name. The value supplied by VAR(*exp*) is a floating-point number.

Example

```
USE PERSONNL
SET TALK ON
CALCULATE MAX(SALARY), MIN(SALARY), AVG(SALARY)
```

CALL

Syntax

CALL *modulename* [WITH *expC/memvar*]

The CALL command executes a binary (assembly language) program that was previously loaded into memory with the LOAD command (see LOAD). The WITH option is used to pass the value of the expression or memory variable to the binary program. The CALL command should be used only with external programs designed as binary modules. Normal executable programs should be accessed with the RUN/! command.

CANCEL

Syntax

CANCEL

The CANCEL command halts execution of a command file and returns FoxPro to the Command window.

CHANGE

Syntax

CHANGE [*scope*] [FIELDS *fieldlist*] [FOR *condition*] [WHILE condition] [NOAPPEND] [NOCLEAR] [NOEDIT] [NODELETE] [NOMENU]

The CHANGE command permits editing of fields listed in *fieldlist*. If the *scope* option is absent, the quantifier ALL is assumed. The FOR/WHILE option allows only those records satisfying the condition to be edited. The NOAPPEND, NOEDIT, and NODELETE options restrict the appending, editing, or deleting of records. The NOCLEAR option leaves the display on the screen after the user exits the CHANGE process. NOMENU prevents the menu display.

Example

To edit the Tapelimit and Expiredate fields in the MEMBERS database, enter

```
CHANGE FIELDS TAPELIMIT, EXPIREDATE
```

CLEAR

Syntax

CLEAR

The CLEAR command erases the screen. CLEAR can also be used as an option of the @ command to clear the screen below and to the right of the location specified by the @ command.

Examples

To erase the entire screen, enter

```
CLEAR
```

To erase the screen below and to the right of the cursor at 12,20, enter

```
@ 12,20 CLEAR
```

CLEAR ALL

Syntax

CLEAR ALL

The CLEAR ALL command closes all open database, memo, index, and format files and resets the current work area to 1.

CLEAR FIELDS

Syntax

CLEAR FIELDS

The CLEAR FIELDS command clears the list of fields specified by the SET FIELDS command. The CLEAR FIELDS command has no effect if SET FIELDS was not previously used to specify fields (see SET FIELDS).

CLEAR GETS

Syntax

CLEAR GETS

The CLEAR GETS command clears all pending GET statements, or all GET statements that have not yet been accessed by a READ command. Use CLEAR GETS to prevent the next READ command in the program from invoking full-screen editing of the fields or variables named in the previous GET.

Example

```
ACCEPT "Enter Y to store entries, N to delete" TO ANS
IF ANS = "N"
  CLEAR GETS
```

```
ELSE
   READ
ENDIF
```

CLEAR MEMORY

Syntax

CLEAR MEMORY

The CLEAR MEMORY command erases all current memory variables.

CLEAR MENUS

Syntax

CLEAR MENUS

The CLEAR MENUS command clears all menus from the screen and erases all menus from memory.

CLEAR POPUPS

Syntax

CLEAR POPUPS

The CLEAR POPUPS command clears all pop-up menus from the screen and erases all pop-up menus from memory.

CLEAR PROGRAM

Syntax

CLEAR PROGRAM

The CLEAR PROGRAM command clears the buffer of any compiled program.

CLEAR PROMPTS

Syntax

CLEAR PROMPTS

The CLEAR PROMPTS command releases all menu prompts created with the @-PROMPT command from a screen or window.

CLEAR READ

Syntax

CLEAR READ[ALL]

The CLEAR READ command terminates the current READ. When CLEAR READ is used, program control returns to the previous READ command (if there is one). The ALL clause, when used, terminates all READS on all levels. The CLEAR READ command may be useful when multiple data entry screens are displayed by using nested levels of @...SAY...GET commands followed by multiple READ statements.

CLEAR TYPEAHEAD

Syntax

CLEAR TYPEAHEAD

The CLEAR TYPEAHEAD command clears the contents of the typeahead buffer (see SET TYPEAHEAD).

CLEAR WINDOWS

Syntax

CLEAR WINDOWS

The CLEAR WINDOWS command clears all active windows from the screen and erases all windows from memory (see DEFINE WINDOW).

CLOSE [ALL]

Syntax

CLOSE *filetype*/ALL

The CLOSE command closes all file types listed in *filetype*, which can be ALTERNATE, DATABASES, FORMAT, INDEX, or PROCEDURE. If the ALL option is used, all open files are closed, including any that may have been opened by using FoxPro's low-level file functions.

CLOSE MEMO

Syntax

CLOSE MEMO *memofield* [ALL]

The CLOSE MEMO command closes an open memo-field window. The ALL option closes all open memo windows.

COMPILE

Syntax

COMPILE *filename*/*skeleton*

The COMPILE command reads a FoxPro program or command file and creates an object (.DBO) file, which is an execute-only FoxPro program file. A skeleton composed of wildcards can be used in place of the file name; for example, COMPILE M*.PRG would compile all .PRG files beginning with the letter M.

Example

```
COMPILE mailer.prg
```

CONTINUE

Syntax

CONTINUE

The CONTINUE command resumes a search started by LOCATE. After LOCATE finds the record matching the criteria specified in the command, you can find additional records that meet the same criteria by entering CONTINUE (see LOCATE).

COPY

Syntax

COPY TO *filename*[*scope*][FIELDS *fieldlist*][FOR *condition*]
[WHILE *condition*][[WITH] CDX I PRODUCTION][NOOPTIMIZE]
[TYPE][DBMEMO3/FOXPLUS/DIF/MOD/SDF/SYLK/WK1/WKS/
WR1/WRK/XLS/DELIMITED [WITH *delimiter*/WITH BLANK/
WITH TAB]]

The COPY command copies all or part of the active database to *filename*. If *scope* is not listed, ALL is assumed. The FIELDS option specifies the fields to be copied. The FOR option copies only those records meeting the condition. The WHILE option copies records as long as the condition is true. Specifying SDF will copy the file in SDF format; specifying DELIM-ITED will copy the file in Delimited format. The DBMEMO3 or FOXPLUS type is used when databases with memo fields must be copied out to dBASE III/III PLUS or FoxBase file format.

Note that additional TYPE options can be used to copy to foreign files. The additional type options, detailed in Chapter 19, are DIF, MOD, SYLK, WK1, WKS, WR1, WRK, and XLS.

Use the WITH CDX or WITH PRODUCTION clause to specify whether a new structural compound index file should be created along with the new database. (Both options perform the same task; include WITH CDX or WITH PRODUCTION if you want the .CDX file created with the database file.) The NOOPTIMIZE clause will disable FoxPro's normal internal optimization technology (also known as Rushmore).

Example

To copy Lastname, Firstname, and City fields from the active database MEMBERS to TOWNS, enter

```
COPY TO TOWNS lastname, firstname, city
```

COPY FILE

Syntax

COPY FILE *sourcefile* TO *destinationfile*

The COPY FILE command creates an identical copy of a file. You must supply the extension in both *sourcefile* and *destinationfile*. Note that you can include a drive and path designation along with the destination if desired.

Example

To copy a file named REPORTER.FRX to a new file named TESTER.FRX, enter

```
COPY FILE reporter.frx TO tester.frx
```

COPY INDEXES

Syntax

COPY INDEXES *indexfilelist*/ALL [TO *.cdx filename*]

The COPY INDEXES command converts single-entry index files (.IDX files) into index tags within a compound index file (.CDX file). If you omit the TO clause, the .IDX index file information is added as tags to the structural compound index file. If you omit the TO clause and no structural compound index file exists, a new one is created with the same name as the database, and the tags are added to that file. If you include the TO clause, the .IDX file index information is added as tags to the .CDX file specified as part of the option.

Example

To copy to the structural compound index file three .IDX files called NAMES, STATES, and ZIPS, you could use the following command:

```
COPY INDEXES names, states, zips
```

COPY MEMO

Syntax

COPY MEMO *memofieldname* TO *filename* [ADDITIVE]

The COPY MEMO command copies the contents of a memo field to a text file. A drive name and path can be included as a part of the file name. If the ADDITIVE option is used, the text of the memo field will be added to the end of an existing file name; if the ADDITIVE option is omitted, any existing file with the same name will be overwritten.

Example

```
USE MEMBERS
GO 4
COPY MEMO preference TO A:COMMENTS.TXT
```

COPY STRUCTURE

Syntax

COPY STRUCTURE TO *filename* [FIELDS *fieldlist*]
[WITH] CDX/PRODUCTION

The COPY STRUCTURE command copies the structure of an active database to *filename*, creating a new, empty database file. Specifying FIELDS with *fieldlist* will copy only those fields to the new structure.

Use the WITH CDX or WITH PRODUCTION clause to specify whether a new structural compound index file should be created along with the new database. (Both options perform the same task.)

COPY STRUCTURE EXTENDED

Syntax

COPY TO *filename* STRUCTURE EXTENDED

The COPY STRUCTURE EXTENDED command creates a new database with records that contain information about the fields of the old database. The new database contains the fields Fieldname, Fieldtype, Fieldlen, and Fielddec. One record in the new database is added for each field in the old database.

COPY TAG

Syntax

COPY TAG *tagname* [OF *.cdx filename*] TO *indexfile*

The COPY TAG command converts a compound index (.CDX) file's tag information into a single-index style (.IDX) index file. If you omit the OF clause, the index information is copied from the tag of the structural compound index file.

Example

To copy the index tag named NAMES from the structural compound index file to an .IDX-style index file called LASTNAME.IDX, you could use the following command:

```
COPY TAG names TO lastname.idx
```

COPY TO ARRAY

Syntax

COPY TO ARRAY *arrayname* [FIELDS *fieldlist*][SCOPE][FOR condition][WHILE *condition*][NOOPTIMIZE]

The COPY TO ARRAY command copies data from the fields of a database into an array. (Note that the COPY TO ARRAY command is compatible with dBASE IV; if you need compatibility with FoxBase Plus, use the SCATTER TO command instead.) For each record in the database, the first field is stored in the first element of the array, the second field in the second element, and so on. (You must first declare the array with the DECLARE command.) If the database has more fields than the array has elements, the contents of extra fields are not stored to the array. If the array has more elements than the database has fields, the extra elements in the array are not changed. Note that memo fields are not copied into the array. The NOOPTIMIZE clause turns off FoxPro's internal optimization techniques (known as Rushmore).

Example

```
USE HOURS
DECLARE ThisWeek [6,5]
COPY TO ARRAY ThisWeek NEXT 5
```

COUNT

Syntax

COUNT [*scope*][FOR *condition*][WHILE *condition*][TO *memvar*][NOOPTIMIZE]

The COUNT command counts the number of records in the active database that meet a specific condition. The *scope* option quantifies the records to be counted. The FOR option can be used to specify a condition that must be met before a record will be counted. If you use the WHILE option, counting will take place until the condition is no longer true. The TO option can be used to store the count to the memory variable *memvar*. The NOOPTIMIZE clause turns off FoxPro's internal optimization techniques (known as Rushmore).

Example

To count the number of records containing the letters MD in the State field and to store that count as the memory variable MTEMP, enter

```
COUNT FOR STATE = "MD" TO MTEMP
```

CREATE

Syntax

CREATE *filename*

The CREATE command creates a new database file and defines its structure. If CREATE is entered without a file name, FoxPro prompts you for one when the structure is saved. If CREATE is followed by a file name, a database with that file name will be created. The file-name extension .DBF is added automatically unless you specify otherwise.

CREATE COLOR SET

Syntax

CREATE COLOR SET *colorsetname*

The CREATE COLOR SET command creates a new color set from the current color settings. When you use this command, all color pairs in every color scheme is saved in the newly created color set. A color set name can be up to ten characters long, and can contain numbers and underscores, but cannot start with a number. After creating the color set, you can load the color set with the SET COLOR SET command.

CREATE FROM

Syntax

CREATE *file1* FROM *file2*

The CREATE FROM command creates a new database with a structure based on a file created earlier with the COPY STRUCTURE EXTENDED command (see COPY STRUCTURE EXTENDED).

CREATE LABEL

Syntax

CREATE LABEL [*filename*]

The CREATE LABEL command creates a label-form file. This file can be used with the LABEL FORM command to produce mailing labels.

CREATE MENU

Syntax

CREATE MENU [*filename*/?][[WINDOW *windowname1*][IN [WINDOW] *windowname2*/IN SCREEN]

The CREATE MENU command activates the FoxPro menu creation utility. After the desired menu is created, information about the menu is stored in a special database with an .MNX extension. For details, refer to a more advanced programmer's text or to your FoxPro programmer's documentation.

CREATE PROJECT

Syntax

CREATE PROJECT [*file*/?][WINDOW *windowname1*][IN [WINDOW] *windowname2*/IN SCREEN]

The CREATE PROJECT command opens a project window, used for the creation of a project database. A *project database* is a special database used to keep track of all parts of a FoxPro project. This command is typically used by programmers when building complete applications. For details, refer to a more advanced programmer's text or to your FoxPro programmer's documentation.

CREATE QUERY

Syntax

CREATE QUERY [*filename*/?]

The CREATE QUERY command displays the RQBE window, allowing the creation of a query. The command is equivalent to choosing New from the File menu and selecting Query in the dialog box. More details about designing and saving queries can be found in Chapter 6.

CREATE REPORT

Syntax

CREATE REPORT [*filename*]

The CREATE REPORT (or, as an alternative, MODIFY REPORT) command creates or allows the user to modify a report-form file for producing reports. Once the report has been outlined with the CREATE REPORT command, the report can be displayed or printed with the REPORT FORM command. As with CREATE LABEL, if you omit a file name, FoxPro will ask for one when you save the report.

CREATE SCREEN

Syntax

CREATE SCREEN [*file* | ?] [WINDOW *windowname1*] [IN [WINDOW] *windowname2*/IN SCREEN]

The CREATE SCREEN command activates the FoxPro Screen Creation utility, used to design custom screen forms in FoxPro. The WINDOW and IN WINDOW clauses may be used to place the screen within a window or within the child window of a parent window. The IN SCREEN command places the screen within the full screen (this is also the default). For more details on the Screen Creation utility, see Chapter 13.

CREATE VIEW [FROM ENVIRONMENT]

Syntax

CREATE VIEW [FROM ENVIRONMENT]

The CREATE VIEW command saves the current environment to a view file. The command operates in the same manner, whether or not the FROM ENVIRONMENT clause is specified. The optional clause is supported for compatibility with dBASE.

DEACTIVATE MENU

Syntax

DEACTIVATE MENU *menuname1*[,*menuname2*...]/[ALL]

The DEACTIVATE MENU command deactivates the named menu and clears it from the screen. The menu remains in memory and can be recalled with the ACTIVATE MENU command. If the ALL clause is included, all menus currently on the screen are removed from the screen.

Example

```
DEACTIVATE MENU mymenu
```

DEACTIVATE POPUP

Syntax

DEACTIVATE POPUP *popupname1*[,*popupname2* ...]/[ALL]

The DEACTIVATE POPUP command deactivates the named pop-up menu and erases it from the screen. The pop-up menu remains in memory and can be recalled to the screen with the ACTIVATE POPUP command. If the ALL clause is included, all pop-up menus currently on the screen are removed from the screen.

Example

```
DEACTIVATE POPUP choices2
```

DEACTIVATE WINDOW

Syntax

DEACTIVATE WINDOW *windowname*/ALL

The DEACTIVATE WINDOW command deactivates the window or windows named within the command and erases them from the screen. The windows remain in memory and can be restored to the screen with the ACTIVATE WINDOW command. If the ALL option is not used, the most recently activated window is deactivated. If a window is underlying the most recent window, it becomes the active window. If the ALL option is included, all active windows are deactivated.

Example

```
DEACTIVATE WINDOW output
```

DECLARE

Syntax

DECLARE *arrayname 1* [*row,col*],[*arrayname2*][*row,col*]

The DECLARE command creates an array. (Note that the DECLARE command is compatible with dBASE IV. If you desire compatibility with FoxBase Plus, use the DIMENSION command instead.) In the definition list, you enter the array name and the dimensions of the array. Array names may be up to ten characters in length. Array dimensions consist of the row and column numbers. If a column number is omitted, FoxPro creates a one-dimensional array. If row and column numbers are used, they must be separated by a comma, and FoxPro creates a two-dimensional array. Arrays declared within programs are private unless declared public with the PUBLIC command.

Examples

To declare a private array, enter

```
DECLARE ARRAY Finance[10,4]
```

To declare an array as public within a program, enter

```
PUBLIC ARRAY Finance[10,4]
```

Note that these examples both declare an array and make it public. You can make a previously declared array public with the syntax PUBLIC *arrayname.*

DEFINE BAR

Syntax

DEFINE BAR *linenumber*/ *systemoptionname* OF *popupname*
PROMPT *expC* [BEFORE *expN*/AFTER *expN*] [KEY *keylabel*]
[MARK *expC*] [MESSAGE *expC*] [SKIP [FOR *expL*]] [COLOR
colorpairslist/COLOR SCHEME *expN*]

The DEFINE BAR command defines one bar option within a pop-up menu. The *popupname* must have been previously defined with the DEFINE POPUP command. *Linenumber* specifies the line number within the pop-up menu; line 1 appears on the first line of the pop-up, line 2 on the second line of the pop-up, and so on. The text specified with PROMPT appears as text in the bar of the menu. The MESSAGE option can be used to specify text that will appear at the bottom of the screen when the specified menu bar is highlighted. The SKIP option causes the bar to appear, but the bar will not be selectable within the menu.

The *systemoptionname* clause can be used to place items that are available from the System menu into your pop-ups. The BEFORE and AFTER clauses determine the physical location of an option, relative to the option number specified by *expN*. The KEY clause assigns another key to a pop-up option. The MARK clause, when used along with the SET MARK command, allows the placement of a check mark besides the pop-up option. Use the COLOR or COLOR SCHEME option to change the colors of the pop-up. Note that in FoxPro for Windows, color commands and options change only the colors used by *user-defined* windows and menus; all other elements under Windows must be changed through the Windows color option in the Control Panel.

Example

```
DEFINE BAR MainMenu FROM 3,10 TO 10,30
DEFINE BAR 1 OF MainMenu PROMPT "Add records"
DEFINE BAR 2 OF MainMenu PROMPT "Edit records"
DEFINE BAR 3 OF MainMenu PROMPT "Delete records"
DEFINE BAR 4 OF MainMenu PROMPT "Print reports"
DEFINE BAR 5 OF MainMenu PROMPT "Exit system"
```

DEFINE BOX

Syntax

DEFINE BOX FROM *printcolumn* TO *printcolumn* HEIGHT
expr [AT LINE *printline*][SINGLE/DOUBLE/
borderdefinitionstring]

The DEFINE BOX command lets you define a box that appears around
printed text. Use the specified options in the command to define the
starting column on the left, the ending column on the right, the height
of the box, and the starting line for the top of the box. The
borderdefinitionstring option lets you specify a character that will be used
as the box border; the default, if this option is omitted, is a single line.

Example

```
DEFINE BOX FROM 4 TO 76 HEIGHT 45 AT LINE 5
```

DEFINE MENU

Syntax

DEFINE MENU *menuname* [BAR [AT LINE *expN*]] [IN [WINDOW]
windowname/IN SCREEN] [KEY *keylabel*] [MARK *expC*]
[MESSAGE *expC*] [NOMARGIN] [COLOR *colorpairslist*/COLOR
SCHEME *expN*]

The DEFINE MENU command defines a bar menu. If the MESSAGE
option is added, the text of the message appears at the bottom of the
screen when the menu is displayed (see ACTIVATE MENU).

   The BAR clause creates a bar-style menu that imitates the style of the
FoxPro System menus. Use the IN WINDOW or IN SCREEN clause to
define whether the defined menu is in a window or in the full screen. (If
the clause is omitted, the window appears in the full screen.) The KEY
clause assigns another key to a pop-up option. The MARK clause, when
used along with the SET MARK command, allows the placement of a

check mark beside the pop-up option. The NOMARGIN clause, when used, omits the extra space that normally appears to the left of each menu pad. Use the COLOR or COLOR SCHEME option to change the colors of the pop-up. Note that in FoxPro for Windows, color commands and options change only the colors used by *user-defined* windows and menus; all other elements under Windows must be changed through the Windows color option in the Control Panel.

Example

```
DEFINE MENU MainMenu
```

DEFINE PAD

Syntax

DEFINE PAD *padname* OF *menuname* PROMPT *expC* [AT *row, col*] [BEFORE *padname*/AFTER *padname*] [KEY *keylabel* [MARK *expC*] [MESSAGE *expC*] [SKIP [FOR *expL*]] [COLOR *colorpairslist*/COLOR SCHEME *expN*]

The DEFINE PAD command defines one pad of a bar menu. Use a separate statement containing this command for each desired pad within the menu. The text specified with PROMPT appears inside the menu pad. If the AT *row,col* option is omitted, the first pad appears at the far left, and each successive pad appears one space to the right of the previous pad. Any text that accompanies the MESSAGE option appears on the message line (see SET MESSAGE TO) when that pad is highlighted within the menu.

The KEY clause assigns another key to a pop-up option. The BEFORE and AFTER clauses determine the physical location of a pad, relative to the pad number specified by *expN*. The MARK clause, when used along with the SET MARK command, allows the placement of a check mark beside the pop-up option. The SKIP clause, when used, causes a pad to be skipped if the logical expression evaluates as true. Use the COLOR or COLOR SCHEME option to change the colors of the menu pad. Note that in FoxPro for Windows, color commands and options change only the colors used by *user-defined* windows and menus; all other elements under Windows must be changed through the Windows color option in the Control Panel.

Example

```
DEFINE MENU MainMenu
DEFINE PAD Adder OF MainMenu PROMPT "Add" MESSAGE "Add new records"
DEFINE PAD Editor OF MainMenu PROMPT "Edit" MESSAGE "Edit records"
DEFINE PAD Eraser OF MainMenu PROMPT "Delete" MESSAGE "Delete records"
DEFINE PAD Printer OF MainMenu PROMPT "Print" MESSAGE "Print reports"
DEFINE PAD Quit OF MainMenu PROMPT "Exit" MESSAGE "Leave application"
```

DEFINE POPUP

Syntax

DEFINE POPUP *popupname* [FROM *row1,col1* [TO *row2,col2*]
[IN WINDOW *windowname*/IN SCREEN] [FOOTER *expC*]
[KEY *keylabel*] [MARGIN] [MARK *expC*] [MESSAGE *expC*] [MOVER]
[MULTI] [PROMPT FIELD *field*/PROMPT FILES [LIKE *skeleton*]
PROMPT STRUCTURE] [RELATIVE] [SCROLL] [SHADOW] [TITLE *expC*]
[COLOR *colorpairslist*/COLOR SCHEME *expN*]

Use the DEFINE POPUP command to define a pop-up menu. The FROM and TO row and column coordinates define the upper-left and lower-right corners of the pop-up. If the TO coordinate is omitted, FoxPro will make the menu as large as needed to contain the prompts within the menu. The PROMPT FIELD, PROMPT FILE, and PROMPT STRUCTURE clauses are optional. These allow you to display selection lists of field contents, file names, or field names from a database structure. The COLOR or COLOR SCHEME option may be used to specify colors for the pop-up. By default, user-defined pop-ups take on the colors of color scheme 2. Note that in FoxPro for Windows, color commands and options change only the colors used by *user-defined* windows and menus; all other elements under Windows must be changed through the Windows color option in the Control Panel. If the optional SHADOW clause is included, a shadow appears beneath the pop-up.

The IN WINDOW and IN SCREEN clauses can be used to define whether the pop-up appears in a window or in the full screen. (If the clause is omitted, the default is the full screen.) The FOOTER clause assigns a text footer, centered in the bottom border of the pop-up. The KEY clause assigns another key as a hot key for the pop-up. The MARGIN clause causes an extra space to appear to the left and the right of each pop-up option. The MARK clause, when used along with the SET MARK command, allows the placement of a check mark beside the pop-up option. The MESSAGE clause displays the specified message, in the position specified by the SET MESSAGE command.

The MOVER clause, when included, allows the movement of pop-up options, using the double-headed arrow that appears at the left edge of the pop-up. The MULTI option allows multiple choices from a single pop-up option. The RELATIVE clause lets you change the order in which items appear in the pop-up. If a menu pop-up is created by using the RELATIVE clause, menu options appear in the order in which they were defined. The SCROLL clause, when included, adds a scroll bar at the right edge of the pop-up; mouse users can use the scroll bar to scroll through the menu options. The TITLE clause adds a title to the border of the pop-up.

Example

```
DEFINE POPUP MainMenu FROM 5,5 TO 14,40
DEFINE POPUP PrintMenu FROM 15,12 TO 30,17
```

DEFINE WINDOW

Syntax

DEFINE WINDOW *windowname1* FROM *row1,col1* TO *row2,col2*/AT *row3,col3* SIZE *row4,col4* [IN [WINDOW] *windowname2*/IN SCREEN/IN DESKTOP] [FONT *expC1* [, *expN1*]] [STYLE *expC2*] [FOOTER *expC3*]

[TITLE *expC4*] [HALFHEIGHT] [DOUBLE/PANEL/NONE/
SYSTEM/*borderstring*] [CLOSE/NOCLOSE] [FLOAT/NOFLOAT]
[GROW/NOGROW] [MDI/NOMDI] [MINIMIZE] [SHADOW]
[ZOOM/NOZOOM] [ICON FILE *expC5*] [FILL *expC6*/FILL FILE
.bmp file][COLOR SCHEME *expN2*/COLOR *colorpairlist*/
COLOR RGB (*colorvaluelist*)]

The DEFINE WINDOW command defines display attributes and screen
coordinates for a window. The FROM and TO coordinates define the
upper-left and lower-right corners of the window. The AT and SIZE
clauses may be used in place of FROM and TO: Use AT to define the
upper-left corner of the window, and use SIZE to define the windows size
in terms of rows and columns. The default border is a single-line box;
you can use the DOUBLE, PANEL, NONE, or *borderstring* option to
specify a different border for the window. (Use ASCII codes for the border
string option.) By default, windows take on the colors of color scheme 1.
Note that in FoxPro for Windows, color commands and options change
only the colors used by *user-defined* windows and menus; all other
elements under Windows must be changed through the Windows color
option in the Control Panel. The expression named with TITLE appears
at the top of the window.

The CLOSE/NOCLOSE option specifies whether the window may be
closed by the System menu or by clicking the close box. If the option is
omitted or NOCLOSE is specified, the window cannot be closed (except
by deactivating it). The SHADOW option causes a shadow to appear
beneath the window. The FLOAT/NOFLOAT and ZOOM/NOZOOM options determine whether the window can be moved (in the case of FLOAT)
or zoomed (in the case of ZOOM). If the options are omitted or if the
NOFLOAT or NOZOOM option is specified, the window cannot be moved
or zoomed. The options GROW/NOGROW specify whether the user will
be permitted to resize the window. If GROW is included, the user can
resize the window; if NOGROW is included, the user cannot.

Use the IN [WINDOW] *windowname2* clause to integrate a child
window with its parent window, restricting the child window from moving
outside the parent window or being sized larger than the parent window.
If the parent window is moved, the child window moves with it. Note that
when a child window is defined within a parent window, the coordinates
specified in the DEFINE WINDOW command are relative to the parent
window, not the screen.

Use the IN SCREEN clause to define the window on screen instead of inside an existing window. Use the IN DESKTOP clause to place a user-defined window on the Windows desktop, outside the main FoxPro window. Use the FONT clause to specify a font (Roman, Script, Symbol, etc.) for text output to the window. The font is specified with *expC1*; include *expN1* to specify a font size (8 point, 10 point, etc.) other than the current font size. As an example, the clause FONT 'ROMAN',16 displays text in the window in 16-point Roman font.

Use the STYLE clause to specify a font style for the output to the window. The styles that are available for a font are determined by your installation of Windows. The font style is specified with *expC2*, using the codes shown below. If *expC2* is not included, the standard font style is used.

Character	Font Style
B	Bold
I	Italic
O	Outline
S	Shadow
-	Strikeout
T	Transparent
U	Underline

You can include more than one character to specify a combination of font styles. As an example, the clause STYLE 'BO' specifies Bold Outline.

In FoxPro for Windows, the FOOTER clause is ignored. It is provided for backwards compatibility with FoxPro for DOS programs.

Use the HALFHEIGHT clause to create windows with half-height title bars. Half-height title bars provide compatibility for windows that were created in FoxPro 2.0 and imported into FoxPro for Windows.

The FILL clause lets you fill the background of a window with the character specified in the character expression.

Example

```
DEFINE WINDOW MyWindow FROM 5,5 TO 7,52 DOUBLE COLOR B/W
ACTIVATE WINDOW MyWindow
@ 1,6 SAY "Are you SURE you want to do this?"
```

DELETE

Syntax

DELETE [*scope*][FOR *condition*][WHILE *condition*][NOOPTIMIZE]

The DELETE command marks specific records for deletion. If DELETE is used without a record number, the current record is marked for deletion. The *scope* option is used to identify the records to be deleted. The FOR option can be used to specify a condition that must be met before a record will be deleted. If you use the WHILE option, records will be deleted until the condition is no longer true. DELETE marks a record for deletion; the PACK command actually removes the record. The NOOPTIMIZE clause will turn off FoxPro's internal optimization techniques (known as Rushmore).

Example

To mark records within the next 24 records for deletion, beginning with the current record and specifying that they have an entry of VA in the State field in order to be deleted, enter

```
DELETE NEXT 24 FOR STATE = "VA"
```

DELETE FILE

Syntax

DELETE FILE *filename.ext*/[?]

The DELETE FILE command deletes a file from the disk. If an extension is present, it must be specified. If the optional question mark is used in place of a file name, a list box of all files in the current directory appears. The user can then select the file to be deleted from the list box.

DELETE TAG

Syntax

DELETE TAG *tagname1* [OF *.cdx file1*][, *tagname2* [OF *.cdx file2*]].../ALL

The DELETE TAG command removes the named tag from a compound index file. If the OF clause is omitted, FoxPro looks in the structural compound index file for the tags to be deleted. The ALL clause causes all tags to be deleted from the compound index file, and the file itself is also deleted.

Example

To delete an index tag named ZIPS stored in a compound index file named ABCSTAFF.CDX, you could use the command

```
DELETE TAG zips OF abcstaff
```

DIMENSION

Syntax

DIMENSION *arrayname 1* [*row,col*][,*arrayname2*] [*row,col*]...[*arraynamex*] [*row,col*]

The DIMENSION command creates an array. (Note that the DIMENSION command is compatible with FoxBase Plus. If you desire compatibility with dBASE IV, use the DECLARE command instead.) In the definition list, you enter the array name and the dimensions of the array. Array names may be up to ten characters in length. Array dimensions consist of the row and column numbers. If a column number is omitted, FoxPro creates a one-dimensional array. If row and column numbers are used, they must be separated by a comma, and FoxPro creates a two-dimensional array.

Example

```
DIMENSION ARRAY Finance[10,4]
```

DIR

Syntax

DIR [*drive*:][*filename*][*skeleton*][TO PRINT[PROMPT]/TO FILE *filename*]

The DIR command displays the directory of all database files or files of a specific type if a file extension is specified. *Drive* is the drive designator, and *filename* is the name of a file with or without an extension. Skeletons composed of wildcards, which are asterisks or question marks, can be used as part of or as a replacement for *filename*. In the case of database files, the display produced by DIR includes the number of records contained in the database, the date of the last update, and the size of the file in bytes. The TO PRINT and TO FILE options may be used to route the directory display to the printer or to a file name. If the PROMPT clause is included with TO PRINT, a dialog box is displayed before printing starts.

Example

To display all index files from the current default drive, enter

```
DIR *.IDX
```

DISPLAY

Syntax

DISPLAY [*scope*][*fieldlist*][FOR *condition*][WHILE *condition*][OFF][TO PRINT[PROMPT]/TO FILE *filename*]

The DISPLAY command displays a record from the active database. You can display more records by including the *scope* option. The FOR option limits the display of records to those satisfying the condition. If you use the WHILE option, records will be displayed until the condition is no longer true. Only the fields listed in *fieldlist* will be displayed; if *fieldlist* is absent, all fields will be displayed. The OFF option will prevent the record number from being displayed. The TO PRINT and TO FILE options may be used to route the display to the printer or to a file called *filename*. Note that when the TO FILE option is used, the default extension for the file is .TXT. If the PROMPT option is included with the TO PRINT clause, a dialog box is displayed before printing starts.

Example

To display the Lastname, Firstname, City, and State fields for ten records beginning with the current record, enter

```
DISPLAY NEXT 10 lastname, firstname, city, state
```

DISPLAY MEMORY

Syntax

DISPLAY MEMORY[LIKE *skeleton*][TO PRINT/TO FILE *filename*]

The DISPLAY MEMORY command displays all active memory variables, their sizes, and their contents. The numbers of active variables and available variables are listed along with the numbers of bytes consumed and bytes available. Wildcards may be used as skeletons; for example, DISPLAY MEMORY LIKE MEM* would display all variables beginning with the letters MEM. The TO PRINT and TO FILE options may be used to route the display to the printer or to a file name. Note that when the TO FILE option is used, the default extension for the file is .TXT. If the PROMPT option is included with the TO PRINT clause, a dialog box is displayed before printing starts.

DISPLAY STATUS

Syntax

DISPLAY STATUS[TO PRINT[PROMPT]/TO FILE *filename*]

The DISPLAY STATUS command displays, for every active work area, the name and alias of the currently open database, any filter condition currently in effect, and the expressions used in any open index files. The current drive designator, function key settings, and settings of SET commands are also displayed. The TO PRINT and TO FILE options may be used to route the display to the printer or to a file name. Note that when the TO FILE option is used, the default extension for the file is .TXT. If the PROMPT option is included with the TO PRINT clause, a dialog box is displayed before printing starts.

DISPLAY STRUCTURE

Syntax

DISPLAY STRUCTURE [IN *alias*] [TO PRINT[PROMPT]/TO FILE *filename*]

The DISPLAY STRUCTURE command displays the structure of the active database, unless the IN *alias* option is used. The complete file name, along with the current drive designator, number of records, date of last update, and name of fields, including their statistics (type, length, and decimal places), is listed. If you have established a fields list with SET FIELDS, a > symbol appears to the left of the selected fields in the structure list. The IN alias option causes the structure of a file open in another work area (as specified by the alias) to be displayed. The TO PRINT and TO FILE options may be used to route the display to the printer or to a file name. Note that when the TO FILE option is used, the default extension for the file is .TXT. If the PROMPT option is included with the TO PRINT clause, a dialog box is displayed before printing starts.

DO

Syntax

DO *filename* [WITH *parameterlist*][IN *filename*]

The DO command starts execution of a FoxPro command file. The file-name extension of .PRG or .DBO is assumed unless otherwise specified. If the WITH option is specified and followed by a list of parameters in *parameterlist*, those parameters are transferred to the command file. The IN *filename* clause can be used to execute a procedure that is stored in a different program file.

DO CASE

Syntax

DO CASE
 CASE *condition*
 commands...
 [*CASE condition*]
 [*commands...*]
 [OTHERWISE]
 [*commands...*]
 ENDCASE

The DO CASE command selects one course of action from a number of choices. The conditions following the CASE statements are evaluated until one of the conditions is found to be true. When a condition is true, the commands between the CASE statement and the next CASE, or OTHERWISE and ENDCASE, will be executed. FoxPro then executes the command following the ENDCASE statement. If none of the conditions in the CASE statements are found to be true, any commands following the optional OTHERWISE statement will be executed. If the OTHERWISE statement is not used and no conditions are found to be true, FoxPro proceeds to the command following the ENDCASE statement.

Example

In the following DO CASE commands, FoxPro chooses from among three possible alternatives: (1) executing a command file named MENU, (2) appending records to the database, or (3) exiting from FoxPro.

```
DO CASE
 CASE SELECT = 1
 DO MENU
 CASE SELECT = 2
 APPEND
 CASE SELECT = 3
 QUIT
ENDCASE
```

DO WHILE

Syntax

DO WHILE *condition*
 commands...
ENDDO

The DO WHILE command repeatedly executes commands between DO WHILE and ENDDO as long as *condition* is true. When FoxPro encounters a DO WHILE command, the condition in that command statement is evaluated: If the condition is false, FoxPro proceeds to the command following the ENDDO command; if it is true, FoxPro executes the commands following the DO WHILE command until the ENDDO command is reached. When the ENDDO command is reached, the condition in the DO WHILE statement is again evaluated. If it is still true, the commands between DO WHILE and ENDDO are again executed. If the condition is false, FoxPro proceeds to the command below the ENDDO command.

Example

To display Lastname, Firstname, City, and State fields for each record until the end of the database, you could use the following program:

```
DO WHILE .NOT. EOF()
   ? lastname, firstname, city, state
   SKIP
ENDDO
```

EDIT

Syntax

EDIT [*scope*][NOAPPEND][NOCLEAR][NOEDIT][NODELETE]
[NOMENU][FIELDS *list*][FOR *condition*][WHILE *condition*]

The EDIT command invokes the FoxPro full-screen Editor. If no record number is specified in the scope, the current record, which is identified by the current position of the record pointer, will be displayed for editing.

The FIELDS option will display only the fields listed in field list. The NOCLEAR option causes the edit display to remain on the screen after the changes are completed. The NOAPPEND, NOEDIT, and NODELETE options restrict appending, editing, or deleting in Edit mode. The NOMENU option prevents access to the Edit menu. The FOR and WHILE options let you specify conditions that must be met before a record will appear in the edit screen.

EJECT

Syntax

EJECT

The EJECT command causes the printer to perform a formfeed.

EJECT PAGE

Syntax

EJECT PAGE

The EJECT PAGE command causes the printer to perform a formfeed. Use the EJECT PAGE command along with the ON PAGE command to handle page ejects for printed reports. The EJECT PAGE command invokes any end-of-page routines you have established with the ON PAGE command, and it increments _PAGENO and resets _PLINENO to 0. Note that the output of the EJECT PAGE command is made available to a disk file or screen if output is being sent to a disk file or screen instead of to the printer.

ERASE

Syntax

ERASE *filename.ext*/[?]

The ERASE command erases the named file from the directory. The name must include the file extension. You can also use the command DELETE FILE *filename.ext* to erase a file. If the file is on a disk that is not in the default drive, you must include the drive designator. If the optional question mark is used in place of a file name, a list box appears. The user can select the file to be deleted from the list box.

EXIT

Syntax

EXIT

The EXIT command exits a DO WHILE, FOR, or SCAN loop and proceeds to the first command following the end of the loop (that is, the command after the ENDDO, ENDFOR, or ENDSCAN command).

Example

The following command-file portion uses EXIT to exit the DO WHILE loop if a part number of 9999 is entered:

```
DO WHILE .T.
    ? "Enter part number to add to inventory."
    ? "Enter 9999 to exit."
    INPUT TO PARTNO
    IF PARTNO = 9999
        EXIT
    ENDIF
    APPEND BLANK
    REPLACE PARTNUMB WITH PARTNO
    EDIT
ENDDO
```

EXPORT

Syntax

EXPORT TO *file* [FIELDS *fieldlist* [*scope*] [FOR *condition*]
[WHILE *condition*] [NOOPTIMIZE] [TYPE] DIF/MOD/SYLK/WK1/
WKS/WR1/WRK/XLS

The EXPORT command exports a database file to a foreign file of the type specified with the TYPE option. (See Chapter 18 for more details on the various type options.) Use the FIELDS clause to limit the fields that are copied to the foreign file. The FOR and WHILE clauses can be used to limit records that are copied to the other file. Use the NOOPTIMIZE clause to disable FoxPro's normal optimization techniques (also known as Rushmore).

EXTERNAL

Syntax

EXTERNAL ARRAY/LABEL/LIBRARY/MENU/PROCEDURE/REPORT/
SCREEN *filename/arrayname*

The EXTERNAL command alerts the FoxPro project manager to an undefined reference. This is an advanced command used in programming; for details, refer to a more advanced programmer's text or to your FoxPro programmer's documentation.

FILER

Syntax

FILER [LIKE *skeleton*][NOWAIT]

The FILER command displays the FoxPro file maintenance utility. Use the LIKE option with a skeleton to display a specific type of file. The NOWAIT option, when used, causes program execution to continue after the Filer utility appears.

FIND

Syntax

FIND *characterstring*

The FIND command positions the record pointer at the first record containing an index key that matches *characterstring.* If there are leading blanks in *characterstring, characterstring* must be enclosed by single or double quotes; otherwise, no quotes are necessary. If the specific character string cannot be found, the EOF value is set to "True" and a NO FIND message is displayed on the screen (if FoxPro is not executing a command file). An index file must be open before you use the FIND command.

FLUSH

Syntax

FLUSH

The FLUSH command flushes all active buffers to disk, without closing the files.

FOR

Syntax

FOR *memvar* = *expN1* TO *expN2* [STEP *expN3*]
 commands...
ENDFOR/NEXT

The FOR and accompanying ENDFOR or NEXT statements set up a loop that repeats a set number of times, as defined by the numeric expressions. The value *expN1* marks the starting point and the value *expN2* marks the ending point. The loop repeats the number of times specified between *expN1* and *expN2*, unless an incremental value other than 1 is specified with the optional STEP clause. Once the set number of repetitions has been accomplished, FoxPro proceeds to the command below the ENDFOR or NEXT command. The NEXT keyword can be used as a substitute for the ENDFOR keyword. If a STEP clause is used, *memvar* is incremented or, if the value of STEP is negative, decremented every time the ENDFOR or NEXT is encountered until *memvar* equals or exceeds *expN2*.

Example

To use the FOR-ENDFOR commands to print Lastname, Firstname, City, and State fields for a specified number of records, you could use the following program:

```
USE MEMBERS
INPUT "Print how many records? " TO COUNTERS
STORE 1 TO BEGIN
FOR BEGIN = 1 TO COUNTERS
    ? lastname, firstname, city, state
    SKIP
ENDFOR
```

FUNCTION

Syntax

FUNCTION *procedurename*

The FUNCTION command identifies a procedure that serves as a user-defined function.

Example

```
FUNCTION StateTax
PARAMETERS SaleCost, TaxRate
Gross = SaleCost + (SaleCost * TaxRate)
RETURN(Gross)
```

GATHER FROM

Syntax

GATHER *memvar* FROM *array*[FIELDS *fieldlist*][MEMO]

The GATHER FROM command moves data from a set of variables or an array of memory variables into a database file. (Note that GATHER FROM is compatible with FoxBase Plus; if you need compatibility with dBASE IV, use APPEND FROM ARRAY instead.) The elements of the array are transferred, beginning with the first element of the array, into the corresponding records of the database file. If there are more elements in the array than fields in the database, the extra elements are ignored. If there are more fields in the database than there are elements in the array, the extra fields remain empty. The FOR clause, which is optional, lets you define a condition that must be met before data in the array will be added to a new record. Note that memo fields are ignored during the data-transfer process unless the MEMO clause is included.

GETEXPR

Syntax

GETEXPR [*expC*] TO *memvar*

The GETEXPR command brings up the Expression Builder. The expression constructed by the user with the Expression Builder is then stored to the memory variable specified as part of the GETEXPR command. The GETEXPR command can be used within a program to allow the user to define selection criteria for printing a report or a set of labels.

GO/GOTO

Syntax

GO or GOTO BOTTOM/TOP/*expN* [IN *alias*]

The GO and GOTO commands position the record pointer at a record. GO TOP moves the pointer to the beginning of a database, and GO BOTTOM moves it to the end of a database. If a numeric value is provided, the pointer moves to that record number. The IN *alias* clause can be used to move the record pointer in a database that is open in another work area; *alias* can be either the file alias or a work-area number.

HELP

Syntax

HELP [*commandname/functionname*]

The HELP command provides instructions on using FoxPro commands and functions, as well as other information. If you enter HELP without specifying a command or function, a menu-driven system of help screens allows you to request information on various subjects. If HELP is followed by a command or function, information about that command or function will be displayed.

HIDE MENU

Syntax

HIDE MENU [[*name1*][,*name2*...]]/[ALL] [SAVE]

The HIDE MENU command hides a current menu bar while retaining the menu bar in memory. If the ALL option is used, all current menu bars are hidden. Use the SAVE option to place an image of the menu bar on the screen or in a window. This option can prove useful when developing or testing programs.

HIDE POPUP

Syntax

HIDE POPUP [[*name1*][,*name2*...]/[ALL] [SAVE]

The HIDE POPUP command hides a current pop-up menu while retaining the pop-up in memory. If the ALL option is used, all current pop-ups are hidden. Use the SAVE option to place an image of the menu bar on the screen or in a window. This option can prove useful when developing or testing programs.

HIDE WINDOW

Syntax

HIDE WINDOW [[*name1*[,*name2*...]]/[ALL][SAVE]

The HIDE WINDOW command hides a current window while retaining the window in memory. If the ALL option is used, all current windows are hidden. Use the SAVE option to place an image of the window on the screen. This option can prove useful when developing or testing programs.

IF

Syntax

IF *condition*
  commands...

[ELSE]
 commands...
ENDIF

IF is a decision-making command that will execute commands when certain conditions are true. If the condition for the IF statement is true, the commands between IF and ENDIF will be executed. Should the condition be false and there is an ELSE, the commands between ELSE and ENDIF will be executed. However, if the condition for IF is not true and there is no ELSE, FoxPro will drop to the ENDIF statement without executing any commands.

IMPORT

Syntax

IMPORT FROM *filename* [TYPE] DIF/FW2/MOD/PDOX/RPD/
SYLK/WK1/WK3/WKS/WR1/WRK/XLS

The IMPORT command imports a foreign file of the type specified with the TYPE option and creates an equivalent database file. Use the TYPE option to specify the format of the foreign file. (See Chapter 19 for more details on the various type options.)

INDEX

Syntax

INDEX ON *expC* TO *.idx filename*/TAG *tagname* [OF *.cdx filename*][FOR *expL*] [COMPACT] [ASCENDING/DESCENDING] [UNIQUE][ADDITIVE]

The INDEX command creates an index file based on an expression (which is usually a field name or a combination of fields) from the active database. Depending on the field, the index file will be indexed alphabetically, numerically, chronologically, or logically. If the index based on the first field has duplicate entries, the duplicates are indexed according to additional fields in *fieldlist*, provided additional fields have been listed.

When the UNIQUE option is used, duplicate entries are omitted from the index. The indexing occurs in ascending order unless you add the DESCENDING option. Use the FOR option to limit records included in the index. The TAG *tagname* and OF *.cdx filename* options can be used to specify that the index should be a tag of a compound index file. If the OF clause is omitted and the TAG clause is included, the tag is added to the structural compound index file; if none exists, one with the same name as the database is created. The COMPACT clause forces the creation of an index file in the compact format.

Example

To create an index file called TOWNS based on the values in a field named City, enter

```
INDEX ON CITY TO TOWNS
```

INPUT

Syntax

INPUT[*expC*][TO *memvar*]

The INPUT command stores an entry that is entered by the user to a memory variable. An optional character expression can display a message to the user during keyboard entry. The expression can be a memory variable or a character string.

Example

To display the prompt "Enter name to search for:" and store the response to the memory variable NEWNAME, enter

```
INPUT "Enter name to search for:" TO NEWNAME
```

INSERT

Syntax

INSERT[BLANK][BEFORE]

The INSERT command adds a new record below the record pointer's position and renumbers the records below the insertion. Specifying BEFORE causes the record to be inserted at the record pointer; thus, if the pointer is at record 3, the new record will be 3 and the records below it will be renumbered. If the BLANK option is omitted, FoxPro allows immediate editing of the new record; otherwise, the record will be blank, but Edit mode will not be entered.

Example

To insert a new record at position 10 in the active database, enter

```
GO 10
INSERT BEFORE
```

JOIN

Syntax

JOIN WITH *alias* TO *filename* FOR *condition* [FIELDS *fieldlist*]
[FOR *condition*][NOOPTIMIZE]

The JOIN command creates a new database by combining specific records and fields from the active database and the database listed as *alias*. The combined database is stored in *filename*. You can limit the choice of records from the active database by specifying a FOR condition. All fields from both files will be copied if you do not include a field list; if you do, only those fields specified in the field list will be copied. Specify fields from the nonactive database by supplying *filename -> fieldname*. The NOOPTIMIZE clause turns off FoxPro's internal optimization (also known as Rushmore).

KEYBOARD

Syntax

KEYBOARD *expC*

The KEYBOARD command stuffs the keyboard buffer with the character expression supplied as *expC*. The data stays in the keyboard buffer until FoxPro looks for input, at which time the buffer is read.

LABEL FORM

Syntax

LABEL FORM *labelfilename*/? [*scope*][SAMPLE][FOR *condition*]
[WHILE *condition*][TO PRINT[PROMPT]][TO FILE
filename][ENVIRONMENT][OFF][PREVIEW][NOOPTIMIZE]

The LABEL FORM command prints mailing labels from a label-form file (extension .LBX). The SAMPLE option allows a sample label to be printed. The FOR option can be used to specify a condition that must be met before a label for a record will be printed. If you use the WHILE option, records will be printed until the condition is no longer true. The TO PRINT option sends output to the printer, and the TO FILE option sends output to a named disk file. If the PROMPT option is included with the TO PRINT clause, a dialog box is displayed before printing starts. The ENVIRON-MENT option causes a view file with the same name as the label file to be used before printing begins. If the question mark is substituted in place of a file name, a box containing a list of all label files appears. The user may then select the label file to print from the list. The OFF option causes the display of labels on the screen to be suppressed while the labels are printed or sent to a file.

The PREVIEW option causes an on-screen preview display of the labels to appear. Use the NOOPTIMIZE clause to disable FoxPro's normal optimization techniques (also know as Rushmore).

Example

To print mailing labels by using a label form named MAILERS for records with State fields containing NM and to restrict printing to the next 25 records beginning at the current record-pointer position, enter

```
LABEL FORM MAILERS NEXT 25 FOR STATE = "NM" TO PRINT
```

LIST

Syntax

LIST [OFF][*scope*][*fieldlist*][FOR *condition*][WHILE *condition*][TO PRINT/TO FILE *filename*]

The LIST command provides a list of database contents. The *scope* option quantifies the records to be listed. If *scope* is absent, ALL is assumed. The FOR option specifies a condition that must be met before a record will be listed. If you use the WHILE option, records will be listed until the condition is no longer true. The OFF option prevents the record number from being listed. If the TO PRINT option is used, the listing will be printed. TO FILE directs the list to a disk file.

LIST FILES

Syntax

LIST FILES [ON *drive/dir* [LIKE *skeleton*][TO PRINT/TO FILE *filename*]

The LIST FILES command displays a list of disk files. Use the ON option to specify a drive and/or directory. Wildcards may be used as skeletons; for example, LIST FILES LIKE *.IDX would display all files with the extension of .IDX. The TO PRINT and TO FILE options may be used to route the list to the printer or to the named disk file.

LIST MEMORY

Syntax

LIST MEMORY [LIKE *skeleton*][TO PRINT/TO FILE *filename*]

The LIST MEMORY command lists the names, sizes, and types of memory variables. Wildcards may be used to define file name skeletons; for example, LIST MEMORY LIKE MEM* would display all variables beginning with the letters MEM. If the TO PRINT option is used, the listing will be printed on the printer. If the TO FILE option is used, the listing will be directed to the named disk file.

LIST STATUS

Syntax

LIST STATUS [TO PRINT/TO FILE *filename*]

The LIST STATUS command lists information on currently open work areas, the active file, and system settings. All open files and open index file names are displayed, along with work-area numbers, any expressions used in index files, the default disk drive, function-key settings, and settings of the SET commands. If the TO PRINT option is used, the listing will be printed on the printer. LIST STATUS does not pause during the listing, which is the only difference between LIST STATUS and DISPLAY STATUS.

LIST STRUCTURE

Syntax

LIST STRUCTURE [TO PRINT/TO FILE *filename*] [IN ALIAS *alias*]

The LIST STRUCTURE command lists the structure of the database in use, including the name, the number of records, all names of fields, and the date of the last update. If the TO PRINT option is used, the listing will be printed on the printer. The TO FILE option may be specified to redirect the output to a file. LIST STRUCTURE does not pause during the listing, which is the only difference between LIST STRUCTURE and DISPLAY STRUCTURE. The IN ALIAS option may be used to list the structure of a file in another work area; *alias* may be either an alias name or a work-area number.

LOAD

Syntax

LOAD *binaryfilename*

The LOAD command is used to load binary (assembly language) programs into memory for future use. An extension is optional; if omitted, it is assumed to be .BIN.

LOCATE

Syntax

LOCATE [*scope*] [FOR *condition*] [WHILE *condition*][NOOPTIMIZE]

The LOCATE command finds the first record that matches *condition*. The *scope* option can be used to limit the number of records that will be searched, but if *scope* is omitted, ALL is assumed. The LOCATE command ends when a record-matching condition is found, after which FoxPro displays the location of the record but not the record itself. Use the CONTINUE command after a LOCATE command to locate additional records meeting the same condition (see CONTINUE). The FOR option specifies a condition that must be met before a record will be located. If you use the WHILE option, a record will be located until the condition is no longer true. The NOOPTIMIZE clause turns off FoxPro's internal optimization (also known as Rushmore).

Example

To locate a record containing the character string Smith in the Lastname field, enter

```
LOCATE FOR lastname = "Smith"
```

LOOP

Syntax

LOOP

The LOOP command causes a jump back to the start of a DO WHILE loop. The LOOP command is normally executed conditionally within an IF statement.

MENU

Syntax

MENU BAR *array1,expN1*
MENU *expN2,array2,expN3[,expN4]*
READ MENU BAR TO *var1,var2*[SAVE]

The MENU BAR, MENU, and READ MENU BAR TO commands create a menu bar system where the menu bar appears in a horizontal format across the top of the screen and each option of the menu, when chosen, displays a list of associated choices in a pop-up menu. (Before creating a menu bar, you must use the DIMENSION command to initialize an array for each list of menu options.)

Use the MENU BAR command to insert the character expressions contained in *array1* into the menu bar; *array1* is a two-dimensional array of character strings. *Array1*(i,1) becomes the menu pad that is displayed on the menu bar at position i. *Array1*(i,2) can be used to define an optional message that will appear at the SET MESSAGE TO location when the pad is selected. *ExpN1* defines the number of pads that appear on the menu bar.

Use the MENU command to insert menu pop-ups into a menu bar. *ExpN2* defines the position on the menu bar where the pop-up being defined will appear; *expN3* defines the number of options on the pop-up menu. *ExpN4*, which is optional, limits the number of menu options shown on the screen at any time. If the number of menu options exceeds this limit, the options scroll within the pop-up menu. *Array2* is a one-dimensional array containing the character strings that are used as menu options. Use a backslash (\) as the first character to make an option nonselectable. Use a backslash followed by a hyphen (-) to draw a graphics bar in place of a menu item.

Use the READ MENU BAR TO command to activate the menu bar defined by the prior commands. Use *var1* and *var2* to control which menu-bar pad and menu options are selected by default when the menu is initially displayed. Once a selection has been made by the user, *var1* and *var2* will contain values that correspond to the menu selection. These values may then be acted on by the program. Use the optional SAVE clause to cause the menu bar to remain on the screen after a menu option has been chosen.

Example

```
*Mainmenu.PRG displays main menu.
SET TALK OFF
SET MESSAGE TO 24 CENTER
*Initialize arrays used for menu bar.
DIMENSION TOPBAR(3,2)
TOPBAR(1,1) = '  ADD  '
TOPBAR(2,1) = ' EDIT  '
TOPBAR(3,1) = ' PRINT '
TOPBAR(1,2) = 'Add data to file'
TOPBAR(2,2) = 'Edit data in file'
TOPBAR(3,2) = 'Print data in file'
*Initialize array used for Add pop-up.
DIMENSION Adder(4)
Adder(1) = 'Add Members   '
```

```
Adder(2) = 'Add Rentals      '
Adder(3) = 'Add Purchases '
Adder(4) = 'Exit this menu'
*Initialize array used for Edit pop-up.
DIMENSION Edits(4)
Edits(1) = 'Edit Members      '
Edits(2) = 'Edit Rentals      '
Edits(3) = 'Edit Purchases '
Edits(4) = 'Exit this menu'
*Initialize array used for Print pop-up.
DIMENSION Print(4)
Print(1) = 'Print Members      '
Print(2) = 'Print Rentals      '
Print(3) = 'Print Purchases '
Print(4) = 'Exit this menu'
*Insert the pop-ups into the menu bar.
MENU BAR TOPBAR,3
MENU 1,Adder,4
MENU 2,Edits,4
MENU 3,Print,4
*Activate the menu system.
READ MENU BAR TO 1,1
```

MENU TO

Syntax

MENU TO *memvar*

The MENU TO command is used along with the @-PROMPT command to implement light-bar menus. See @-PROMPT for a complete explanation of the use of the MENU TO command.

MODIFY COMMAND/MODIFY FILE

Syntax

MODIFY COMMAND/FILE *filename* [*skeleton*][NOEDIT][NOWAIT]
[RANGE *expN1*[,*expN2*][WINDOW *windowname*][SAME][SAVE]

MODIFY COMMAND or MODIFY FILE starts the FoxPro Editor, which can be used for editing command files or ASCII text files. If MODIFY COMMAND is used, the file name will be given the extension .PRG unless a different extension is named. If MODIFY FILE is used, no extension is added unless one is specified in the file name. The WINDOW option may be used to open the file in a previously defined window. The *skeleton* option may be used to open windows for all files that match the file skeleton supplied. The NOEDIT option causes the text to be displayed, but editing is not allowed. The NOWAIT option causes program execution to continue as soon as the window is opened. The RANGE option may be used to open an editing window with a range of characters selected for editing. The characters selected begin with the position specified in *expN1* and continue for *expN2* characters. If *expN2* is omitted, editing begins at the character position specifed by *expN1*. If a window for editing is already open, the SAME clause prevents the new window from becoming the active window. The SAVE option causes the window to remain visible after editing is completed.

MODIFY GENERAL

Syntax

MODIFY GENERAL *generalfield* [*,generalfield2...*]

The MODIFY GENERAL command opens an editing window in the specified general field of the current record. When the window is open, you can insert, modify, or delete linked or embedded objects. *Generalfield* specifies the name of the general field to open. You can open an editing window for a general field in a table that is open in a different work area by including the table's alias with the field name. To open multiple general fields, include a list of general fields, separated by commas.

Example

```
MODIFY GENERAL photo1, photo2
```

MODIFY LABEL

Syntax

MODIFY LABEL *filename*/? [[WINDOW *windowname1*] [IN [WINDOW] *windowname2* | IN SCREEN]] [NOENVIRONMENT] [NOWAIT] [SAVE]

The MODIFY LABEL command creates or allows editing of a label-form file. This file can be used with the LABEL FORM command to produce mailing labels. The file name will be given the extension .LBX. If the question mark is used in place of a file name, FoxPro displays a list of all label files in the current directory. The user may then select a label file for editing from the list. The SAVE option causes the label-design window to remain visible after changes to the label are completed.

The WINDOW and IN WINDOW clauses can be used to specify that the label design should take place in a window or in the child window of a parent window. The IN SCREEN clause forces label design to use the full screen; this is also the default if no WINDOW clause is used. The NOENVIRONMENT clause is used when you do not want to restore the environment that was in place when you originally created the labels. The NOWAIT clause, used within programs, causes program execution to continue after the label-design screen or window has appeared.

MODIFY MEMO

Syntax

MODIFY MEMO *memofield1*[,*memofield 2*...][NOEDIT][NOWAIT] [RANGE *expN1*[,*expN2*]][WINDOW *windowname*][SAVE]

MODIFY MEMO places the contents of a memo field in the FoxPro Editor. The WINDOW option may be used to open the memo field in a previously defined window. The NOEDIT option causes the text to be displayed, but editing is not allowed. The NOWAIT option causes program execution to continue as soon as the window is opened. The RANGE option may be used to edit a memo field with a range of characters selected for editing. The characters selected begin with the position specified in *expN1* and continue for *expN2* characters. If *expN2* is omitted, editing begins at the character position specified by *expN1*. The SAVE option causes the memo window to remain visible after editing is completed.

MODIFY MENU

Syntax

MODIFY MENU [*filename*/?] [[WINDOW *windowname*] [IN [WINDOW] *windowname2* | SCREEN]] [NOWAIT] [SAVE]

The MODIFY MENU command modifies an existing menu. The command brings up the FoxPro menu-creation utility. See CREATE MENU for additional details.

MODIFY PROJECT

Syntax

MODIFY PROJECT [*filename*/?] [[WINDOW *windowname*] [IN [WINDOW] *windowname2*/SCREEN]] [SAVE]

The MODIFY PROJECT command modifies an existing project. The command opens the Project window. See CREATE MENU for additional details.

MODIFY QUERY

Syntax

MODIFY QUERY [*file*/?] [NOWAIT]

The MODIFY QUERY command modifies an existing query. The command causes the RQBE window to be displayed, containing the previously stored query. For more details on designing and saving queries, see Chapter 6.

MODIFY REPORT

Syntax

MODIFY REPORT *filename*/? [[WINDOW *windowname1*][IN [WINDOW] *windowname2* | IN SCREEN]][NOENVIRONMENT][NOWAIT][SAVE]

The MODIFY REPORT command allows you to use the Report Generator to create or modify a report-form file for producing reports. The file names produced will be given the extension .FRX. If the question mark is used in place of a file name, FoxPro displays a list of all report-form files in the current directory. The user may then select a report file for editing from the list. The SAVE option causes the report design to remain visible after changes to the report are completed.

The WINDOW and IN WINDOW clauses can be used to specify that the report design should take place in a window or in the child window of a parent window. The IN SCREEN clause forces report design to use the full screen; this is also the default if no WINDOW clause is used. The NOENVIRONMENT clause is used when you do not want to restore the environment that was in place when you originally created the report. The NOWAIT clause, used within programs, causes program execution to continue after the report-design screen or window has appeared.

MODIFY SCREEN

Syntax

MODIFY SCREEN [*filename*/?] [[WINDOW *windowname1*] [IN [WINDOW] *windowname2*/IN SCREEN]] [NOENVIRONMENT] [NOWAIT] [SAVE]

The MODIFY SCREEN command modifies an existing screen form, created with the CREATE SCREEN command. See CREATE SCREEN for additional details.

MODIFY STRUCTURE

Syntax

MODIFY STRUCTURE

The MODIFY STRUCTURE command allows you to alter the structure of the active database. After the structure has been modified, a backup copy containing the original data remains on disk with the same file name but with the extension .BAK.

MODIFY WINDOW

Syntax

MODIFY WINDOW *windowname*/SCREEN FROM *row1,col1*
TO *row2,col2*/AT *row3,col3* SIZE *row4,col4*
[FONT *expC1* [, *expN1*]] [STYLE *expC2*] [TITLE *expC3*]
[HALFHEIGHT] [DOUBLE/PANEL/NONE/SYSTEM]
[CLOSE/NOCLOSE] [FLOAT/NOFLOAT] [GROW/NOGROW]
[MDI/NOMDI] [MINIMIZE] [ZOOM/NOZOOM] [ICON FILE *expC4*]
[FILL FILE *.bmp file*] [COLOR SCHEME *expN2*/COLOR
colorpairlist/COLOR RGB (*colorvaluelist*)]

The MODIFY WINDOW command changes the attributes of an existing user-defined window or the main FoxPro window. (Use the DEFINE WINDOW command to create user-defined windows.) Note that you cannot use MODIFY WINDOW to change the attributes of FoxPro system windows (such as the Command window, Browse windows, and the Filer).

Use MODIFY WINDOW to change the location, default font, title, border, controls, and color of a user-defined window or the main FoxPro window. You can change any of these attributes by including the options shown above. As an example, include the TO and FROM or AT and SIZE clauses to specify a new location or size for a user-defined window. To prevent a user-defined window from being moved, include the NOFLOAT option.

Use *windowname* to specify the user-defined window you wish to modify. (The specified window must first be created with the DEFINE

WINDOW command.) Use SCREEN instead of a window name to modify the attributes of the main FoxPro window. (To later return the main FoxPro window to its startup configuration, use the MODIFY WINDOW SCREEN command without any additional options.

For additional information about the MODIFY WINDOW options, see DEFINE WINDOW in this appendix.

MOVE POPUP

Syntax

MOVE POPUP *popupname* TO *row,col*/BY *deltarow,deltacol*

The MOVE POPUP command moves a pop-up to a different screen location.

Examples

To move a pop-up to the starting position of row 14, column 18, you could use the command

```
MOVE POPUP MyPop TO 14,18
```

To move the pop-up six lines down and four lines to the right, you could use the command

```
MOVE POPUP MyPop BY 6,4
```

MOVE WINDOW

Syntax

MOVE WINDOW *windowname* TO *row,col*/BY *deltarow,deltacol*

The MOVE WINDOW command moves a predefined window to a new location on the screen.

Examples

To move the window to the starting position of row 15, column 20, enter

```
MOVE WINDOW MyWindow TO 15,20
```

To move the window six lines down and four lines to the right, enter

```
MOVE WINDOW MyWindow BY 6,4
```

NOTE/*/&&

Syntax

NOTE/*/&&

The NOTE or * or && command is used to insert comments in a command file. Use && to add a comment at the end of an existing statement. Use NOTE or * at the beginning of a line when the entire line is to be a comment. Text after the *, the &&, or the word NOTE in a command file will be ignored by FoxPro.

ON

Syntax

ON ERROR *command*
ON ESCAPE *command*
ON KEY *command*

This command causes a branch within a command file, specified by *command*, to be carried out when the condition identified by ON (an error, pressing the ESC key, or pressing any key) is met. If more than one ON condition is specified, the order of precedence is ON ERROR, ON ESCAPE, and then ON KEY. All ON conditions remain in effect until another ON condition is specified to clear the previous condition. To clear an ON condition without specifying another condition, enter ON ERROR, ON ESCAPE, or ON KEY without adding a command.

Examples

To cause program control to transfer to another program called ERRTRAP if an error occurs, enter

```
ON ERROR DO ERRTRAP
```

To cause the program to display a customized error message if an error occurs, use the following form:

```
ON ERROR ? "A serious error has occurred. Call J.E.J.A. Tech
Support for instructions."
```

To cause the program to call another program, HELPER.PRG, if the ESC key is pressed, enter

```
ON ESCAPE DO HELPER
```

To halt processing within a program and transfer program control to a program named HALTED.PRG if any key is pressed, enter

```
ON KEY DO HALTED
```

If the ON KEY syntax is used, the key that is pressed will be stored in the keyboard buffer. The routine that is called by the ON KEY command should use a READ command or INKEY function to clear the buffer.

ON BAR

Syntax

ON BAR *expN* OF *popupname1* [ACTIVATE POPUP *popupname2*/ ACTIVATE MENU *menuname*]

The ON BAR command activates a pop-up or a bar menu when a particular bar of a pop-up is selected. Use *expN* to specify the desired bar that, when chosen, will activate the other pop-up or menu. The corresponding ACTIVATE POPUP or ACTIVATE MENU clause specifies the pop-up or the menu that is activated as the result of the choice.

ON KEY =

Syntax

ON KEY = *expN* [*command*]

The ON KEY = *expN* command branches to a subroutine when the user presses the key that has the ASCII code indicated by the expression.

ON KEY-LABEL

Syntax

ON KEY [LABEL *keylabel*] [*command*]

The ON KEY-LABEL command branches to a subroutine when the specific key identified by the key label is pressed.

ON PAD

Syntax

ON PAD *padname* OF *menuname*
[ACTIVATE POPUP *popupname*]
[ACTIVATE MENU *menuname*]

The ON PAD command ties a given pad within a bar menu to a specific pop-up menu. When the named pad is selected from the menu, the associated pop-up menu appears. Use the ACTIVATE MENU clause to activate a bar menu.

Example

```
ON PAD Add OF MainMenu ACTIVATE POPUP AddRecs
ON PAD Edit OF MainMenu ACTIVATE POPUP EditRecs
ON PAD Print OF MainMenu ACTIVATE POPUP PrintRec
```

ON PAGE

Syntax

ON PAGE [AT LINE *expN command*]

The ON PAGE command executes the command named after the ON PAGE command whenever FoxPro reaches the designated line number or encounters an EJECT PAGE command. The ON PAGE command is generally used to call a procedure that prints a footer, ejects a page, and prints a header. Using ON PAGE without any clauses cancels the effects of the previous ON PAGE command.

Example

```
ON PAGE AT LINE 58 DO FOOTERS
SET PRINT ON
LIST LASTNAME, FIRSTNAME, SALARY, HIREDATE
(...more commands...)

PROCEDURE FOOTERS
?
? " Salary listing--for personnel use only."
EJECT PAGE
? " SALARY LISTING "
?
? DATE()
RETURN
```

ON READERROR

Syntax

ON READERROR [*command*]

The ON READERROR command runs a program or executes a named command or procedure after testing for an error in input. The ON READERROR command is called in response to invalid dates, improper responses to a VALID clause, or improper entries when a RANGE clause is in effect. ON READERROR without the *command* clause cancels the previous ON READERROR command.

ON SELECTION BAR

Syntax

ON SELECTION BAR *expN* OF *popupname* [*command*]

The ON SELECTION BAR command links a program, a procedure, or a command to a specific bar of a bar menu. When the bar identified by the value *expN* is chosen from the menu, the command, procedure, or program named is executed.

ON SELECTION BAR without the rest of the expression cancels the effects of the previous ON SELECTION BAR command.

Example

```
ON SELECTION BAR 2 OF MyPop DO REPORTER
```

ON SELECTION MENU

Syntax

ON SELECTION MENU *menuname*/ALL [*command*]

The ON SELECTION MENU command links a program, a procedure, or a command to any pad of a bar menu. When any pad is chosen from the menu, the command, procedure, or program named is executed.

ON SELECTION MENU without the rest of the expression cancels the effects of the previous ON SELECTION MENU command.

Example

```
ON SELECTION MENU OF MyPop DO SUBMENU2
```

ON SELECTION PAD

Syntax

ON SELECTION PAD *padname* OF *menuname* [*command*]

The ON SELECTION PAD command links a program, procedure, or command to a specific pad of a bar menu. When the named pad is chosen from the menu, the command, procedure, or program named within the ON SELECTION statement is executed. ON SELECTION PAD without the *padname* clause cancels the previous ON SELECTION PAD command.

Example

```
ON SELECTION PAD Print OF MainMenu DO REPORTER
```

ON SELECTION POPUP

Syntax

ON SELECTION POPUP *popupname*/ALL [*command*]

The ON SELECTION POPUP command names a program, procedure, or command that executes when a selection is made from a pop-up menu. If no command or procedure is named, the active pop-up is deactivated. If the ALL option is used, the command or procedure applies to all pop-ups. ON SELECTION POPUP without the *popupname* clause cancels the previous ON SELECTION POPUP command.

Example

```
ON SELECTION POPUP Print DO Reporter
```

PACK

Syntax

PACK [MEMO] [DBF]

The PACK command removes records that have been marked for deletion by the DELETE command and rebuilds any open index files. Because the command involves recopying much of the active database, it can be time-consuming with large files.

You can add the MEMO or DBF clause to specifically pack just the database file without packing the memo fields, or to pack just the memo-field file without packing the database. The MEMO clause causes a pack of the memo-field file, but the database file is not packed. The DBF clause causes a pack of just the database file, but the memo-field file is not packed. If you omit both clauses, both the database file and the memo-field file are packed.

PARAMETERS

Syntax

PARAMETERS *parameterlist*

The PARAMETERS command is used within a command file to assign variable names to data items that are received from another command file with the DO command. The PARAMETERS command must be the first command in a command file. The number, order, and data types of the items in the parameter list must match the list of parameters included with the WITH option of the DO command that called the command file.

Example

The following portion of a command file shows the use of the PARAMETERS command to receive a location for displaying an error message, along with the contents of the message:

```
PROCEDURE ErrMessage
PARAMETERS Row, Message
@ Row, 36-(LEN(TEXT)/2) SAY Text
RETURN
```

PLAY MACRO

Syntax

PLAY MACRO *macroname* [TIME *n seconds*]

The PLAY MACRO command plays a previously stored macro. Use the optional TIME clause to specify a time interval, in seconds, between keystrokes of the macro.

PRINTJOB/ENDPRINTJOB

Syntax

PRINTJOB
commands
ENDPRINTJOB

The PRINTJOB command places stored print-related settings into effect for the duration of a printing job. Desired values must be stored to print-system memory variables before the PRINTJOB command is encountered. When PRINTJOB is executed, starting codes stored to _pscodes are sent to the printer; a formfeed is sent if _peject contains BEFORE or BOTH; _pcolno is initialized to 0; and _plineno and ON PAGE are activated. When the printing process is complete and the ENDPRINTJOB command is encountered, any ending print codes stored to _pecodes are sent to the printer; a formfeed is sent if _peject contains AFTER or BOTH; FoxPro returns to the PRINTJOB command if the _pcopies variable contains more than 1 (set to more than one copy of the report); and _plineno and ON PAGE are deactivated.

Example

```
*Sets compressed print on for Epson with ESC code 018.
*Ejects page after end of each report.
*Spools two copies of report to printer.
STORE 018 to _pcodes
STORE "AFTER" to _peject
STORE 2 to _pcopies
PRINTJOB
REPORT FORM Payroll TO PRINT
END PRINTJOB
```

PRIVATE

Syntax

PRIVATE ALL [LIKE/EXCEPT *skeleton*]/
memvarlist/ARRAY *arraydefinitionlist*]

This command sets specified variables to private, hiding values of those variables from all higher level parts of a program. Skeletons are file-name patterns that include the acceptable DOS wildcards of asterisk (*) and question mark (?). Memory variables are private by default.

Examples

To hide all variables, excluding BILLPAY, from higher level parts of the program, enter

```
PRIVATE ALL EXCEPT BILLPAY
```

To hide all variables with eight-character names that end in TEST from higher level parts of the program, enter

```
PRIVATE ALL LIKE ????TEST
```

To hide only the variable named PAYOUT from higher level parts of the program, enter

```
PRIVATE PAYOUT
```

PROCEDURE

Syntax

PROCEDURE *procedurename*

The PROCEDURE command identifies the start of each separate procedure within a procedure file.

Although using a one-line procedure is inefficient (procedures should be at least two lines long), the following example demonstrates a simple procedure:

Example

```
PROCEDURE ERROR1
@ 2,10 SAY "That is not a valid answer. Try again."
RETURN
```

PUBLIC

Syntax

PUBLIC *memvarlist*/ARRAY *arraydefinitionlist*

This command sets named variables or arrays to public, making the values of those variables or arrays available to all levels of a program.

Example

To make the variables named BILLPAY, DUEDATE, and AMOUNT available to all modules of a program, enter

```
PUBLIC BILLPAY, DUEDATE, AMOUNT
```

QUIT

Syntax

QUIT

The QUIT command closes all open files, leaves FoxPro, and returns you to the operating system prompt.

READ

Syntax

READ [CYCLE] [ACTIVATE *expL1*] [DEACTIVATE *expL2*] [MODAL]
[WITH *windowtitlelist*] [SHOW *expL3*] [VALID *expL4/expN1*]
[WHEN *expL5*] [OBJECT *expN2*] [TIMEOUT e*xpN3*] [SAVE]
[NOMOUSE] [LOCK/NOLOCK] [COLOR [*colorpairslist*]/COLOR
SCHEME *expN4*]

The READ command allows entry from an @ command with a GET option. Normally, a READ command clears all GETs when all data entry or editing is completed. The SAVE option is used to avoid clearing all GETs after completion of data entry or editing.

The CYCLE clause is used to leave the READ active when moving past the last or first GET. The ACTIVATE clause is executed when READ is issued and whenever the current READ window changes. (ACTIVATE can be considered to be a window-level WHEN clause.) The DEACTIVATE clause is executed if you bring another window forward (or whenever the value of WONTOP( ) changes). DEACTIVATE can be considered to be a window-level VALID clause. The SHOW clause is used along with the SHOW GETS command (see SHOW GETS). The SHOW clause is executed whenever the SHOW GETS command is issued.

The optional VALID clause is evaluated when you exit from the READ. The WHEN clause can be used to determine whether the READ will take place, depending on the value of the logical expression. The OBJECT specifies which object is initially selected within the READ. Use the TIMEOUT clause to specify how long (in seconds) a READ will be in effect if no key is pressed. Normally, all GETS are cleared following a READ;

use the SAVE statement to reissue a READ without reissuing the GETS. The NOMOUSE option prevents objects from being selected with the mouse, and the COLOR and COLOR SCHEME options can be used to specify colors for the READ. Note that in FoxPro for Windows, color commands and options change only the colors used by *user-defined* windows and menus; all other elements under Windows must be changed through the Windows color option in the Control Panel.

READ MENU

Syntax

READ MENU TO *memvar* [SAVE]

The READ MENU TO command activates a pop-up menu defined with the @-MENU command (see @-MENU). The SAVE option causes the menu to remain visible after a menu selection has been made.

RECALL

Syntax

RECALL [*scope*] [FOR *condition*] [WHILE *condition*][NOOPTIMIZE]

The RECALL command unmarks records that have been marked for deletion. If *scope* is not listed, ALL is assumed. The FOR option can be used to specify a condition that must be met before a record will be recalled. If you use the WHILE option, deleted records will be recalled until the condition is no longer true. The NOOPTIMIZE clause turns off FoxPro's internal optimization techniques (also known as Rushmore).

REINDEX

Syntax

REINDEX [COMPACT]

The REINDEX command rebuilds all open index files in the current work area. If any changes have been made to the database while its index file was closed, you can update the index file with REINDEX.

All tags in all open compound index files are updated. Also, the COMPACT option can be used to cause the reindexed files to use the compact file format.

RELEASE

Syntax

RELEASE *memvarlist*/ALL [LIKE/EXCEPT *wildcards*]
RELEASE MODULE *modulename*/MENUS *menunamelist*/POPUP
popupnamelist/WINDOW *windownamelist*
RELEASE BAR *barlist*/RELEASE PAD *padname* OF *menuname*

The RELEASE command removes all or specified memory variables from memory. Wildcards, which are asterisks or question marks, are used with the LIKE and EXCEPT options. The asterisk can represent one or more characters, the question mark one character. The RELEASE MENUS, RELEASE POPUP, RELEASE WINDOW, RELEASE BAR, and RELEASE PAD variations of the command release the named objects from active memory. The RELEASE MODULE command releases any binary files loaded with the LOAD command from memory.

Example

To release all memory variables except those ending with the characters TAX, enter

```
RELEASE ALL EXCEPT ???TAX
```

RENAME

Syntax

RENAME *filename.ext* TO *newfilename.ext*

The RENAME command changes the name of a file. The name must include the file extension. If the file is on a disk that is not in the default drive, the drive designator must be included in *filename.ext.*

REPLACE

Syntax

REPLACE [*scope*] *field* WITH *expr* [...*field2* WITH *expr2*...] [FOR *condition*] [WHILE *condition*] [ADDITIVE][NOOPTIMIZE]

The REPLACE command replaces the contents of a specified field with new values. You can replace values in more than one field by listing more than one *field* WITH *expr;* be sure to separate each field replacement with a comma. The FOR option can be used to specify a condition that must be met before a field in a record will be replaced. If you use the WHILE option, records will be replaced until the condition is no longer true. If the *scope,* FOR, or WHILE option is not used, the current record (at the current record-pointer location) will be the only record replaced. The ADDITIVE option can be used when replacing a memo field to add the expression to the existing text in the field. FoxPro will automatically insert a carriage return between the old text and the new. Use the NOOPTIMIZE clause to disable FoxPro's optimization techniques (also known as Rushmore).

Example

To replace the contents of a field called Salary at the current record with a new amount equal to the old amount multiplied by 1.05, enter

```
REPLACE SALARY WITH SALARY * 1.05
```

REPORT FORM

Syntax

REPORT FORM *filename*/? [*scope*] [FOR *condition*] [WHILE *condition*] [PLAIN] [HEADING *characterstring*] [SUMMARY]

[NOEJECT] [TO PRINT[PROMPT]/TO FILE *filename*] [OFF]
[PREVIEW] [NOCONSOLE] [NOOPTIMIZE]

The REPORT FORM command uses a report-form file (previously created with the CREATE REPORT command) to produce a report. A file name with the extension .FRX is assumed unless otherwise specified.

The FOR option can be used to specify a condition to be met before a record will be printed. If you use the WHILE option, records will be printed until the condition is no longer true. If *scope* is not included, ALL is assumed. The PLAIN option omits page headings. The HEADING option (followed by a character string) provides a header in addition to any header that was specified when the report was created with CREATE REPORT. The NOEJECT option cancels the initial formfeed. The SUMMARY option causes a summary report to be printed. TO PRINT directs output to the screen and the printer, while TO FILE directs output to a disk file. If the question mark is substituted for a file name, a list of all report files appears. The user may then select the report to print from the list. The optional OFF clause, when used, turns off the normal screen output while the report is being printed. If the PROMPT option is included with the TO PRINT clause, a dialog box is displayed before printing starts. The PREVIEW option causes an on-screen preview display of the labels to appear. The NOCONSOLE option disables the output that is normally sent to the screen. Use the NOOPTIMIZE clause to disable FoxPro's normal optimization techniques (also known as Rushmore).

RESTORE

Syntax

RESTORE FROM *filename*/MEMO *memofield* [ADDITIVE]

The RESTORE command reads memory variables into memory from a memory-variable file or from a memo field. When used with files, RE-STORE FROM assumes that *filename* ends with .MEM; if it does not, you should include the extension. If the ADDITIVE option is used, current memory variables will not be deleted.

RESTORE MACROS

Syntax

RESTORE MACROS FROM *macrofilename*/MEMO *memofield*

The RESTORE MACROS command restores macros that were saved in a macro file or in a memo field to memory. If the MEMO clause is used, the macros are restored from a memo field. If any existing macros are assigned to the same keys, they will be overwritten when you use this command.

RESTORE SCREEN

Syntax

RESTORE SCREEN [FROM *memvar*]

The RESTORE SCREEN command restores a screen from the buffer or from the named memory variable (see SAVE SCREEN).

RESTORE WINDOW

Syntax

RESTORE WINDOW *windownamelist*/ALL FROM *filename*/
MEMO *memofield*

The RESTORE WINDOW command restores window definitions that were saved in a file or in a memo field with the SAVE WINDOW command. If the MEMO clause is used, the windows are restored from a memo field.

RESUME

Syntax

RESUME

The RESUME command is a companion to the SUSPEND command. RESUME causes program execution to continue at the line following the line at which program operation was suspended (see also SUSPEND).

RETRY

Syntax

RETRY

The RETRY command returns control to a calling program and executes the same line that called the program containing the RETRY command. The function of RETRY is similar to the function of the RETURN command; however, where RETURN executes the next successive line of the calling program, RETRY executes the same line of the calling program. RETRY can be useful in error-recovery situations, where an action can be taken to clear the cause of an error and repeat the command.

Example

```
*Printing program includes error recovery.
WAIT "Press a key to start the report."
ON ERROR DO PROBLEMS
REPORT FORM MyFile TO PRINT
ON ERROR
RETURN

*...more commands...

*PROBLEMS.PRG
*Error trapping for printer program.
CLEAR
? "Printer is NOT READY."
? "Take corrective action, then press any key."
WAIT
RETRY
RETURN
```

RETURN

Syntax

RETURN [TO MASTER/*expr*/TO *procedurename*]

The RETURN command ends execution of a command file or procedure. If the command file was called by another command file, program control returns to the other command file. If the command file was not called by another command file, control returns to the command level. If the TO MASTER option is used, control returns to the highest level command file. If the TO *procedurename* option is used, control returns to the named procedure. The *expr* option is used to return the value in a user-defined function to another procedure or command file.

RUN/!

Syntax

RUN [/*N*] *filename*
! [/*N*] *filename*

The RUN command executes a non-FoxPro program from within the FoxPro environment, provided there is enough available memory. The program must be an executable file (having an extension of .COM, .EXE, or .BAT). When the program completes its execution, control is passed back to FoxPro. You can also execute DOS commands with RUN. The exclamation point (!) can be substituted for the word RUN. The /*N* option can be used to specify an amount of memory to be freed, where *N* is a numeric value. If *N* is omitted, RUN frees a standard amount of memory (which varies, depending on your system). If *N* is 0, RUN frees as much memory as possible, swapping large portions of FoxPro out to disk. Any value other than 0 is interpreted as memory needed in kilobytes, and as much of FoxPro as necessary is swapped out to disk to provide the memory.

SAVE

Syntax

SAVE TO *filename*/MEMO *memofieldname* [ALL LIKE/EXCEPT *skeleton*]

The SAVE command copies memory variables to a disk file or to the contents of a memo field. Wildcards, which are asterisks or question marks, are used with parts of file names as skeletons, along with the LIKE and EXCEPT options. The asterisk can represent one or more characters, the question mark one character.

Example

To save all existing six-letter memory variables ending in the letters TAX to a disk file named FIGURES, enter

```
SAVE TO FIGURES ALL LIKE ???TAX
```

SAVE MACROS

Syntax

SAVE MACROS TO *macrofilename*/MEMO *memofield*

The SAVE MACROS command saves macros currently in memory to a macro file. If the MEMO option is used, the macros are saved to the named memo field of the current record.

SAVE SCREEN

Syntax

SAVE SCREEN [TO *memvar*]

The SAVE SCREEN command saves the current screen image to the buffer. If the TO clause is included along with a variable name, the screen image is saved to the named memory variable. You can later use RESTORE SCREEN to redisplay the screen.

SAVE WINDOW

Syntax

SAVE WINDOW *windownamelist*/ALL TO *windowfilename*/
MEMO *memofield*

The SAVE WINDOW command saves the windows named in the list to a disk file. If the ALL option is used, all windows in memory are saved to a file. If the MEMO option is used, the windows are saved to the named memo field of the current record. The windows can be restored to memory by using the RESTORE WINDOW command.

SCAN

Syntax

SCAN [*scope*] [FOR *condition*] [WHILE *condition*]
[*commands...*]
[LOOP]
[*commands*]
[EXIT]
ENDSCAN

The SCAN and ENDSCAN commands are simplified alternatives to the DO WHILE and ENDDO commands. The SCAN-ENDSCAN commands cause the file in use to be scanned, processing all records that meet the specified conditions.

Example

```
USE MEMBERS
SCAN FOR EXPIREDATE <= DATE()+60
   SET PRINT ON
   ? "Dear: "
   ?? trim(FIRSTNAME) + " " + LASTNAME
   ?
   ? "Your membership expires within the next 60 days."
   ? "Please call 555-1212 to renew your membership."
   EJECT
   SET PRINT OFF
ENDSCAN
```

SCATTER TO

Syntax

SCATTER *memvar* [FIELDS *fieldlist*] TO *array*

The SCATTER TO command moves data from the current record of a database file or from memory variables into an array. (Note that SCATTER TO is compatible with FoxBase Plus; if you need compatibility with dBASE IV, use COPY TO ARRAY instead.) The fields of the current record are transferred, beginning with the first field of the record, into the corresponding elements of the array. If the database has more fields than the array has elements, the contents of extra fields are not stored to the array. If the array has more elements than the database has fields, the extra elements in the array are not changed. Note that memo fields are ignored during the data-transfer process.

SCROLL

Syntax

SCROLL *row1,col1,row2,col2,expN1,expN2*

The SCROLL command causes a rectangular portion of the screen to scroll. The upper-left corner of the portion is designated by *row1,col1* and the lower-right corner is designated by *row2,col2*. The numeric expression indicates the number of lines of the area to scroll. A negative number forces a scroll downwards, and a positive number forces a scroll upwards.

Use *expN2* to scroll horizontally. A positive value scrolls to the right by *N2* columns. A negative value scrolls to the left by *N2* columns.

SEEK

Syntax

SEEK *expr*

The SEEK command searches for the first record in an indexed file whose field matches a specific expression. If *expr* is a character string, it must be enclosed by single or double quotes. If *expr* cannot be found and FoxPro is not executing a command file, the EOF value is set to "True" and a "No find" message is displayed on the screen. An index file must be open before you can use the SEEK command.

Note the use of two related commands, SET EXACT and SET NEAR. Use SET EXACT to tell FoxPro to find a precise match. Use SET NEAR to tell FoxPro that if a match cannot be found, the record pointer should be positioned at the closest record rather than the end of the file.

SELECT

Syntax

SELECT *n/alias*

This variation of the SELECT command chooses from among ten possible work areas for database files. When FoxPro is first loaded into the computer, it defaults to work area 1. To use multiple files at once, you can select other work areas with the SELECT command; other files can then be opened in those areas. Acceptable work areas are the numbers 1 through 10.

Example

To open a file named TAXES in work area 5, enter

```
SELECT 5
USE TAXES
```

SELECT-SQL

Syntax

SELECT [ALL/DISTINCT][*alias.*]*select_item*[AS
col_name][, [*alias.*]*select_item*[AS *col_name*]...]
FROM *database* [*local_alias*][*database*[*local_alias*]...]
[[INTO destination]/[TO FILE filename [ADDITIVE]/TO
PRINTER]] [NOCONSOLE][PLAIN][NOWAIT][WHERE *joincondition*
[AND *joincondition*...][AND/OR *filtercondition*][AND/OR
filtercondition...]]][GROUP BY *groupcol*[, *groupcol*
[ORDER BY *order_ite*m[ASC/DESC][, *order_item*[ASC/
DESC]...]]

This variation of the SELECT command retrieves data from a table (made
up of fields from one or more FoxPro database files). SELECT commands
can be entered manually in the Command window, or you can create
them by designing a query in the RQBE window. The use of the SELECT-
SQL statement is an advanced topic, beyond the scope of this text; for
more information, refer to your FoxPro documentation or to a text on the
SQL Data Retrieval language.

SET

Syntax

SET

This command causes the View window to be displayed. The View window
options (at the left edge of the window) can then be used to view and
modify most available SET parameters within FoxPro.

SET ALTERNATE

Syntax

SET ALTERNATE ON/OFF
SET ALTERNATE TO *filename* [ADDITIVE]

The SET ALTERNATE TO command creates a text file with the extension .TXT and, when activated by SET ALTERNATE ON, stores all keyboard entries and screen displays to the file. The SET ALTERNATE OFF command halts the process, after which CLOSE ALTERNATE is used to close the file. (You can SET ALTERNATE OFF temporarily, and turn it on again later before using CLOSE ALTERNATE, to resume sending output to the file.) If the ADDITIVE option is used, SET ALTERNATE appends to the end of any existing file.

Example

To store the actions of the LIST command to a text file, enter

```
SET ALTERNATE TO CAPTURE
SET ALTERNATE ON
LIST LASTNAME, FIRSTNAME
SET ALTERNATE OFF
CLOSE ALTERNATE
```

SET ANSI

Syntax

SET ANSI ON/OFF

The SET ANSI command determines how comparisons of strings of different lengths are made with FoxPro's SQL commands. When SET ANSI is ON, character strings are compared for the full length of the string. Hence, "Derek " and "Derek" do not match if SET ANSI is ON. When SET ANSI is OFF, strings are compared character by character only until the shorter string ends. Hence, "Derek " and "Derek" match if SET ANSI is OFF.

SET AUTOSAVE

Syntax

SET AUTOSAVE ON/OFF

The SET AUTOSAVE command, when turned on, causes FoxPro to save changes to disk after each I/O operation. This reduces the chances of data loss due to power or hardware failure. The default for SET AUTOSAVE is OFF.

SET BELL

Syntax

SET BELL ON/OFF

The SET BELL command controls whether audible warnings will be issued during certain operations. SET BELL ON enables the bell, and SET BELL OFF disables the bell.

SET BELL TO

Syntax

SET BELL TO *frequency/duration*

The SET BELL TO command controls the frequency and duration of the bell. The frequency is the desired tone in hertz, and each unit of duration is approximately .0549 seconds. Available frequency is from 19 to 10,000 and available duration is from 1 to 19.

SET BLINK

Syntax

SET BLINK ON/OFF

The SET BLINK command determines whether screen elements (borders, shadows, text) can be made to blink on EGA or VGA monitors. SET BLINK ON enables blinking of selected elements. Use the Color option of the Window menu or the SET COLOR OF command to change the actual elements to blinking.

SET BLOCKSIZE

Syntax

SET BLOCKSIZE TO *expN*

The SET BLOCKSIZE command defines the size of blocks used to store memo fields on disk. Each block is 512 bytes, and *expN* can be a value from 1 to 32. If e*xpN* is greater than 32, disk space for memo fields is allocated in bytes rather than in 512-byte blocks. The default value for SET BLOCKSIZE is 64.

SET BORDER

Syntax

SET BORDER TO [SINGLE/DOUBLE/PANEL/NONE/
borderdefinitionstring1] [,*borderdefinitionstring2*]

The SET BORDER command redefines the border, which is a single line. The SINGLE option defines a single line; the DOUBLE option defines a double line; the PANEL option defines a panel built with the ASCII 219 character; and NONE defines no border. The *borderdefinitionstring* option may contain up to eight ASCII values separated by commas. Value 1 defines the top of the border; value 2 the bottom; values 3 and 4 the left and right edges; and values 5, 6, 7, and 8 the upper-left, upper-right, lower-left, and lower-right corners, respectively. By default, *borderdefinitionstring1* is also used for the active window. The optional *borderdefinitionstring2* defines the appearance of the border if the window is not active.

SET CARRY

Syntax

SET CARRY ON/OFF

The SET CARRY command controls whether data will be copied from the prior record into a new record when APPEND or INSERT is used. By default, SET CARRY is OFF.

SET CENTURY

Syntax

SET CENTURY ON/OFF

This command determines whether the century is displayed in dates. For example, a date that appears as 12/30/86 will appear as 12/30/1986 after the SET CENTURY ON command is used.

SET CLEAR

Syntax

SET CLEAR ON/OFF

The SET CLEAR command determines whether the screen will be cleared after a SET FORMAT TO or a QUIT command. If SET CLEAR is OFF, the screen will not be cleared upon execution of SET FORMAT TO or QUIT. The default for SET CLEAR is ON.

SET CLOCK

Syntax

SET CLOCK ON/OFF

The SET CLOCK command defines whether the system clock will appear. SET CLOCK ON displays the clock, and SET CLOCK OFF hides the clock.

SET CLOCK TO

Syntax

SET CLOCK TO *row,col*

The SET CLOCK TO command determines the location of the system clock, as defined by the row and column coordinates provided.

SET COLOR OF

Syntax

SET COLOR OF NORMAL/MESSAGES/TITLES/BOX/ HIGHLIGHT/INFORMATION/FIELDS TO [*colorpairslist*]

The SET COLOR OF command can be used to define colors for standard items, such as messages, titles, boxes, and highlights. *Colorpairslist* is one to ten color pairs, with foreground and background values separated by a slash and each color pair separated by a comma. Note that in FoxPro for Windows, color commands and options change only the colors used by *user-defined* windows and menus; all other elements under Windows must be changed through the Windows color option in the Control Panel.

SET COLOR OF SCHEME

Syntax

SET COLOR OF SCHEME *expN* TO [*colorpairslist*]

The SET COLOR OF SCHEME command sets the colors of the numbered scheme to the color list identified in *colorpairslist; expN* is a numeric expression from 1 to 11 or from 17 to 24. (Schemes 12 through 16 are reserved by FoxPro.) Schemes 17 through 24 can be user-defined. Schemes 1 through 11 apply to the following objects:

Scheme	Object
1	User windows
2	User menus
3	Menu bar
4	Pop-up menus
5	Dialog boxes
6	Dialog pop-ups
7	Alert boxes
8	Windows
9	Window pop-ups
10	Browse window
11	Report Layout window

The color-pairs list is one to ten color pairs, with foreground and background values separated by a slash and each color pair separated by a comma. Note that in FoxPro for Windows, color commands and options change only the colors used by *user-defined* windows and menus; all other elements under Windows must be changed through the Windows color option in the Control Panel.

SET COLOR OF SCHEME TO

Syntax

SET COLOR OF SCHEME *expN1* TO [SCHEME *expN2*]

The SET COLOR OF SCHEME TO command copies the colors of the first color scheme to the second color scheme. The *expN* is a numeric expression from 1 to 11 or from 17 to 24. (Schemes 12 through 16 are reserved by FoxPro.) Schemes 17 through 24 can be user-defined. If SCHEME *expN2* is omitted, colors will be copied from the last named color set.

SET COLOR SET TO

Syntax

SET COLOR SET TO [*colorsetname*]

The SET COLOR SET TO command loads a color set that was defined and saved previously. Use the Create Color Set command to define and save a color set.

SET COLOR TO

Syntax

SET COLOR TO *colorpairslist*

The SET COLOR command is used to select screen colors and display attributes. *Colorpairslist* is one to ten color pairs, with foreground and background values separated by a slash and each color pair separated by a comma. Note that in FoxPro for Windows, color commands and options change only the colors used by *user-defined* windows and menus; all other elements under Windows must be changed through the Windows color option in the Control Panel.

SET COMPATIBLE

Syntax

SET COMPATIBLE ON/OFF

The SET COMPATIBLE command turns on or off compatibility with FoxBase Plus. When SET COMPATIBLE is OFF, FoxBase Plus programs run in FoxPro without modification. When SET COMPATIBLE is ON, dBASE IV programs that use some commands run without modification.

SET CONFIRM

Syntax

SET CONFIRM ON/OFF

The SET CONFIRM command controls the behavior of the cursor during editing. When SET CONFIRM is ON, the ENTER key must be pressed to move from one field to another when editing in a highlighted field, even if you completely fill the field. When CONFIRM is OFF, the cursor automatically advances when you fill a field.

SET CONSOLE

Syntax

SET CONSOLE ON/OFF

The SET CONSOLE command turns output to the screen on or off, controlling the display. SET CONSOLE does not control output to the printer. Use SET CONSOLE within a program when you want to hide any screen display, but also leave the keyboard active (during the typing of a user's password, for example).

SET CURRENCY

Syntax

SET CURRENCY TO [*expC*]

The SET CURRENCY command changes the symbol used for currency. A character expression containing up to nine characters may be used as the currency symbol.

SET CURRENCY LEFT/RIGHT

Syntax

SET CURRENCY LEFT/RIGHT

The SET CURRENCY LEFT/RIGHT command changes the placement of the currency symbol, allowing the symbol to appear to the left or the right of the value.

SET DATE

Syntax

SET DATE AMERICAN/ANSI/BRITISH/ITALIAN/FRENCH/GERMAN/ JAPAN/USA/MDY/DMY/YMD

This command sets the display format for dates. American and MDY display as *MM/DD/YY*; ANSI displays as *YY.MM.DD*; British, French, and DMY display as *DD/MM/YY*; Italian displays as *DD-MM-YY*; German displays as *DD.MM.YY*; Japan and YMD display as *YY/MM/DD*; and USA displays as *MM-DD-YY*. The default value is American.

SET DECIMALS

Syntax

SET DECIMALS TO *expN*

The SET DECIMALS command changes the number of decimal places that are normally displayed during calculations.

SET DEFAULT

Syntax

SET DEFAULT TO *drive:directory*

This command changes the default drive and/or directory used in file operations.

SET DELETED

Syntax

SET DELETED ON/OFF

With SET DELETED set OFF (as it is by default), all records marked for deletion will be displayed when commands such as LIST and REPORT FORM are used. With SET DELETED set to ON, deleted records are omitted from the output of LIST, DISPLAY, LABEL FORM, and REPORT FORM commands. They are also omitted from the Edit and Browse displays, unless you explicitly move the record pointer to a deleted record with a GOTO command before issuing the EDIT or BROWSE command.

SET DEVELOPMENT

Syntax

SET DEVELOPMENT ON/OFF

The SET DEVELOPMENT command, when on, tells FoxPro to compare creation dates of .PRG files and compiled .DBO files; then, when a program is run, an outdated .DBO file will not be used. The FoxPro Editor automatically deletes old .DBO files as programs are updated, so the SET DEVELOPMENT command is not needed if you use the FoxPro Editor. If you use another editor to create and modify program files, add a SET DEVELOPMENT ON statement at the start of your programs.

SET DEVICE

Syntax

SET DEVICE TO PRINTER/SCREEN/FILE *filename*

The SET DEVICE command controls whether @ commands are sent to the screen or the printer. SET DEVICE is normally set to SCREEN, but if PRINTER is specified output will be directed to the printer. The FILE option directs output to the named disk file.

SET DISPLAY TO

Syntax

SET DISPLAY TO
MONO/COLOR/CGA/EGA25/EGA43/MONO43/VGA25/VGA43/
VGA50

The SET DISPLAY TO command sets the font used to display information. (This command is provided primarily for compatibility with programs written for FoxPro for DOS.) CGA switches the main FoxPro window font to 9-point FoxFont. COLOR has no effect in FoxPro for Windows, but the option is included for backwards compatibility with FoxPro/DOS programs. EGA25 switches the main FoxPro window font to 7-point FoxFont. EGA43 switches the main FoxPro window font to 9-point FoxFont. MONO has no effect in FoxPro for Windows, but the option is included for backwards compatibility with FoxPro/DOS programs. VGA25 switches the main FoxPro window font to 7-point FoxFont. VGA50 switches the main FoxPro window font to 9-point FoxFont.

SET DOHISTORY

Syntax

SET DOHISTORY ON/OFF

The SET DOHISTORY command turns on or off the storage of commands from command files in the Command window. When DOHISTORY is ON, program file commands are stored in the Command window as they are executed. You can later edit and re-execute those commands as if they had been entered at the command level.

SET ECHO

Syntax

SET ECHO ON/OFF

The SET ECHO command determines whether instructions from command files will be displayed or printed during program execution. Setting ECHO to ON can be useful when debugging programs. The default for SET ECHO is OFF.

SET ESCAPE

Syntax

SET ESCAPE ON/OFF

The SET ESCAPE command determines whether the ESC key will interrupt a program during execution. The default for SET ESCAPE is ON.

SET EXACT

Syntax

SET EXACT ON/OFF

The SET EXACT command determines how precisely two character strings will be compared. With SET EXACT OFF, which is the default case, comparison is not strict: A string on the left of the test is equal to its substring on the right if the substring acts as a prefix of the larger string. Thus, "turnbull" = "turn" is true even though it is clearly not. SET EXACT ON corrects for this lack of precision. Note that SET EXACT determines whether you can use FIND or SEEK for the first part of an index key. If SET EXACT is OFF, you can search for the first part of the key; if SET EXACT is ON, you must search for the entire key expression.

SET FIELDS

Syntax

SET FIELDS ON/OFF

This command respects or overrides a list of fields specified by the SET FIELDS TO command.

SET FIELDS TO

Syntax

SET FIELDS TO [*fieldlist*/ALL [LIKE/EXCEPT *skeleton*]]
ADDITIVE]

This command sets a specified list of fields that will be available for use. The ALL option causes all fields present in the active database to be made available. The LIKE/EXCEPT *skeleton* options select fields that match or do not match the skeleton. The ADDITIVE option adds the fields to a prior list of fields.

SET FILTER

Syntax

SET FILTER TO [*condition*]

The SET FILTER command displays only those records in a database that meet a specific condition.

Example

To display only those database records that contain the name "Main St." in the Address field during a DISPLAY or LIST command, enter

```
SET FILTER TO "Main St." $ ADDRESS
```

SET FIXED

Syntax

SET FIXED ON/OFF

The SET FIXED command sets the number of decimal places used within a numeric display.

SET FORMAT TO

Syntax

SET FORMAT TO *filename*/?

The SET FORMAT TO command lets you activate a format file called *filename* to control the format of the screen display used during EDIT, CHANGE, and APPEND operations. If *filename* has the extension .FMT, you need not supply the extension. The SET FORMAT command without a specified file name cancels the effects of the previous SET FORMAT command. The question mark, if used, causes a list of format files to appear.

SET FULLPATH

Syntax

SET FULLPATH ON/OFF

The SET FULLPATH command specifies whether full path names appear with file names returned by the DBF and NDX functions. If SET FULLPATH is OFF, only the drive designator and file name are returned by the functions. If SET FULLPATH is ON, the drive designator, path name, and file name are returned by the functions.

SET FUNCTION

Syntax

SET FUNCTION *expN*/*keylabel* TO *characterstring*

The SET FUNCTION command resets a function key to a command or sequence of commands of your choice. The maximum width of a command sequence is 75 characters. You can view the current settings with the DISPLAY STATUS command.

Example

To change the function of the F5 key to opening a file named MEMBERS and entering Append mode, enter

```
SET FUNCTION "5" TO "USE MEMBERS;APPEND;"
```

The semicolon (;) represents a carriage return.

SET HEADING

Syntax

SET HEADING ON/OFF

The SET HEADING command determines whether column headings appear when the LIST, DISPLAY, CALCULATE, AVERAGE, or SUM command is used.

SET HELP

Syntax

SET HELP ON/OFF
SET HELP TO *filename*

The SET HELP command turns on or off the FoxPro on-line help feature. When SET HELP is ON, pressing F1 or entering HELP as a command displays the Help window. When SET HELP is OFF, the Help window is not available.

All help commands are stored in a database file named FOXHELP.DBF. You can use the SET HELP TO *filename* command to specify a different database file. This can be useful if you are designing a custom help system for an application.

SET HELPFILTER

Syntax

SET HELPFILTER [AUTOMATIC] TO *expL*

The SET HELPFILTER command permits the display of a subset of help topics in the Help window. Only those records that meet the logical condition specified by the expression will be available in the Help window. The AUTOMATIC clause causes the filtering effect to be canceled after the Help window is closed. (You can also cancel the effects of SET HELPFILTER by issuing another SET HELPFILTER TO command without specifying an expression.)

SET HOURS

Syntax

SET HOURS TO [12/24]

The SET HOURS command changes the time display to the desired format, 12 or 24 hours. If you choose the 12-hour clock, AM or PM is displayed along with the time.

SET INDEX

Syntax

SET INDEX TO [*indexfilelist*/? [ORDER *expN*/
.idx *indexfile*/[TAG] *tagname* [OF .cdx *file*]] [ASCENDING
/DESCENDING][ADDITIVE]

The SET INDEX command opens the index file *filename*. If your file has the .IDX extension, you do not need to include the extension in the command. If a question mark is substituted in place of a file name, a list of all index files appears. The user may then select the index file to activate from the list.

You can use the ORDER, TAG, and ASCENDING/DESCENDING clauses. Use ORDER and TAG to specify a master index file or a master tag in a compound index file. Use ASCENDING or DESCENDING to specify whether the records should be accessed in ascending or descending order. For example, if an index file was originally created in ascending order, you use the DESCENDING option to force the records to be displayed or retrieved in descending order.

SET INTENSITY

Syntax

SET INTENSITY ON/OFF

The SET INTENSITY command determines whether reverse video is on or off during full-screen operations. SET INTENSITY is ON when you begin a session with FoxPro. If you change SET INTENSITY to OFF, you should generally turn on the delimiters to mark the boundaries of the data-entry area for each field.

SET KEYCOMP

Syntax

SET KEYCOMP TO DOS/WINDOWS

The SET KEYCOMP command determines whether FoxPro uses the keystroke and keystroke combinations of FoxPro for Windows or those of FoxPro for DOS. If you are familiar with FoxPro for DOS, you can enter the command SET KEYCOMP TO DOS to navigate menus and dialog boxes using the same keystrokes used by FoxPro for DOS. If you are familiar with Windows and prefer to use the keystrokes used by Windows, enter the command SET KEYCOMP TO WINDOWS.

SET LIBRARY

Syntax

SET LIBRARY TO *filename* [ADDITIVE]

The SET LIBRARY command opens external API (Application Program Interface) libraries. The use of API libraries is an advanced topic that is beyond the scope of this book; for details, refer to a more advanced programmer's text or to your FoxPro programmer's documentation.

SET LOGERRORS

Syntax

SET LOGERRORS ON/OFF

The SET LOGERRORS command determines whether FoxPro stores compilation errors in a file.

SET MARGIN

Syntax

SET MARGIN TO *expN*

The SET MARGIN command resets the left printer margin from the default of 0.

SET MARK

Syntax

SET MARK TO *expC*

The SET MARK command specifies the delimiter used to separate the month, day, and year of a date. The character expression must be a single character enclosed by quotes.

Example

```
SET MARK TO "#"
```

SET MARK OF

Syntax

SET MARK OF MENU *menuname*
 TO *expC1*/*expL1*

SET MARK OF PAD *padname*
 OF *menuname*
 TO *expC2*/*expL2*

SET MARK OF POPUP *popupname*
 TO *expC3*/*expL3*

SET MARK OF BAR *expN*
 OF *popupname*
 TO *expC4*/*expL4*

The SET MARK OF command places a check-mark character before each pad or option in user-defined menus. The character used for the check mark is specified by the character expression. The value of the logical expression may be used in the program to toggle the check mark on and off.

SET MEMOWIDTH

Syntax

SET MEMOWIDTH TO *expN*

SET MEMOWIDTH controls the width of columns containing the display or printed listings of memo-field contents. The default value provided if this command is not used is 50.

SET MESSAGE

Syntax

SET MESSAGE TO *expC*

This variation of the SET MESSAGE command identifies a user-definable message that appears at the position specified earlier with SET MESSAGE TO (see the next command).

Example

To display the message "Press F1 for assistance." on the message line, enter

```
SET MESSAGE TO "Press F1 for assistance."
```

SET MESSAGE TO

Syntax

SET MESSAGE TO [*expN*/LEFT/CENTER/RIGHT]

This variation of the SET MESSAGE command specifies the screen or window line and the optional left, center, or right placement for screen messages when the MENU TO command is used.

SET MOUSE

Syntax

SET MOUSE TO *expN*

The SET MOUSE command adjusts the sensitivity of the mouse. Values from 1 to 10 are permissible, with 1 being the least sensitive and 10 being the most sensitive. The default for the SET MOUSE command is 5.

SET NEAR

Syntax

SET NEAR ON/OFF

The SET NEAR command can be used to position the record pointer at the nearest record when a FIND or a SEEK operation is unsuccessful. If SET NEAR is ON, the record pointer is placed at the next record when the expression is not located. If SET NEAR is OFF, the record pointer is placed at the end of the file when the expression is not found.

SET ODOMETER

Syntax

SET ODOMETER TO [*expN*]

The SET ODOMETER command tells FoxPro how often commands that display a record count (such as APPEND and COPY) should update the screen display. The default value is 100, and the maximum value is 32,767. Setting ODOMETER to a higher value can speed up command execution slightly.

SET OPTIMIZE

Syntax

SET OPTIMIZE ON/OFF

The SET OPTIMIZE command enables or disables FoxPro's query-optimization techniques (also called Rushmore). FoxPro uses Rushmore, along with commands that support FOR clauses, to enhance performance. In rare cases where Rushmore should be disabled, use the SET OPTIMIZE OFF command. Note that some commands in FoxPro also support a NOOPTIMIZE option; this option disables Rushmore for the specific command.

SET ORDER

Syntax

SET ORDER TO [*expN* | *.idx indexfile*/[TAG] *tagname* [OF *.cdx file*][IN *workarea* | *alias*][ASCENDING | DESCENDING]] [ADDITIVE]

This command makes the specified index file the active index without changing the open or closed status of other index files.

You can use the TAG, IN and ASCENDING/DESCENDING clauses. Use TAG to specify a master tag in a compound index file. Use ASCENDING or DESCENDING to specify whether the records should be accessed in ascending or descending order. For example, if an index file was originally created in ascending order, you can use the DESCENDING option to force the records to be displayed or retrieved in descending order. Use the IN clause to designate the master index file or tag for a database that is open in another work area.

Example

If three index files, NAME, CITY, and STATE, have been opened in that order and STATE is the active index, to change the active index to CITY, enter

```
SET ORDER TO 2
```

SET PATH

Syntax

SET PATH TO *pathname*

The PATH command identifies a search path that will be searched for files if a file is not found in the current directory. Note that the PATH command does not alter an existing DOS path; it merely specifies a search path for database and related FoxPro files.

Example

To change the path from the default path to a path named FoxPro on drive C, enter

```
SET PATH TO C:
```

For more information on search paths, read your DOS manual (version 2.1 or later).

SET POINT

Syntax

SET POINT TO *expC*

The SET POINT command changes the character used as the decimal point. The specified expression can be any single character enclosed by quotes.

Example

```
SET POINT TO ","
```

SET PRINTER

Syntax

SET PRINTER ON/OFF

The SET PRINTER command directs output to the printer as well as to the screen. The default for SET PRINTER is OFF. (The SET PRINT ON/OFF command is identical to this command.)

SET PRINTER TO

Syntax

SET PRINTER TO LPT1/COM1/COM2/*otherDOSdevice*/*filename*

SET PRINTER TO reroutes printer output to the device or disk file specified.

SET PROCEDURE

Syntax

SET PROCEDURE TO *procedurefilename*

The SET PROCEDURE command opens a procedure file. SET PROCEDURE is placed in the command file that will reference the procedures in a procedure file or in its calling program.

SET RELATION

Syntax

SET RELATION TO [*expr1* INTO *alias*] [ADDITIVE]
[[,*expr2* INTO *alias*] [ADDITIVE]...]

The SET RELATION command links the active database to an open database in another area. If the key-expression option is used, the active file must contain that key, and the other file must be indexed on that key. The ADDITIVE option may be used to specify multiple relations out of a single work area.

Example

To set a relation between the active database and a database named PARTS using a key field named CUSTNO, enter

```
SET RELATION TO CUSTNO INTO PARTS
```

SET RELATION OFF

Syntax

SET RELATION OFF INTO *alias*

The SET RELATION OFF command breaks an existing relation between two databases. The parent database must be the currently selected database, and *alias* indicates the related (child) database; *alias* may be the alias name or a word-area number.

SET RESOURCE

Syntax

SET RESOURCE ON/OFF

The SET RESOURCE command tells FoxPro whether to save any changes made to the FoxPro environment before exiting the program. Changes are saved to the resource file (FOXUSER.DBF). If SET RESOURCE is OFF, changes will not be saved upon exiting FoxPro.

SET RESOURCE TO

Syntax

SET RESOURCE TO *filename*

The SET RESOURCE TO command tells FoxPro to use a different file as the resource file. By default, the resource file is a database named FOXUSER.DBF. You can provide another file name along with the SET RESOURCE TO command to cause that file to be used as the resource file.

SET SAFETY

Syntax

SET SAFETY ON/OFF

The SET SAFETY command determines whether a confirmation message will be provided before existing files are overwritten by commands such as SORT or COPY, or before a ZAP command is executed. SET SAFETY is normally set to ON.

SET SEPARATOR

Syntax

SET SEPARATOR TO *expC*

The SET SEPARATOR command specifies the symbol that should be used to separate hundreds in numeric amounts. The default is the comma, which is standard in U.S. currency. The expression may be any single character enclosed by quotes.

Example

```
SET SEPARATOR TO "."
```

SET SHADOWS

Syntax

SET SHADOWS ON/OFF

The SET SHADOWS command enables or disables shadows underneath windows.

SET SKIP

Syntax

SET SKIP TO [*alias1* [,*alias2*...]]

You SET SKIP command, which you use along with SET RELATION, lets you access all records within the linked file that match a particular index-key value in the parent file. Use SET SKIP to identify one-to-many relationships, where one record in the parent file is related to many records in the related, or child, file. When you use SET SKIP, subsequent LIST, DISPLAY, REPORT FORM, and LABEL FORM commands will process all records that match the expression used to define the relation, rather than just the first matching record.

SET SPACE

Syntax

SET SPACE ON/OFF

The SET SPACE command, when ON, tells FoxPro to add a space between expressions printed with the ? and ?? commands. The default for SET SPACE is ON.

Example

```
SET SPACE ON
USE ABCSTAFF
GO 1
? LASTNAME, FIRSTNAME
Morse Marcia
SET SPACE OFF
? LASTNAME, FIRSTNAME
MorseMarcia
```

SET STATUS

Syntax

SET STATUS ON/OFF

The SET STATUS command turns on or off the status display at the bottom of the screen.

SET STATUS BAR

Syntax

SET STATUS BAR ON/OFF

Use the SET STATUS BAR command to determine whether the Windows-style status bar that normally appears in FoxPro for Windows is visible. (The Windows-style status bar is displayed at the bottom of the FoxPro desktop.) Enter the command SET STATUS BAR ON to display the Windows-style status bar, or enter the command SET STATUS BAR OFF to remove it from the desktop.

SET STEP

Syntax

SET STEP ON/OFF

This is a debugging command that determines whether processing will stop each time a command in a command file is executed. The default of SET STEP is OFF.

SET STICKY

Syntax

SET STICKY ON/OFF

The SET STICKY command affects the operation of menu pads and menu pop-ups when the mouse is used. When SET STICKY is ON and a menu pad is selected with the mouse, the associated menu pop-up remains open on the screen until an option is selected (or ESC is pressed). When SET STICKY is OFF and a menu pad is selected with the mouse, the associated menu pop-up closes as soon as the mouse button is released.

SET SYSMENU

Syntax

SET SYSMENU ON/OFF/AUTOMATIC/TO [*systemmenupopuplist/ systemmenupadlist*]/TO [DEFAULT]

The SET SYSMENU command controls access to the FoxPro System menus within a program. Use ON to enable menu access, and use OFF to disable menu access. The AUTOMATIC option makes the menus visible during program execution, and options are either enabled or disabled as appropriate, depending on the current command within your program. You can use the TO clause to specify that only certain menu pads or pop-ups are available from the FoxPro System menus.

SET TALK

Syntax

SET TALK ON/OFF/WINDOW

The SET TALK command determines whether results of FoxPro commands (such as the current record number after a SKIP or LOCATE, or the results of a SUM or AVERAGE command) are displayed on the screen. The default for SET TALK is ON. The WINDOW option can be used to direct the output of SET TALK to a small window at the upper-right corner of the screen.

SET TEXTMERGE

Syntax

SET TEXTMERGE [ON/OFF] [TO [*file*] [ADDITIVE]] [WINDOW *windowname*] [SHOW/NOSHOW]

The SET TEXTMERGE command enables or disables the evaluation of database fields, variables, or the results of expressions using a text-merge operation. If SET TEXTMERGE is ON, database fields, variables, and expressions enclosed by the text-merge delimiters are evaluated and output when placed after the or \ command, or when placed between TEXT and ENDTEXT. If SET TEXTMERGE is OFF, the fields, variables, or expressions are not evaluated; instead, the actual names for the fields, variables, or expressions are output. Use the TO clause to direct the output of a text-merge operation to a file; use the ADDITIVE clause to add the output to an existing file. Use the WINDOW clause to direct output to the named window. To suppress visual output, use the NOSHOW clause; the SHOW clause can later be used to restore visual output.

SET TEXTMERGE DELIMITERS

Syntax

SET TEXTMERGE DELIMITERS [TO] [*expC1* [,*expC2*]]

Use the SET TEXTMERGE DELIMITERS command to change the default text-merge delimiters. (The default delimiters are double sets of angle brackets.) If just *expC1* is specified, the specified character is used for both delimiters. If you specify *expC1* and *expC2*, then *expC1* becomes the left delimiter and *expC2* becomes the right delimiter.

SET TOPIC

Syntax

SET TOPIC TO [*expC/expL*]

The SET TOPIC command determines how help topics are displayed. When Help is selected, a list of available topics is normally displayed; if you enter SET TOPIC TO *expC* where *expC* is the name of a help topic, that particular topic will be displayed whenever Help is selected. The logical expression *expL* is used when creating a user-defined help system.

SET TYPEAHEAD

Syntax

SET TYPEAHEAD TO *expN*

This command sets the size, in number of keystrokes, of the typeahead buffer. The default value is 20. The size of the typeahead buffer can be increased so that fast typists do not outrun the keyboard. An acceptable value is any number between 0 and 32,000.

SET UNIQUE

Syntax

SET UNIQUE ON/OFF

This command is used with the INDEX command to create lists that are free of duplicates. (The list may not be indexed adequately if there are duplicates.) When you build an index with UNIQUE set ON, there is only one index entry for each unique index key. (Note that you can achieve the same effect by adding the UNIQUE clause to the INDEX ON command.) The default setting for SET UNIQUE is OFF.

SET VIEW

Syntax

SET VIEW ON/OFF

The SET VIEW command enables or disables the View window.

SET VIEW TO

Syntax

SET VIEW TO *filename*

The SET VIEW TO command activates the named view file, placing all settings in that view file (open databases, indexes, relations, and filters) into effect.

SET WINDOW OF MEMO

Syntax

SET WINDOW OF MEMO TO *windowname*

The SET WINDOW command sets a window for use when editing the contents of memo fields. The window listed as *windowname* must have been previously defined with the DEFINE WINDOW command.

SHOW GET

Syntax

SHOW GET *variable*[, *expN* [PROMPT *expC*]] [ENABLE/ DISABLE] [LEVEL *expN*] [COLOR *colorpairslist*/COLOR SCHEME *expN*]

The SHOW GET command redisplays a single GET field or object. When the field or object is redisplayed, editing can be enabled or disabled with the ENABLE/DISABLE clauses. The PROMPT clause can be used to display a character expression as a prompt for the object. Use the LEVEL clause to display a field or object on a READ level other than the current one. Use the COLOR or COLOR SCHEME clause to set the colors for the object. Note that in FoxPro for Windows, color commands and options change only the colors used by *user-defined* windows and menus; all other elements under Windows must be changed through the Windows color option in the Control Panel.

SHOW GETS

Syntax

SHOW GETS *variable* [ENABLE/DISABLE] [LEVEL *expN*] [WINDOW *windowname*] [COLOR *colorpairslist*/COLOR SCHEME *expN*]

The SHOW GETS command redisplays all GET fields or objects. When the fields or objects are redisplayed, editing can be enabled or disabled with the ENABLE/DISABLE clauses. The WINDOW clause can be used to display the fields or objects in a window. Use the LEVEL clause to display fields or objects on a READ level other than the current one. Use the COLOR or COLOR SCHEME clause to set the colors for the objects. Note that in FoxPro for Windows, color commands and options change only the colors used by *user-defined* windows and menus; all other elements under Windows must be changed through the Windows color option in the Control Panel.

SHOW MENU

Syntax

SHOW MENU *menuname*/ALL [PAD *padname*] [SAVE]

The SHOW MENU command displays a menu without activating the menu. The command is primarily used in the program-design process to check the visual appearance of a menu. The ALL option causes all menus to be shown. The SAVE option places images of menus on the screen. This option is normally used for testing and debugging programs.

SHOW OBJECT

Syntax

SHOW OBJECT *expN* [PROMPT *expC*] [ENABLE/DISABLE] [LEVEL *expN*] [COLOR *colorpairslist*/COLOR SCHEME *expN*]

The SHOW OBJECT command redisplays a single GET field or object. The SHOW OBJECT command differs from SHOW GET in that SHOW OBJECT refers to the field or object by the object number; SHOW GET refers to the field or object by name (field name, variable name, or array-element name). When the field or object is redisplayed, editing can be enabled or disabled with the ENABLE/DISABLE clauses. The PROMPT clause can be used to display a character expression as a prompt for the object. Use the LEVEL clause to display a field or object on a READ level other than the current one. Use the COLOR or COLOR SCHEME clause to set the colors for the object. Note that in FoxPro for Windows, color commands and options change only the colors used by *user-defined* windows and menus; all other elements under Windows must be changed through the Windows color option in the Control Panel.

SHOW POPUP

Syntax

SHOW POPUP *popupname*/ALL [SAVE]

The SHOW POPUP command displays a pop-up menu without activating the menu. The command is primarily used in the program-design process to check the visual appearance of a menu. The ALL option causes all pop-ups to be shown. The SAVE option is used to place images of pop-ups on the screen. This option is normally used for testing and debugging programs.

SHOW WINDOW

Syntax

SHOW WINDOW *windowname*/ALL [SAVE] [TOP/BOTTOM/SAME]

The SHOW WINDOW command displays a window without activating the window. The command is primarily used in the program design process to check the visual appearance of a window. The ALL option causes all windows to be shown. Use BOTTOM or TOP to place a window at the bottom or top of a stack of existing windows. The SAME option applies only to windows previously hidden with DEACTIVATE WINDOW or HIDE WINDOW. Use SAME to put the previously hidden window back in the same position it occupied earlier. The SAVE option places images of the window on the screen. This option is normally used for testing and debugging programs.

SIZE POPUP

Syntax

SIZE POPUP *popupname* TO *expN1,expN2*
SIZE POPUP *popupname* BY *expN3,expN4*

The SIZE POPUP command resizes a pop-up menu. If the TO clause is used, the pop-up will be changed to the new size, where *expN1* is the new size in rows and *expN2* is the new size in columns. If the BY clause is used, the pop-up will be changed relative to its existing size, with *expN3* representing rows and *expN4* representing columns; for example, the command SIZE POPUP BY 4,3 would make an existing pop-up four rows larger and three columns wider.

SKIP

Syntax

SKIP *expN* [IN *aliasname*]

The SKIP command moves the record pointer. SKIP moves one record forward if no value is specified. Values can be expressed as memory variables or as constants. The IN *aliasname* option can be used to move the record pointer within a file in another work area.

Example

To skip two records back, enter

```
SKIP -2
```

SORT

Syntax

SORT TO *filename* ON *field1* [/A][/C][/D] [*,field2* [/A][/C][/D]...] [ASCENDING/DESCENDING] [*scope*] [FOR *condition*] [WHILE *condition*] [FIELDS *fieldlist*][NOOPTIMIZE]

The SORT command creates a rearranged copy of a database. The order of the new database depends on the fields and options specified. The /C option creates a sorted file in dictionary order, where there is no differentiation between upper- and lowercase. Use /A for ascending order on a specific field, /D for descending order on a specific field. Use the ASCENDING or DESCENDING options to specify ascending or descending order for all fields. (The /A or /D option can be used with any field to override the effects of the ASCENDING or DESCENDING option.) The FIELDS option may be used to specify fields to be included in the sorted file; if omitted, all fields are included. You can sort up to 10 fields in a single sort; you cannot sort on memo fields or on logical fields. The NOOPTIMIZE clause turns off FoxPro's internal optimization (also known as Rushmore).

Example

To sort a database on the Lastname and then Firstname field, both in descending order, and output the sorted file to a file named NEWNAME, enter

```
SORT TO NEWNAME ON LASTNAME, FIRSTNAME DESCENDING
```

STORE

Syntax

STORE *expr* TO *memvarlist/arrayelementlist*

The STORE command creates a memory variable and stores a value to that variable or to the named array.

Example

To multiply a field called Salary for the current record by 1.05 and store it in the new memory variable named NEWAMT, enter

```
STORE SALARY * 1.05 TO NEWAMT
```

SUM

Syntax

SUM [*scope*] [*fieldlist*] [TO *memvarlist*] [TO ARRAY *arrayname*] [FOR *condition*] [WHILE *condition*][NOOPTIMIZE]

The SUM command provides a sum total of *fieldlist* involving numeric fields. If the TO option is not used, the sum is displayed (assuming SET TALK is ON) but not stored in memory. If the TO option is used, the sum is displayed (assuming SET TALK is ON) and is stored as the specified memory variable. If the *scope* option is not used, ALL is assumed by FoxPro. The FOR option can be used to specify a condition that must be met before an entry in a field can be summed. If you use the WHILE option, records will be summed until the condition is no longer true. The TO ARRAY option stores the values summed to the elements of the named array. Use the NOOPTIMIZE clause turns off FoxPro's internal optimization (also known as Rushmore).

Example

To total the contents of two specified fields (Salary and Taxes) and store those sums to the memory variables A and B, enter

```
SUM SALARY, TAXES TO A,B
```

SUSPEND

Syntax

SUSPEND

The SUSPEND command suspends execution of a command file or procedure and returns program control to the command level, while leaving current memory variables intact. Execution of the command file or procedure can be restarted where it was interrupted, with the RESUME command.

TEXT

Syntax

TEXT
text to be displayed
ENDTEXT

The TEXT command displays blocks of text from a command file. If SET PRINT is ON, the text will be printed.

Note that expressions (including field names), memory variables, and functions placed between TEXT and ENDTEXT statements will be evaluated if SET TEXTMERGE is ON. If SET TEXTMERGE is OFF, expressions, variables, and functions are output as literal characters, including the text-merge delimiters. For example, a line between a TEXT and ENDTEXT statement containing the expression <<TIME( )>> would appear as <<TIME( )>> if SET TEXTMERGE were OFF. The same expression would appear as the current time according to the computer's clock if SET TEXTMERGE were ON.

Example

```
TEXT
Press the RETURN key to run the payroll.
Or press the ESCAPE key to exit.
ENDTEXT
```

TOTAL

Syntax

TOTAL TO *filename* ON *key* [*scope*] [FIELDS *fieldlist*] [FOR *condition*] [WHILE *condition*][NOOPTIMIZE]

The TOTAL command adds the numeric fields in a database and creates a new database containing the results. The file to be totaled must be indexed or sorted on the key field. If the FIELDS *fieldlist* option is used, fields totaled will be limited to those fields named in the list. If the *scope* option is not used, the quantifier of ALL is assumed, meaning all records in the database will be totaled unless you use the FOR or WHILE option. The FOR option can be used to specify a condition that must be met for the fields to be totaled. If you use the WHILE option, records will be totaled until the condition is no longer true. Use the NOOPTIMIZE clause to turn off FoxPro's internal optimization (also know as Rushmore).

Example

To total the Salary, Fedtax, Statetax, and Fica fields in a database named PAYROLL and store those totals to a second database named RECORDS, you could use commands like these:

```
USE PAYROLL
TOTAL TO NEWFIL ON FIELDS SALARY, FEDTAX, STATETAX, FICA
```

TYPE

Syntax

TYPE *filename.ext* [TO PRINT/TO FILE *filename*] [NUMBER]

The TYPE command displays the contents of a disk file on screen. If the TO PRINT option is used, the file will be printed. The TO FILE option directs the output of the TYPE command to a named disk file. The NUMBER option causes line numbers to be included.

UPDATE

Syntax

UPDATE [RANDOM] ON *keyfield* FROM *alias* REPLACE *field* WITH *expr* [*,field2* WITH *expr2...*]

The UPDATE command uses data from a database specified by *alias* to make changes to the database in use. The value in the matching record in the file you are updating from is added to the value in the active file.

Example

To update the Rentamt field in a database named WORLDWIDE, based on the contents of the Rentamt field in a database named CURRENCY, enter

```
SELECT 2
USE CURRENCY
SELECT 1
USE WORLDWIDE INDEX LASTNAME
UPDATE ON LASTNAME FROM CURRENCY REPLACE RENTAMT
WITH CURRENCY->RENTAMT RANDOM
```

Both files must be sorted or indexed on the key field unless RANDOM is included, in which case only *alias* need be indexed.

USE

Syntax

USE [*databasefile*/?] [IN *workarea*] [AGAIN] [INDEX *indexfilelist*/? [ORDER [*expN*/.*idx indexfile*/[TAG] *tagname* [OF .*cdx file*] [ASCENDING/DESCENDING]]]] [ALIAS *alias*] [EXCLUSIVE] [NOUPDATE]

The USE command opens a database file and related index files in a work area. If the ? is used in place of the database file name, a list of available files appears. Use the INDEX option to specify index files that will be open or active. Use the ALIAS option to open the file in a different work area. Entering the USE command without specifying a file name will close the file that is currently open.

Use the AGAIN clause to open the same database simultaneously in a different work area. The ORDER and TAG clauses can be used to designate the master index file or the master tag of a compound index file. The ASCENDING and DESCENDING clauses may be used to determine whether records are displayed and retrieved in ascending or descending order. For example, if the index file opened with the database was originally created in descending order, the ASCENDING clause would cause the records to be accessed in ascending order.

The ALIAS clause may be used to assign an alternate name, or alias, to the database. Work areas may then be selected by referring to the word-area number, the database name, or the alias. The EXCLUSIVE clause has an effect only under FoxPro/LAN; it causes the database to be opened for exclusive use, and other network users cannot use the database until it is closed. The NOUPDATE clause prevents changes to the database file.

WAIT

Syntax

WAIT [*expC*] [TO *memvar*]

The WAIT command halts operation of a command file until a key is pressed. If a character expression is included, it will be displayed on the screen. If the TO option is used, the key pressed will be stored as a memory variable.

ZAP

Syntax

ZAP

The ZAP command removes all records from the active database file. The ZAP command is equivalent to a DELETE ALL command followed by a PACK command.

ZOOM WINDOW

Syntax

ZOOM WINDOW *windowname* MIN/MAX/NORM [AT *row1,col1*/ FROM *row1,col1* [SIZE *row2,col2*/TO *row2,col2*]]

The ZOOM WINDOW command changes the size of a window. Windows can be reduced to minimum size (minimized), enlarged to maximum size (maximized), or sized anywhere in between. The MIN clause minimizes the named window, and the MAX clause maximizes the named window. Note that if a window is a child window (a window within a window), the window can maximized only up to the size of the parent window. The NORM clause can be used to return a window to its original size, after it was minimized or maximized.

The AT and FROM clauses can be used to restore a minimized or maximized window to a different location. The *row1,col1* coordinates specify the upper-left corner of the window. The optional *row2,col2* coordinates specify the lower-right corner of the window. If the second set of coordinates is omitted, the window takes on the same size as it had before it was minimized or maximized.

APPENDIX

Glossary of Functions

This appendix summarizes the FoxPro functions. Following the name of each function is the function's syntax and a description of its purpose. For a similar summary of FoxPro commands, see Appendix A.

Because this is a beginning-to-intermediate level text, some functions and options relating to advanced programming are not covered in detail here. Refer to your FoxPro documentation for additional information about these functions.

Glossary Symbols and Conventions

1. All functions are printed in UPPERCASE, although you can enter them in either upper- or lowercase letters.

2. The term *expC* indicates a character expression, *expN* indicates a numeric expression, and *expL* indicates a logical expression. Where data type does not matter, the term *expr* is used.

3. Whenever a function calls for or permits an *alias* argument, you can use the alias name (in quotes), or you can use the work-area number or letter.

4. Any part of a parameter that is enclosed by [ ] (left and right brackets) is optional.

5. An ellipsis (...) following a parameter means that the parameter can be repeated infinitely; that is, until you exhaust the memory of the computer or reach the limit of 1024 characters on a single program line.

Summary of Functions

ABS

Syntax

ABS(*expN*)

The ABS function returns the absolute (positive) value of the specified numeric expression.

ACOPY

Syntax

ACOPY(*array1, array2* [, *expN1* [, *expN2* [, *expN3*]]])

The ACOPY function copies elements of the array named in *array1* to the elements of the array named in *array2*. The number of elements copied to the destination array is returned if the copy is successful; otherwise, a value of –1 is returned. *ExpN1*, which is optional, denotes the starting position in the source array. *ExpN2* is the number of elements to copy, beginning with *expN1*. If *expN2* is omitted, the copying begins at the first element of the array. *ExpN3*, which is also optional, denotes the starting element in the target array. If *expN3* is omitted, the copying begins at the first element in the target array.

ACOS

Syntax

ACOS(*expN*)

The ACOS function returns the arccosine of *expN*, as measured in radians between 0 and +pi (3.14159). Allowable values for *expN* are from +1 to –1.

ADEL

Syntax

ADEL (*array*, *expN* [,2])

The ADEL function deletes a single element within an array, or it deletes a row or column from a two-dimensional array. If the deletion is successful, a value of 1 is returned; otherwise, –1 is returned. *Array* denotes the name of the array, and *expN* identifies the element to delete. For example, if *expN* is 3, the third element in the array is deleted. Also note that when an array element is deleted with ADEL, the element is not left blank; instead, the contents of all remaining elements after the deleted element are shifted forward by one element, leaving the last element unused and set to a logical "False" (.F.) value. The optional ,2 argument is used to specify that the deletion take place in a two-dimensional array rather than a one-dimensional array. When the option is used, a column is deleted rather than a single element.

ADIR

Syntax

ADIR(*array* [,*expC1* [, *expC2*]])

The ADIR function fills array elements with information from a disk directory. *Array* is the name of the array where the file information is to be stored. *ExpC1* is any DOS file skeleton. The array will be filled with file names, sizes, creation dates and times, and DOS attributes for all files matching the skeleton. *ExpC2*, which is optional, specifies additional information that is to be returned—D for subdirectory information, H for hidden files, S for system files, and V for volume names.

AELEMENT

Syntax

AELEMENT(*array*, *expN1* [, *expN2*])

The AELEMENT function returns the element number of an array element, based on the row and column location for that element. (Array elements can be referred to in one of two ways: by element number or by row-and-column location. Use AELEMENT to convert a row-and-column location to an element number.) *Array* is the name of the array; *expN1* is the row location; and *expN2*, which is used with two-dimensional arrays, is the column location.

AFIELDS

Syntax

AFIELDS(*array*)

The AFIELDS function fills array elements with four field attributes—name, type, length, and number of decimal places—from the current work area. These attributes are the contents of the four columns that normally appear as a result of the LIST STRUCTURE command. Field names are stored in the first column, and the contents of the column will be character elements. Field types are stored in the second column, and the contents of the column will be character elements containing a single letter—C for character, D for date, L for logical, M for memo, N for numeric, or F for floating. Field lengths are stored in the third column, and the contents of the column will be numeric elements. The number of decimal places for the fields is stored in the fourth column, and the contents of the column will be numeric elements.

AFONT

Syntax

AFONT(*array* [,*expC* [,*expN*]])

The AFONT function places the names of available Windows fonts into an array. You can also use AFONT to determine available font sizes, or if a font is scalable. (Use GETFONT() to display a dialog box containing available Windows fonts, and font sizes and styles.) *Array* is the name of the array that receives the names of the available Windows fonts. If the specified array does not exist, FoxPro creates it; if the array exists but is not large enough to contain all the fonts, the size of the array is automatically increased as needed. If the array is successfully created, AFONT() returns a logical "True" (.T.); otherwise AFONT() returns a logical "False" (.F.).

Use the optional *expC* to create an array that contains the available font sizes for a specific font. If the font you specify in *expC* does not support scalable fonts, the available font sizes are stored to the array and

AFONT() returns a logical "True" (.T.). If the font you specify in *expC* is scalable (it supports fractional font size values), a single element containing -1 is stored to the array, and AFONT() returns a logical "True" (.T.). If the font you specify in *expC* is not available, a single element containing "False" (.F.) is stored to the array and AFONT() returns a logical "False" (.F.).

Include *expN* to determine if a specific font size is available for a font. If the font size *expN* is available for the font specified in *expC*, a single element containing a logical "True" (.T.) is stored to the array, and AFONT() returns a logical "True" (.T.). If the font size is not available for the specified font, a single element containing "False" (.F.) is stored to the array, and AFONT() returns a logical "False" (.F.).

AINS

Syntax

AINS(*array*, *expN* [,2])

The AINS function inserts a new element into an existing array. *Array* is the name of the array that receives the new element, and *expN* is an element number for one-dimensional arrays or a row number or column number for two-dimensional arrays. The optional ,2 argument specifies that the insertion takes place in a two-dimensional array rather than a one-dimensional array. When the option is used, a column is inserted rather than a single element.

Note that when the new element is inserted, the last element of the array is discarded, and all remaining elements following the new element are moved back by one position. If the insertion is successful, a value of 1 is returned; otherwise, a value of –1 is returned.

ALEN

Syntax

ALEN(*array* [, *expN*]

The ALEN function returns the number of elements, rows, or columns in an array. *Array* is the array name, and *expN* denotes whether the function should return the number of elements, rows, or columns. If *expN* is 0 (or if *expN* is omitted), the number of elements is returned. If *expN* is 1, the number of rows is returned. If *expN* is 2, the number of columns is returned.

ALIAS

Syntax

ALIAS([*expN*/*expC*])

The ALIAS function returns the alias of the database open in the work area specified by *expN*, or the work-area number specified by *expC*. If *expN* or *expC* is omitted, ALIAS returns the alias of the current work area.

ALLTRIM

Syntax

ALLTRIM(*expC*)

ALLTRIM returns the character expression *expC* minus any leading and trailing blanks.

ANSITOOEM

Syntax

ANSITOOEM(*expC*)

The ANSITOOEM function is used to move data from FoxPro for Windows to FoxPro for DOS. ANSITOOEM( ) converts each character in *expC* to a corresponding character in the MS-DOS (OEM) character set. The character expression *expC* should contain characters from the ANSI character set.

If a character in *expC* has no MS-DOS equivalent, the character is converted to a similar MS-DOS character.

ASC

Syntax

ASC*(expC)*

The ASC function returns the decimal ASCII code for the leftmost character in *expC*.

ASCAN

Syntax

ASCAN(*array, expr* [, *expN1* [, *expN2*]])

The ASCAN function scans an array, searching for a particular value. *Array* names the array to be scanned, and *expr* denotes the data to search for. The expression can be any data type. *ExpN1*, which is optional, denotes the starting element where the search will begin; if it is omitted, ASCAN begins with the first element. *ExpN2*, which is also optional, denotes the number of elements that should be searched; if it is omitted, ASCAN searches to the end of the array.

ASCAN returns a numeric value, indicating the position of the data in the array. If ASCAN cannot find the data, a value of 0 is returned.

Note that ASCAN does respect the status of SET EXACT. If SET EXACT is ON, the contents of the array element must precisely match the contents of *expr*, both in length and content. If SET EXACT is OFF, the contents of *expr* are tested from left to right until a match is found; any remaining characters in the array element are ignored.

ASIN

Syntax

ASIN(*expN*)

The ASIN function returns the arcsine of *expN*, as measured in radians between –pi/2 and +pi/2 (SY-1.57079 to 1.57079). Acceptable values for *expN* are from +1 to –1.

ASORT

Syntax

ASORT(*array* [, *ExpN1* [, *expN2* [, *expN3*]]])

The ASORT function sorts an array, arranging the array elements in ascending order. *Array* denotes the name of the array. *ExpN1*, which is optional, is a numeric value that denotes the element at which to start the sort. If *expN1* is omitted, the sort begins with the first element. *ExpN2*, which is used along with *expN1*, is a numeric value that denotes the column where sorting starts; when *expN2* is used, *expN1* is then assumed to be the row where sorting starts. *ExpN3* denotes a sort order—0 for ascending or 1 for descending.

ASUBSCRIPT

Syntax

ASUBSCRIPT(*array*, *expN1*, *expN2*)

The ASUBSCRIPT function returns the row or column location of an array element, based on an element's number. (Array elements can be referred to in one of two ways: by element number or by row-and-column location. Use ASUBSCRIPT to convert an element number to a row-and-column location.) *Array* is the name of the array. *ExpN1* is the element number.

ExpN2, which is used with two-dimensional arrays, must be 1 if the row location is desired, or 2 if the column location is desired.

AT

Syntax

AT(*expC1*, *expC2* [, *expN*])

The AT function finds *expC1* in *expC2*. (Note that *expC2* may be a memo field.) The function returns as an integer the starting position of *expC1*. If *expC1* is not found, the function returns a 0. If the optional *expN* is used, the *expN*th occurrence of *expC1* is searched for.

ATAN

Syntax

ATAN(*expN*)

The ATAN function returns the arctangent of *expN*, as measured in radians between –pi/2 and +pi/2 (–1.57079 to 1.57079). *ExpN* can be any value.

ATC

Syntax

ATC(*expC1*, *expC2*[,*expN*])

The ATC function searches a character string *expC1* for another character string *expC2*. If *expC1* is not found, the function returns a 0. If the optional *expN* is used, the *expN*th occurrence of *expC1* is searched for. The ATC function operates just like the AT function, but the ATC function is not case sensitive.

ATCLINE

Syntax

ATCLINE(*expC1*, *expC2*)

The ATCLINE function finds *expC1* within *expC2* and then returns the line number where it was found. *ExpC2* can be a memo field. If *expC1* is not found in *expC2*, the function returns a 0. ATCLINE is not case sensitive; the ATLINE function performs the same task but is case sensitive. ATCLINE is usually used to locate text within a memo field and return the line number containing the desired text.

ATLINE

Syntax

ATLINE(*expC1*, *expC2*)

The ATLINE function finds *expC2* within *expC1* and then returns (as an integer) the line number where it was found. If *expC1* is not found in *expC2*, the function returns a 0.

ATN2

Syntax

ATN2(*expN1*, *expN2*)

The ATN2 function returns the arctangent angle (as measured in radians) for all four quadrants. You specify the X and Y coordinates (or sine and cosine of the angle) instead of specifying the tangent value as with the ATAN function. *ExpN1* is the X coordinate or sine of the angle, and *expN2* is the Y coordinate, or cosine of the angle.

BAR

Syntax

BAR()

The BAR function returns the number of the option most recently selected from the active pop-up menu. Use the DEFINE BAR command to assign each menu item a number. If no pop-up menu is active, the BAR function returns a 0.

BETWEEN

Syntax

BETWEEN(*expr1*, *expr2*, *expr3*)

The BETWEEN function returns a logical "True" (.T.) if *expr1* is greater than or equal to *expr2* and less than or equal to *expr3;* otherwise, the function returns a logical "False" (.F.). The expressions used must be of the same type.

BOF

Syntax

BOF([*alias*])

The BOF function returns a logical "True" (.T.) if the record pointer is at the beginning of file (above the first record in the database file). Use the optional *alias* to test for the beginning of the file in a different work area.

CAPSLOCK

Syntax

CAPSLOCK([*expL*])

The CAPSLOCK function turns the CAPS LOCK keyboard mode on or off, or it returns the current state of CAPS LOCK. The CAPSLOCK(.T.) function turns the CAPS LOCK mode on, and CAPSLOCK(.F.) turns the CAPS LOCK mode off. If *expL* is omitted, the status of CAPS LOCK is returned without changing the state of the keyboard.

CDOW

Syntax

CDOW(*expD*)

The CDOW function returns the name of the day of the week for the given date expression.

CDX

Syntax

CDX(*expN* [, *alias*])

The CDX function returns the names of open compound index (.CDX) files. Note that the CDX function is identical in operation to the MDX function. *ExpN* is a numeric value that identifies the desired compound index file, according to the following possibilities. If the database has a structural compound index file and *expN1* is 1, the name of the structural compound index file is returned. If *expN1* is 2, the name of the first .CDX compound index file (as identified by the INDEX clause of the USE command, or the SET INDEX command) is returned. If *expN1* is 3, the second .CDX compound index file name is returned, and so forth. If *expN1* is greater than the number of open .CDX compound index files, the function returns a null string.

If the database does not have a structural compound index file and *expN1* is 1, the name of the first .CDX compound index file (as identified by the INDEX clause of the USE command, or by the SET INDEX command) is returned. If *expN1* is 2, the second .CDX compound index file name is returned, and so forth. If *expN1* is greater than the number of open .CDX compound index files, the function returns a null string.

Use the *alias* option to return the names of compound index files open in different work areas.

CEILING

Syntax

CEILING(*expN*)

The CEILING function returns the nearest integer greater than or equal to *expN*. Positive numbers with decimals are rounded up to the next highest number, and negative numbers with decimals are rounded up to the number next closest to 0.

CHR

Syntax

CHR(*expN*)

The CHR function returns the character whose decimal ASCII code is equivalent to *expN*.

CHRSAW

Syntax

CHRSAW([*expN*])

The CHRSAW function checks the keyboard buffer for the presence of a character and returns a logical "True" (.T.) if a character is found there. The optional *expN* specifies the number of seconds to wait for a keypress before returning the value.

CHRTRAN

Syntax

CHRTRAN(*expC1*, *expC2*, *expC3*)

The CHRTRAN function translates the characters of *expC1*. The strings in *expC2* and *expC3* are used as a translation table. Any occurrences of the first character in *expC2* are replaced by the first character in *expC3*, the second character in *expC2* by the second character in *expC3*, and so forth.

CMONTH

Syntax

CMONTH(*expD*)

The CMONTH function returns the name of the month that corresponds to the date expression.

CNTBAR

Syntax

CNTBAR(*popupname*)

The CNTBAR function returns the number of bars in the named pop-up menu.

CNTPAD

Syntax

CNTPAD(*popupname*)

The CNTPAD function returns the number of menu pads in the named menu bar.

COL

Syntax

COL()

The COL function returns the current column location of the cursor.

COS

Syntax

COS(*expN*)

The COS function returns the cosine of *expN* as measured in radians. To convert an angle from degrees to radians, use the DTOR function.

CTOD

Syntax

CTOD(*expC*)

The CTOD function returns the date value that corresponds to *expC* in the default date format (generally *MM/DD/YY*). Use the SET DATE and SET CENTURY commands to change the default format.

CURDIR

Syntax

CURDIR([*expC*])

The CURDIR function returns the current DOS directory on the drive identified by *expC*. If no such drive exists, CURDIR returns a null string. If *expC* is omitted, the default drive is assumed.

DATE

Syntax

DATE()

The DATE function returns the current system date.

DAY

Syntax

DAY(*expD*)

The DAY function returns the numeric day of the month that corresponds to the date expression.

DBF

Syntax

DBF([*alias*])

The DBF function returns the database file name for the file open in the specified work area. If no *alias* is specified, the DBF function returns the file name for the currently selected work area. If no file is open in the work area, the function returns a null string.

DDE functions

The DDE (Dynamic Data Exchange) functions listed below can be used in the exchange of data between FoxPro for Windows and other Windows applications. These are complex functions used in advanced programming; for more details on these functions, refer to your FoxPro documentation.

Function	Use
DDEAbortTrans()	Abort an asynchronous DDE transaction
DDEAdvise()	Establish a warm or hot link to a server application
DDEEnabled()	Set or return the DDE status
DDEExecute()	Send an execute message to a server application
DDEInitiate()	Open a DDE channel to a server application

DDELastError()	Return an error code for the last error caused by a DDE function
DDEPoke()	Send data to a client or server application
DDERequest()	Request data from a server application
DDESetOption()	Change or return DDE settings
DDESetService()	Add, remove, or change the status of services
DDESetTopic()	Associate a topic with a service
DDETerminate()	Close a DDE channel

DELETED

Syntax

DELETED([alias])

The DELETED function returns a logical "True" (.T.) if the current record is marked for deletion; otherwise, it returns a logical "False" (.F.). Use the optional alias to test for deleted records in an unselected work area.

DIFFERENCE

Syntax

DIFFERENCE(expC1, expC2)

The DIFFERENCE function returns a numeric value between 0 and 4, representing the phonetic difference between two character strings, expC1 and expC2. The DIFFERENCE function can be useful for searching databases when the precise spelling of an entry is not known.

DISKSPACE

Syntax

DISKSPACE()

The DISKSPACE function returns the number of bytes available on the default drive.

DMY

Syntax

DMY(*expD*)

The DMY function returns a date expression in European format (*DD-Month-YY*) for the given date expression.

DOW

Syntax

DOW(*expD*)

The DOW function returns the numeric day of the week corresponding to the date expression. The value returned ranges from 1 (for Sunday) to 7 (for Saturday).

DTOC

Syntax

DTOC(*expD* [,1])

The DTOC function returns a character string containing the date that corresponds to the date expression. Use the SET DATE and the SET CENTURY commands to change the format of the string. The optional ,1 argument causes DTOC to return the string in the *YYYYMMDD* format, similar to the DTOS function.

DTOR

Syntax

DTOR(*expN*)

The DTOR function converts the angle specified by *expN* from degrees to radians.

DTOS

Syntax

DTOS(*expD*)

The DTOS function returns a character string in the format *YYYYMMDD* for the given date expression. This function is useful when indexing on a date field.

EMPTY

Syntax

EMPTY(*expr*)

The EMPTY function returns a logical "True" (.T.) if the expression *expr* is blank. The function will also return a value of "True" if the expression is a numeric expression with a value of 0 or a logical expression with a value of "False."

EOF

Syntax

EOF([*alias*])

The EOF function returns a logical "True" (.T.) if the end-of-file marker is reached (the record pointer passes the last record in the database, or a FIND, LOCATE, or SEEK command was unsuccessful). Use the optional *alias* to test for the end-of-file marker in a different work area. Note that if you establish a relation with SET RELATION and the related file does not contain a record with the key matching the current record, the record pointer will be at the end-of-file marker in the related file.

ERROR

Syntax

ERROR()

The ERROR function returns the number of the error causing the ON ERROR condition. An ON ERROR routine must be in effect for the ERROR function to return a value other than 0.

EVALUATE

Syntax

EVALUATE(*expC*)

The EVALUATE function evaluates a character expression and returns the result. The expression must be a character string enclosed in quotes, and the character string may contain a character expression, variable, or database field name.

EXP

Syntax

EXP(*expN*)

The EXP function returns the value of e raised to *n*th power. *ExpN* is the exponent, *N*, in the equation e ^ N. The value of e is roughly 2.71828 (the base of natural logarithms).

FCHSIZE

Syntax

FCHSIZE(*expN1, expN2*)

The FCHSIZE function changes the size of a file opened with a low-level file function. *ExpN1* is the file handle, returned by the FOPEN() function when you open a file for low-level use or by FCREATE() if you have just created the file. (If a file is opened with FOPEN(), it must be opened with write or read/write privileges to change its size.) *ExpN2* is the size you want the file to be. If *expN2* is less than the original file size, the file will be truncated. If *expN2* is greater than the original file size, the file's size is increased as needed.

The FCHSIZE function returns the final size of the file, in bytes. If FCHSIZE is unable to change the file size (usually due to insufficient disk space, or because an invalid file handle has been specified) the function returns a value of -1.

FCLOSE

Syntax

FCLOSE(*expN*)

The FCLOSE function flushes to disk the buffers for the file with the numeric file handle specified by *expN*, and closes the file. Use the FCREATE or FOPEN function to assign a file handle to the file.

FCOUNT

Syntax

FCOUNT([*alias*])

The FCOUNT function returns the number of fields in a database. Use the [*alias*] option to return the number of fields in a database that is open in an unselected work area.

FCREATE

Syntax

FCREATE(*expC*[, *expN*])

The FCREATE function creates a new file named *expC* and opens the file for use. If a file with the name *expC* already exists, the existing file is overwritten. FCREATE also assigns the file a numeric "handle" to identify the file when other low-level file functions are used. By default, the file will have a DOS read/write attribute assigned. The optional numeric expression can be used to specify the attribute of the file created, using one of the following values:

0	Read/write (default)
1	Read-only
2	Hidden
3	Read-only/hidden
4	System
5	Read-only/system
6	System/hidden
7	Read-only/system/hidden

FEOF

Syntax

FEOF(*expN*)

The FEOF function returns a logical "True" (.T.) if the file pointer is positioned at the end-of-file (EOF) marker. *ExpN* indicates the numeric handle of the file that you wish to test for the end-of-file marker.

FERROR

Syntax

FERROR()

The FERROR function tests whether a low-level file function has been successful. FERROR returns a 0 if the last low-level function was successfully performed. If the last function was not successful, a value not equal to 0 is returned.

FFLUSH

Syntax

FFLUSH(*expN*)

The FFLUSH function flushes the file whose handle is *expN*. If the file was written to, FFLUSH writes all data in the buffers to disk.

FGETS

Syntax

FGETS(*expN1*1[, expN2])

The FGETS function returns a series of bytes from the file having the file handle specified by *expN1*. FGETS returns a series of bytes from a file until a carriage return is encountered. The optional numeric argument *expN2* can be used to specify the number of bytes that the function will return.

FIELD

Syntax

FIELD(*expN1*[, *alias*])

The FIELD function returns the name of the field in the active database that corresponds to the numeric position specified in the expression. If there is no corresponding field in the active database, FIELD returns a null string. Use the optional *alias* to return a field name from a database that is open in an unselected work area.

FILE

Syntax

FILE(*expC*)

The FILE function returns a logical "True" (.T.) if the character expression matches the name for an existing file in the default directory. If no such file can be found, the FILE function returns a logical "False" (.F.).

FILTER

Syntax

FILTER([alias])

The FILTER function returns the filter expression of the current work area. Use the optional alias to return a filter from an unselected work area. If no filter is in effect, a null string is returned.

FKLABEL

Syntax

FKLABEL(expN)

The FKLABEL function returns the name of the function key that corresponds to expN.

FKMAX

Syntax

FKMAX( )

The FKMAX function returns the number of programmable function keys available on your keyboard.

FLOOR

Syntax

FLOOR(expN)

The FLOOR function returns the nearest integer value less than or equal to the numeric expression. All positive numbers with a decimal will be rounded down to the next lowest number, and all negative numbers with a decimal will be rounded down to the next number farther from 0.

FONTMETRIC

Syntax

FONTMETRIC (*expN1*, [,*expC1*, ,*expN2*, [,*expC2*,]])

The FONTMETRIC function returns font attributes for the current font for the desktop or active output window. To return font attributes for a specific font, include *expC1* to specify the font, *expN2* to specify the font's size, and *expC2* to specify a special font style.

The following table shows the values for *expN1* and the corresponding font attribute that is returned:

expN1	Attribute
1	Character height in pixels
2	Character ascent (units above baseline) in pixels
3	Character descent (units below baseline) in pixels
4	Leading (space between lines) in pixels
5	Extra leading in pixels
6	Average character width in pixels
7	Maximum character width in pixels
8	Font weight
9	Italic (0 = No, Nonzero = Yes)
10	Underlined (0 = No, Nonzero = Yes)
11	Strikeout (0 = No, Nonzero = Yes)
12	First character defined in the font
13	Last character defined in the font
14	Default character (substituted for characters not in the font)
15	Word break character
16	Pitch and family
17	Character set
18	Overhang (extra added width)

| 19 | Horizontal aspect for the font device |
| 20 | Vertical aspect for the font device |

To return an attribute for a specific installed font, include the font's name in *expC1*. Include the font's size (in points) in *expN2* for the font specified with *expC1*.

Include a font style code in *expC2* to return an attribute for a specific font style. If *expC2* is omitted, the attribute is returned for the normal font style. The following table shows the values for *exp2:*

Character	Font style
B	Bold
I	Italic
N	Normal
O	Outline
S	Shadow
-	Strikeout
T	Transparent
U	Underline

FOPEN

Syntax

FOPEN(*expC* [, *expN*])

The FOPEN function opens the file named by *expC*. *ExpC* may include a full path name for files on drives or in directories that are not in the current search path. The optional numeric expression can be used to specify an attribute of read-only, read/write, or write-only. Use 0 for read-only (the default), 1 for write-only, or 2 for read/write. If a file named by FOPEN is not found, the function returns a value of –1.

FOUND

Syntax

FOUND([*alias*])

The FOUND function returns a logical "True" (.T.) if the last CONTINUE, FIND, LOCATE, or SEEK command was successful. A logical "False" (.F.) is returned if the search command was unsuccessful. Note that if you have established a relation with SET RELATION and you specify the related file with *alias*, the function returns a logical "True" if the pointer is on a record with a key value matching that of the current record in the active database.

FPUTS

Syntax

FPUTS(*expN1*, *expC* [, *expN2*])

The FPUTS function writes the character string within *expC* to the file whose file handle is *expN1*. FPUTS is different from FWRITE in that FPUTS adds a carriage return and linefeed to the end of each line. The entire character string identified as *expC* is written, unless the optional numeric argument *expN2* is used; the value of *expN2* specifies the number of characters to write.

FREAD

Syntax

FREAD(*expN1*, *expN2*)

The FREAD function returns as a character string a specified number of bytes from a file whose file handle is *expN1*. The numeric value of *expN2* is the number of bytes to read, starting from the current position of the file pointer. (Use the FOPEN function to open the file.)

FSEEK

Syntax

FSEEK(*expN1*, *expN2*[, *expN3*])

The FSEEK function moves the file pointer within a file. *ExpN1* is the file's handle (returned from the FOPEN function), and *expN2* is the number of bytes the file pointer must be moved. If *expN2* is positive, the file pointer is moved toward the end of the file. If *expN2* is negative, the file pointer is moved toward the beginning of the file. The number of bytes moved is normally relative to the beginning of the file. The optional argument specified in *expN3* can be used to change this relative position. If *expN3* is 0, movement is relative to the start of the file (the default). If *expN3* is 1, movement is relative to the current position of the file pointer. If *expN3* is 2, movement is relative to the end of the file.

FSIZE

Syntax

FSIZE(*field*[, *alias*])

FSIZE returns the size of the specified *field* in bytes. Use the optional *alias* to select a field from a file in an unselected work area.

FULLPATH

Syntax

FULLPATH(*file*[, 1 / *file2*])

FULLPATH returns the full DOS path name for the given *file*. If the file is not found in the default directory, FULLPATH will search the FoxPro path for the file. If the optional argument , 1 is added, the search will use the DOS path.

A second file name can be used in place of the optional argument ,1, in which case the function returns the relative path between the two files.

FV

Syntax

FV(*expN1*, *expN2*, *expN3*)

The FV function returns the future value of an investment. FV calculates the future value of a series of equal payments earning a fixed interest rate. The future value is the total of all payments plus the interest. *ExpN1* is the payment amount, *expN2* is the interest rate, and *expN3* is the number of periods. If the payments are compounded monthly and the interest rate is compounded yearly, divide the interest rate by 12 to get the proper results.

FWRITE

Syntax

FWRITE(*expN1*, *expC* [, *expN2*])

The FWRITE function lets you write to a file whose handle is *expN1*. The numeric value of *expN2* is the number of bytes to write, starting from the current position of the file pointer. (Use the FOPEN function to open the file and assign a handle.)

GETBAR

Syntax

GETBAR(*expC*, *expN*)

The GETBAR function returns the number of a bar at a specific position in a pop-up menu. This function can be useful when pop-up options have been added, removed, or rearranged. *ExpC* denotes the pop-up name, and *expN* denotes a position within the pop-up.

GETDIR

Syntax

GETDIR([*expC1* [, *expC2*]])

The GETDIR function displays the Select Directory dialog box. You can use this dialog box to choose a directory. The function returns the name of the directory you choose as a character string. If you do not choose a directory (you click Cancel or press ESC), the GETDIR function returns a null string.

Use *expC1* to define a prompt for the directory list that appears in the dialog box. Use *expC2* to specify the directory that is displayed by default in the dialog box.

GETENV

Syntax

GETENV(*expC*)

The GETENV function returns a character string that contains the contents of the DOS environmental variable named as the character expression.

GETFILE

Syntax

GETFILE([*expC1*][, *expC2*])

The GETFILE function causes the FoxPro Open File dialog box to be displayed. Using the dialog box, a file may be chosen. The function then returns the name of the chosen file. *ExpC1* is an optional extension; if used, only files with that extension will appear in the list box. *ExpC2* is an optional prompt that appears at the top of the Open File dialog box.

GETFONT

Syntax

GETFONT()

The GETFONT function displays the FoxPro for Windows Font dialog box. You can use the dialog box to choose an installed Windows font. The function returns the name, size, and style of the font that you choose in the dialog box. Your choice is returned as a character string with the font name, size, and style separated by commas. If you do not choose a font in the dialog box (you click Cancel or press ESC), the GETFONT function returns a null string.

GETPAD

Syntax

GETPAD(*expC*, *expN*)

The GETPAD function returns the name of a menu pad at a specific position in a bar menu. This function can be useful when menu pads have been added, removed, or rearranged. *ExpC* denotes the menu name, and *expN* denotes a position within the menu.

GOMONTH

Syntax

GOMONTH(*expD*, *expN*)

The GOMONTH function returns a date that is *expN* months before or after *expD*. If *expN* is positive, the date returned is *expN* months after *expD*. If *expN* is negative, the date returned is *expN* months before *expD*.

HEADER

Syntax

HEADER([*alias*])

The HEADER function returns the number of bytes in the header of the database open in the current work area. If no database is open in the specified work area, 0 is returned. Use the optional *alias* to return the bytes in the header of a file open in an unselected work area.

IIF

Syntax

IIF(*expL, expr1, expr2*)

The IIF function (Immediate IF) returns the value of *expr1* if the logical expression is true and returns the value of *expr2* if the logical expression is false. *Expr1* and *expr2* must be of the same data type.

INKEY

Syntax

INKEY([*expN*][,*expC*])

The INKEY function returns an integer value between 0 and 255, corresponding to the decimal ASCII code for the key that was pressed. If no key has been pressed, a 0 will be returned. Include the optional *expC* to show or hide the cursor. If expC is the letter S, the cursor is shown (or visible). If expC is the letter H, the cursor is hidden.

INLIST

Syntax

INLIST(*expr1*, *expr2*[, *expr3*...])

The INLIST function determines if an expression is contained in a series of expressions. INLIST returns a logical "True" (.T.) if *exp1* is contained in the list of expressions *expr2*, *expr3*, and so on. The expressions must all be of the same data type.

INSMODE

Syntax

INSMODE([*expL*])

The INSMODE function changes the insert/overwrite mode based on *expL*. If *expL* is omitted, the function returns the insert mode setting.

INT

Syntax

INT(*expN*)

The INT function returns the integer portion of *expN*. No rounding occurs; any decimal values are simply dropped.

ISALPHA

Syntax

ISALPHA(*expC*)

The ISALPHA function returns a logical "True" (.T.) if the first character of *expC* is a-z or A-Z. A logical "False" (.F.) is returned if *expC* begins with a nonalphabetic or numeric character.

ISCOLOR

Syntax

ISCOLOR()

The ISCOLOR function returns a logical "True" (.T.) if the system has color capability (whether or not a color monitor is being used) and returns a logical "False" (.F.) if the system has monochrome capability.

ISDIGIT

Syntax

ISDIGIT(*expC*)

The ISDIGIT function returns a logical "True" (.T.) if the first character of *expC* is a digit (0-9).

ISLOWER

Syntax

ISLOWER(*expC*)

The ISLOWER function returns a logical "True" (.T.) if the first character in *expC* is a lowercase letter, or a logical "False" (.F.) if the first character is anything other than a lowercase letter.

ISUPPER

Syntax

ISUPPER(*expC*)

The ISUPPER function returns a logical "True" (.T.) if the first character in *expC* is an uppercase character, or a logical "False" (.F.) if the first character is anything other than an uppercase character.

KEY

Syntax

KEY([*.cdx filename,*] *expN* [, *alias*])

The KEY function returns the index expression of the specified index file. The numeric expression identifies the index file, where 1 is the first index file opened, 2 is the second index file opened, and so on. Use the *alias* option to return the key expression for an index file that is open in an unselected work area.

The *.cdx filename* option can be used to specify an index tag in a compound index file.

LASTKEY

Syntax

LASTKEY()

The LASTKEY function returns the decimal ASCII value for the last key pressed. (The LASTKEY function returns the same ASCII values as the INKEY function.)

LEFT

Syntax

LEFT(*expC*, *expN*)

The LEFT function returns the leftmost number of characters specified in *expN* from the character expression *expC*, starting with the first or leftmost character.

LEN

Syntax

LEN(*expC*)

The LEN function returns the length of a character string expression specified in *expC*. *ExpC* can be a memo field name, in which case the length of the text stored within the memo field is returned. Note that in the case of character fields, LEN returns the length of the field, not the length of the text within the field. With character fields, you must add a TRIM function to get the length of the text stored in the field.

LIKE

Syntax

LIKE(*expC1*, *expC2*)

The LIKE function compares two character expressions and returns a logical "True" (.T.) if the character string in *expC2* contains the

characters in *expC1*. The pattern can include the wildcard characters
* (representing any sequence of characters) and ? (representing any
single character).

LINENO

Syntax

LINENO( )

The LINENO function returns the line number of the next statement in
the program that is currently running.

LOCFILE

Syntax

LOCFILE(*expC1* [, *expC2*] [, *expC3*])

The LOCFILE function locates a disk file and returns the file name along
with the complete search path. To be found, the file must be in the
current directory, or somewhere in the FoxPro path. If the specified
file cannot be found, the Open File dialog box appears so a manual
search can be attempted. *ExpC1* indicates the file name. The optional
expC2 specifies extensions of files to be displayed in the Open File
dialog box. The optional *expC3* is a prompt to be displayed at the top
of the Open File dialog box.

LOG

Syntax

LOG(*expN*)

The LOG function returns the natural logarithm of a number specified by *expN*. *ExpN* must be greater than 0. Use the SET DECIMALS command to specify the number of decimal places returned.

LOG10

Syntax

LOG10(*expN*)

The LOG10 function returns the common (base 10) logarithm of a number specified by *expN*. *ExpN* must be greater than 0. Use the SET DECIMALS command to specify the number of decimal places returned.

LOOKUP

Syntax

LOOKUP(*field1*, *search expr*, *field2* [, *expC*])

The LOOKUP function searches a database for a record and returns a value from a specified field when the record is found. *Field1* is the name of the field from which the value is to be returned. *Search expr* is the expression used as the basis for the search. *Field2* specifies the name of the field you want to search. The optional *expC* specifies the name of a compact index tag that can be used to speed up the search.

LOWER

Syntax

LOWER(*expC*)

The LOWER function converts all uppercase letters in *expC* to lowercase. The function will not affect nonalphabetic characters. The LOWER function does not change the way the data is stored unless you use it as part of a STORE or REPLACE command. The function is generally used for finding or comparing data whose case in unknown.

LTRIM

Syntax

LTRIM(*expC*)

The LTRIM function trims all leading blanks from the character expression defined as *expC*.

LUPDATE

Syntax

LUPDATE(*alias*)

The LUPDATE function returns the last update of the active database. Use the optional *alias* to return the last update for a file open in an unselected work area.

MAX

Syntax

MAX(*expr1*, *expr2* [, *expr3*...])

The MAX function returns the maximum value from the list of expressions. The expressions must all be of the same data type.

MCOL

Syntax

MCOL([expC])

The MCOL function returns a value representing the column location of the mouse pointer in the screen or within a window. The optional expC denotes the name of a window. If expC is omitted, the column coordinate of the mouse pointer relative to the entire screen is returned by the function. If the mouse pointer lies outside a window and the window is named in expC, the function returns a value of -1.

MDOWN

Syntax

MDOWN()

The MDOWN function returns the state of the left mouse button. If the left mouse button is depressed when MDOWN() is executed, a logical "True" (.T.) is returned. Otherwise, a logical "False" (.F.) is returned.

MDX

Syntax

MDX(expN [, alias])

The MDX function returns the names of open compound index (.CDX) files. Note that the MDX function is identical in operation to the CDX function. ExpN is a numeric value that identifies the desired compound index file, according to the following possibilities: If the database has a structural compound index file and expN1 is 1, the name of the structural compound index file is returned; if *expN1* is 2, the name of the first .CDX compound index file (as identified by the INDEX clause of the USE command or by the SET INDEX command) is returned; if *expN1* is 3, the second .CDX compound index file name is returned; and so forth. If *expN1* is greater than the number of open .CDX compound index files, the function returns a null string.

If the database does not have a structural compound index file and *expN1* is 1, the name of the first .CDX compound index file (as identified by the INDEX clause of the USE command or by the SET INDEX command) is returned. If *expN1* is 2, the second .CDX compound index file name is returned, and so forth. If *expN1* is greater than the number of open .CDX compound index files, the function returns a null string.

Use the *alias* option to return the names of compound index files open in different work areas.

MDY

Syntax

MDY(*expD*)

The MDY function returns a *Month DD, YY* (or *Month DD, YYYY*) character string for a given date expression. The month is always spelled out, and the day always takes the *DD* format. If SET CENTURY is OFF, the year takes the *YY* format; otherwise, the year takes the *YYYY* format.

MEMLINES

Syntax

MEMLINES(*memofield*)

The MEMLINES function returns the number of lines in the named memo field for the current record. Note that the number of lines in the memo field will be affected by the current value of SET MEMOWIDTH.

MEMORY

Syntax

MEMORY()

The MEMORY function returns the amount of free conventional memory as a numeric value in kilobytes.

MENU

Syntax

MENU()

The MENU function returns the name of the currently active menu. If a menu is not active, MENU returns a null string.

MESSAGE

Syntax

MESSAGE([1])

The MESSAGE function returns the current error message, which is useful for situations in which FoxPro detects an error within a program. The MESSAGE function can be used along with the ON ERROR command for error-trapping and recovery purposes. The optional argument 1 tells FoxPro to return the actual program code for the last line that caused the ON ERROR condition.

MIN

Syntax

MIN(*expr1*, *expr2*[, *expr3*...])

The MIN function returns the minimum value expression from the list of expressions. The expressions must all be of the same data type.

MLINE

Syntax

MLINE(*memofield, expN* [, *expN2*])

The MLINE function returns the specified line *expN* from the named memo field in the current record. Note that the value of SET MEMOWIDTH will affect the number of lines in a memo field. The optional argument *expN2* denotes any offset from the start of the memo-field line.

MOD

Syntax

MOD(*expN1, expN2*)

The MOD function returns the remainder when *expN1* is divided by *expN2*. A positive number is returned if *expN2* is positive, and a negative number is returned if *expN2* is negative. If there is no remainder, a 0 is returned.

MONTH

Syntax

MONTH(*expD*)

The MONTH function returns the numeric month (1 to 12) that corresponds to the date expression. The numbers 1 through 12 correspond to January through December.

MRKBAR

Syntax

MRKBAR(*ExpC,ExpN*)

The MRKBAR function returns a logical value, indicating whether a specific bar of a pop-up menu is marked. (The SET MARK command can be used to mark or unmark a pop-up bar.) *ExpC* is the name of the pop-up menu. *ExpN* is the number that identifies the specific bar of the menu. If the bar is marked, the function returns a logical "True" (.T.); otherwise, the function returns a logical "False" (.F.).

MRKPAD

Syntax

MRKPAD(*expC1,expC2*)

The MRKPAD function returns a logical value, indicating whether a specific pad of a bar menu is marked. (The SET MARK command can be used to mark or unmark a menu pad.) *ExpC1* is the name of the menu bar. *ExpC2* is the pad name. If the pad is marked, the function returns a logical "True" (.T.); otherwise, the function returns a logical "False" (.F.).

MROW

Syntax

MROW([*expC*])

The MROW function returns a value representing the row location of the mouse pointer in the screen or within a window. The optional *expC* denotes the name of a window. If *expC* is omitted, the row coordinate of the mouse pointer relative to the entire screen is returned by the function.

If the mouse pointer lies outside a window and the window is named in *expC*, the function returns a value of -1.

MWINDOW

Syntax

MWINDOW([*windowname*])

The MWINDOW function returns a logical "True" (.T.) if the mouse pointer is positioned over a window specified by *windowname*. If the mouse pointer is not positioned over the specified window, a logical "False" (.F.) is returned. If the MWINDOW function is used without an optional window name, the name of the window that the mouse pointer is positioned over is returned. If the mouse pointer is not positioned over any window, a null string is returned.

NDX

Syntax

NDX(*expN*[, *alias*])

The NDX function returns the name of an open index file in the current work area. The numeric expression specifies the order of the index file, 1 being the first index file opened, 2 the second index file opened, and so on. Use the optional *alias* to return the name of an open index file in an unselected work area.

NUMLOCK

Syntax

NUMLOCK([*expL*])

The NUMLOCK function changes the NUM LOCK keyboard mode or returns the status of the NUM LOCK mode. NUMLOCK(.T.) turns on NUM LOCK, and NUMLOCK(.F.) turns off NUM LOCK. If the logical expression is omitted, NUMLOCK returns the status of the NUM LOCK mode.

OBJNUM

Syntax

OBJNUM(*variable* [, *expN*])

The OBJNUM function returns the object number of a GET object. (GET objects such as fields, check boxes, push buttons, and radio buttons are assigned object numbers, in the order in which they are created.) *Variable* is the name of the variable used to create the GET object. When nested READs are used, the optional argument of *expN* can be used to specify an object at a different READ level.

OCCURS

Syntax

OCCURS(*expC1*, *expC2*)

The OCCURS function returns an integer that represents the number of times *expC1* occurs in *expC2*. If *expC1* is not found in *expC2*, the function returns a 0.

OEMTOANSI

Syntax

OEMTOANSI(*expC*)

The OEMTOANSI function is used to move data from FoxPro for DOS to FoxPro for Windows. OEMTOANSI() converts each character in *expC* to a corresponding character in the FoxPro for Windows (ANSI) character set. The character expression *expC* should contain characters from the OEM character set.If a character in *expC* has no Windows equivalent, the character is converted to a similar Windows character.

ORDER

Syntax

ORDER([*alias*])

ORDER returns the name of the master (or active) index file in the current work area. Use the optional *alias* to return the name of the active index in an unselected work area.

OS

Syntax

OS()

The OS function returns the name and version of the operating system.

PAD

Syntax

PAD()

The PAD function returns the name of the pad last chosen from the active menu bar. The function returns a null string if no menu is active.

PADC, PADL, PADR

Syntax

PADC(*expr, expN[, expC]*)
PADL(*expr, expN[, expC]*)
PADR(*expr, expN[, expC]*)

These functions pad the expression *expr* with a designated character on the left side, the right side, or on both sides. *ExpN* specifies the total length of the resultant string. The expression is padded with blanks unless an optional character is supplied as *expC*; if provided, the optional character is used to pad the expression. Use PADC to pad an expression on both sides; use PADL to pad an expression on the left side; and use PADR to pad an expression on the right side. You can pad character, date, or numeric expressions with these functions.

PARAMETERS

Syntax

PARAMETERS( )

The PARAMETERS function returns a numeric value indicating the number of parameters passed to the procedure most recently called.

PAYMENT

Syntax

PAYMENT(*expN1, expN2, expN3*)

The PAYMENT function returns the amount of a loan payment. PAYMENT assumes that the interest rate is constant and that payments are made at the end of each period. *ExpN1* is the principal amount, *expN2* is the interest rate, and *expN3* is the number of payments. If the payments are compounded monthly and the interest rate is compounded yearly, divide the interest rate by 12 to get the proper results.

PCOL

Syntax

PCOL()

The PCOL function returns the current column position of the printer.

PI

Syntax

PI()

The PI function returns the numeric constant pi (approximately 3.14159).

POPUP

Syntax

POPUP()

The POPUP function returns the name of the active pop-up menu.

PRINTSTATUS

Syntax

PRINTSTATUS()

The PRINTSTATUS function returns a logical "True" (.T.) if the printer is ready and a logical "False" (.F.) if it is not.

PRMBAR

Syntax

PRMBAR(*expC*, *expN*)

The PRMBAR function returns the prompt text for a specific option of a pop-up menu. *ExpC* denotes the pop-up name, and *expN* denotes the bar number of the pop-up menu.

PRMPAD

Syntax

PRMPAD(*expC1*, *expC2*)

The PRMPAD function returns the prompt text for a specific pad of a bar menu. *ExpC1* denotes the menu name, and *expC2* denotes the pad name in the bar menu.

PROGRAM

Syntax

PROGRAM([*expN*])

The PROGRAM function returns the name of the program currently running or the program that was running when an error occurred. The optional numeric expression can be used for nesting programs (calling a program from a program). When used, the value *expN* indicates how many levels back FoxPro should go to get the program name.

PROMPT

Syntax

PROMPT()

The PROMPT function returns the prompt for the last option chosen from the active menu pad or pop-up menu. The function returns a null string if no pop-up menu is active.

PROPER

Syntax

PROPER(*expC*)

The PROPER function returns the character expression specified in *expC* with initial capitals. Each word in the character string has the first letter capitalized and the remaining letters lowercased.

PROW

Syntax

PROW()

The PROW function returns the current row position of the printer. Note that when an EJECT command is issued, PROW is reset to 0.

PUTFILE

Syntax

PUTFILE([*expC1*][, *expC2*][, *expC3*][, *expC4*])

The PUTFILE function displays the Save As dialog box. The user can enter or choose a file name, and the file name is returned as a character expression by the function. The optional *expC1* argument is a prompt string that, if used, appears above the text box. The optional *expC2* argument is a default file name that appears in the text box. The optional *expC3* argument is a default file extension. The optional *expC4* replaces the text in the Save push button.

PV

Syntax

PV(*expN1*, *expN2*, *expN3*)

The PV function returns the present value of an investment, or the amount that must be invested to earn a known future value. *ExpN1* is the payment made each period, *expN2* is the interest rate, and *expN3* is the number of periods. If the payments are compounded monthly and the interest rate is yearly, divide the interest rate by 12 to get the proper results.

RAND

Syntax

RAND([*expN*])

The RAND function returns a random number between 0 and 1. The optional numeric expression can be used to provide a seed different than the default for generating the random number. A given seed will always produce the same sequence of random numbers; you can vary the sequence of random numbers by varying the seed. If *expN* is negative, the seed is taken from the system clock.

To obtain a random number in a particular range, multiply the result of the RAND function by a chosen value. For example, you could get a random number between 50 and 100 by using (RAND*50)+50.

RAT

Syntax

RAT(*expC1, expC2*[, *expN*])

The RAT function (Reverse AT) searches *expC2*, starting from the right, for the *expN*th occurrence of the character string *expC1*. The function returns as an integer the position where *expC1* is found. If *expC1* is not found in *expC2* the specified number of times, the function returns a 0. If *expN* is omitted, the default is 1.

RATLINE

Syntax

RATLINE(*expC1, expC2*)

The RATLINE function (Reverse ATLINE) searches *expC2* for the last occurrence of *expC1*. The function returns the number of the line where *expC1* was found. If *expC1* is not found in *expC2*, the function returns a 0. Note that *expC2* can be a memo field.

RDLEVEL

Syntax

RDLEVEL()

The RDLEVEL function returns a numeric value representing the level of the current READ. (READs can be nested up to four levels deep in FoxPro 2.)

READKEY

Syntax

READKEY()

The READKEY function returns an integer value that indicates the key pressed when exiting from the editing commands APPEND, BROWSE, CHANGE, CREATE, EDIT, INSERT, MODIFY, and READ. READKEY provides a value between 0 and 36 if no changes were made to the data, or a value between 256 and 292 if changes were made to the data.

RECCOUNT

Syntax

RECCOUNT([*alias*])

The RECCOUNT function returns the number of records in the database open in the current work area. If no database is open, RECCOUNT returns a 0. Use the optional *alias* to return the number of records in a database open in an unselected work area.

RECNO

Syntax

RECNO([*alias*])

The RECNO function returns the current record number. Use the optional *alias* to return the current record number in a database open in an unselected work area. Note that RECNO(0) can follow an unsuccessful

SEEK to determine what record number to return. If a SEEK is unsuccessful, the use of RECNO(0) immediately after the SEEK returns the record number of the closest matching record.

RECSIZE

Syntax

RECSIZE([*alias*])

The RECSIZE function returns the size of the database record in the current work area. Use the optional *alias* to return the size of the database record for a database open in an unselected work area. If no database is open, RECSIZE returns a 0.

RELATION

Syntax

RELATION(*expN*[, *alias*])

The RELATION function returns the relational expression for the *N*th relation of the work area identified by *alias*. Use the optional *alias* to specify an unselected work-area number, work-area letter, or alias name. If no relation exists, the function returns a null string.

REPLICATE

Syntax

REPLICATE(*expC*, *expN*)

The REPLICATE function returns a character string consisting of *expC* repeated *expN* times.

RIGHT

Syntax

RIGHT(*expC*/*memvar, expN*)

The RIGHT function returns the rightmost part of the character string *expC* or memory variable *memvar*. Use the numeric expression *expN* to specify the number of characters that will be returned.

ROUND

Syntax

ROUND(*expN1, expN2*)

The ROUND function rounds off the number supplied in *expN1*. Use *expN2* to specify the number of decimal places to round off to. If *expN2* is negative, the rounded number returned is a whole number.

ROW

Syntax

ROW()

The ROW function returns the current row location of the cursor.

RTOD

Syntax

RTOD(*expN*)

The RTOD function converts radians to degrees. The numeric expression is the value in radians, and the value returned by the function is the equivalent value in degrees.

RTRIM

Syntax

RTRIM(*expC*)

The RTRIM function strips the trailing spaces from the named character string. The RTRIM function is identical to the TRIM function.

SCHEME

Syntax

SCHEME(*expN1* [, *expN2*])

The SCHEME function returns a color-pair list or a color pair from a color scheme. To return the complete color-pair listing for a color scheme, provide the color-scheme number as *expN1*. To return a single pair listing from a color scheme, provide the position of the color pair in the color-pair list as the optional argument *expN2*.

SCOLS

Syntax

SCOLS()

The SCOLS function returns the number of columns available on the display screen.

SECONDS

Syntax

SECONDS()

The SECONDS function returns the value of the system clock, using a *seconds.thousandths* format.

SEEK

Syntax

SEEK(*expr*[, *alias*])

The SEEK function returns a logical "True" (.T.) if the search expression can be found in the active index. If the search expression is not found, the function returns a logical "False" (.F.), and the record pointer is placed at the end of the file. Use the optional *alias* to search an open index in an unselected work area.

SELECT

Syntax

SELECT()

The SELECT function returns the number of the current work area (assuming SET COMPATIBLE is OFF). If SET COMPATIBLE is ON, the function returns the number of the highest unused work area.

SET

Syntax

SET(*expC*[,1])

The SET function returns the status of the various SET commands. The character expression contains the name of the desired SET command. Note that you need to use quotes around *expC* if it is a character string rather than a memory variable. Using SET without the optional argument returns the ON/OFF setting. Using SET with the optional argument ,1 returns the SET TO setting.

SIGN

Syntax

SIGN(*expN*)

SIGN returns a numeric value that represents the sign of the numeric expression. If *expN* is positive, SIGN returns a value of 1. If *expN* is negative, SIGN returns a value of SY-1. If *expN* is 0, SIGN returns a 0.

SIN

Syntax

SIN(*expN*)

The SIN function returns the sine of *expN*, where *expN* is an angle measured in radians. To convert degrees to radians, use the DTOR function.

SKPBAR

Syntax

SKPBAR(*expC*, *expN*)

The SKPBAR function returns a logical value that indicates if an option (bar) on a menu pop-up is enabled or disabled. If the specified pop-up option is disabled, "True" (.T.) is returned. If the pop-up option is enabled, "False" (.F.) is returned. Use *expC* to indicate the name of the menu pop-up that contains the option. Use *expN* to indicate the pop-up option number for which you want to test the enabled or disabled status.

SKPPAD

Syntax

SKPPAD(*expC1*, *expC2*)

The SKPPAD function returns a logical value that indicates if a menu pad on a menu bar is enabled or disabled. If the specified menu pad is disabled, "True" (.T.) is returned. If the menu pad is enabled, "False" (.F.) is returned. Use *expC1* to indicate the name of the menu bar that contains the pad. Use *expC2* to indicate the name of the menu pad for which you want to test the enabled or disabled status.

SOUNDEX

Syntax

SOUNDEX(*expC*)

The SOUNDEX function returns a four-character string that represents the phonetic SOUNDEX code for the character expression *expC*. The four-character code returned by the SOUNDEX function can be useful for finding similar-sounding names or for building an index to perform lookups based on the sound of a word.

SPACE

Syntax

SPACE(*expN*)

The SPACE function returns a character string containing the specified number of blank spaces. The maximum number of spaces that can be specified by *expN* is 65,504.

SQRT

Syntax

SQRT(*expN*)

The SQRT function returns the square root of the numeric expression *expN*. The numeric expression must be a positive number.

SROWS

Syntax

SROWS( )

SROWS returns the number of rows available on the screen.

STR

Syntax

STR(*expN1*[, *expN2*[, *expN3*]])

The STR function converts a numeric expression to a character expression, where *expN1* is the numeric expression to be converted to a character string. Use the optional *expN2* to specify a length (including the decimal point and decimal places), and use the optional *expN3* to specify a number of decimal places.

STRTRAN

Syntax

STRTRAN(*expC1*, *expC2*[, *expC3*][, *expN1*][, *expN2*])

The STRTRAN function performs a search-and-replace operation on a character string. The function returns the given expression *expC1*, with occurrences of *expC2* replaced with *expC3*. Replacements start at the *expN1*th occurrence and continue for a total of *expN2* replacements.

STUFF

Syntax

STUFF(*expC1*, *expN1*, *expN2*, *expC2*)

The STUFF function inserts or removes characters from any part of a character string. *ExpC1* is the existing character string, *expN1* is the starting position in the string, *expN2* is the number of characters to remove, and *expC2* is the character string to insert.

SUBSTR

Syntax

SUBSTR(*expC*, *expN1*[, *expN2*])

The SUBSTR function extracts a portion of a string from a character expression. *ExpC* is the character expression to extract the string from, *expN1* is the starting position in the expression, and *expN2* is the number of characters to extract from the expression.

SYS

Syntax

SYS(*expN*)

The SYS functions return character-string values that contain various system data. *ExpN* is a numeric value that corresponds to the appropriate system function. The more commonly used system functions are shown here; consult your FoxPro documentation for a complete listing.

Function	Returns
SYS(1)	The current system date
SYS(2)	The number of seconds since midnight
SYS(3)	A unique legal file name
SYS(5)	The current default device
SYS(6)	The current print device
SYS(7)	The name of the current format file
SYS(9)	Your FoxPro serial number
SYS(12)	The amount of free memory
SYS(13)	The printer status
SYS(23)	The amount of EMS memory used by FoxPro
SYS(24)	The EMS limit specified in CONFIG.FP
SYS(2003)	The current directory name
SYS(2006)	The type of graphics hardware in use

SYSMETRIC

Syntax

SYSMETRIC(*expN*)

The SYSMETRIC function returns the size of a Windows display element. (In FoxPro for Windows, display elements include the screen, menus, windows, window controls, and the cursor.) The values provided by the function are returned in pixels unless otherwise noted. Note that the values can vary for different display drivers and hardware.

The following table shows values for *expN* and corresponding screen elements:

expN	Display Element
1	Windows screen width
2	Windows screen height
3	Width of sizable window frame
4	Height of sizable window frame
5	Width of scroll arrows on vertical scroll bar
6	Height of scroll arrows on vertical scroll bar
7	Width of scroll arrows on horizontal scroll bar
8	Height of scroll arrows on horizontal scroll bar
9	Height of window title
10	Width of nonsizable window frame
11	Height of nonsizable window frame
12	Width of DOUBLE or PANEL window frame
13	Height of DOUBLE or PANEL window frame
14	Thumb width on horizontal scroll bar
15	Thumb height on vertical scroll bar
16	Minimized window icon width
17	Minimized window icon height
18	Maximum cursor width
19	Maximum cursor height
20	Single-line menu bar height
21	Maximized window width
22	Maximized window height
23	Kanji window height
24	Minimum sizable window width
25	Minimum sizable window height
26	Minimum window width
27	Minimum window height
28	Window controls width

29	Window controls height
30	1 if mouse hardware present, 0 otherwise
31	1 for Windows debugging version, 0 otherwise
32	1 if mouse buttons swapped, 0 otherwise

TAG

Syntax

TAG([*.cdx filename*,] *expN* [, *alias*])

The TAG function returns tag names from compound index (.CDX) files, or it returns the names of open index (.IDX) files. The *.cdx filename* argument, when used, lets you return the tag names from a specific compound index file. *ExpN* denotes the order of the tag: If *expN* is 1, the name of the first tag in the compound index file is retrieved; if *expN* is 2, the name of the second tag in the compound index file is retrieved; and so on. Use the *alias* clause to return tag names from index files open in different work areas.

If the *.cdx filename* argument is omitted, the TAG function first returns names of the .IDX files (based on their order specified by the USE command or by the SET INDEX command). Next, the function returns tag names from the structural compound index file, if there is one. Finally, the function returns tag names from other compound index files, in the order that the tags were created and in the order the compound index files were identified with the USE and/or SET INDEX commands.

TAN

Syntax

TAN(*expN*)

The TAN function returns the tangent of *expN*, where *expN* is measured in radians. To convert degrees to radians, use the DTOR function.

TARGET

Syntax

TARGET(*expN*[, *expr*])

The TARGET function returns the alias of the work area that is the target of the *N*th relation from the work area specified by *expr*. Use the optional *expr* to specify another work area by alias, number, or letter. If *expr* is omitted, the current work area is used. If the relation specified by the function does not exist, a 0 is returned.

TXTWIDTH

Syntax

TXTWIDTH(expC1 [, *expC2, expN* [, *expC3*]])

The TXTWIDTH function returns the length of a character expression as it appears in the font used by the active window. *ExpC1* is the character expression, and the value returned by the function is the number of characters the expression will occupy using the current font of the active window. (If no window is active, the value returned is determined by the current font used by the main FoxPro window.)

Include the optional *expC2, expN,* and *expC3* arguments to identify a specific font, font size, or font style. The name of the font (such as Script or Roman) is specified by *expC2*. The font size, in points, is specified by *expN*. Include a font style code in *expC3* to specify a font style. If *expC2* is omitted, the normal font style is used.

The following table shows the values for *expC3*. Note that you can include more than one character to specify a combination of styles; for example, IU specifies italic underline.

Character	Font style
B	Bold
I	Italic
N	Normal

O	Outline
-	Shadow
-	Strikeout
T	Transparent
U	Underline

TIME

Syntax

TIME([*expN*])

The TIME function returns the current system time in the format *HH:MM:SS* (if SET HOURS is set to 24) or in the format *HH:MM:SS am/pm* (if SET HOURS is set to 12). If you include the numeric argument *expN*, the function's result includes hundredths of a second. (Note, however, that maximum accuracy of the clock is about 1/18 of a second.)

TRANSFORM

Syntax

TRANSFORM(*expr, expC*)

The TRANSFORM function formats character strings or numbers with PICTURE options without using the @-SAY command. *Expr* is the variable or field to format; *expC* is a character expression that contains the PICTURE clause.

TRIM

Syntax

TRIM(*expC*)

The TRIM function trims trailing spaces from a character string. If the character string is composed entirely of spaces, TRIM returns a null string. The TRIM function is identical to the RTRIM function.

TYPE

Syntax

TYPE(*expC*)

The TYPE function returns a single character indicating the data type of the expression named in *expC*. The character C denotes character type, L denotes logical type, N denotes numeric type, D denotes date type, M denotes memo type, and U denotes an undefined type.

UPDATED

Syntax

UPDATED()

The UPDATED function returns a logical "True" (.T.) if any data was changed in the associated GETs when the last READ command was processed.

UPPER

Syntax

UPPER(*expC*)

The UPPER function converts all alphabetic characters in *expC* to uppercase letters. The UPPER function does not change the way the data is stored unless you use the function as part of a STORE or REPLACE command. It is generally used for finding or comparing data whose case is unknown.

USED

Syntax

USED([*expr*])

The USED function returns a logical "True" (.T.) if a database is open in the current work area. Use the optional *expr* to identify a different work area by its alias, number, or letter. If no database is open in the specified work area, a logical "False" (.F.) is returned.

VAL

Syntax

VAL(*expC*)

The VAL function converts a character expression containing numbers into a numeric value. Starting at the leftmost character and ignoring leading blanks, VAL processes digits until a nonnumeric character is encountered. If the first character of *expC* is not a number, VAL returns a value of 0.

VARREAD

Syntax

VARREAD()

The VARREAD function returns the name of the field or variable currently being edited. The function can be useful when designing context-sensitive help systems, allowing you to specify different help messages for different fields.

VERSION

Syntax

VERSION()

The VERSION function returns a character string indicating the version number of FoxPro.

WBORDER

Syntax

WBORDER([*windowname*])

The WBORDER function returns a logical "True" (.T.) if the window specified by *windowname* has a border.

WCHILD

Syntax

WCHILD([*windowname/expN1*])

The WCHILD function returns the number of child windows in a parent window, or the names of the child windows in a parent window. The *windowname* argument is the name of the desired window; if this argument is omitted, the function assumes the use of the current window. If a window name is specified, the optional numeric expression *expN1* can also be used. When *expN1* is used, the name of the child window is returned. If the names are returned, they are returned in the order that they were stacked in the parent window. The value of *expN1* corresponds to the desired child window, varying from 0 (denoting the child window at the bottom of the stack) up to the number of child windows in the stack.

WCOLS

Syntax

WCOLS([*expC*])

The WCOLS function returns the number of columns available in the active window. Use the optional *expC* to name a window other than the currently active window.

WEXIST

Syntax

WEXIST(*expC*)

The WEXIST function returns a logical "True" (.T.) if the window named in *expC* has been previously defined.

WFONT

Syntax

WFONT(*expN* [, *windowname*])

The WFONT function returns font attributes for the font currently used by the active window, or by a specific window if one is named with the optional *windowname* clause. Use *expN* to specify the font attribute to be returned; *expN* can be a value of 1, 2, or 3. Use 1 to return the name of the current font. Use 2 to return the current font size, in points. Use 3 to return a code indicating the current font style. The following table shows the values returned when 3 is used as the value of *expN:*

Character	Font style
B	Bold
I	Italic
N	Normal
O	Outline
S	Shadow
-	Strikeout
T	Transparent
U	Underline

WLAST

Syntax

WLAST([*windowname*])

The WLAST function returns the name of the window that was active prior to the current window, or returns a logical "True" (.T.) if the named window was active prior to the current window.

WLCOL

Syntax

WLCOL([*windowname*])

The WLCOL function returns a numeric value representing the column location of the upper-left corner of a window. Use the optional *windowname* to identify the window by name. If *windowname* is omitted, the function returns the column location of the upper-left corner of the currently active window.

Because windows can be positioned partially off the screen, it is possible to retrieve negative values from WLCOL(). If a window's upper-left corner is located to the left of the screen, negative values are returned by WLCOL().

WLROW

Syntax

WLROW([*windowname*])

The WLROW function returns a numeric value representing the row location of the upper-left corner of a window. Use the optional *windowname* to identify the window by name. If *windowname* is omitted, the WLROW function returns the row location of the upper-left corner of the currently active window.

Because windows can be positioned partially off the screen, it is possible to retrieve negative values from WLROW(). If a window's upper-left corner is located to the left of the screen, negative values are returned by WRCOW().

WMAXIMUM

Syntax

WMAXIMUM([*windowname*])

The WMAXIMUM() function returns a logical "True" (.T.) if the specified window is maximized. If the specified window is not maximized, a logical "False" (.F.) is returned. If the optional *windowname* is omitted, a logical value is returned indicating whether the currently active window is maximized.

WMINIMUM

Syntax

WMINIMUM([*windowname*])

The WMINIMUM() function returns a logical "True" (.T.) if the specified window is minimized. If the specified window is not minimized, a logical "False" (.F.) is returned. If the optional *windowname* is omitted, a logical value is returned indicating whether the currently active window is maximized.

WONTOP

Syntax

WONTOP([*expC*])

The WONTOP function returns the name of the window that is frontmost on the screen. If the optional *expC* is used to name a window, the function returns a logical "True" (.T.) if the named window is frontmost.

WOUTPUT

Syntax

WOUTPUT([*expC*])

The WOUTPUT function returns the name of the window currently receiving output. If the optional *expC* is used to name a window, the function returns a logical "True" (.T.) if output is currently being directed to the window named in *expC*. If output is not being directed to a window, the function returns a null string.

WPARENT

Syntax

WPARENT([*windowname*])

The WPARENT function returns the name of the parent window of a specific child window. The optional *windowname* argument denotes the child window for which the name of the parent window is desired. If the argument is omitted, the function assumes the use of the current window. If the current window is not a child window, the function returns a null string.

WREAD

Syntax

WREAD([*windowname*])

The WREAD function returns a logical "True" (.T.) if the specified window is participating in the current READ. If the specified window is not involved in the current read, a logical "False" (.F.) is returned.

WROWS

Syntax

WROWS([*expC*])

The WROWS function returns the number of rows available in the active window. Use the optional *expC* to return the number of rows available in the window named in *expC*.

WTITLE

Syntax

WTITLE([*windowname*])

The WTITLE function returns the title of the specific window named in *windowname*. If the optional *windowname* clause is omitted, WTITLE returns the title of the topmost window.

WVISIBLE

Syntax

WVISIBLE(*expC*)

The WVISIBLE function returns a logical "True" (.T.) if the window named in *expC* has been activated and is not hidden. The function returns a logical "False" (.F.) if the window has not been activated, has been deactivated, or is hidden.

YEAR

Syntax

YEAR(*expD*)

The YEAR function returns the numeric year corresponding to the date expression.

Index